A Decade of Economic Reforms in India

A Decade of Economic Reforms in India

Edited by
Raj Kapila & Uma Kapila

AF
ACADEMIC FOUNDATION

Academic Foundation
www.academicfoundation.com

The Editors :

RAJ KAPILA
Director and Chief Editor, Academic Foundation, Delhi.

UMA KAPILA
Reader, Department of Economics, Miranda House, University of Delhi.

Published in 2002 by
ACADEMIC FOUNDATION
AF House,
B - 5, Chandra Nagar,
Delhi-U.P. Border,
T.H.A. Ghaziabad - 201011. India

TEL : 0120-4621793, 4611015

FAX : 0120-4611016

{from Delhi (local call), please dial
91 - instead of the STD code 0120-}

MOBILE : 98103 21661

E-MAIL : academic@vsnl.com

www : academicfoundation.com

City Office :
S-202, 2nd Floor, Chetan Complex, Plot No. 6,
Shreshtha Vihar LSC, New Delhi - 110 092.

A Decade of Economic Reforms in India
Raj Kapila & Uma Kapila, ed.

ISBN 81-7188-240-4

Laser- Typeset at AF's DTP Division.
Printed at Print Perfect, New Delhi.

Dedicated To
All Those Engaged In
The Development Of India's Economy

CONTENTS

...Contd...

...Contd...

...Contd...

ACKNOWLEDGEMENT

The editors are indeed grateful to the contributors mentioned overleaf, for their papers/articles that have been published in this volume.

AUTHORS / CONTRIBUTORS

C. Rangarajan. .... *Governor, Andhra Pradesh; Ex-Governor, Reserve Bank of India, Mumbai.*

Ashok V. Desai. .... *Consulting Editor, Business Standard, New Delhi; formerly, Chief Economic Consultant, Ministry of Finance, Govt. of India.*

Bimal Jalan. .... *Governor, Reserve Bank of India, Mumbai.*

Jagdish Bhagwati. .... *Professor of Economics, International Economics Research Centre, Columbia University, New York.*

Kirit Parikh. .... *Ex-Director and Professor Emeritus, Indira Gandhi Institute of Development Research, Mumbai.*

Y.V. Reddy. .... *Dy. Governor, Reserve Bank of India, Mumbai.*

Raja Chelliah. .... *Chairman, Madras School of Economics, Chennai.*

Montek S. Ahluwalia. .... *Director (EvO), IMF, Washington; Ex-Member, Planning Commission; formerly, Finance Secretary, Govt. of India.*

Vijay L. Kelkar .... *Executive Director, International Monetary Fund (IMF); Ex-Chairman, Tariff Commission; formerly, Finance Secretary, Govt. of India, New Delhi.*

V.S. Vyas .... *Professor Emeritus; Chairman, Governing Board, Institute of Development Studies, Jaipur.*

Murasoli Maran .... *Union Minister of Commerce and Industry, Government of India, New Delhi.*

Nagesh Kumar .... *Senior Fellow, Centre for Research & Information System for the Non-Aligned and other Developing Countries (RIS), New Delhi.*

Rajesh Chadha .... *Senior Consultant, National Council of Applied Economic Research (NCAER), New Delhi; Reader, Hindu College, University of Delhi.*

V. Ratna Reddy .... *Centre for Economic and Social Studies, Hyderabad.*

Ajay Shah .... *Prof., Indira Gandhi Institute of Development Research, Mumbai.*

Editors :

Raj Kapila .... *Director and Chief Editor, Academic Foundation, Delhi.*

Uma Kapila .... *Reader, Department of Economics, Miranda House, University of Delhi.*

1

Introduction :

Consensus on Economic Reforms

Reflecting on the millennium that has just ended, Bimal Jalan notes with surprise as to how recent is the story of economic growth. Quoting from Paul Krugman, he points out that economic growth that raises living standards is in fact a modern invention. While in a few western countries like England, Germany, France and the United States, per capita incomes were increasing on a sustained basis, the so-called underdeveloped or Third World countries were the exporters of primary products and importers of industrial products with stagnant, and in some cases, declining per capita incomes. The development strategies of the newly independent and developing countries, including India, in the mid-twentieth century were framed against this background. The role of speeding up the process of industrialisation was assigned to the State with the need for the Government to occupy the commanding heights and to lead from the top. India, at that time, played a pioneering role in giving expression to the aspirations of the newly independent Third World countries in the economic field. In 1956, India's Five Year Plan outlined the goals of development strategy in the following terms:

"The pattern of development and the structure of socio-economic relations should be so planned that they result not only in appreciable increases in national income and employment but also in greater equality in incomes and wealth. Major decisions regarding production, distribution, consumption and investment — and in fact all significant socio-economic relationships — must be made by agencies informed by social purpose."

In practice, it meant, that all allocation decisions were to be made by the Government or its agencies. The primary emphasis was to be on increasing the domestic savings rate by suppressing consumption, by high taxation, and by appropriating profits through ownership of commercial enterprises.

Shift in the Development Paradigm

After pursuing an inward-looking development strategy with the state assuming an all important role for more than four decades, in 1990-91, in the midst of grave balance of payments crisis, India embarked on a comprehensive reform of the economy that would transform India from a controlled to a fairly open economy which is integrated with the world economy and in which the market would be given the prime role in the allocation of resources.

The reforms of the nineties saw some significant achievements. Decontrol of industries, external sector reforms, tariff reductions, financial liberalisation, etc. The state monopoly has been abolished in virtually all sectors. India has done away with quantitative restrictions. Our highest tariff rates have come down from 400 per cent to 35 per cent with the average rate declining to approximately 25 per cent.

Now that ten years have passed, one may ask: were the reforms done right? Could they have been better? What have been the flaws? Where have we gone wrong? What is to be the agenda for the second generation reforms? This volume is an attempt to provide insights into these questions in the writings of eminent economists.

A Sequencing Error

"We in this country tend to think of reforms as we do of domestic repairs: call a plumber to fix a leak, an electrician to deal with a misbehaving tubelight, a mason to stop a leak. This is the thinking reflected in government announcements: there are labour reforms, and power reforms, and insurance reforms, all isolated, stand-alone improvements" remarks Ashok Desai.

Actually, an economy is a machine rather than a house; everything in it is interconnected with everything else. So if one fixes a leak in one place, it may burst a valve somewhere else; if one is to avoid expensive mistakes, one has to understand the economy as a whole, emphasises Dr. Desai. He points out that there was an error of sequencing. Industries that boomed in the early 1990s are suffering today. Industrial licensing was removed first; trade liberalization came much later. The result was that domestic producers were still focussed on the domestic market in the early 1990s; in their view, the landscape of the markets was little different from the 1980s. The economy was a largely closed one; so the growth of industry was based on domestic market expectations. And because it was closed, the growth of one domestic industry created the market for another; all sorts of industries grew up, efficient and inefficient, high-cost and low-cost.

The present economic crisis, points out Desai, is not due to the reforms in industry, trade and capital markets, but due to the undone reforms in industrial protection, exchange rate policy, and infrastructure.

The Next Wave of Reforms

The curse of our persistent poverty, according to Kelkar, is due to lower growth rates. In other words, what India faces is the problem of low productivity across the sectors as well as of the low growth in this productivity. After analysing the factors that could have contributed to this relative low productivity and low growth impasse, he recommends the launching of next wave of reforms — the second generation of reforms. According to him, "the first wave of reforms launched in 1991 by Dr. Manmohan Singh and Shri Narasimha Rao were essentially crisis-driven. This time round we can have consensus-driven reforms so that we can act in anticipation of a crisis which could definitely visit on us if the present trends are allowed to continue".

The reform measures required are macro-economic, meso-economic and micro-economic. Macro-economic reforms are required to ensure fiscal health. A very important area of reforms, according to Kelkar, would be redefining the role of Government and down-sizing the Government while improving the quality of governance. The down-sizing of the Government will also mean privatisation of non-strategic public sector enterprises including banking sector. Meso-economic reforms would include: major infrastructure sectoral reforms such as energy, transport, telecom and reforms of universities and other higher institutions of learning. Micro-economic reforms will be to promote competition in product markets and services sector by allowing free entry and freer international trade. Micro-economic reforms should also encompass factor markets, such as labour markets, land markets, capital markets, and natural resources market.

Strengthening and Deepening of Reforms

A policy agenda for the future should be determined by looking at existing strength and weaknesses, and building on the strength while correcting the weaknesses, says Montek Ahluwalia. According to him our strength lies in:

(i) Growth performance which is now much better than the frustratingly low 3.5 per cent to 4 per cent which characterised the first three decades after independence. The growth rate in the 1990s has been around 6 per cent. If we focus on the 1980s and 1990s, India has been one of the ten fastest growing economies in the world !

(ii) A rise in literacy rate from 18.3 per cent in 1951 to 62 per cent in 1996-97 and

(iii) Population growth appears to be declining (from above 2 per cent for a long period, India's population is expected to slow down to 1.5 per cent in the next decade).

According to Montek Ahluwalia these positive developments have important implications for our prospects in the next decade. He would classify the reform agenda ahead of us into three categories.

(i) The first item on this agenda on which there is a great deal of agreement must be to restore fiscal discipline. This is actually a first generation reform, which we have not been able to carry out as planned.

(ii) The second category consists of first generation reforms which are still to be completed. Reforms in this areas would involve: (i) Industrial deregulation; (ii) further opening the economy to trade; (iii) Disinvestment and privatisation; (iv) Financial sector reforms; and (v) Private financing of infrastructure.

(iii) The last category consists of what can be called genuine second generation reforms, which take the reform process to new areas not addressed thus far. These are: (i) extending reforms to the states; (ii) labour legislation (iii) the functioning of the legal system.

Revitalise the Governance

According to Bimal Jalan, compared with the record of the first 40 years of development, there is very little doubt that India's economy — by any standard of measurement — is stronger and more resilient today than was the case a decade ago. In his judgement, the phenomenal changes that have taken place in the world economy, the present direction of policies to make India more open and more competitive is right and deserves to be accelerated. In addition to economic reforms, it is now important to embark on an urgent programme to revitalise the governance and public delivery systems at all levels of Government — centre, state and districts. Without strengthening the ability of the Government to do what it alone can do, and narrowing the focus of its activities to what matters most for the future development of the country— education, health, clean environment, and a functioning infrastructure — India cannot adequately seize the opportunities that lie ahead.

Information Technology

Globalization is no longer an option: it is a fact, remarks Kirit Parikh. The revolution in information technology is transforming the global economic structure. This provides an opportunity to developing countries to leap-frog and catch up with the developed world. To leap-frog, however, the frog has to come out of the well. Telecommunication reforms that lead to a competitive telecom sector are critical if India is to benefit fully from the new information technology.

Economic Reforms and Poverty

There is a frequent assertion by critics what went wrong in

our assault on poverty in the past, and hence, what is wrong with reforms today, is that our planners were interested in growth as the objective, not in poverty. But Economists such as Jagdish Bhagwati argue that growth was, and is, desired *because* it would reduce poverty. There are three central reasons:

(i) it creates jobs that 'pull up' the poor into gainful employment by providing more economic opportunity;

(ii) it provides the revenues with which we can build more schools and provide more health facilities for the poor; and

(iii) it creates the incentives that enable the poor to access these facilities and also for the advancement of progressive social agendas generally.

In short, sometimes all good things go together: growth improves incomes, pulls up people out of poverty, improves literacy, helps spend more on public health, and does much more along these lines. And economic reforms, aimed at a reversal of the anti-globalisation, anti-market, pro-public-enterprise attitudes and policies that produced our dismal growth performance, are therefore the most important thing that we need to do, says Jagdish Bhagwati.

Human Development Index

According to Vijay Kelkar, in terms of human development index developed by United Nations, while we are amongst the lowest 20 percent, the East Asian countries are in the highest 20 percent. However, while making such international comparisons there is one interesting and an important point: although India lags behind in the levels of living as measured in per-capita income terms or human development index terms, in equity indicator such as 'Gini Index' which summarises the distribution of income or consumption of an economy, India is in the top ten amongst all developing countries. The latest World Development Report of the World Bank shows that our consumption distribution is perhaps less inequitable even compared to the distribution obtained in the United States! According to this Report, the Gini-index for India in 1997 was 0.378 as compared to major developing countries such as China at 0.403, Thailand 0.414, Malaysia 0.485, Mexico

0.537 and Brazil 0.600. This is an important point because many analysts on the left of the ideological spectrum have regarded India to be one of the worst sufferers from income inequalities and it is said to be getting worse. Obviously, data do not support this.

The Balance Sheet of Reforms

The balance sheet of economic reforms in India in the 1990s is mixed, says Nagesh Kumar. The overall post-reform growth rate of output has been robust at an average of 6.8 per cent. The observed growth rate for the 1990s is not only significantly higher than that recorded during the 1980s but it is also more sustainable in terms of parameters of fiscal and current account. He further points out that Indian industry has relied more on technology imports and affiliations with outside multinational companies and less on in-house R&D activity. Increased dependence on imported technology and industrial consolidation, however, have not yet resulted in any measurable productivity improvement. The neglect of in-house R&D is a matter of concern for sustaining industrial growth and competitiveness. Another area of concern, according to Nagesh Kumar, is that the fiscal adjustment has been achieved by pruning capital expenditure rather than by containing current expenditure of the government. The decline in public investment in physical and social infrastructure questions the sustainability of growth.

In Raja Chelliah's view, the obstacles to reform are, to some extent (i) lack of understanding, (ii) short-term political considerations and (iii) lack of financial resources. The economic reform strategy for the next decade will be dictated and determined by three basic objectives. (a) 6 to 6.5 per cent annual rate of growth of GDP; (b) considerable emphasis on human development and (c) reversing the trend of worsening regional disparities.

State and the Market

Reforms have not reduced the role of the state. In some areas, the role has expanded and in some others, it has contracted. According to Rangarajan, more market does not mean less government but only different government. The need for expanded state intervention in areas of education, health and sanitation cannot be underestimated. But it is only an efficient economy that will generate the necessary surplus which will enable the state to fulfil its socio-economic obligations. Efficiency and equity should not be posed as opposing considerations.

Agriculture

Analysing the approach to reforms in agriculture, Vyas and Reddy state that our long term goals as well as contemporary developments, suggest a cautious approach to reforms in agriculture without losing sight of distributional aspects within the sector and vis-a-vis other sectors of the economy. In order to achieve the objectives of a dynamic surplus generating agriculture, ensuring equitable distribution and, providing safety nets for the vulnerable sections, the role of the non-price factors, especially the institutional factors, is important. There is need for building and strengthening delivery systems and local initiatives.

Public Finances

On the subject of restructuring of public finances, Y.V. Reddy points out that today, fiscal and monetary options are no longer driven by domestic compulsions alone; they have to broadly conform to certain internationally acceptable norms of what constitutes the sound fundamentals of an open and competitive economy. We do not have much option to deviate from these standards in the medium and long-term.

There is now an increasing realisation about the importance of monetary policy, and the autonomy in the conduct of monetary policy as well as efficiency in monetary transmission mechanism. These require, according to Reddy, drastic reduction in the high level of government borrowing which has a significant bearing on fiscal and revenue deficits.

Centre and States

Economic reform in a broader sense would also encompass re-aligning of relative functions of Centre and States towards achieving economic prosperity. This would mean, according to Y.V. Reddy, greater emphasis on development of social infrastructure and physical infrastructure, which lie in the domain of States compared to Centre. Expenditure responsibility of States is likely to grow in social sectors; particularly education, health, sanitation and nutrition. Thus, as the reforms progress, relative balance between Centre and States tends to tilt in favour of States.

Changing Multilateral Trade Discipline

Apart from the impact of various unilateral economic reforms undertaken since 1991, India's economy also had to reorient itself to the changing multilateral trade discipline within the newly written GATT/WTO framework, points out Rajesh Chadha in chapter-10. The unilateral trade policy measures have encompassed exchange-rate policy, foreign investment, external borrowing, import licensing, custom tariffs and export subsidies. The multilateral aspect of India's trade policy refers to India's WTO commitments with regard to trade in goods and services, trade related investment measures, and intellectual property rights. The multilateral trade liberalisation under the WTO negotiations is aimed at reducing tariff and non-tariff barriers on international trade.

In multilateral trade negotiations, under the auspices of WTO the real thing is that market power talks. Those who are powerful call the shots. The reality is that a majority of the members are from the developing world, but they are not united. If we, in the developing world, stand together and work together no one can harm us, remarks Murasoli Maran.

Banking and Financial Sector Reforms

Following the recommendations of the Committee on Financial System (CFS) which reported in 1991 and the second Report of the Narasimham Committee in 1998, a considerable ground has been covered in putting in place a financial system which can meet the requirements of a more competitive and open economy.

The Report of the Narasimham Committee (April 1998) provides a framework for the current phase of reforms — the second generation of reforms — which could be conveniently looked at in terms of three broad inter-related issues:

(i) Actions that need to be taken to strengthen the foundations of the banking system;

(ii) Streamlining procedures, upgrading technology and human resource development; and

(iii) Structural changes in the system.

Reserve Bank of India has already acted on many of the recommendations and in this connection has submitted a report (Oct. 31, 2001) outlining the action taken on the recommendations of the Committee and the areas where no action has been taken (chapter-17).

Political Consensus

Prime Minister's Economic Advisory Council in its report, *Economic Reforms: A Medium Term Perspective* has briefly catalogued the rationale for economic reforms and the specific areas which need to be addressed in the second generation reforms in major sectors of the economy.

The report stresses the need to develop a political consensus around the core reform programme so that specific reform measures enjoy support cutting across party lines. India has demonstrated that there exists broad political support to the reform programme, as has been proved by the transition of several Governments in the last five years. The world at large now believes that the reform process in India is irreversible, but certainly there has to be an acceleration in its momentum so that the goals that seem so easily within reach can be rapidly attained.

The reform process has also to be accelerated in the States. It is heartening to note that in the past few years several political parties in various States continue to sustain bold reform programmes embracing a wide range of activities. Thus a nation-wide consensus for reforms is already in place. What is required now is to build on this consensus in terms of policy and implementation.

2

A Decade of Reforms

ASHOK V. DESAI

The reforms are now 10 years old. In the early days, they were the subject of bitter partisan debate. I remember the time when Manmohan Singh went to Calcutta for a public debate with Jyoti Basu and the leftists. We were greeted with black flags, and just escaped being attcked with sticks by CPM activists. I also remember the vile attacks Manmohan Singh faced in Parliament. He was a sensitive man, and used to show it; Atal Behari Vajpayee advised him to develop a thick skin.

Now that ten years have passed, the reforms are passing into folklore. Soon students will be writing long doctoral dissertations on the reforms. Manmohan Singh will join the pantheon of Hindu gods. That will be the time to leave the reforms to history and to turn to more interesting topics.

But I think there is still time to ask: were the reforms done right? Could they have been done better? The questions have a particular resonance because of the bad times through which the economy is passing. Industrial growth has slumped. Industrialists view the future with great gloom; as a result, they are not investing. Exports have fallen this year. The government is clueless about what to do, and has been asking industrialists; industrialists are asking economists for a change. But no one has a clear answer. Could it be that we were brought to this pass by the reforms?

We in this country tend to think of reforms as we do of domestic repairs: call a plumber to fix a leak, an electrician to deal with a misbehaving tubelight, a mason to stop a leak. This is the thinking reflected in government announcements: there are labour reforms, and power reforms, and insurance reforms, all isolated, stand-alone improvements, each adding to the beauty of the house of India.

Actually, an economy is a machine rather than a house; everything in it is interconnected with everything else. So if one fixes a leak in one place, it may burst a valve somewhere else; if one is to avoid expensive mistakes, one has to understand the economy as a whole. And we in the finance ministry in 1991 were not just trying to fix a leak; we were trying to improve the machine so that it would work better for all time. Such basic repairs give excellent results if they succeed; but they are also more risky. And then, the economy is a machine that acts slowly; one may do something today, and the effects may become evident years later. Hence one has to understand not just the mechanics, but also the dynamics of the economy. It is a terribly complicated machine; not even the best economists understand it quite fully. And let me say, quite frankly, that we who undertook the reforms were not the best economists. Manmohan Singh used to call himself an extinguished economist. He was extremely intelligent, and he had an instinctive grasp of economics; but he was right, his economics was out of date. I was more of a practitioner; but I had made my living by doing bits of economics for which people were prepared to pay - economics of industry, trade, energy, etc. India had been in the hands of socialists for forty years. They ran the economy by their theological principles; there was no point in a non-socialist learning to run the economy, and no chance of getting any practice. So we came to the job ill equipped. Not that better preparation would have made much difference. For we faced tremendous opposition; we did what we could, not what we thought needed to be done; and when, after toiling for two years, I found that nothing worthwhile could be done, I left. Mistakes were made, and I want to ask today: could we have done better? Would the economy be in a better shape if we had? Time is limited; let me take up three questions:

1. The splendid industrial boom of the early 1990s was cut short by a credit squeeze in 1996; industry has never recovered momentum since. Could a softer landing have been devised?

2. Precisely those industries that boomed in the early 1990s are doing badly; in this sense, the investment in those years was misguided. Could it have been guided better?
3. The momentum has slackened so much by now that the economy looks ready to lapse back into the Hindu rate of growth of 3½ per cent. Is that not the ultimate failure of the reforms? Why has growth slumped? How can it be raised again?

The Credit Squeeze of 1996

The reason for the credit squeeze was that Manmohan Singh felt the economy was overheating and inflation was going up. The balance of payments was still in good conditions; but if inflation rose, and domestic shortages developed, the balance of payments deficit could lead to another crisis. By that time I was in Business Standard. I disagreed with the finance ministry's assessment, and was against the deflationary measures. But I would not say that Manmohan Singh was wrong. He had some facts on his side. He also had to worry that inflation would make the Congress unpopular and lead to its defeat in the general election. There will always be times when the government feels the economy is overheating and has to cool it down. Could it have been done more skilfully?

The 1996 squeeze bit so deep because it was largely a squeeze on the quantity of credit. Industrial producers had ordered machinery from abroad; just as it started arriving, they were told there was no credit to finance them. Producers had begun to ship production to the market; just then there was no money to finance the pipeline inventories. Must it be done that way?

One obvious improvement would be to act more on the price of credit and less on the quantity. Interest rates did go up to unprecedented levels in 1996; the financial institutions were borrowing from the public at 18-20 per cent. But bank's lending rates (which were then in the 20s) moved little. In general, interest rates move slowly and insufficiently in response to changes in liquidity.

If one wants to bring in interest rates as a policy variable, then the government should become neutral to them. And it will not so become unless it brings down its borrowings considerably. So reduction of the fiscal deficit is essential if the credit markets are to function smoothly. Reducing it is not difficult. It could cause havoc if done suddenly, but if planned over a few years, it can be easily done by small changes in the rates of growth of revenue and expenditure. It has not happened because no government wanted to do it.

Local Credit Markets

But I have a solution that does not require such radical change: it is to create local markets for credit instruments. The Reserve Bank should organize and regulate these local markets, and encourage banks to participate in them. Just now, only big companies raise money on commercial paper and certificates of deficit; and the market for these instruments is confined to the banks. Actually, banks should be lending less in the form of loans and overdrafts, and should invest more in hundis issued by borrowers. It is quite wrong to ask banks to invest in shares; hundis are much better. Investment in hundis would enable banks to spread risk. Available for different period, they would help banks choose their maturity profile; and individual borrowers' record of default would give everyone information about their creditworthiness and be reflected in the interest they have to pay. Local businesses could also use hundis to borrow directly from investors. And differences in local interest rates would pave the way for flow of funds between cities and regions outside the banking system. Local credit markets are the easiest and most important reform of the financial markets possible today.

Electronic Payments System

The other easy and important reform is to create a national electronic payments system. The Reserve Bank has unaccountably dragged its feet on this. The result is that it is easier to transfer securities between investors than it is to transfer cash. The Reserve Bank would like the system to be a monopoly of the banks; and most banks are in such poor shape that they are incapable of taking on technical changes. That was the sorry story of bank computerization, and it is of electronic transfer.

Actually, electronic transfer can be a stand-alone business outside banks; just as anyone can set up a depository participant, so should it be possible for anyone to set up an electronic cash transfer business. These two changes – local credit markets and a network of cash transfer agents – would introduce flexibility in the financial system, and reduce its vulnerability to shocks.

The introduction of electronic cash dealers could be a first step towards the separation of two functions now combined in banks - cash holding and investment. Cash holding is a riskless activity, but also one that brings no return. One should be able to keep one's cash in an account, but for just that service, one should pay for the safe keeping rather than earn interest. There can be any number of safe-keepers; they do not have to be banks, and do not have to be as strictly regulated as banks. Just as Sam Pitroda unveiled the era of street-corner telephone kiosks, I would like to see street-corner ATMs servicing everybody who paid an annual fee, irrespective of whether they had a bank account or not.

Investment institutions must be regulated; but they do not have to mix up all investments, bear all risks and give investors an average, net rate of interest as banks do at present. If they pass on risks to the investors, as mutual funds do, they can be run very cheaply. So I would like to think of banks functioning like mutual funds, bundling their borrowers into risk classes and offering them to depositors with full disclosure of risk.

It is a general perception that precisely the industries that boomed in the early 1990s are suffering today. The perception is implicit in the distinction people draw between the old economy, tired and faltering and the new economy, bursting with energy. Some of the momentum has gone out of the new economy, and it looks ready to join the old economy. But it is true that there has been a massacre of companies that did well till 1996.

A Sequencing Error

I see a number of reasons for this phenomenon. First, there was an error of sequencing. Industrial licensing was removed first; trade liberalization came much later. The result was that domestic producers were still focussed on the domestic market in the early 1990s; in their view, the landscape of the markets was little different from the 1980s. The economy was a largely closed one; so the growth of industry was based on domestic market expectations. And because it was closed, the growth of one domestic industry created the market for another; all the markets grew together, and gave no signals about which ones were going to grow and shrink in the long run. This is the trouble with closed economies; growth has nothing to do with international comparative advantage, and all sorts of industries grow up, efficient and inefficient, high-cost and low-cost.

Thus I would attribute the crisis in traditional industries to delayed and incomplete opening up; and in this respect, I see things going from bad to worse. The present government is close to industrialists and responsive to their demands, and is giving higher protection to everyone who goes and ask for it. The relative costs in this country are becoming less related to international prices. An industry with 50 per cent protection can never become internationally competitive. If we again have an industrial boom, industries will grow up which will collapse equally spectacularly in the future slump. High and unequal tariffs build up inefficient production. They make industry less competitive, narrow the range of exports and worsen the balance of payments; and thereby they reduce the long-run growth rate. And they raise the growth rate of imports over that of exports, and make periodic payments crises inevitable.

The Massacre of Machine-Building

There are a couple of side stories to this major theme of incomplete trade liberalization. The first is the reduction of duties under EPCG schemes until, by the mid - 1990s, machinery could be imported duty-free. The export obligation was a fig-leaf. To this day there are thousands of firms that reneged on their export obligations. The Department of Revenue Intelligence sends ruffians to them from time to time, harasses them, seals their premises and so on. But virtually none has been convicted, for the government failed to fulfil many of the preconditions required for exports. Anyway, EPCG meant duty-free imports of machinery. It brought in much new technology; and duty-free machinery for protected production meant higher profits. But it annihilated the machinery industry. Machinery output actually fell over the early

1990s. We know this of the output the government measures; the decline of small-scale machinery production, which it does not measure, was much more severe. And since it came to power, the present government has blatantly discriminated in favour of steel producers and awarded them high import duties; so the discrimination against equipment manufacture has worsened.

Metal-based industries have led the current industrial slowdown. But this is not just a point about total production. India's engineering industry was an excellent instrument for bringing down costs of machinery and for diffusing technology. Small manufacturers quickly imitated imported models and produced cheap copies; and all manufactures kept tinkering with the machinery, improving it and adapting it to local conditions. With the decline of the engineering industry, this vehicle of technological improvement has shrunk.

Financial Conservatism

The other side story relates to the financing of industrial growth. It is remarkable to what an extent the booming old industries in the early 1990s were financed by the government financial institutions and the nationalized banks - and how closely they are responsible for the latter's sickness. This incestuous relationship puzzles me; I am not clear at all why the government institutions should have stuck so close to the established industrialists. It could be conservatism, inertia, corruption, or a broader nexus between the political, industrial and financial establishments.

I have talked to some chiefs of the financial institutions. They thought there was no alternative. Very few enterprises in this country are rated; amongst those few, a minority are good risks. When everyone wanted to borrow and there was a shortage of credit, credit institutions would naturally prefer those that are large, old and established; that is what the financial institutions did. I am in the end disinclined to see conspiracies, and tend to think that the lending to large borrowers in traditional industries was the rational strategy for large, risk-averse financiers.

But I cannot help but remark on a number of features of the Indian financial system. First, such a high proportion of finance that is mediated is debt finance, and so little is equity. The primary equity market has more or less died after the reforms; and even if one takes into account private placements, mergers and acquisitions, debt finance dominates. Second, so much of the debt finance is mediated by government financial institutions. Governments consequently get a first charge on all that credit; no wonder they borrow so much. And finally, total equity investment is not negligible; it is just invested in small enterprises by industrialists and their friends. It is unmediated and unmarketed. Most enterprises are owner-managed, single-product and incapable of attracting risk capital. So owners become rentiers; they build a big house for the joint family, and live on the income from the enterprise year after year - until a catastrophe sweeps it away. This technological stagnancy in family-owned industry has much to do with India's industrial sluggishness and with the general fear of external influences. The small businessman has a deadly fear of the taxman, of his ability to close down and ruin businesses; so he bribes him, and avoids joining the ranks of regular taxpayers. Thus, I would link both Indian governments' chronic deficits and Indian xenophobia to the shape of its financial system.

Such comprehensive diagnoses immediately call forth radical and revolutionary solutions, such as abolition of the government. For today, I am not in that business. For the moment, I would stress three things.

First, the importance of abolishing import duties. Abolition of import duties would make all import replenishment schemes for exporters redundant, and permit them to set up import-based export production of any product without the permission of the two great enemies of exports, the customs and the directorate general of foreign trade. Once they are abolished, the exchange rate must be so varied as to keep the bulk of industry competitive. And if the exchange rate is to be manipulable by policy, restrictions on capital flows will be necessary. The simplest such control would be variable Tobin tax on foreign exchange transactions. To obstruct capital flows, the Tobin tax should be raised; to encourage them, it should be reduced. If it is actively used, both portfolio and direct investment can be entirely free.

Second, the importance of localizing the supply of credit. The financial system is too concentrated just now; it channels financial flows to a small number of large enterprises. We need local markets and local financial institutions. Chidambaram had the right idea in Local Area Banks, but such small localized banks cannot survive the competition of large, government-backed banks. Let us first try out local hundi markets; then market makers for the hundis will emerge. Let us try out local cash dealers; then the cash dealers may be allowed to offer their clients investment options such as mutual funds: they can become portfolio investment managers.

Finally, the importance of broadening the equity market. The sanitized market SEBI has created can never be broadened; it can only serve large, respectable, conservative firms. They are not going to bring an industrial revolution to India. What we need is outside equity for young entrepreneurs, for small companies; the model for their provision must be the venture capitalist. Maybe once the hundi dealers and portfolio investment managers have grown to a certain size and accumulated a track record, they can be allowed to start venture capital businesses.

Back to the Hindu Rate?

The weak and worsening economic performance since 1996 must raise the question in some minds: did the reforms do some lasting damage to the growth process? Some of those minds will have ready-made answers to the question: for instance, that growth in India is constrained by purchasing power, that purchasing power is determined by income distribution, and that liberalization must have worsened distribution. Such explanations were given after growth slowed down in 1965. It was wrong then; income distribution had changed little, and the lower growth was due to the rise of inefficient public enterprises that absorbed much investment and produced little. This time, slack demand is more evident as a factor in the slowdown, so it is time for leftists to start cranking the gramophone.

Distribution changes little and slowly, and is almost never the cause of cyclical changes. But 1965 bears interesting parallels with today. Then also, heavy industrial investment had been made which was mismatched with the emerging demand pattern: the followers of Mahalanobis invested in capital goods industry, but people wanted consumer goods. Then too there had been two poor agricultural years. Then too bad times lasted for five years, from 1966 till 1970. Then too a devaluation had been followed by trade liberalization, but bureaucrats soon reversed it. Then too Pakistan had been hit worse than India, and had a coup. Then too the thoughts of politicians haunted by a bad economy had turned to war.

But there are differences. Then the exchange rates were fixed; so if import duties were raised, their effect persisted. Today, if import duties are raised, the balance of payments improves, and the Rupee appreciates; not only is the degree of protection eroded by the appreciation, but exports become less profitable. And unlike them, there has been a software export boom, which has reinforced the tendency of the rupee to appreciate and of traditional industries to become less competitive. The troubles of the old industries are also accentuated by the fact that both transport and power are owned by governments, and that the real costs of both for Indian industries are higher than abroad. Energy-intensive industries suffer from high costs; and since all metals are energy-intensive, all the metal and machinery industries are under stress. And because the railways are so inefficient, it is cheaper to import wheat into Madras from Australia than from Punjab, cheaper to import Italian marble into Bombay than marble from Rajasthan.

This is my explanation of the present economic crisis: it is not due to the reforms in industry, trade and capital markets, but to the undone reforms in industrial protection, exchange rate policy, railways and transport.

M.A. Master Memorial Lecture at Indian Merchants' Chamber, Bombay, October 19, 2001.

3

Economic Reforms Agenda

Micro, Meso and Macro Economic Reforms

VIJAY KELKAR

During the 1990s, India has been among the fastest growing economies of the world. This year would be the third consecutive year when the real GDP growth would be six percent or higher. This has been accompanied by exchange rate stability and low inflation rate. For instance, currently, the underlying core inflation rate remains only three percent per annum. Still, the great question remains, namely, will the present trend of growth acceleration continue to enable India to meet the strategic objectives of (i) eradication of poverty, and (ii) playing our rightful role in the world by becoming a source of growth and stability for the global economy? To analyze this, it is necessary to look at the Indian economy in somewhat longer and in a global perspective. This is essential to identify the necessary policy reforms.

In India's economic history, our Independence marks a major discontinuity. Since Independence, India has achieved remarkable progress in overcoming the long-term Colonial stagnation and economic backwardness. We were indeed fortunate that in the formative years our destiny was guided by a group of remarkably talented leaders led by India's First Prime Minister Pandit Jawahar

These are personal views of the Author and need not reflect the views of the organizations with which he is associated.

Lal Nehru. They had a well-defined world view and equally well articulated strategy. The aspiration of national leadership was clear: they wanted to create a vibrant self-reliant national economy and eradicate poverty as rapidly as possible. Given the weaknesses and the limited social base of the entrepreneurial class and the absence of well-functioning capital markets, the State was assigned the twin roles of leading the process of primitive capital accumulation and of an entrepreneur particularly for creating the heavy and basic industries. Consequently, the public sector became the leading agent for industrialisation.

This strategy did pay off. It substantially accelerated the growth rate from the virtual stagnancy of the pre-Independence era. It created the social and industrial infrastructure and the technological base for defence production as well as in the sophisticated and strategic nuclear and space fields. This, not only paved the way for future growth, but also provided the required policy autonomy to pursue national security objectives in a Nuclear Age.

In implementing the strategy one of the major problems soon to be faced was the failure on the agricultural front, leading to growing dependence on PL-480 food imports. This strategic shortcoming was quickly overcome by Smt. Indira Gandhi by launching the Green Revolution to achieve the objective of self-reliance in food security.

These achievements are indeed historic when we recognize that all this was achieved under a democratic form of governance, without any colonial exploitation and while facing the challenges of demographic explosion. Population of India which was less than 400 million in 1951, crossed one billion mark in 2001. This meant during the second half of the century, India added as much as 600 million people!

Our development performance is outstanding when compared to our own historical standards, but seen in the context of the contemporary experience of other economies of Asia, such as, China, Japan or Korea, our performance is perhaps far short. India, at the time of Independence, had almost similar levels of per-capita income as that of China or Korea but since then both these economies have surpassed India in terms of per-capita incomes or even in terms of share in the global economy whether in manufacturing output or in global trade. The per-capita income in Korea was US$ 8490 in 1999 while ours was still US$ 450. The Gross National Product of China which in the year 1999 was US$ 980 billion which was more than twice that of ours. In both China and Korea, it was achieved through a sustained growth rate of more than 8 percent per annum over more than two decades. The picture looks even less flattering when one moves away from the traditional indicators to the broader developmental outcomes in the areas of health and education. We, in India, are never tired of boasting of our pool of scientists and engineers, yet, the ground reality is that even here the scientists and engineers per million population in India is less than one fourth of that of China or one tenth of Korea. China and the east Asian economies have uniformly and significantly out-performed India. While we see an outstanding performance of these economies in overcoming poverty, we have the dubious distinction of housing the world's largest number of poor. In terms of human development index developed by United Nations, while we are amongst the lowest 20 percent, the east Asian countries are in the highest 20 percent.

While making such international comparisons there is one interesting and an important point to which I want to invite your attention : although India lags behind in the levels of living as measured in per-capita income terms or human development index terms, in equity indicator such as 'Gini Index' which summarizes the distribution of income or consumption of an economy, India is in the top ten amongst all developing countries. The latest World Development Report of the World Bank shows that our consumption distribution is perhaps less inequitable even compared to the distribution obtained in the United States! According to this Report, the Gini-index for India in 1997 was .378 as compared to major developing countries such as China at .403, Thailand .414, Malaysia .485, Mexico .537 and Brazil .600. There is also a recently published paper by Prof. Hashim, showing that in India the "Gini Index" may have been, in fact, improving over the plan periods, albeit, marginally. This is an important point because many analysts on the left of the ideological spectrum have regarded India to be one of the worst sufferers from income inequalities and it is said to be getting worse. Obviously, data do not support this. This brings us to the heart of our economic problem, namely, for the curse of our poverty the villain is the low per capita income due to the comparatively lower growth rates. In other words, what India faces is the problem of low productivity across the sectors as well as of the low growth in this productivity. I would submit that this is the crux of India's persistent cruel poverty.

Now an important issue is how did we get into this situation when otherwise, the development process seems to have done the trick, namely, that of transforming a low savings economy into high-savings/ high-investment economy. Over the last 50 years, the rate of savings and investment which were only 10.4 percent and 10.2 percent respectively in 1951-52 have been more than doubled reaching almost 25 percent of the GDP in the decade of 90s. In other words, the Indian people have made great sacrifices for making large investments but the total rate of return on these resources has not been adequate either to catch up with the dynamic developing economies or making available resources to eradicate poverty.

I think many factors have contributed to this relatively low productivity and low growth impasse. The first strategic error was the relative neglect of international trade. By neglecting international trade we precluded the possibilities of exploiting productivity enhancing exchanges. In the manufacturing sector we opted for an across-the-board import substitution strategy where we sought to produce everything in a production chain whether the product was a commercial vehicle or a steel mill. And by this, the weakest link decided the fate of the strength of the whole production chain. We entered into production of a number of activities in which we just did not possess the competitive edge. It resulted in a loss of efficiency for the entire industry. For instance, forcing the Indian fertilizer industry to use only Indian designed catalyst, the entire fertilizer industry's productivity suffered. Same was the case for electronics sector where our software industry took time to take off because of the insistence on the use of domestic computer hardware. What all these examples show is that we just did not allow international trade to enlarge the possibilities of using our own resources more efficiently and we ended up taxing our own productive sectors. Increased international trade would not only have given boost to aggregate demand and provided a source of growth but also would have increased the productivity through technology infusion by making available state-of-the-art capital goods as well as intermediate inputs. Such an enhanced participation in international competition would have also promoted innovation and creativity-a key requirement to succeed in the emerging knowledge-driven world economy. Greater international trade is of strategic importance for yet another reason. India is very resource-poor country in terms of per capita availability of important natural resources. This means that the international trade is the only way India can meet its growing resource needs such as energy or metals.

The second strategic limitation was the relative neglect of agriculture. Not only did we neglect investments in agriculture and in related activities such as irrigation, but we also manipulated the terms of trade against agriculture. This was a copy book revisit to the debate between Joseph Stalin and Bukharin. I think the recent arguments of Shri Sharad Joshi have considerable merit when he argues for liberating India's agricultural sector from the present regime of controls which deny the exciting possibilities of employment expansion from value added agriculture. This neglect also had a profound impact on the growth process itself. Prof. Sukhamoy Chakravarty has shown how the consequent failure on the food economy front consequently led to stop / go policies regarding public investment inducing sharper business cycles and thereby reducing the underlying growth rate.

The third weakness has been the working of our public sector. In designing the policies for public sector we did not adequately think of the role of incentives, particularly incentives provided for the management or the bureaucracy to ensure that the shareholder value or national wealth is maximized. Our legal system may have further aggravated the problem by treating public sector as an extension of the state, which meant that we finally robbed the public sector of any risk taking ability; a key hallmark of an entrepreneur. Consequently, public sector which was supposed to be the primary force of capital accumulation became a drain on fiscal resources.

There is yet another major source adversely affecting the long term growth rate. This is what I call the curse of growing subsidisation and cross subsidisation. The growth in subsidies has been very high. In 1971, the total explicit subsidy provided in the budget amounted to 3 per cent of Gross Domestic Product and within three decades or so this share has increased four fold, now exceeding 12 per cent of GDP. Of course, not all subsidies are bad. There are these merit subsidies, where social benefits are higher than the social costs. But these are even less than 1/3rd of the total subsidies. Subsidies essentially imply under recovery of costs. These are being showered by both Centre and States through direct budgetary outgo or through foregone revenues. These subsidies preempt resources from needed investments. Similarly, there are implicit subsidies through under-performing of public sector as well as other forms of indirect subsidies through cross subsidization. Let us take the example of non-performing public sector enterprises. By 1998-99 the stock of the Central Government investments even at book value has increased to 2740 billion rupees. What is the post-tax rate of return on these investments? It is less than three percent. If these investments had achieved comparable returns as efficient enterprises do, then the rates of return would have been at least two/three times higher. The difference between these is also an implicit subsidy ultimately borne by the tax-payers.

If direct subsidies are bad enough, the impact of the curse of indirect subsidisation is deleterious. Not only are these subsidies non-transparent, as these are not made out from the Budget, being effected through differential pricing of public sector produced goods and services but also lead to loss of international competitiveness of many of our major industries. The working of the curse of cross-subsidisation can be seen in all major sectors, such as, electricity, railway transport, petroleum sector, telecommunications and so on and so forth. It is felt that charging prices differently to different class of consumers promotes the goal of social justice. Ruefully, what happens is exactly opposite. Giving power free to the agricultural sector not only knocks out any incentive for efficient use of electricity on demand side, but also on supply side, it leads to a deterioration in the quality of electricity supplies. In a market economy, you can either fix price or fix quantity but cannot do both over a long period of time. Consequently, farmers get intermittent power supplies which adversely affects his economics while simultaneously affecting the SEB's financial health. This has further adverse implications for the industrial sector. The electricity charges for industrial sector are many times higher than that paid by agricultural and household sector. Such a mark-up phenomenon is seen perhaps only in India and not elsewhere. Similar phenomena exist in railways where the rail freight rates are pegged much higher than costs to cross-subsidize passenger travel. These policies adversely affect the competitive strength of our industry and once again weakens industrial growth, exports, employment and productivity growth.

Finally, one of the biggest drags on India's development has come from the growth of Government consumption which is expenditure on current consumption. This is because of the size of the Government and the compensation given to employees of government and employees of semi-government organisations. With successive Pay Commissions, the compensation of the Government employees has been revised upwards not always consistent with the States' capacity to pay or with the underlying quality of supplies.

With the recent Pay Commission decision, the public consumption will go up by as much as 2 per cent of the Gross Domestic Product and this has become the major source of fiscal stress for both the Centre and State Government finances.

What are the implications of these developments? These have led to enormous fiscal stress to Central and the State Governments. The combined fiscal deficits of the Central and State Governments are now as high as ten percent of GDP. This is one of the highest ratios in the world and the consequences of these fiscal deficits, if continued, will be profound. For instance, currently the National debt is as much as 82 percent of GNP and is increasing at a rapid pace which, if unchecked, can lead to an internal debt trap. Already, these growing revenue deficits and fiscal deficits have led to massive market borrowing by the Government. This means higher interest rates and crowding out of private sector investment. Currently, almost 80 percent of private financial savings are being absorbed by public sector borrowing. Consequently, a cruel choice is between higher inflation by printing of money or higher interest rates which choke investment and employment growth. The ultimate outcome, of course, is non-sustainability of recent dynamism leading to considerable lowering of growth rates.

Clearly, the key to India's prosperity lies in reversing these trends.

If the analysis presented so far is correct, then the policy initiatives that are required are obvious. I would suggest that what is necessary now is the launching of the next wave of reforms, described as the second generation of reforms by the Finance Minister, Shri Yashwant Sinha. The first wave of reforms launched in 1991 by Dr. Manmohan Singh and Shri Narasimha Rao were essentially crisis-driven. This time round we can have consensus-driven reforms so that we can act in anticipation of a crisis which could definitely visit on us if the present trends are allowed to continue.

The foremost reform measures that are required are macroeconomic reforms to ensure fiscal health. Parliament needs to quickly adopt the proposed Fiscal Responsibility Act, which would limit the revenue deficits and budgets deficits and safeguard the economy from a debt trap. Such a strategy has been successfully deployed by a number of countries. Of course, merely passing the Fiscal Responsibility Act will not achieve the fiscal balance. What is required is simultaneous action both at the Centre and the States to increase user charges particularly of intermediate inputs such as electricity, water, transport, etc. so as to cover long run marginal costs which will ensure that resources are generated to increase investments and also to improve the quality of these services. These measures would encourage private investment in these sectors enlarging the supplies of much needed infrastructural inputs while reducing the costs for consumers. There is also a need to increase the tax-GDP ratio through (i) improved tax administration by using information technology, (ii) drastically pruning the tax exemptions, e.g., small scale sector exemptions from excise taxes, and (iii) bringing services sector in the value added tax (VAT) system of taxation. Presently, India's tax-GDP ratio is lower than the Asian and OECD economies.

Of course, one of the most important reform would be redefining the role of Government and down-sizing the Government while improving the quality of governance. The down-sizing of the Government will also mean privatisation of non-strategic public sector enterprises including banking sector.

To my mind, the only strategic public sector enterprises should be those dealing with atomic energy, space and defence production. In all other areas, we should privatise the public sector enterprises.

The privatization process, of course, will have to be handled carefully. First and foremost, it has to be transparent and it should lead to an industrial structure that is competitive while reducing the concentration of economic power. To facilitate this, the privatization process would need to ensure that the major public sector undertakings such as oil companies, telecom companies, steel companies etc. become widely held, professionally managed organizations observing the best standards of corporate governance, a key hallmark of modern capitalism. Such a strategy would also give fresh impetus to deepen and widen domestic equity markets providing further impetus to new investments. Privatizing public sector undertakings by selling them to strategic investors, whether domestic or foreign, can be a possible route. But this has a very limited role at least in near future as the political economy of India requires a somewhat different strategy for privatization from those adopted by the countries of Latin America, or East Asia, or Central Europe.

The most important outcome of the fiscal correction would be reduction of both short-term and long-term real interest rates in the economy. Currently they are at unprecedented levels of between 6-8 per cent. No country in the world has achieved sustained growth rate with such high interest rates. Bringing the real interest rates in the neighbourhood of 3-4 per cent can trigger a spectacular investment boom throughout the economy. Such a reduction in the long-term interest rates will also be essential for maintaining exchange rate regime that is supportive of trade liberalization, i.e., avoid over-valuation of rupee. Thus, the reduced interest rate and competitive exchange rate can become the proverbial "Archimedean" lever to propel the economy on a higher growth path.

In the next wave of reforms what is going to be crucial is the launching of meso-economic reforms, i.e., major infrastructure sectoral reforms such as energy, transport, telecom and reforms of universities and other higher institutions of learning. In a growing economy, these sectors will require enormous amount of new investments. Currently, all these sectors are under public sector and in some cases these are monopolies. If in these sectors we introduce both privatization of public sector enterprises and entry of private sector, the gains to the economy are likely to be quite spectacular. Even in the advanced economies, such as, United States which liberalized over the last twenty years, transport sector, energy sector, the efficiency gains have been as high as 10 to 15 percent of the sectoral GDP. The other countries' experience is similar. My own study at the Tariff Commission suggests that to the Indian economy the benefits of these meso-economic reforms could be as high as 3-4 per cent of GDP per annum. Mind you, these annual gains are only static efficiency gains and to capture these gains very little capital is required. Moreover, they will also provide the spring board for further dynamic gains particularly by bringing new private investments and productivity growth. In this list of meso-economic reforms, I want to especially emphasize the reform of higher education, i.e., college and universities. Today, there are severe entry barriers to start a private university in India. This needs to change. Here, collaboration or alliance with great academic institutions like this University can play a great role in India's future.

A major implication of the proposed meso-economic reforms is a need to create a new institutional architecture for the management of the Indian economy recognizing that we are now aiming to become a full-fledged modern market economy, where stability, predictability and transparency of policies are of fundamental importance. Such a new institutional architecture will have an independent monetary authority by giving greater independence to Reserve Bank of India on the lines of autonomy enjoyed by the Federal Reserve in USA or the Bank of England in U.K.

The new institutional architecture will also imply strengthening of independent regulatory agencies such as SEBI, TRAI, CERC etc. and start treating their independence at par with the independent judiciary. This will inspire confidence amongst both investors and consumers and promote competition in these sectors and what we also will be achieving is the reduction in counter-productive politics of cross-substitution.

Now, let me turn to the required micro-economic reforms. The center piece of microeconomic reforms will be to promote competition in product markets and services sector by allowing free entry and freer international trade. This also means giving level playing field to all entities, i.e., private sector and public sector. To achieve this, one of the foremost policy measure would be to reduce our tariff barriers. Today, India has one of the world's highest tariff barriers – where the dynamic Asian economies have average rate of tariff of 5 percent or so, ours is nearly 25 percent. We need to accelerate the program of tariff reduction and bring tariffs at par with the Asian level. The recent policy measure of the removal of all non-tariff barriers is, of course, of great importance as it means removing all import controls against consumer goods and agricultural products and opening the doors for the winds of competition to flow everywhere. In the coming years, there could be pressures to make increased use of "anti-dumping" measures. These need to be resisted by observing the letter and spirit of WTO anti-dumping codes. This will enhance the credibility of our trade policies vis-a-vis our trading partners and also encourage shift of resources towards more efficient use.In addition, we will need to replace present MRTP Act with a new Competition Law to bring our Competition Policy at par with the emerging international trends.

Finally, the next wave of micro-economic reforms should encompass factor markets. In the 1991 reforms, the emphasis was on reforms of product markets by abolishing industrial licensing and import barriers. These reforms left the factor markets such as labour markets, land markets, capital markets, natural resources market such as water and institutions somewhat untouched. Notice that I am including "institutions" as a factor of production. The term "Institutions" includes State and quasi-State institutions as well as judiciary and civil society. These institutional reforms would strengthen the "social capital" base in addition to strengthening of the physical and human capital base of the economy. Although, many leading mainstream economists are somewhat skeptical of the concept of "social capital", for the one like me coming from India, I find this concept further elaborated by Mr. Fukayama quite appealing.

The reforms of labour markets are particularly important. The new post-industrial revolution requires flexibility in all operations.

This means flexibility in labour markets is of phenomenal importance so that companies can respond with speed to the changing market conditions. Our present laws of bankruptcy and corporate control also require reforms so that the market for corporate control become competitive. Factor market reforms would also need to cover financial markets – the mother of all markets. The financial sector reforms would involve reforms of banking sector, equity markets, debt markets and foreign exchange markets. In this, privatization of state-owned banks is perhaps the most essential. But this needs to be preceded by strengthening of the regulation and supervision of financial institutions and of capital markets. The recent developments in the Indian stock market vividly show how actions of one private bank, one cooperative bank and a major stock exchange management can have deleterious impact on national equity markets and particularly on small shareholders. Such developments can be avoided only by strong regulations and supervision. As the economy liberalizes and integrates with the world economy, the downside risks of globalization get amplified if the financial sector is weak. This has been the main lesson of the Asian crisis or the recent crisis of Turkey.

I would like to make one more point regarding the next phase of reforms. In the first phase of reforms, the reforms essentially concentrated on reforms at Central Government. Now these have to be taken to the level of our States. Almost 40 per cent of our revenue and fiscal deficits is because of the State finances. They need to be rectified. Similarly, a number of reforms are required for improving the delivery system since all basic services such as Education, Health, are delivered at State level. The State-level Reforms are of particular importance to promote regional equity; the matter of fundamental significance for a federal polity like India. Here, one cannot over-emphasize the importance of education particularly of primary education and of literacy. In some sense, it is this sector which will ultimately make or break India. Fortunately, a number of States are now taking initiatives for improving the quality of governance. There are interesting developments taking place in the States of Madhya Pradesh, Rajasthan, Himachal Pradesh, Kerala, etc. in the fields of Education and Health delivery. There are a number of states accepting the dictum to "think-global but act local" and consequently there is growing competition amongst State Governments to give better and improved services. Ruefully, very few of these States are in Indo-gangatic plains and here lies one of our most daunting challenges. This great issue of regional inequality I have not addressed in this lecture not because it is not important : On the contrary it is so important and merits a separate and detailed discussion.

All these measures will lead to higher growth rate by increasing the rate of investment, allocative efficiency, employment and thus remove poverty more rapidly. But, as I mentioned earlier, given the size of India, the removal of poverty cannot be the only objective for our economic policies. I think playing a rightful role in the world so as to provide growth and stability to the global economy should also be an important goal. But to achieve this in the age of globalization revolves not just on the growth rate of the gross national product but more on what you contribute to the global pool of knowledge and technological progress. Here, our performance so far worries a great deal as when it comes to the creation of knowledge or new technology, or new products, our performance has been quite dismal. For instance, if you take patents as one of the quantitative indicators of innovation or growth of knowledge those in the year 1999 the most recent year for which data are available, the number of patents India obtained in United States was only 114 as compared to Taiwan or South Korea which are as high as 4000. For the developed countries such as USA, Germany or Japan, these are much higher. Even in case of domestic patents, in India, they were only 1660 while in China these were 12000 or so and in Japan they were 3,00,000. In terms of the growth of total factor productivity which is an important indicator of technological progress, our performance has been lower than the countries such as China, Japan, Korea or the United States. Even the Research and Development (R&D) expenditure which India devotes as a percentage of GDP is much lower than Japan, Korea and other developed countries. When it comes to education, whether in terms of literacy or the amount of support to the universities, our performance, vis-a-vis other high performing developing countries such as China and Korea is woefully inadequate. In other words, what I am trying to argue is that this knowledge or innovation deficit is an even bigger problem which we will have to overcome if we want to successfully compete in the emerging knowledge-based world economy and become a source of technological progress for the world. In a paper written with Professor Bowonder, we have argued that India will have to strengthen the national innovation system to meet this challenge.

Given the ubiquitous presence of failures in the markets for the generation and diffusion of knowledge or technical innovation, there is a need to have public policy to promote generation and diffusion of innovation in addition to promoting competition. A coherent framework for such a set of policies is given by the concept of national innovation system. Such an analytical approach to the science and technology policies was first developed by Prof. R. Nelson and this has been recently further elaborated by the OECD. According to the National Innovation System concept, firms, which are key actors in the implementation and development of new technology, are seen as embedded in a larger national, institutional and cultural system that includes universities, financial institutions, R&D laboratories, labour markets, technology alliances, intellectual property right regime, bodies of law that mould and constrain what firms can do as well as government policies that support technological advance and assist national business firms. In other words, a national innovation system is that set of distinct institutions which jointly and individually contribute to the development and diffusion of new technologies and which provides the framework within which governments form and implement policies to influence the innovation process. We will also need to make much faster progress on social policies to promote social equality in terms of caste or gender. This will further release the latent creative energies of the society.

I now come to my final point regarding the launching of next wave of reforms. We need to show greater vigour and greater sense of urgency. The reason for emphasizing the urgency is due to the unique state of our demographic transition. In the next couple of decades India will have once in a life time chance of having a population structure where we will have the largest share of working population. Happily, such a demographic structure with its accent on youth also augurs well for promoting creativity and innovation. After these decades, however, the process of aging will catch and the vigour and the size of the working population would decline particularly as India's population is expected to reach a steady state over the next few decades. Like a satellite when it is put to the orbit, it requires high velocity to ensure exit from the Earth's gravitational force, if our economy is to exit from the gravitational pull of poverty, it also requires a high exit velocity of double-digit growth rate over the next two decades. We cannot afford to lose this unique opportunity.

Such sustained high growth is now feasible, as other miracle economies achieved it precisely when the share of working population was highest, maintaining high savings and investment rates and also increasing labour supply and productivity.

As we enter into the new century, the Indian economy stands at cross roads. Either it can take the "business as usual" road which means continued poverty and a low growth trap or take the high road to achieve prosperity, global prominence and more egalitarian society through accelerated reforms and by energizing the national innovation system.

Experience and economic theory tell us that the impact of such micro-meso-macro economic reforms can be multiplicative exploiting their synergy. Hence, I am quite confident that with these reforms Indian economy can grow at eight to nine percent per annum over the next two decades or so. This would make India's economy by the year 2020 world's fourth largest, i.e., after United States, China and Japan overtaking all the major European economies such as Germany, France or the U.K and India's per capita income would exceed US$ 2000. Presently, we are in the bottom twenty amongst all the countries in terms of Human Development Index. By the year 2020, we can be amongst the first twenty and thus fulfil that long awaited promise which Jawaharlal Nehru so eloquently described as our "tryst with destiny".

Annual Fellows Lecture at University of Pennsylvania, April 24, 2001.

4

Before and After Ten Years of Economic Reforms

BIMAL JALAN

The Post-Independence Development Record, 1950-1990

As we reflect on the history of human civilization in the millennium that has just ended, it is surprising to recall just how recent is the story of economic growth. As Paul Krugman has noted in a recent book, "economic growth, at least economic growth that raises living standards, is a modern invention. From the dawn of history to the Eighteenth century, the world was essentially Malthusian. Improvements in technology and capital investments were always overtaken by population growth; the number of people slowly increased, but their average standards of living did not."[1] Up to about the end of the Nineteenth century, the only countries where per capita incomes were increasing on a sustained basis for any length of time were the Western countries, particularly, England, Germany, France and the United States. During this entire period, the then so-called under-developed or Third World countries continued to be exporters of primary products and importers of industrial products with stagnant, and in some cases, declining per capita incomes. A large number of

Parts of this Lecture draw on some of my previous publications, particularly *India's Economic Crisis: The Way Ahead*, (Oxford University Press, 1991); *India's Economic Policy: Preparing for the 21st Century*, (Viking/Penguin, 1996); and *Finance and Development: Which Way Now?* (Administrative Staff College of India, Hyderabad, 1999).

them were also colonies of the Western powers, and the connection between these two situations — the colonial state and income stagnation — was not missed by their leaders and intellectuals.

The development strategies of the newly independent and developing countries, including India, in mid-Twentieth century were framed against this background. The central and the leading role for breaking away from the colonial legacy and for speeding up the process of industrialisation was assigned to the State. The need for the Government to occupy the commanding heights and to lead from the top received further support from the astounding success of the Soviet Union in emerging as a rival centre of political and industrial power within a very short period. India, at that time, played a pioneering role in giving expression to the aspirations of the newly independent Third World countries in the economic field. Thus, in 1956, India's Second Five Year Plan outlined the goals of development strategy in the following terms:

> "The pattern of development and the structure of socio-economic relations should be so planned that they result not only in appreciable increases in national income and employment but also in greater equality in incomes and wealth. Major decisions regarding production, distribution, consumption and investment — and in fact all significant socio-economic relationships — must be made by agencies informed by social purpose."

In practice, it meant, that all allocation decisions were to be made by the Government or its agencies. The need of raising resources for development was, of course, considered important. However, the primary emphasis was to be on increasing the domestic savings rate by suppressing consumption, high taxation, and appropriating profits through ownership of commercial enterprises. Accelerated capital accumulation through these means was considered to be the key to development. In a celebrated observation which guided many a planner and policy maker in developing countries, Professor W. Arthur Lewis observed that:

> "The central problem in the theory of economic development is to understand the process by which a community which was previously saving and investing 4 to 5 per cent of its national income or less, converts itself to an economy where voluntary saving is running at about 12 to 15 per cent of national income and more. This is the central problem because the central fact of economic development is rapid capital accumulation (including knowledge and skills with capital)".[2]

In the process of capital accumulation, the role of financial system was essentially limited, as allocation decisions were to be made by the central planning authorities and not by the financial markets. To a large extent, financial system also had a limited role in providing incentives for savings and capital accumulation as interest rates were controlled, and generally "repressed", and household savings were pre-empted through high levels of statutory reserve and liquidity ratio. New banks and financial institutions were set up, and old ones were taken over, in order to act primarily as deposit taking agencies and providers of credit and finance for designated and centrally determined purposes.

While the reasons for adopting a centrally directed strategy of development were understandable against the background of the colonial rule, it, however, soon became clear that actual results of this strategy were far below expectations. Instead of showing high growth, high public savings and a high degree of self-reliance, India was actually showing one of the lowest rates of growth in the developing world with rising public deficits and periodic balance of payments crises. According to one calculation, in 30 out of 35 years between 1956 and 1991, India had balance of payment problems of varying intensity. Thankfully, public memories are short! However, looking back, it is hard to believe that for as long as 40 years between 1950 and 1990, India's growth rate averaged less than 4 per cent per annum, and per capita income growth was less than 2 per cent per annum. This was at a time when the developing world, including the Sub-Saharan Africa and other least developed countries, showed a growth rate of 5.2 per cent per annum.

In my view, however, the most striking failure was not in terms of growth, or even in the precarious situation of the balance of payments. Although the argument is not convincing, it could still be argued by some that the low growth outcome was due to a number of factors beyond India's control, such as, the border wars, severe droughts, periodic oil shocks, and — finally — inhospitable global environment! The balance of payments difficulties could also — with some imagination — be attributed to the global woes of primary producers, and the struggle of a poor developing country like India to industrialise and become self-reliant in heavy industry (which hitherto was the monopoly of the rich industrialised countries). The most conspicuous failure, in my view, for which there is no alibi, and the responsibility for which lies squarely and indisputably at our doors, is the erosion in public savings and the inability of the public sector to generate resources for investment or provision of public services.

It will be recalled that an important assumption in the choice of post-independence development strategy was the generation of public savings, which could be used for higher and higher levels of investment. However, this did not happen, and the public sector-instead of being a generator of savings for the community's good — became, over time, a consumer of community's savings. This reversal in roles had become evident by the early Seventies, and the process reached its culmination by the early Eighties. By then, the Government began to borrow not only to meet its own revenue expenditure but also to finance public sector deficits and investments. During the period 1960-1975, total public sector borrowings (including Government) averaged 4.4 per cent of GDP. These increased to 6 per cent of GDP by 1980-81, and further to 9 per cent by 1989-90. Thus, the public sector, which was supposed to generate resources for the growth of the rest of the economy, gradually became a net drain on the society as a whole. It is interesting to note that the Central Government's total internal public debt by the year 1994-95 was close to Rs.5,00,000 crore, and nearly one-third of it was accounted for by assets held in the public sector. The interest payments on public debt amounted to nearly Rs.40,000 crore, which was financed by new net borrowings, and represented nearly 70 per cent of the Centre's fiscal deficit. In effect, by 1994-95, one-third of the interest payments was on account of the Government's past investment in the public sector. In the last five years since then, the Centre's internal debt has almost doubled to Rs.9,70,000 crore in 1999-2000. This sharp increase in internal debt is partly accounted for by the need to borrow higher and higher amounts to service the past debt.

A large part of the cherished "family silver" has thus been financed out of borrowings, and kept polished with further borrowings by an impoverished family.[3] In the annals of development history, it is hard to find another example of a perfectly sensible idea — the need for higher public investment for greater public good — leading to exactly the opposite result, i.e. higher public consumption with diminishing returns for the public!

The 1990s — A Shift in the Development Paradigm

The State-dominated development paradigm has shifted rather sharply in recent years. Almost all developing countries have moved towards a more market-determined strategy of development. There were several factors which contributed to this change in perception. First and the foremost reason for questioning the earlier strategy, as mentioned above, was the simple fact that actual results in terms of growth of incomes or industrial development were well below expectations. While saving rates were rising, as per the Arthur Lewis model, so were capital-output ratios because of inefficiencies in the allocation and use of resources. Paradoxically, a strategy which was expected to reduce dependency on foreign aid and foreign trade, also resulted in greater dependence on aid and emergency assistance from abroad.

An equally important factor contributing to the change in perceptions was the astonishing success of Japan and the East Asian countries in accelerating their rates of growth by relying on market - oriented pattern of industrialisation (with, of course, varying degrees of "guidance" by the State). Japan's per capita rate of growth of 8 per cent per annum during 1953 - 1973 was unprecedented in the history of economic development. No economy had ever grown at that rate before, and Japan emerged from the ruins of war to become the world's second largest economy. Similar was the record of industrialisation in East Asia particularly in countries like Hong Kong, Singapore, Taiwan and South Korea. In the Fifties, their per capita incomes or the degree of industrialisation was no different from those of the rest of Asia. However, within a period of 30 years, they were able to catch up with the industrialised countries of the West. A final and decisive development leading to the demise of the old strategy was the collapse of the Soviet Union and the acceptance of market-led development strategies by all countries of Eastern Europe.

Beginning in 1991, when India was in the midst of an acute economic crisis, the Government of India also introduced a number of measures to improve the working of the economy. These measures, spread over a number of years, had two broad objectives. One was the reorientation of the economy from a statist, centrally directed and highly controlled economy to what is referred to in the current jargon as a 'market-friendly economy'. A reduction in direct controls and physical planning was expected to improve the efficiency of the economy. It was to be made more 'open' to external trade and external flows through a reduction in trade barriers and liberalisation of foreign investment policies. A second objective of the reform measures was macro-economic stabilisation. This was to be achieved by substantially reducing fiscal deficits and the government's draft on society's savings.

Compared with the historical trend, the impact of these policies has been positive and significant. The growth rate of the economy during 1992-93 to 1999-2000 was close to 6.5 per cent per annum. The balance of payments position has also substantially improved. Despite several unfavourable external developments, including the imposition of sanctions in 1998 and sharp rise in oil prices more recently, foreign exchange reserves are at a record level. Exports have done well, current account deficits have been moderate, and India's external debt (as a percentage of GDP) and the debt servicing burden have actually come down since the early Nineties. There is also evidence of considerable restructuring in the corporate sector with attention being given to cost-competitiveness and financial viability. Industrial growth increased sharply during the period 1993 to 1996 to over 9 per cent per annum. The industrial growth rate came down to 5.5 per cent per annum in the next two years, but increased again to 8 per cent upto the end of 1999-2000. The rate of inflation also came down sharply — from 10.3 per cent in 1990-91 to a modest 3.3 per cent in 1999-2000. Fiscal deficit has also come down somewhat — from 8.3 per cent in 1990-91 to 5.6 per cent in 1999-2000.

There has been considerable debate in the country about the content, the pace and the results of the reform process. I do not propose to enter this particular debate, except to say that compared with the record of the first 40 years of development, there is very little doubt that India's economy — by any standard of measurement — is stronger and more resilient today than was the case a decade ago. I leave you to judge whether this outcome is due to the reform process, astute short-term economic management, favourable external circumstances, or just plain old good luck! There is also little doubt that India's "potential" for growth combined with external and domestic financial stability is greater today — at the beginning of the Twenty-First century than was the case 20, 50 or 100 years ago.

India in the New Global Economy

A most remarkable feature of the so-called "New Economy" is the role of the services sector (of which the IT or Information Technology sector is a part) in generating growth of income and employment. It will be recalled that the focus of attention in conventional economics, including development economics, was on production of goods – manufactured products and agricultural commodities. It was, of course, recognised that the services sector (which includes transport, communication, trade, banking, construction and public administration, etc.) was an important source of income and employment in most economies. However, overall, the growth of services was perceived at best as a byproduct of developments in the primary and secondary sectors, and at worst as a drag on the prospects for long-term economic growth. Services were believed to be mainly non-tradable activities with slow productivity growth and low employment potential. In developing countries, the conventional view of the growth of the services sector was even worse. It was seen to divert scarce resources away from production of goods, and contribute to accentuation of income inequalities.

In the last few years, there has been a phenomenal change in the conventional view of services and their role in the economy. The development of certain services is now regarded as one of the preconditions of economic growth, and not as one of its consequences. The boundary between goods and services is also disappearing, as services of various kinds are delinked from the manufacturing process and become essential elements of the productive structure. Many industrial products are not only manufactured — they are also designed, marketed, advertised, distributed, leased and serviced. A significant and rising part of the value added by manufacturers now consists of services.

The change in the image and role of services has been brought about by unprecedented and unforeseen advances in computer and communication technology in the last two decades. An important aspect of the "services revolution" is that geography and levels of industrialisation are no longer the primary determinants of the location of facilities for production of services. As a result, the traditional role of developing countries is also changing — from mere recipients to important providers of long-distance services.

From India's point of view, some of the recent global developments, which provide opportunities for substantial growth, are the following:

- The fastest growing segment of services is the rapid expansion of knowledge-based services, such as, professional and technical services. India has a tremendous advantage of the supply of such services because of a developed structure of technological and educational institutions, and lower labour costs.
- Progress in information technology is making it increasingly possible to unbundle the production and consumption of information-intensive service activities. These activities — research and development, computing, inventory management, quality control, accounting, personnel administration, secretarial, marketing, advertising, distribution, and legal services – are performed in all economic sectors.
- Unlike most other prices, world prices of transport and communication services have fallen dramatically. By 1960, sea transport costs were less than a third of their 1920 level, and they have continued to fall. The cost of a telephone call fell more than ten-fold between 1970 and 2000. Moreover, the cost of communication is also becoming independent of distance. The most dramatic example in this area is, of course, provided by the 'Internet'. India's geographical distance from several important industrial markets (for instance, North America) is no longer an important element in the cost structure of skill-based services.
- Further, India does not necessarily have to be a low-cost producer of certain types of goods (e.g., computers or

discs) before it can become an efficient supplier of services embodied in them (e.g., software or music). It is possible now to provide value added services without waiting to 'catch up' in technology for production of sophisticated equipment or products.

- The decline in the share of manufacturing in the output of rich countries implies a relative decline in their demand for industrial raw materials and fuels. This means that growth in exports of developing countries in the future will depend less on natural resource endowments and more on efficiency in providing services and service-intensive goods.

As a result of the above developments, the sources of comparative advantage of nations are vastly different today from what they were 50 or even 20 years ago. And, there are very few developing countries which are as well placed as India to take advantage of the phenomenal changes that have occurred in production technologies, international trade, capital movement, and deployment of skilled manpower. India today has the knowledge and the skills to produce and process a wide variety of industrial and consumer products and services. Another important factor in India's favour is the international capital mobility and integration of global financial markets. Domestic savings continue to be important for development. However, scarcity of domestic capital is no longer a binding constraint. Increased mobility of capital has ensured that global resources would flow to countries which can show high growth and high returns. It is possible now for India to take advantage of a virtuous circle of higher growth, higher external capital inflows, and higher domestic incomes and savings, which in turn can lead to further growth.

At the same time, it must be recognised that the "death of distance" and the growing integration of global product, services and financial markets in recent years has also presented new challenges for management of the national economy — not only in India but all over the world. The trend towards integration of markets, particularly financial markets, is by no means an unmixed blessing. Unlike the old days, a heavy price may have to be paid by national economies for somnolence, sloth and non-conformity to generally accepted international norms and standards of macro-economic management, disclosure, transparency and financial accountability. If a country does not put its financial house in order, fresh investments, trade and technology are likely to pass it by. Faced with this situation, only a few countries, with certain special advantages and resource endowments, may still manage to grow at an acceptable rate. Other countries which need capital and external flows to meet their trade or current account deficits, are likely to find it increasingly difficult to meet their import requirements of essential commodities (such as, oil), raw materials and machines.

Another consequence of recent global trends is the greater vulnerability of national economies to developments outside their own borders. In addition to the direct effects (which are currently most visible in the volatile stock markets), the indirect effects due to "contagion" can be quite serious. A crisis in any one or a group of countries, can be transmitted to other countries - including countries which may not have any strong economic linkages with crisis-affected countries. Thus, the Nineties have been marked by a large number of currency crises (for example, in Mexico, Russia, Asia and Brazil); substantial swings in exchange rates (including the exchange rate of three leading currencies – the dollar, the Euro and the Yen); and run ups in asset prices followed by sharp collapse (for example, in Japan and East Asia). While the crises initially occurred in one or two specific countries, their adverse effects were felt across the world.

The lessons of recent developments are clear. Advances in IT, the increasing role of services, the integration of financial and capital markets, and the diminished role of distance, provide tremendous new opportunities for countries like India. At the same time, like other countries, we are also likely to be subject to greater vulnerability and new risks. Thus, at the beginning of the new century, the challenge before us is in two directions — how to seize the new opportunities, while at the same time, protecting ourselves against unanticipated risks? Insularity or isolation is not the answer, as such an approach would promote neither growth nor stability.

India has to move vigorously to take advantage of expanding opportunities in trade and become a location of choice for IT and other industries and services so that growth rates, along with employment, are substantially enhanced. It must also keep some safety nets handy by building a diversified and efficient financial system which can aid and protect the development process at all times — good and bad. Can these objectives be met? This is the real question to ponder for the future.

Tryst With Destiny

There has been a fair amount of debate in the country on the implications of the new directions in India's economic policy. As far as I can see, there is no major disagreement with the ends or objectives of new economic policies. Most, though not all, commentators seem to agree that efficiency in the use of resources and growth performance of the economy need to be improved. There is also broad agreement that the Government's fiscal deficits should be reduced, that exports should be increased, and that more should be done for improving the health and education of the poor. There is, however, a substantial difference of views on the instruments that should be used to achieve these objectives, and whether current policies will succeed in raising the growth rate of the economy in the long run. Concern has also been expressed on certain political and social implications of the new policies, particularly whether they will make the country more amenable to external pressures and hurt the development of the country's domestic resources. These issues are important, and deserve to be fully considered in the evolution of India's economic policy in the Twenty-First century.

In considering these issues, it is not possible to escape from the responsibility of paying attention to the nature and character of our State apparatus, and to our previous record. We cannot decry the widespread corruption and 'criminalisation of politics' – a phrase which has figured prominently in Parliament in recent years – on the one hand, and ask for more discretionary powers for the State on the other. To do so is to suffer from a form of 'cognitive dissonance'. It is also important to remember that, as pointed out in the earlier part of this talk, the results of India's old policies in promoting growth or reducing poverty were highly unsatisfactory, and in any case, far worse than those registered by more open and competitive economies. As for external pressures, there is hardly any doubt that an aid-dependent economy with persistent balance of payments crises (as was the case in India from 1956 to 1991) is likely to be much more vulnerable than a country which is not so dependent on aid or emergency assistance from abroad.

In my judgement, keeping in view the actual economic and non-economic results of the old strategy, the phenomenal changes that have taken place in the world economy, and India's present comparative advantage, the present direction of policies to make India more open and more competitive is right and deserves to be accelerated. Without a major transformation of our economic policies and effort to align them with contemporary realities of global trade, investment and technology, it is not feasible for India to occupy the high ground and realise its full potential for growth and development.

A decisive move towards more and deeper economic reforms is the first strategic priority for the future. However, it will be a grave mistake to misconstrue the need for economic reforms with a call for less role for Government or public policy in widening opportunities and creating a positive environment for equitable development. In developing countries, such as India, with massive illiteracy and underdevelopment of infrastructure, Government must continue to have an important and crucial role in creating the necessary conditions for growth through investments in areas, such as, education, health, water supply, irrigation, infrastructure, etc. These tasks cannot be taken over by the market. Successful economic reforms must result in strengthening the ability of Governments to do what they need to do by helping to generate higher growth, higher revenue and higher productivity. As the recent experience of several transitional and emerging market economies shows, economic reforms are necessary but by no means a sufficient condition for growth and development.

In this connection, a core issue, with multiple dimensions, which would need to be resolved in years to come is what can perhaps be described as growing "public-private" dichotomy in our economic life. It is a striking fact of our present situation that economic renewal and positive growth impulses are now occurring largely outside the public sector — at the level of private corporations (e.g. software companies), autonomous institutions (e.g. IIMs or IITs), or individuals at the top of their professions in India and abroad. In the Governmental or public sector, on the other hand, we see a marked deterioration at all levels — not only in terms of output, profits and public savings (to which I made a reference earlier), but also in the provision of vital public services in the fields of education, health, water and transport. These two elements — fiscal deterioration and inability to provide essential services — are, of course, intimately connected. Most of our public resources are now dissipated in payment of salaries or interest on past debt with little or no resources available for expansion of public or publicly supported services in vital sectors.

In considering the reasons for the decay and deterioration that is taking place in our public services, I am reminded of an observation by A.H.Hanson nearly 40 years ago on the reasons for the then prevailing crisis of Indian Planning. He was an admirer of Indian planners, but after seeing the results on the ground, he was compelled to ask:

> "The men are able, the organization is adequate, the procedures are intelligently devised. Why, then, have the Plans, since 1956, so persistently run into crisis?"

Hanson's answer to this question is also revealing:

> "For various reasons, Indian Planners have never treated the 'objective function' with sufficient respect. Their tendency is to give themselves the fullest benefit of every possible doubt ... Too many of their aims are contingent upon the adoption, by various sections of the Indian community, of attitudes they are exceedingly unlikely to adopt ....."[4]

That was 1963! Today, in 2001, and after more than 50 years of experience of independent administration, we still seem to be giving ourselves the benefit of doubt. Over time, our problems in the management of public resources at different levels have only become more and more intractable. Let us look at some of the problems that now bedevil our public delivery systems:

- We can be justifiably proud of the fact that the "rule of law" prevails in our country, and that even the mightiest are not above the law. The delays in the judicial process may be legendary, but there is a widespread respect for the "rule of law". However, for historical reasons, it is also a fact that our legal system provides full protection to the private interests of the so-called "public servant", often at the expense of the public that he or she is supposed to serve. In addition to complete job security, any group of public servants in any public sector organisation can go on strike — hospitals, universities, schools, banks, buses, post offices, railways, municipalities — in search of higher wages, promotions and bonuses for themselves irrespective of the costs and inconvenience to the public (in whose name they have been appointed in the first place). Problems have only become worse over time and there is little or no accountability of the public servant to perform the public duty.

- The "authority" of Governments at, both Centre and States, to enforce their decisions has eroded over time. Governments can pass orders, for example, for relocation of unauthorised industrial units or other structures, but implementation can be delayed if they run counter to the private interests of some (at the expense of the general public interest). Similarly, Governments may decide to restructure public utilities to cut down waste or output losses, but these decisions do not necessarily have to be implemented if they adversely affect the interests of public servants employed in these organisations.
- Governments at different levels may announce plans and programmes to provide social services (such as, expand literacy), but these initiatives are unlikely to be implemented on the ground because of fiscal stringency. For example, in 1994, the Tenth Finance Commission projected a rate of growth in real terms of 2.5 per cent for expenditure on elementary education upto the end of the century in respect of four States where the incidence of poverty and illiteracy was among the highest in the country. This projected rate of growth in expenditure was lower than the growth of population in the relevant age group, and grossly insufficient to cover new programmes of adult literates. In the five years since the Tenth Finance Commission's report, it is interesting to note that the real expenditure on elementary education, outside of salaries of Government teachers, in these four States has actually been negative!

- The process and procedures for conducting business in Government and public service organisations, over time have become non-functional. There are multiplicity of Departments involved in the simplest of decisions, and administrative rules generally concentrate on the process rather than results. There is very little decentralisation of decision-making powers, particularly financial powers. Thus, while local authorities have been given significant authority in some States for implementing national programmes, their financial authority is limited. Transfers to local authorities for health spending, for example, average less than 15 per cent of State Government budgets.
- The multiplicity of functions and responsibilities placed upon ill-equipped and ill-trained staff in public offices and local institutions make it almost impossible to deliver services with any degree of efficiency, particularly in rural areas. For example, a "multi-purpose" female health worker is required to perform as many as forty-seven tasks to be undertaken on a regular basis!

Let us also ponder, for a moment, who suffers the most from fiscal stringency and the atrophy of the public delivery systems. It is certainly not the affluent classes, or persons elected or appointed by the people to serve them. They can always go to private hospitals, private schools, autonomous universities or institutes of higher education, and have similar alternative means of meeting their other requirements. The worst affected are likely to be the poor, the unemployed, and the illiterate who are dependent on public services, public investment and public programmes. It is useful to keep this perspective in mind as a fair amount of defence of the "status quo" in respect of the public sector is done in the name of the weaker sections of the society.

In addition to economic reforms, which already figure prominently in the national discourse, it is now important to embark on an urgent programme to revitalise the governance and public delivery systems at all levels of Government — centre, state and districts. Without strengthening the ability of the Government to do what it alone can do, and narrowing the focus of its activities to what matters most for the future development of the country — education, health, clean environment, and a functioning infrastructure — India cannot adequately seize the opportunities that lie ahead.

In my view, this is really the harder part of the so-called second generation reforms. The non-governmental sector now has a dynamism and momentum of its own. While there will be problems, and there will be arguments for and against a particular policy to liberalise, to open up, or to introduce more competition, I am confident that progress in the desired direction is unavoidable and irreversible. At the same time, it is also clear that unless we put our fiscal house in order and improve our public delivery systems, no amount of macro-policy reforms by themselves will be sustainable or yield permanent results. If lakhs of primary schools run by Government agencies, thousands of primary health centres set up by district authorities, and hundreds of Central and State Universities continue to under-perform or decline, two or three hi-tech cities and one or two new business schools and technical institutes cannot make up for the gigantic loss of human resources. It is simply a question of relative proportions, and inextricable linkages between public good and private progress.

In order to overcome some of the problems that I mentioned a little while ago, we need to move on a number of fronts. We need legal reform to focus sharply on the interests of the public, and not those of the public servant, in the functioning of the governmental and public delivery systems. Clear mechanisms for establishing accountability for performance are essential, and all forms of special protection for persons working for Government or public sector agencies (except for armed forces or agencies engaged in maintenance of law and order) deserve to be eliminated. We need institutional reform. All public monopolies should be eliminated, and there should be no purchase preference for public sector enterprises or agencies. Government should be free to engage the services of non-governmental organisations or private service providers at competitive costs to ensure effective delivery of essential services. We need freedom of information and full disclosure of all financial decisions made by Governments and its multifarious agencies on a daily rather than quarterly or annual basis. We need a new "political-bureaucratic" compact based on well-defined division of responsibility and accountability. The public system cannot function without respect for conventions and mutual trust and harmony among different agencies of the state. Above all, we need fiscal empowerment as, without financial resources, it is not feasible to lay a road or build a school. The last is a most difficult task in view of the deadweight of the past, but it can no longer be avoided.

Let me end with two prognostications about India's potential for long-term growth that I came across recently. The first is by a well known Indian economist with a distinguished record of forecasting. He has observed that, "it is possible for India to have a per capita income of US $ 30,000 by the year 2047. If the Indian economy does as well as some of the world's fast-growing economies have done, it could be even higher."[5] The second projection is by a Professor in business management in the United States. He estimates that, by the year 2025, India's GDP would exceed that of Japan and India would then be the third largest economy in the world (behind US and China).

Both forecasts, independently arrived at in two different parts of the world, are, of course, contingent on a number of factors. There is, however, no doubt that, if we have the will, and we are able to realise even half our potential in the next 20 or 25 years, India's poverty would have become a distant memory.

Notes

1. Paul Krugman, *The Return of Depression Economics*, The Penguin Press, London, 1999.
2. W.A. Lewis, "Economic Development with Unlimited Supplies of Labour", *Manchester School,* Vol.22, 1954.
3. It may be mentioned that some parts of the public sector, particularly oil and telecommunications have been quite profitable. This partly reflects their erstwhile monopoly position and the administered price regimes. These profitable sectors have been largely self-financing without the need for budget transfers.
4. Hanson A.H., "The Crisis of Indian Planning", Political Quarterly, October-December 1963, reprinted in Hanson A.H., *Planning and Politicians,* London: Routledge and Kegan Paul, 1969.
5. Kirit Parikh, "Economy" in *India Briefing – A Transformative Fifty Years*, published by M.E.Sharp Inc., New York, 1999, for Asia Society. Parikh's per capita income forecasts assume a dollar-rupee exchange rate based on purchasing power parity.
6. Rosensweig J.A., *Winning the Global Game,* The Free Press, New York, 1998. Rosensweig's forecasts are also on purchasing power parity basis.

From: *C.D. Deshmukh Memorial Lecture*, January 2001, India International Centre, New Delhi.

5

Economic Reforms A Policy Agenda for the Future

MONTEK S. AHLUWALIA

I

Some Positive Features

A policy agenda for the future should be determined by looking at existing strength and weaknesses and building on the strength while correcting the weaknesses. It is natural that public discussion usually focuses on our weaknesses which therefore always look daunting. But to put matters in perspective, I would like to begin by acknowledging that we enter the new millennium with some important strengths. Let me just mention three :

(i) First, our growth performance is now much better than the frustratingly slow 3.5 per cent to 4 per cent growth which characterised the first three decades after independence. India's GDP grew at an average rate of 5.8 per cent in the 1980s. It accelerated to around 6.5 per cent in the Eighth Plan period (1992-93 to 1996-97) and this is expected to be maintained in the Ninth Plan period. This record suggests that the Indian economy is adjusting well to the new policies. It is not generally realised that if we focus on the 1980s and 1990s, India has been one of the ten fastest growing economies in the world !

(ii) The educational deficiencies of our population have long been a drag on our growth potential. We have always taken pride in the quality of our highly skilled personnel, our scientists, our managers and more recently our software wizards. But the general level of education for the bulk of our population has long been extremely low. Adult literacy was only 18.3 per cent in 1951 and only increased to 28.3 per cent by 1960 and 34.4 per cent by 1971. This was undoubtedly one of the reasons for our persistently low growth in the years. The most recent estimates by the NSS show that literacy had increased to 62 per cent in 1996-97. This is still low, but it is now in the range which is consistent with achieving growth rates of 7 to 8 per cent.

(iii) Population growth, which for long remained stubbornly above 2 per cent, at last appears to be declining. Kerala's justly celebrated achievements in this area have been matched by Tamil Nadu and it appears that Andhra Pradesh and Karnataka are not far behind. Birth rates are much higher in the northern States but even in these States they are declining. India's population in the next decade is expected to slow down to 1.5 per cent.

These positive developments have important implications for our prospects in the next decade. If GDP growth can be pushed up from around 6.5 per cent at present to say 7 per cent at the start of the decade, and then to 8 per cent by the end of the decade, it would give us an average growth of around 7.5 per cent for the decade as a whole. With population growing at 1.5 per cent, this means per capita income would grow at about 6 per cent per year. Growth of this order is much higher than we have experienced in the past and can create many virtuous circles. If it is reasonably well distributed, it would guarantee a sharp reduction in the level of poverty by the end of the next decade. One can go further and say that unless we can achieve growth of this order, we cannot expect to see a significant improvement in the conditions of living of the mass of our people.

What are the policies we need to follow to achieve such growth and especially to make it broad-based? Fortunately, a substantial consensus has now emerged in professional and even in political circles on economic policies. There is general agreement that the process of economic reforms must be strengthened and deepened and this is sometimes described as implementing "the second generation of reforms". I am not entirely comfortable with this description. It implies that we have successfully completed the first generation of reforms, and must now move on to the next hierarchical level. The reality is somewhat different. I would classify the reform agenda ahead of us into three categories.

- The first item on this agenda on which there is a great deal of agreement must be to restore fiscal discipline. This is actually a first generation reform, which we have not been able to carry out as planned.
- The second category consists of first generation reforms which are more or less on track, but are still to be completed because of our deliberate choice of gradualism as a reform strategy.
- The last category consists of what can be called genuine second generation reforms, which take the reform process to new areas not addressed thus far.

II

Fiscal Discipline

Let us begin with fiscal discipline, which is a first generation reform which got lost somewhere on the way. The seriousness of the fiscal problem facing the country is now so widely recognised that it is useful to put it in some perspective.

In 1991, when the economic reforms began, we faced an exceptionally severe crisis and the Central Government's fiscal deficit – which had reached 8.3 per cent of GDP in the preceding year – was seen as a root cause of the crisis. This gave a sense of urgency to the need for fiscal correction and we were able to reduce the deficit to around 6 percent of GDP in the very first year. It was recognised at the time that even this was too high and further reduction was needed to release resources into the economy and reduce interest rates, both very necessary to stimulate private investment. The medium term objective, outlined in a discussion paper circulated by the Finance Ministry in 1993, was to reduce the fiscal deficit to around 3 per cent by 1996-97. Unfortunately this target was never achieved. The actual deficit was 5.2 per cent in 1996-97, it deteriorated to 6 per cent in 1997-98, and has remained at about that level subsequently. The result has been that interest rates remain very high.

Meanwhile, the fiscal position of the States, including the so called better administered States, has deteriorated significantly. Unlike the Centre, the States are not allowed to borrow freely and this puts an automatic limit on their fiscal deficit. However, this only means that their fiscal weaknesses are reflected in an uncontrolled growth in non-Plan expenditure, and mounting losses on the supply of various economic services. The scale of the problem can be judged by the fact that the losses of all the State Electricity Boards amounted to about Rs. 11,000 crores in 1997-98. The losses on account of irrigation are about Rs. 2000 crores even if we count only the maintenance cost of the systems. If interest on capital invested in irrigation is included, the losses would be much higher. Losses in the State Road Transport Corporations are about Rs. 1000 crores.

With such large losses it is not surprising that the States are unable to meet their targets for Plan expenditure. In the Eighth Plan period (1992-93 to 1996-97) Plan expenditure by the States in real terms was 20 percent lower than targeted. The position has worsened in the Ninth Plan because of the impact of the Fifth Pay Commission. Besides, what is shown as Plan expenditure in the States' Budgets exaggerates the actual extent of new development projects. This is because Plan projects which have been almost completed continue to be shown as ongoing projects, which enables the salary and running costs of these projects, which should normally be covered by the non-Plan budget, to be financed from the Plan budget. In effect, therefore, a large portion of Plan expenditure is not financing new development projects but only covering salaries and rising costs of old projects. The situation in some States is such that they find it difficult to meet salary payments.

The consequences of not correcting this situation are self-evident. The high deficit will perpetuate the present high interest rates which hurt investments in the economy and indeed hurt the small producers the most. The low level of Plan expenditure will jeopardise much needed public investment in critical areas and jeopardise our growth objective. I am not saying that growth depends only on Plan expenditure, or that all Plan expenditure is sacrosanct. Most of the investment needed to achieve our targeted 7 to 8 per cent growth can and should come from the private sector, and there are many areas where Plan expenditure can be effectively replaced by private investment. However, the ratio of Plan expenditure of the Centre and States combined was 11.3 per cent of GDP in 1990-91 and has declined to a little over 9 percent today. This has squeezed investment in many areas which are critical for accelerating growth to 7-8 per cent.

This resource squeeze has direct implications for our ability to accelerate growth in agriculture. Faster agricultural growth and broad based rural development is central to our strategy for reducing poverty. To achieve this, we have to expand investment in irrigation, land development, soil and moisture conservation, agricultural research, development of agricultural marketing facilities, and finally, expansion and maintenance of rural and district roads to improve rural connectivity. These basic investments in rural infrastructure can only be undertaken by the public sector but unfortunately the level of these expenditures has probably declined in real terms because of the severe fiscal problems of the States.

Much larger investments are also needed in health and education, especially in rural areas, to bring our social development indicators up to respectable levels comparable with other developing countries. This again has to come from public sector. In other infrastructure areas such as power generation and distribution, ports, airports, telecommunications and national highways, the private sector can play a much larger role than it has in the past, and this must be encouraged. However, even in these areas, public investment will continue to be extremely important in the foreseeable future and we have large gaps to fill.

The fiscal objective for the next decade must therefore have two dimensions. We must reduce the fiscal deficit to release resources for private investment but we must simultaneously increase public investment in critical areas. This suggests that the scale of fiscal effort needed is very large. The combined fiscal deficit of the Centre and the States was around 8.5 per cent of GDP in 1998-99. The Finance Minister has already said that we should try to reduce the Centre's fiscal deficit (as recently redefined) to around 2 per cent over the next three years. This would suggest that the combined fiscal deficit of the Centre and the States should be reduced to say 4.5 per cent over a three year period. Simultaneously, we should aim to increase total Plan expenditure of the Centre and the States taken together by say 1.5 per cent of GDP from the present level. The total fiscal improvement required to achieve these twin objectives is around 5.5 per cent of GDP over a three year period i.e. around 1.8 percentage points per year.

This improvement has to be achieved partly by the Centre and partly by the States. I will not go into the issue of what should be the exact balance between the two. The important point to note is that a fiscal correction of 5.5 percentage points of GDP over the next three years is an extremely difficult task in any situation. It cannot be achieved by acting on one or two instruments. Action will be needed on several fronts. Let me mention some :

i) Improving Tax Administration to Raise Larger Revenues

Anyone who has studied the Indian tax system, both at the Central and the State level, is struck by the fact that the system is archaic with complex and cumbersome procedures, a multiplicity of rates, numerous exemptions and large areas of discretion, all of which lends itself to evasion by tax payers and harassment by tax authorities. The system also lends itself to corruption at all levels, which explains the relatively low levels of tax realisation. Experience of other countries shows that a tax reform which brings about a system change could generate additional revenues of 3 per cent of GDP in a relatively short period without necessarily increasing tax rates. Half the fiscal adjustment needed could therefore come from effective implementation of tax reform. This can be done if we can translate general statements about "improving tax administration" and "widening the tax" into specific proposals for removal of exemptions, simplifying the system by reducing the number of rates and also modernising procedures. Hopefully, the new Tax Reforms Committee, referred to in the President's Address, can quickly come up with specific recommendations in this regard.

ii) Reducing Subsidies

Almost everyone is willing to endorse general statements about reducing subsidies, but agreement vanishes as soon as one focuses on specific proposals. And yet the total volume of direct and indirect subsidies in our system has risen to unsustainable levels. The major direct subsidies in the Central Government are the subsidies on fertilizer, food and sugar and these amount to Rs. 24,000 crores according to the Budget Estimates for 1999-2000 though they may turn out to be higher. In addition, there are large implicit subsidies such as massive undercharging for higher education and for hospital services, undercharging for railway passengers, undercharging for postal services, etc. The subsidy on kerosene is Rs. 8000 crores and on LPG around Rs. 4000 crores. These subsidies are not technically borne by the Budget, but are covered by overcharging for other petroleum products such as petrol and aviation turbine fuel. However, this clearly represents a loss of potential resources since the cross subsidy element built into the high price of some petroleum products could otherwise be mopped up in the form of tax revenue. These subsidies are not specifically targeted at the poor but actually accrue to relatively higher income groups, or at best to the average consumer. However, the subsidy burden effectively prevents the government from spending on programmes which would stimulate broad based growth that would have a large beneficial effect which is probably better distributed.

The State sector too is burdened by massive subsidies which could be reduced. Electric power is supplied to farmers at 10 to 20 percent of the cost of production in most States and free in some. Household consumers of electricity are also undercharged as is water for irrigation, passenger bus services and, of course, higher education.

I must emphasise that what is needed is not complete elimination of all these subsidies, but only a substantial reduction combined with better targeting. This will release resources which will enable us to finance some of the critical expenditures which need to be increased to meet our development objectives.

iii) Downsizing of Government

This is another area where we can save some resources. Government departments, including the Railways and Posts, have long been overmanned. There are also too many government departments. A liberalised economy needs far fewer Ministries and Departments than a controlled and regulated economy and some steps have to be taken in this direction. The Fifth Pay Commission, an expert body, had estimated that a 30 per cent reduction in government staff should be achieved over time. Proposals to downsize government are sometimes resisted because it is perceived that unemployment is a serious problem and government employment helps to meet demands for jobs. However redirecting resources from paying for surplus manpower in order to build much needed economic and social infrastructure will create many more jobs in the rest of the economy. We have to recognise that the purpose of government is to provide essential services efficiently, and not to create employment.

iv) Bolder Privatisation

Many developing countries have been able to bring about a substantial improvement in their fiscal position by undertaking major privatisation of public sector enterprises.This option is also open to us and should be aggressively followed not only by the Centre, which has begun the process, but also by the States. I will say more on this subject later in this lecture.

v) Reprioritize Plan Schemes

Finally, it is necessary to re-prioritize Plan expenditure to eliminate schemes which are of doubtful value. Detailed post evaluation studies show that many of our Plan schemes, though well intentioned, simply do not achieve their stated objectives, or do so only to a limited degree, making the schemes cost-ineffective. This is due to a combination of poor design of the schemes and inadequate administrative capability. Unfortunately, such schemes continue to remain in operation, absorbing resources which could be deployed in other areas. The administrative agencies responsible for these schemes become strong vested interest for their continuation and criticism of the effectiveness of the scheme only leads to demands to "strengthen" the schemes through better administration and monitoring, which usually means more staff and more resources. A thorough re-examination of all Plan schemes, with a drastic elimination of schemes which are demonstrated to be ineffective, would release resources which would enable the more important and more cost-effective schemes to be fully funded. Strict application of such tests of effectiveness in a framework of formal zero based budgeting would automatically ensure better design of schemes and also appropriate mid-course restructuring, to ensure that they remain funded.

Implementing reforms along these lines is obviously not a simple matter. Each of these proposals viewed in isolation is bound to generate controversy. But then, a fiscal correction of 5.5 percent of GDP cannot be achieved without such effort. Unfortunately, our present system, with its tradition of secrecy about the Budget, makes it very difficult to confront these choices. Difficult decisions cannot be taken if they have to be kept secret from everyone except a very small group, and then suddenly unveiled on the last day of February to be subjected to instant analysis by TV experts! It will be necessary to prepare the ground by actively debating the available options, and more importantly, identifying the implications of not pursuing them.

The need for taking these difficult decisions would become much clearer if we were to adopt the practice followed in some countries of presenting budgets with projections for subsequent years also. This would present a comprehensive picture of the scale of effort needed if we want to get to where we want in the next three years. In this framework the effort needed today can be reduced only if we explicitly plan for a much larger effort tomorrow.

Whatever we do, we can be sure of one thing. If we do not make a move on most, if not all, of the issues I have listed, we will not see significant progress on the fiscal front. This in turn will mean a continuing erosion of public investment in critical areas, continuation of high interest rates limiting the flow of funds for private investment, and an international rating which remains below investment grade. It is unlikely that we can achieve 7 to 8 per cent growth in such circumstances.

III

Completing First Generation Reforms

Having emphasised the overwhelming importance of fiscal correction, let me now turn to my second category which consists of reforms which have proceeded more or less in the gradualist manner originally envisaged, but which need to be completed, or in some cases modified to reflect new developments.

i) Industrial Deregulation

Liberalisation of industrial licensing and opening up industry to foreign investment was an important part of first generation reforms. This element has progressed fairly well as far as Central Government controls are concerned. Investors still face many problems in implementing projects, but these are largely at the State level, which is a second generation area. However, there are some areas of industrial deregulation where further action is needed.

The sugar industry is one such area. Sugar is an extremely important agro-based industry and the second largest industrial employer in the country after cotton textiles. If liberalisation is beneficial to industry it should be beneficial to sugar also. Yet this industry remains subject to extensive control associated with the existing dual price system. State advised prices to be paid to farmers are often unconnected with market conditions, a portion of the production has to be surrendered as levy sugar at an unremunerative price, the so called free market sugar is also subject to release control, and the industry complains of a non-level playing field against imports which do not suffer from the levy. There is a strong case for decontrolling sugar and opening up this area to market competition. If it is felt necessary to retain sugar in the PDS, this should be done by purchase of sugar at market prices with a separate subsidy from the budget. However, I would argue that the sugar subsidy is very poorly targeted and benefits mainly urban middle income consumers. There is a very strong case for removing sugar from the PDS.

Coal is another area where industrial de-regulation should be extended. This is a critical energy source, where private investment is not allowed at present except for captive mining. If we have opened up petroleum to the private sector, there is no reason why coal should not be opened up also. The additional coal production needed to meet the country's energy demands in the next decade is so large that it simply cannot be met by the nationalised coal industry. Failure to increase coal production will only make us more dependent on oil where we are already heavily dependent on imported supplies. The need to allow private investment in this sector is therefore urgent. Private investment will add a competitive spur to the industry, and also bring in new technology which is important in view of the fact that environmental considerations are likely to impose restrictions of various kinds on coal and coal quality. Since coal mining is a difficult area where environmental clearances are bound to take time and the development of a mine also takes several years, we need to act now if we want additional production in six to seven years time!

Another area of industrial policy which needs to be addressed relates to the policy of reservation of certain products for the small scale sector. Many experts have argued that reservation is not the best way of helping small scale industry and their arguments are persuasive. In fact, it is not generally realised that the sectors which are reserved for SSIs have grown more slowly than the unreserved SSI sector. Nevertheless, I recognise that this is a sensitive issue on which it will take time to build a consensus. However, there is a strong case for immediately de-reserving certain areas which have a strong export potential such as garments, toys, and leather footwear. Let me just illustrate the point by looking at two items which in India are reserved for SSI production. In 1997, whereas India's exports of toys and sporting goods were US$ 70 million, China's exports were US$ 8 billion. In other words, China exported 120 times the amount India did! The story in footwear is nearly the same. We exported about US$ 350 million whereas China exported US$ 8 billion, or about twenty two times our level. Continuing with small scale reservation in these areas is preventing us from developing a dynamic export sector which we desperately need, and which would generate high quality employment. We complain about lack of market access for our exports, but the fact is that in critical areas where we have a strong comparative advantage our own policies have prevented us from penetrating world markets.

(ii) Opening the Economy to Trade

Opening up the economy to foreign trade was another important part of the reform agenda and the reforms in this area are now more than half complete. Government has announced that all quantitative restrictions (QRs) will be removed by the year 2003 and this is being done in a phased manner. The time frame of the transition has been made quite clear and has been well accepted by Indian industry. However, we do not have an equally clear time frame for tariff reduction. The government has given a broad indication that tariff rates will be reduced to bring them in line with East Asian countries in about three years time. It would be desirable to give Indian industry a clearer idea of what is intended. Industry is also rightly concerned that tariff reduction should not create tariff anomalies in which tariffs on inputs remain high while tariffs on outputs are reduced.

The time has come for us to quantify our intentions more clearly. We could, for example, indicate that the average tariff level, which is around 30 per cent at present, will be reduced to say 15 per cent over a three year period. This would imply an annual reduction of approximately 5 per cent per year on average, which could be easily absorbed by Indian industry. We should also clearly identify the major tariff anomalies and lay down a phased programme for their elimination. Our anti-dumping mechanisms and procedures should also be strengthened in parallel to reassure industry that they will not be subjected to unfair competition.

There are some who fear that Indian industry will not be able to survive foreign competition if tariffs are reduced further. Personally, I think this is a mistaken view. Indian industry has been able to adjust to large tariff reductions in the past few years and there is no reason to believe that the process cannot be pushed further, especially since the market determined exchange rate will ensure that any excessive pressure of imports will produce an offsetting depreciation which will help domestic industry, while also helping exports. Reduced tariffs on inputs will obviously help domestic industry to become more competitive.

iii) Disinvestment and Privatisation

Disinvestment is another first generation area where the reforms are poised to be carried to the next higher level. The reforms began with "disinvestment" which would still leave the government with a majority stake in PSUs. The United Front Government indicated a willingness to reduce the government's stake to a minority in the non-core and non-strategic area. The present government has gone further still, with a clear declaration that we will go down to 26 per cent in the generality of cases. Disinvestment proposals involving a change in management are currently being processed for Modern Foods and Balco, and for the introduction of a strategic partner in IPCL.

Nevertheless, uncertainties remain in the public mind about the extent to which the government should go. Many people believe that while sale and transfer of management is acceptable for weak PSUs, we should not give up majority control in the so-called "navaratnas". Others believe that the revenues from disinvestment should be used to strengthen other public sector units. As far as the issue of majority ownership is concerned, the fact is that we cannot achieve the desired fiscal correction if we do not off-load a majority stake in the equity of many of the navaratnas. The public must therefore be persuaded that such disinvestment or privatisation is desirable and will help to pay for the creation of socially more useful assets such as schools and hospitals and other forms of rural infrastructure. Nor should we assume that the revenues from disinvestment will necessarily be ploughed back into other PSUs. We have to consider what is the best use for these resources and if hospitals and schools and roads are more important, that is surely what we should build.

The fiscal problem facing us suggests that we should try to achieve disinvestment levels exceeding, if possible, the Rs. 10,000 crores budgeted for 1999-2000, though I recognise that even this level has never been reached in any single year. A business as usual approach to disinvestment will not do. We should move away from annual planning of disinvestment and indicate the scale of effort needed over the next three years. On this basis we should clearly identify the companies and also the extent of disinvestment in those companies which is needed to achieve our target. The Government has indicated that it is considering a new mechanism for implementing disinvestment including the setting up of a separate unit. This is a very welcome development. The key to its success will be our willingness to take the PSUs to be privatised out of the administrative control of the administrative Ministry and transfer it to the new unit. The Ministry's views will of course be taken into account but the critical decisions on the pace and manner of disinvestment and privatisation should be with the new unit.

The manner of the disinvestment, i.e. whether it should involve retail sale to broad based investors or an outright sale to a single buyer, or the induction of a strategic partner will of course vary depending on the enterprise, and the rationale of the specific choice can be made transparent. We should also explain to the public that there is no reason to be alarmed because we are reducing government equity to a minority stake. Our objective should be to ensure that the navaratnas are strengthened as corporate entities, and not that they do not slip out of government control. In fact, a strong case can be made that ending government control over these enterprises is essential if they are to have the commercial autonomy and flexibility they need to survive in competitive markets. No one seriously believes that the presence of the government as an owner adds any value to the company from a commercial point of view. This is as true of Maruti as it is of SAIL or IOC.

iv) Financial Sector Reforms

The financial sector is another area where first generation reforms are well underway but the process needs to be accelerated. The Reserve Bank of India has made commendable progress in upgrading prudential and regulatory standards in our banking system to meet the international standards laid down by the Basle Committee. This is an area where all developing countries will be under much greater international scrutiny in future given the increased concern about financial sector weaknesses in the aftermath of the East Asian crisis. Fortunately, although we still have some way to go, the gaps that remain are easily bridged.

However, the next step is, in some ways, more difficult : how to make sure that our banks, especially the public sector banks, can meet the new prudential standards and compete effectively against foreign banks and private sector banks while doing so. Competition in the banking system will be intensified by technological change, especially the introduction of information technology. The more dynamic banks which take to the new technology will be able to increase their market share without having an extensive branch network. The public sector banks, whose great strength has been their branch network, must be ready to meet this challenge. They will need autonomy and flexibility to restructure in many ways. They will need flexibility in recruiting and promoting personnel, the ability to negotiate wage agreements which reflect productivity and profitability in individual banks and flexibility to redeploy staff and deal with excess staff through voluntary retirement. They will also need flexibility to close loss making branches.

These are difficult issues on which the first reaction of many of the interest groups involved, and even of the general public, may be negative. However we need to develop greater understanding on the part of these groups of the necessity for making these changes in the interest of the banking system itself together with assurances that these changes can be achieved without too much disruption. Some of these problems have to be faced in the near future as the difficult problem of the three weak banks identified by the Verma Committee is addressed.

An important positive development in the financial sector is the opening of the insurance sector to private investment. This will enable new private sector entrants to come into this sector sometime in the year 2000. A strong and competitive insurance industry will strengthen long-term contractual savings, improve service quality to customers, and also serve as a vehicle channeling long term finance, which is relatively scarce at present, to the capial market. This is of course absolutely essential to finance infrastructure. Even so, we have to remember that it will take 5 to 6 years for the new entrants to reach any credible size. Substantial flows of finance from new insurance companies to infrastructure can therefore only be expected in the second half of the decade. This only underscores the urgency of beginning the process as soon as possible.

v) Private Financing of Infrastructure

Private investment in infrastructure is another critical area which was part of first generation reforms but where a major push is needed to carry the reforms forward. Achieving rapid growth in today's more open and competitive environment requires a much higher level of international competitiveness. This in turn requires a very high quality of infrastructure. Unfortunately, our infrastructure, whether we look at roads, power, ports or telecommunications, is clearly inadequate. There are severe shortages in quantity and equally serious deficiencies in quality. Public investment will continue to have an important role in all these areas, but the scale of the need is such that it must be supplemented by private investment. Private investment is especially helpful in the effort to improve quality.

The power sector and telecommunications were opened up to private investment as part of first generation reforms and this was extended to ports, airports and roads. The results so far have been mixed. The good news – and there is some – is that it has been possible to attract investment in all these sectors. About 9000 MW of power capacity has come up, or is under construction, in the private sector. There has also been substantial private investment in cellular phones and other value added segments of telecommunications. Significant private investment has come in ports and the first joint sector airport was recently commissioned in Cochin. Sceptics who say that nothing has happened are clearly misinformed. However, the results achieved thus far are less than was expected and there have been serious implementation problems in all these areas for different reasons.

In the power sector the financial condition of the State Electricity Boards makes it difficult for private power generators to raise the necessary financing as long as the SEBs are seen to be unreliable paymasters because of unviable tariffs and large transmission and distribution losses, much of which is just due to theft and corruption at the distribution end. In retrospect, it would have been better to start the power sector reforms with reforming tariffs and privatising distribution to improve the financial viability of the sector. In telecom there have been other sorts of problems, first because of the inability of new private investors to meet their obligations regarding license fees, and then because of continuing disputes on the jurisdiction and the powers of the regulatory authority.

I do not propose to go into these issues in detail. I would only say that we must recognise that attracting private investment into regulated infrastructure sectors is much more complex than we had realised. Private investors in infrastructure are subject to price regulation and also have to deal with other large public sector organisations in a monopoly situation. Price regulation can cause problems if the tariffs are not sufficiently remunerative, or if they are perceived to be unfair by the public. Dealing with public sector organisations in a monopoly situation poses its own problems. Private telecommunication companies have to deal with the public telecommunication system for interconnection. Private ports have to deal with the Railways to get rail connectivity. It is necessary to provide an environment in which private investors can have reasonable certainty about the rules of the game and which is also seen to be fair to consumers and the public. This calls for strong and credible regulatory agencies which can ensure fairness in fixing regulated tariffs and also provide assurance of fair treatment for private investors.

We need to review our policies and benchmark them against best international practice. This may require changes in many areas to bring our policies in line with best practice. In telecommunications, the government has announced that it will amend the law to strengthen the Telecom Regulatory Authority of India (TRAI). This is a very important decision which should be speedily implemented on the basis of experience elsewhere. We should also look at the other regulatory authorities in the system – the SERC, the TAMP etc. – to see whether similar strengthening is needed.

IV

Second Generation Reforms

Let me now turn briefly to what I would call the real second generation reforms, i.e. reforms that have not formed part of the explicit reform agenda thus far, but now need to be brought to the top of the agenda for the next decade.

i) Extending Reforms to the States

First, there is the issue of extending the reforms process to the State Governments. There has been much discussion and public debate about reforms in the Central Government, but the need for parallel reforms at State government level has not received enough attention. And yet, most of the areas where the common man interfaces with the government agencies lie in the State government area. Health, education, agricultural extension and agriculture related services, irrigation, power distribution, rural, state and district roads, municipal services in urban areas, are all areas where the quality of government output directly affects the lives of the people. All these areas are in the purview of State Governments.

Some State Governments have recognised the need for reforms in particular sectors, e.g. in the power sector, and this is indeed a welcome development. The number of such States is still small, but hopefully it will expand. The key to success in this area, as in many others, is the willingness to introduce reasonable user charges which make the sector financially viable. This is true for power and also for many other services. If States can take significant steps in this area, it would take care of some of the most critical constraints in the next stage of development.

Many of the developmental problems in the State sector are a reflection of the fiscal crisis facing State governments and corrective action in this area, along the lines mentioned earlier, would help resolve these difficulties. However, resources are not the only problem. Additional resources will not improve education if the system tolerates teachers who do not teach, or even attend school. It is a sad fact that efficiency levels in our governmental system have deteriorated greatly in many parts of the country. This is partly due to the fiscal crisis itself because underfunding leads to loss of elan and morale. However it is also in large part a reflection of a deterioration in governance standards which has led to a decline in accountability and performance. One should of course beware of generalisation. Some States perform much better than others. Individuals can always make a huge difference everywhere. However the system as a whole is becoming dysfunctional. Administrative reforms designed to improve performance and increase accountability are therefore essential if resources are to be translated into effective developmental work. The specific solutions needed will vary from State to State. I share the view of many people that greater involvement by the people at the ground level will on the whole improve the responsiveness and efficiency of the system.

State Governments also need to undertake liberalisation of their controls and procedures. The number of separate permissions needed to set up a small business in most States ranges between thirty and forty, and each one of these becomes an occasion for harassment and corruption. What is worse, these burdens fall especially heavily on small businesses increasing transactions costs for them enormously. A serious effort to reduce the rigours of "inspector raj" at the State level would be a major boon to small business and would encourage investment. States would achieve much more by way of attracting investment if they tried to compete with each other in providing an investor friendly environment and in providing superior infrastructure than in the usual effort to offer sales tax incentives.

ii) Labour Legislation

An area that has not been touched by the reforms thus far, but which must now be addressed urgently, relates to reforms in the labour markets and especially labour laws. Economists have long known that India's labour laws deny firms the flexibility they need to operate successfully in highly competitive markets. Enterprises do not have the flexibility to retrench labour or to close down a particular unit in the company in response to changing market conditions without getting prior government permission. The labour laws also specify the "service rules" which govern employment and which cannot be changed very easily. This can make it difficult even to redeploy workers to different activities when needed.

The intention behind these laws was to protect employment. However in trying to protect existing employment they actually discourage growth of new employment. This was less of a problem in earlier years, when the economy was closed and even domestic competition was limited, and the additional costs could simply be passed on to consumers in the form of higher prices. This is no longer possible in an open economy, especially one subject to strong competition from imports. Indian industry needs flexibility to deal with the new and much more competitive situation. They need flexibility to downsize when needed and also to restructure and reorganise businesses through sale, acquisition and merger. The present labour laws are a serious impediment to this process. The resulting inflexibility discourages businesses from expanding freely, and also prevents restructuring which would improve efficiency and create a basis for future expansion of employment.

The provisions relating to contract labour also need to be amended. They make it difficult for establishments to contract out services which have to be performed on the premises - e.g. gardening, cleaning, security and cafetaria. Greater flexibility in this area would lead to a profusion of smaller businesses providing services to existing firms which are otherwise unwilling to increase their own labour force. It would contribute to total employment generation and even to enterprise development.

The time has come to amend our labour laws to bring them in line with practices in other countries. It should be kept in mind that the existing laws apply only to the organised sector labour force, which constitutes only 8 per cent of the total labour force. Ninety-two percent of the labour population derive no benefit from these laws. In fact these laws actually discourage the growth of high quality employment in the organised sector and to that extent are against the interest of those who are seeking employment.

iii) The Functioning of the Legal System

My final candidate for second generation reforms is the legal system. If we want to integrate with the world and to benefit from large inflows of foreign investment we need a well functioning legal system in which contractual rights and obligations can be effectively enforced. The legal system must be one in which the laws are clear and transparent, procedures are speedy, the judiciary is independent of politics and outcomes are perceived to be fair. I have no doubt that we score very well on independence of the judiciary and fairness, but not on clarity or the speed of procedures.

I must confess that I am not professionally competent to pronounce on legal infirmities but I would like to mention some commonly perceived problems.

- First, there is no doubt that we have a plethora of outdated laws, many of which need to be scrapped.
- Second, the laws that are not outdated are often drafted in a manner that is open to multiple interpretations and the resulting lack of clarity has been the subject of a surprising amount of unnecessary legislation. Bibek Debroy in a recent study has highlighted some particularly absurd examples arising out of lack of clarity in the excise law. In 1959 the Supreme Court had to pronounce whether charcoal is coal. On Several other occasions it has had to pronounce on whether betel leaf, chillies, lemons and green ginger are vegetables because if they were, they would be free of tax. My favourite example is the one in 1985 when the Supreme Court had to decide on the vegetable status of coconut - it led to a split decision!
- Third, our legal procedures are enormously time consuming. They seem to be designed to help those seeking postponements. If justice delayed is justice denied there is not much justice in our system.
- Finally, the Government itself has a voracious appetite for litigation and routinely appeals all decisions against it, even decisions by its own appellate bodies! An important motivating factor behind such appeals is the perception that failure to appeal may impunge the integrity of the relevant administrative authority.

The end result of all this is that our courts are clogged with cases and litigation takes an enormously long time. Interestingly it is ordinary citizens and small businesses that are hurt most by these problems. Large corporations, with a battery of lawyers, are much less vulnerable. Drastic change in this area is desperately needed.

I am conscious that there are many important issues of policy which I have not touched upon. One cannot be comprehensive and still observe the normal time constraints of a lecture. My objective was only to outline the broad agenda of reform that we must address in the coming years. As you can see the agenda is fairly large and some of it quite difficult. I would only say that if we can make significant progress in most of the areas I have mentioned, we would be well set to achieve 7 to 8 percent growth over the next decade, and what is more, a growth which will be distributionally balanced and will dramatically reduce poverty.

13th Jawaharlal Nehru Memorial Lecture (IFFCO), November, 1999.

6

Second Generation Reforms

KIRIT S. PARIKH • AJAY SHAH

The first phase of reforms, in the early 1990s, took place in an environment where there was a well-developed consensus among economists about the first-order problems which then afflicted Indian economic policy. Today, as we contemplate the second phase of reforms, it is important to place the economic policy problems in the context of the problems and opportunities for economic growth of India in the coming decade.

The revolution in information technology is transforming the global economic structure, especially in the light of the post-industrial service orientation of modern economies. Economic concentration and the role of transnational corporations are increasing. Financial integration into the unprecedentedly sophisticated global financial system offers new opportunities. Globalization is no longer an option: it is a fact.

The Decline of Traditional Industrial Mass Production

The bulk of income in post-industrial societies is generated in the services sector: once one has enough food, one wants it cooked by the best cooks; once one has enough clothes, one wants designer clothes.

This gives an appeal to brand names. Brand names add tremendous value to a product. A silk tie may cost only \$ 5 to make, but the 'P' (Pierre Cardin) on it allows it to sell for \$ 150! Going beyond this, the super-rich go for designer clothes – one of a kind, or limited edition clothes.

Modern information technology makes it possible to provide 'mass-produced personalized products': MPPPs. The advantage of MPPPs is that they satisfy the urge for individuality, and do it at affordable costs to the masses. Thus the future will belong to MPPPs where a great deal of value addition is done in the services sector. The MPPPs will supersede the branded products of today.

At the same time, growing global prosperity gives people more leisure and increases the demand for entertainment. Entertainment is the ultimate 'superior good', in the sense that all marginal income, beyond a point, is spent on it. The creativity of our writers, artists, and entertainers is a resource which has a potentially vast global market.

Increasing Economic Concentration

The modern industrial economy is sustained by mass consumption. To sustain growth of such an economy one needs growing demand, which is ensured by the growing variety and improving quality of goods and services. When economies of scale exist, in production or innovation, this gives advantages to large firms. Two important characteristics of a modern economy are that it is mass market driven and it is technology dominated.

How long can demand keep growing? Since the large bulk of global population has a level of consumption that is way below that in industrialized nations, the scope for demand growth is very large. But even in industrialized countries, demand keeps growing, for human wants are insatiable. Also, the ensure ever increasing demand, manufacturers build in obsolescence in their products.

The insatiability of wants is not just confined to material goods. It is also for power and dominance. Firms want to be ever bigger, not just because economies of scale dominate but also because the chief executives want to be number one. Another important characteristic of present development patterns is the dominance by a few large firms with monopoly power. While a large firm with economies of scale has the potential to supply goods cheaply, a monopoly has little incentive to do so.

Investors in stock markets who gather more information about firms can make better investment decisions and earn higher rates of return. However, the cost of collection of information does not depend on how much one has to invest. Whether one wants to invest Rs. 10,000 or Rs. one million it is the same. Naturally, one who has a million rupees to invest would collect more information and could obtain a higher percentage return. Thus the fixed costs of information gathering generate increasing returns to scale.

These factors combine to give large, global firms. We have seen how, even in software production, which is dominated by artisans chipping away at code instead of assembly lines, a few large firms play a very large role.

Accelerating Technological Progress: More Power for the Powerful?

Technical knowledge has become the central factor of production. A firm's competitiveness depends on its command over technology. In the traditional world of economists, with only capital and labour as factors of production, every country has a comparative advantage in some products, no matter how inefficient its production system is (in a technical sense). In this world, a country with relatively more labour would export more labour-intensive products and import more capital intensive products. Even if a country has an absolute advantage in the production of both kinds of goods, i.e. it uses less labour and less capital in producing both kinds of goods compared to the other country to trade with the other country; the exchange rate would adjust so that mutually beneficial trade takes place.

Technical knowledge and innovation change the comparative advantage of a nation. A country can compete with other exporters when innovations reduce the domestic cost of production. Increased demand for a country's products can make its currency stronger. A country's competitive advantage, thus, rests on its ability to create an environment in which productivity growth is rapid.

Innovations depend on the stock of knowledge. The stock of knowledge is rapidly growing; the number of scientists doing research today exceeds the total number of scientists who ever existed earlier. Consequently new ideas, new products, new processes, new innovations, and new inventions are coming out at an unprecedented rate.

As a consequence of the increasing pace of technical innovations, products become obsolete long before they are worn out. The product cycle has become shorter and shorter. Firms have to recover their investment in research and re-tooling in a shorter and shorter period. This in turn requires a large market. Globalization is the way through which the massive global market – rather than any subset of it – is harnessed for this rapid recouping of investments.

The information technology that has swept through the world in the last decade is changing the world in profound ways. It affects production processes. Automation is now ubiquitous. Computer chips are everywhere, from refrigerators to washing machines to cars. The computer chips embedded by General Motors in their cars makes them the largest buyer of computer chips in the world.

These changes have made information a vital input into economic activities. Information provides a competitive edge to firms. A firm that knows more about customers is able to devise products which better cater to their interests. With better information about suppliers and availability, a firm can cut the cost of inputs. Good information technology can reduce the capital blocked in holding inventories to a fifth of traditional Indian norms for inventory.

With greater analysis about future possibilities, a firm can take more effective hedging actions using derivatives to reduce its risk. This is particularly important given the high price volatility that is seen on modern financial markets.

Unequal access to information and analysis will lead to growing inequality in the world. At the same time the information revolution and explosion is greatly stimulated by private initiatives with much beneficial impact. The challenge is to use it in a way that would benefit the poor and help reduce the inequity rather than accentuate it.

The information revolution provides an opportunity to developing countries to leapfrog and catch up with the developed world. To leapfrog, however, the frog has to come out of the well. A *koop-mandook* cannot leapfrog. We have not only to embrace this technology but make it universally accessible. This calls for cheap telecommunication facilities. Telecommunication reforms that lead to a competitive telecom sector are critical if India is to benefit fully from the new information technology.

The Advantages of an Open Society

Consider the largest economy in the world today, the US. It has a great advantage in developing new technologies: it is a society that encourages individuality; it has an excellent educational system; it has a large pool of science and technology personnel and a system that provides research support on merit. Government and industry spend a lot of money on research and development. Property rights are associated with knowledge and creators of knowledge obtain large monetary benefits.

The US attracts the best and the brightest from all over the world. Culturally, it cherishes diversity and avoids sectarian or ethnic discrimination. Finally it has a unique financial system, which is able to award resources to good projects, is willing to take risks, and offers the means (derivatives) through which risks can be shared and transferred. Venture capitalists play an important role in the knowledge-based economy: they help finance the process of bringing new ideas to commercial success, provide managerial support, take the risk of failure, and often make a killing. All this has produced many innovator millionaires and some billionaires, a record unmatched by any other country.

In India, today, we have many of these ingredients needed for becoming a knowledge-driven society, and a major source of innovations. This is in contrast to many Third World countries, which suffer from authoritarian or religious societies. We have a democratic society where individualism can flourish. Generally, modern workplaces are blind to differences between people of diverse ethnic, religious, caste, or national backgrounds. Women are not barred from public spaces in India. We have a tradition of respect for learning. We have many educated and trained people who have proven themselves on a global scale; they have demonstrated their ability for creativity and enterprise around the world, including the Silicon Valley. Hence we can aspire to become the innovators, the designers, the thinkers, and the artists of the world.

Globalization: A Fact, Not An Option

Communications technology reaches a large part of the world's population. The World Cup final was watched by billions of people around the world. This integration brings awareness about what is possible and what is available, and the demand for new products and pleasures arises. A global market has developed.

Globalization is now a fact, not an option. The communications revolution has turned the world into a global 'village' where everyone knows what is going on and what is available.

Trade in goods as a percentage of GDP generated by production of goods has increased from 64 per cent to 94 per cent over the decade 1986-96. For high income countries, this ratio has grown from 70 to 179 per cent, which illustrates how globally integrated these economies have become. The emergence of multinational firms and a global market has also led to a deeper integration of production. Parts and components are sourced from different countries and intra-firm trade has become a large part of global trade. A modern car or a computer would generally have components coming from scores of countries. The ease of communication and ubiquitous large computing power have made possible such widespread integration. The diseconomies of scale have been pushed back as IT has made it possible to manage larger firms efficiently. This has accelerated the growth of large transnational corporations (TNCs).

The telecommunication and IT revolution has opened up a new set of opportunities. So far, only global manufacturing had shown deep integration whereby links in the production chain spanned several countries. The same is now possible for the services sector which, as noted earlier, is much larger and growing faster. The size and scope of trade in services are much larger than is commonly perceived (see Box 1). Free trade in services will help us export skilled white collar labour services, just as free trade in manufactured goods permits us to export blue collar labour services.

The benefits of free trade go beyond the volumes of goods and services traded. The opportunity to trade freely imposes a strong discipline on local producers. Competition from imported goods improves quality and lowers cost of domestic products.

This disciplinary impact is a function of the prices at which trade is possible and not the volumes traded. As long as international markets are competitive, free trade benefits a country but with the growing power of TNCs, countries may need to impose 'optimal tariffs'. However, just because a tariff may be acceptable in some cases, there is no justification for imposing it arbitrarily. The case for each particular tariff must be clearly made. This requires refined skills in policy analysis.

Box – 1

The Export of Services Using Modern Telecommunications

Low price telecommunications open up a new breed of opportunities through which firms located in India can export services.

- The dominant export in the services sector, of course, is computer software, where the work of hundreds of thousands of people in India is exported. It is not an accident that the software boom in India really took off after Internet services first became available in India, no matter how clumsy and expensive.
- Scientific research and development is cheaper in India. This has motivated a number of multinational firms to come to India, especially in the areas of computer software, integrated circuits, and pharmaceuticals.
- Doctors outside India usually dictate notes after routine checkup of patients. Secretarial services are cheap in India. There exists an arrangement whereby doctors in Canada dial a special number which instantly connects them to a pool of secretaries in India who are trained in medical jargon. The doctor dictates a log about the patient for a couple of minutes while the secretary takes notes which are typed into a computer and sent to the doctor's computer in Canada via Internet. Thus a secretary in India works for a doctor in Canada.
- Database and information services based in India can create and package products demanded in international markets.
- Many financial sector activities are location independent. Firms such as GE Capital and AIG have commenced moving some of their international operations to India. Indians excel in finance worldwide: hence we can aspire to become an international centre of finance in the manner of Singapore or Hong Kong.

- There are companies in the US where 'technical support' for highly skill-intensive technology products is done from India. A customer in the US dials a toll-free 1-800 number and the call is shunted to a customer support centre which is physically located in India. The customer in the US is not even aware that his call has been fielded by someone across the globe.

Each of these illustrates the 'labour arbitrage' which is made possible by employing highly skilled workers in India, who can earn much higher wages once adequate telecommunications facilities exist.

The size and scope of these activities is enormous. Some observers have expressed the view that service exports cannot be large when compared to India's macroeconomy. We may observe that even though we have one of the worst telecom services in the world, software companies today account for a remarkable one-sixth of the market capitalization of India's corporate sector – the bulk of the revenues of India's software industry are derived from exports. (This calculation ignores all other kinds of service exports.) This is a remarkable outcome – most of these companies are less than a decade old and require minuscule amounts of capital when compared the rest of India's corporate sector.

Financial Sector Integration

Globalization has become most visible in the financial markets. Today, there is phenomenal flow of financial capital across countries. Private capital flows for direct investment and portfolio investment to developing countries have grown rapidly from $ 25 billion in 1990 to $ 150 billion in 1997. For low income countries, net private inflows have reached 4 per cent of GDP. With a reasonable capital-output ratio, this should mean an additional growth rate of 1 percentage point.

Foreign exchange trading has seen a dramatic growth from about $ 15 billion a day in 1973, to an average of $ 1260 billion a day in 1995, seventy times larger than world trade per day. These flows, which helped some countries develop rapidly, can cause a meltdown if domestic financial institutions are not properly supervised or if short-term borrowings are used for long-term investments. Integration with the global economy provides the country opportunities for efficiency and growth but entails risks. The country gets exposed to international shocks and policy mistakes of other countries. However, does global integration improve human welfare? Are the gains of growth more than the pains of added volatility? Are there ways in which a country can globalize while shielding itself against the ill-effects? We do not have clear, generally accepted answers yet.

The process of globalization is a central source of change in the world today. It can lead to widely shared inclusive prosperity or highly uneven development from which a significant number of countries and people are excluded. To benefit fully from it, to turn it into an opportunity, India has to adapt its policies. We have to carry out the second generation of reforms.

Outward Orientation

In the 1960s and the 1970s, a debate was played out amongst economists about the importance of an 'outward orientation'. Economies which emphasized exports of manufactured goods have often fared better than inward-oriented economies, for a wide variety of reasons. India chose to walk along an inward-looking path and missed out on the enormous expansion of global trade.

Today, the growth of manufacturing exports from India faces three basic hurdles: poor infrastructure, a high cost of capital, and high barriers to imports. While these problems should be attacked, it may be years before they are fully addressed.

In contrast, the area of service exports is remarkable since it requires only limited infrastructure and is not capital intensive. Telecommunications infrastructure is central to these opportunities and it is the cheapest kind of infrastructure to build. High interest rates do not deter investments in India's service sector (where India's comparative advantage is higher) as much as they deter investments in the manufacturing sector.

Hence an accent on the export of knowledge-oriented services could be a remarkable niche for India to exploit. This will be particularly appropriate if the expansion of global trade in services in the coming decade proves to be something like the growth of world merchandise trade in the preceding decades.

If India is able to obtain an outward orientation with an accent on service exports, all the benefits of outward orientation would accrue to us. Individuals in India would earn high wages.

Competing in global markets would drive the pace of knowledge acquisition. Exports growth would generate confidence, reduce the archaic fears of 'shortage of foreign exchange', and pave the way for further import liberalization.

Facing the New Millennium: The Second Generation of Reforms

The reforms initiated in June 1991 sought to make the Indian economy a fast-growing one. Rapid growth was desired in order to better deal with the problems of poor human development. It was to be realized through more efficient use of resources. For efficiency, both domestic and international competition were considered essential. What are the major accomplishments so far?

- The most rapid progress has been made in the domestic deregulation of industry. The system of industrial licensing and production controls has been dismantled. Indian firms are now free to decide what, how much, where, and how to produce except for eight strategic or environmentally critical industries. Foreign manufacturers now compete on Indian soil. Thus domestic competition has been greatly enhanced.
- Trade has been liberalized considerably. Many goods can now be imported on 'open general licence', i.e. without a licence. There is now partial convertibility on the current account. Tariff rates have dropped significantly. The maximum rate is now 40 per cent as compared to levels like 250 per cent earlier. The variation of tariff rates across goods is also reduced. these rates will be brought down further as part of our commitment to the World Trade Organization (WTO).
- A government must impose taxes to provide many social services that it can provide best. Yet taxes distort relative prices and incentives. An efficient tax structure is thus critical for an efficient economy. Income tax reforms have been more or less accomplished and the maximum marginal tax rate at 30 per cent (with a 'temporary' 10 per cent surcharge) is comparable to international levels. Significant simplifications have been made in excise rates in the budget of February 1999.

- Many steps have been taken in financial sector liberalization. Interest rates have been partially freed. Private entry in banking has taken place. Banks are required to satisfy prudential norms to reduce the chances of bank failure. Dramatic institutional change has taken place in securities markets in the form of electronic trading, a clearing corporation (CC), and a depository. The open electronic market which we see in India's equity market is the most transparent form of market organization in the world. These changes, put together, have yielded some of the lowest transactions costs on India's equity market, by world standards. These reforms make the financial markets more efficient, reduce the cost of capital, and serve to direct it to most productive uses.

What has been accomplished is significant. Yet much more needs to be done to reap the full benefit of what has so far been done. The new millennium offers us a world of opportunity to partake fully in the global trade of MPPPs and of white collar services, to sell designer services, to entertain the leisure class with creative output. The second generation reforms should aid Indian firms to grow and become multinationals, to let the creativity of our people flourish to acquire a technological pre-eminence in selected areas and to encourage them to exploit to the full opportunities provided by a global world of knowledge industries. This will not only help turn India into a fast growing economy, but also a humane society with the highest levels of sustainable human development.

What reforms are needed for this?

Exploiting the Knowledge-based Global Economy

Telecom

The first and foremost area for progress towards a knowledge-based economy is telecommunications. As highlighted above, integration into the world economy, and export of services, hinges on low price and high quality telecom services being available. India's telecom sector has failed in producing these services. Some telecom services in India cost 10 to 100 times more than comparable services abroad. We have talked about reforms in telecom since the early 1990s but have made limited progress. Box 2 summarizes the vital inputs that should go into telecom reforms.

Box – 2

The Agenda for Telecom Reforms

- The Department of Telecommunication's (DoT) draconian 'Closed User Group' policy, which is incompatible with sensible economics and with the basic idea of a liberal democracy, should be abolished. All interconnections between the citizens of India should be permissible and free of censorship.
- Videsh Sanchar Nigam Limited's (VSNL) monopoly on international telecommunications needs to be replaced by unrestricted competition, without requiring licence fees.
- Domestic long-distance telecom should similarly be a market with unrestricted competition where private and foreign firms face no entry barriers.
- Licence fees for basic services and mobile telecom should be abolished. New technologies, such as cable vendors, should be able to offer telecom services, such as Internet access, without permission requirements or licence fees.
- The electromagnetic specturm is a vital resource which enables many telecom services. The defence services have appropriated an inordinately large fraction of this scarce resource and a lot of these frequencies should be freed up for civilian use. They should be auctioned off to the private sector. Frequencies should be tradeable on an exchange, just like shares. The Government should enforce property rights for the owner of a frequency, just as a squatter is prevented from misappropriating a piece of land.
- The Telecom Regulatory Authority of India (TRAI) should be strengthened and it should address the problems of interconnectivity and minimum standards of service quality. All discriminatory pricing, where prices of telecom services are higher for 'profit making entities' such as Internet service providers, should be abolished.
- The state should embark upon building public infrastructure for high speed data networking. This should be a wholesale facility through which anyone can obtain a 2 Mb/s leased line for domestic networking, for a total price like Rs. 30,000 per month.

- The institutional landscape, which presently consists of DOT, TRAI, Mahanagar Telephone Nigam Limited (MTNL), and VSNL should be altered. The bulk of DOT, which is a telecom services company, should be converted into a limited liability company. The TRAI should be a strong regulator. A small 'Department of Telecommunications' should continue to work on policy questions, with no operational involvement in the telecom industry.

Higher Education

The modern economy, certainly the knowledge economy, requires highly educated people. Primary education is critical and its importance cannot be overemphasized. For running a technology-intensive economy, we need to go beyond primary education and build institutions for higher education. Our experience of recent years has shown that a few high quality engineers and managers have made strong impact in various industries and on the economy as a whole. It is not an exaggeration to give credit for India's software revolution principally to seven institutions: the five IITs, NCST, and the IISc.

The institutions today face enormous constraints in terms of finance and operational autonomy. Their student intake is pitifully small when compared to the size of India's economy. A large increase in the number of institutions *of this quality* would have powerful impact upon our economic growth. Such 'elitist' institutions are consistent with democracy as long as admissions are open to people of all classes. In fact, they provide a way for bright persons from poor and backward classes to advance themselves. The government should fund the capital expenditure of such institutions and give annual support only to needy students.

Intellectual Property Rights: If Indian creativity is to flourish, it has to be rewarded. A system of intellectual property rights (IPR) will open up possibilities of huge rewards for innovators. We should establish a good IPR regime.

Venture Capital: The traditional culture of banks and bank-like institutions in India is oriented towards capital-intensive industrial projects, and they are ill-equipped to take risks in knowledge-intensive projects. New methods of operation in the financial sector, such as venture capital and 'private equity funds', are better suited to the risky projects of the knowledge-based economy.

The Growing Indian Transnational Corporations

Flexibility: If Indian firms are to compete with global TNCs, they have to be flexible in entry and in exit. They must be able to start new activities and also to close down unsuccessful ones. They need the freedom to redeploy resources and exit from unprofitable activities.

- This requires amending the Industrial Relations Act (the inability to retrench workers reduces efficiency by reducing the motivation of workers; this also slows down the process of re-allocation of resources in the economy; of course, workers should be protected against arbitrary retrenchment and the law should establish a due process for the retrenchment of staff).

Trade: Trade reforms are essential to directing resources in India to their most productive uses. Tariff levels should be brought down to internationally comparable levels. All quantitative restrictions, except for environmental and health safety reasons, should be eliminated. What is important is to realize that the ability to import freely is critical for exporters. The ingenuity of Indian entrepreneurs will find myriad ways to exploit these opportunities.

Barriers to Intra-Indian Commerce

Free domestic trade is as important as free international trade. Anything that obstructs it should be eliminated. Thus all restrictions on movement, storage, and trade of agricultural commodities should be removed. Both farmers and consumers will benefit if they do not have to bear the cost of inefficient monopolistic public sector trading organizations.

Equally important for free domestic trade is the removal of indirect barriers imposed by octroi and differential state taxes, which should be high on the agenda. Octroi should be replaced by a property tax. However, this will not work if property prices are artificially depressed due to rent control. Measures to rationalize the rent act are needed. Rents should be adjusted with inflation. Unearned gains in property values should be largely captured by the municipal authorities.

Till such a time that property tax can replace octroi, a surcharge on diesel should replace octroi. Since truck operators claim that the total efficiency costs of octroi are far greater than collections, this can reduce transport cost as well as increase municipal revenue, a truly win-win outcome.

Risk-Taking

The knowledge based economy has a fast-paced environment with rapidly changing prices. Firms and individuals would find it difficult to operate in this environment without tools to hedge against these risks. This is especially true for technically skilled first-generation entrepreneurs, who do not have a well-diversified conglomerate of family businesses to cushion them from risk. An entrepreneur takes enormous risks when he chances everything on one project. Markets for risk, or derivatives markets, give people an opportunity to take greater control of their risks. We should build options and futures markets which permit larger number of people to hedge their risks.

In addition, a proliferation of index funds will provide small investors less risky ways to supply risk capital on the stock market.

Box – 3

The Agenda for Financial Sector Reforms

The financial sector has to support the growth of firms with low-cost access to debt and equity capital. It has to be a discerning source of capital, supporting robust projects while avoiding others: offering capital at a low price to low-risk projects and demanding a high price when faced with high-risk projects. The agenda for reforms on India's financial sector, today, may be summarized as follows:

- On the equity spot market, a conversion to 'rolling settlement' is the last major step required for a world class equity market.
- A liquid debt market does not yet exist in India. The institution building that has taken place on the equity market in recent years can be rapidly applied towards this.

- The introduction of options and futures on the equity index has been delayed for three years. The process must be hastened. Additionally, such markets should be developed for interest rates, the dollar-rupee exchange and for commodities.
- The banking system presents severe challenges in terms of coping with the risk of bankruptcy and impending bank failures. The viability of banks would greatly improve by permitting less risk taking. We also need to start planning for possible bank failures of the next few years, in order to cope with this contingency.
- Venture capital funds and private equity funds are the most effective means of financing innovative firms in the new knowledge-based economy. Their growth should be greatly encouraged.
- Progress towards capital account convertibility will reduce the cost of capital for projects in India on both debt and equity markets.

Capital Account Convertibility

Indian investors should have a level playing field with foreign firms. They should have the same access to international capital markets. We should liberalize and move towards capital account convertibility. While the East Asian crisis has put convertibility on the back burner, we should learn from their mistakes and move towards it, albeit with caution (see box 4).

Box – 4

Is the Case for Capital Account Convertibility Sound?

In the aftermath of the East Asian crisis, many economists have voiced concerns about capital account convertibility (CAC). Is the case for CAC still sound, and what do we need to do to avoid the crises that have engulfed Thailand, Indonesia, and Korea? From India's point of view, the relevant question is 'Can India augment its resources by opening up to international capital flows?' The answer to this must be yes.

East Asian economies – Malaysia, Thailand, Indonesia, Philippines, and China – have seen large inflows of foreign capital which have surely boosted their growth rates. Even with partial liberalization in 1997-98, India got FDI and portfolio investments amounting to 1.7 per cent of its GDP. We could attract much more. The potential gain can be very large. An inflow of US $ 20 billion, if it results in additional investment of that magnitude, could raise India's GDP by 2 per cent.

Does CAC help in attracting more FDI? By itself, financial liberalization is not adequate to do so. One needs other complementary policies. India is an attractive place to invest, and with appropriate policies we could benefit a lot. But what are the dangers? Financial markets have been characterized by 'manias, panics and crashes'. How can a country obtain the benefits of CAC, while protecting itself against the over-reacting herd mentality of financial traders?

This is a problem only for financial trades because these are now almost instantaneous, and not so much for commodity trades which still take time. Foreign financial flows come in three forms: loans or borrowings, portfolio investment, and direct investment; each has its problems.

The most obvious way a crisis can develop is when domestic banks borrow internationally and lend domestically for unproductive activities. Specifically, Indonesia and Malaysia have been accused of 'crony capitalism'. But this had provided years of high growth and cannot be called dubious lending by itself. A bank may be lending to cronies and yet may be meeting prudential norms. The danger of lending to cronies is that one becomes lax in assessing the risks, thus leading domestic banks to make poor loans which can result in crises.

Similarly, when bank loans finance a real estate boom or a stock market boom, there are risks. If the boom is a bubble, with valuations far out of reach of the real underlying values, a collapse is inevitable. Banks loaning against real estate or stocks as collateral get into trouble when the bubble bursts.

Another way a liquidity crisis can develop is similar to bank run. If domestic banks of a country borrow from international markets on short term and loan domestically on long term, a term structure mismatch develops. Even with creditworthy projects, if a rumour induces panic and herd behaviour, it may lead to a liquidity crisis and, eventually, to devaluation if domestic reserves are not adequate.

Portfolio investment can increase volatility in domestic stock markets, but it also has the potential to be self stabilizing. If foreign investors all want to pull out at the same time, it would lead to a fall in stock prices; that would discourage them from going out. If they still decide to withdraw despite their losses, a country with inadequate reserves might have an exchange crisis leading to devaluation.

Finally, direct foreign investment can also lead to an exchange crisis, depending on the terms on which the investment is made. For instance, consider a power plant. If a foreign investor in the project is given a guaranteed rate of return that is greater than the social rate of return, then the investment can be immiserizing. For example, the first agreement signed by the Maharashtra government with the Enron Corporation guaranteed an internal rate of return exceeding 30 per cent on its claimed equity which may have been inflated. This, of course, was conditional on Enron generating electricity as promised, something that involved little risk.

In all these scenarios, crisis leads to devaluation, disruption in the growth process, and much social pain. The country's productive assets are sold dirt cheap in a distress sale. this is particularly troublesome when the real values of the assets are higher than the nominal value because of distorted prices and unrealistically low exchange rates.

In these possibilities, the common thread is that herd behaviour can turn a crisis into a catastrophe if a counry does not have adequate reserves. Since we cannot do anything about herd behaviour, we need measures to withstand it. The obvious way is to limit short-term borrowing and ensure 'adequate' reserves. If the RBI holds reserves to protect against a crisis associated with short-dated capital inflows, then these reserves are effectively a form of free insurance against short-term currency volatility, and serve to encourage short-term inflows. RBI should finance the cost of holding additional reserves by imposing a tax on short-term inflows.

It is worth noting that the CAC committee of the RBI had, along with stringent fiscal discipline, banking sector reforms, and/or a flexible exchange rate policy, recommended that foreign exchange reserves should account for short-term debt in addition to import needs and possible changes in the lead-lag relationship between import payments and export realizations. These preconditions would be even more beneficial than CAC. Albeit cautiously, India should move towards CAC.

Equity and Debt Markets: India's equity market has made enormous progress. Only one element (rolling settlement) stands between India's equity market and the best international standards. At the same time, the debt market remains hobbled by archaic institutions. A liquid, long-term debt market would greatly enable the growth of firms and the financing of infrastructure.

High Growth of Agriculture

Liberalization in Agriculture: Indian farmers are no different than other entrepreneurs -- they adopt new technologies enthusiastically, respond to price signals, and grab opportunities to increase their own well-being. The principal reform needed is to free farmers from all domestic restrictions on storage, transport, and sale of agricultural products. The present policy of low output prices and subsidized (low) input prices puts a net tax on farmers; we should change to a system of internationally competitive prices for both inputs and outputs. To protect poor consumers, it is much better to provide an effective targeted safety net rather than distort food prices which has high costs as compared to the benefits.

The Role of the State: The responsibility of the government is to ensure that adequate public investments are made in irrigation, agricultural research, and infrastructure that ensure well-functioning markets and facilitate exports. For providing food security, the government should follow a mixed strategy of modest buffer stocks supplemented by occasional trade on the world market.

Empowering the Poor

A Safety-Net that works: We can eliminate poverty by consolidating our various anti-poverty measures, of indifferent effectiveness, into a coherent targeted safety net for the poor. Employment programmes are the most effective kind of anti-poverty programme. If wages are kept below the minimum, such programmes are self-targeting, self-liquidating, and self-adjusting. The government has made a good beginning by announcing its intention to combine the various programmes into one and give village panchayats the power to implement these. While eliminating poverty is an important goal in itself, an effective safety net would additionally help enable other reforms which might temporarily worsen poverty.

Old-Age Security

We need to set up a system for old age income security. The increase in life expectancy, the breakdown of the joint family system, and the desire for modern medical care have created several problems for the aged. The present system of provident funds (PFs), even for those few who have that facility, is grossly inadequate largely because of excessive early withdrawals and low rates of returns. The PF system has earned an abysmal real return of 2 per cent in the last decade. The long run average real return on the equity index has been 12 per cent.

We need to set up an effective system of saving with high rates of return, which can also reach the unorganized sector. In addition, poverty alleviation programmes for the elderly are also needed; these would need to be distinct from the employment programmes mentioned above. Yet, an approach to old age income security based on empowering people through a lifetime of saving is preferable to one that emphasizes receiving a dole in old age.

Human Development

Elementary Education: The new age of knowledge industries requires an educated population. Public policy should put a great accent upon expanding the quality and quantity of educational services in the country. Universal and compulsory primary education is only the first step. Empowerment of parents and local government is the key through which expenditures on primary education can yield the best results.

- Primary schools should be put under full control of *panchayats* to ensure effective functioning.
- Private sector initiatives in the *production* of educational services would fit well with the desire on the part of the government to *fund* education. The best way to achieve this is to empower parents. Instead of the Rs. 3000 per child per year which is spent by the state in running a poor quality primary school system, parents should be

given a voucher of Rs. 3000 per child which they can use to pay to a school *of their choice*. This would spur private sector initiatives in offering educational services, and provide competition to government run schools which would need to improve their functioning to attract students and hence obtain vouchers.

A Clean Environment

Environmental Damage: Environmental sustainability is not a luxury for the rich. It is doubtful if economic growth along with environmental degradation increases social welfare at all. We need to institute effective policies to preserve and regenerate environmental resources. Use of economic incentives, a system of public hearings and public pressure backed up by right to information and full liability laws can clean up our air and water. At the same time, degraded land and forests can be regenerated through participatory programmes.

Effective policies for cleaning up air require controlling industrial, vehicular, and household emissions. The state pollution control boards are unable to enforce the present standards for industry emissions for want of effective measurement and monitoring facilities. Once such facilities are available, a more effective policy to provide appropriate economic incentives to industry, would be a pollution tax related to the amount of pollutants discharged. If the measurements are made public, popular pressures would induce firms to clean up their emissions. These monitoring and measurement services could be out-sourced to chartered environmental auditors. These environmental audits could then be made compulsory.

For transport sector emissions, the most effective solution is the expansion of public transport. Emission standards for private vehicles must be enforced and stricter emission standards for new vehicles should be stipulated.

The use of dirty bio-fuels leads to half a million premature deaths each year. We should be able to provide cleaner fuels to all.

Improvements to Governance

Public Finance: Public finance reforms should get high priority in the second generation reforms. Only that can provide the needed funds to the government to expand social services and avoid financial sector distortions when the state pre-emptively obtains these resources. The first-order issues in public finance have, so far, been *aggregate* expenditure, tax revenue, and fiscal deficit. However, it is equally important to take stock of expenditure patterns and measure the cost-benefit ratios of the myriad schemes and projects which have been accumulated over the years. We are suffering from very low quantity and quality of *outcomes* in the creation of public goods, given the levels of *expenditures* on them. One after another, governments have initiated schemes but not closed down enough of the failures. The myriad poorly run government programs are symptomatic of the poor governance which we have in India today.

Power Sector Reforms: The unfinished agenda of rationalizing electricity prices and eliminating subsidies to farmers and domestic consumers should be high on the reforms agenda. Without it, even private power will not become available. We are in a fragile situation today, where if industry goes massively for captive power plants, the present power systems will go into a state of near-breakdown.

Legal Reforms: Accountability and the enforcement of contracts requires that we have a legal system that dispenses justice quickly, inexpensively, and sensibly. Reform of our legal system to make it so is vital for economic progress as well as social justice. These should work at two levels: the administrative problem of how courts work, and the basic problem of redrafting fossilized legislation.

Box – 5

The Agenda for Reforms in Public Finance

- Completion of the tax reforms that have been begun: reduce tariffs, change to value added tax (VAT), harmonize state taxes, abolish octroi, amend rent control acts, and impose pollution taxes.
- Widen the tax net; introduce agricultural income tax.
- Sell public sector units (PSUs) and retire public debt.
- Remove non-merit subsidies and price economic services provided by the government appropriately. Such pricing reforms are critical in electricity, water, and fertilizer for the agricultural sector. Farmers should be compensated by higher output prices and more public investment in agricultural infrastructure. The poor consumers whose real income would go down when food prices increase, should be compensated by self-targeting programmes of income support, such as employment guarantee schemes.
- We need to take a comprehensive look at government spending today, with the objective of eliminating projects and schemes which fare poorly in a cost-benefit sense. The potential for expenditure reduction in this fashion could be as large as 50 per cent of expenditure.

In Conclusion

These reforms are feasible. There is also a large political consensus regarding them. Lobbies of vested interests, and vocal minorities, would certainly object to some, but if we show courage and carry them out, India's development can accelerate dramatically.

India Development Report, 1999-2000, Indira Gandhi Institute of Development Research, Mumbai.

7

Growth, Poverty and Reforms

JAGDISH BHAGWATI

At the outset, let me address and counter the frequent assertion that what went wrong in our assault on poverty in the past, and hence, what is wrong with reforms today, is that our planners were interested in growth as the objective of their planned developmental efforts, not in poverty. This assertion, if true, would be pretty serious and could undermine the reformers since they wish to improve the policies that have undermined growth and *hence,* in their view, the reduction of poverty. In short, while the critics say that growth was an objective desired in *itself* by planners indifferent to poverty, economists such as myself argue that growth was, and is, desired *because* it would reduce poverty.

I will argue presently that growth helps to reduce poverty because of three central reasons:

- it creates jobs that 'pull up' the poor into gainful employment by providing more economic opportunity;
- it provides the revenues with which we can build more schools and provide more health facilities for the poor; and
- it creates the incentives that enable the poor to access these facilities and also for the advancement of progressive social agendas generally.

But many of the critics of reforms today choose not to engage these substantive arguments (which in fact favour, not destroy, the case for economic reforms), but to pretend that India's problem has been that growth, not poverty reduction, was the target of our efforts and that they are correcting that mistake. I simply urge you to throw that assertion back in the face of the critics, so that we can focus on the substantive, not illusory, issues at hand. Ask them to read, from a vast literature, the writings of Dadabhai Naoroji in 1901, and of our great leaders such as Gandhiji and Pandit Nehru. If they think these had no relevance to our planning, ask them to take down from the library shelves the successive Five Year Plans from the first in 1950 and, prior to that, the documents of the National Planning Committee of Mahatma Gandhi's Indian National Congress and its 1940 resolve, in Pandit Jawaharlal Nehru's words in 1946, to:

> "insure an adequate standard of living for the masses; in other words, to get rid of the appalling poverty of the people...[To] insure an irreducible minimum standard for everybody, the national income had to be greatly increased... We calculated that a really progressive standard of living would necessitate the increase of wealth by 500 or 600 per cent. That was however too big a jump for us, and we aimed at a 200 to 300 per cent increase within ten years."

I believe that the truth of the matter is that few serious politicians and economists ever thought of growth as anything except as an instrument for reducing poverty. The focus on poverty was always there, at least in India. Indeed, when I joined the Planning Commission, right after finishing my education abroad in 1961, my first task was to help Pitambar Pant, a great planner, devise the strategy for raising the 'minimum incomes' of the poorest third of the population: and I led him to the view that growth was a critical component of that strategy. True, we could redistribute incomes, assuming that was politically possible, but we had to think of *sustainable* attack on poverty, not a one-shot effect. The difficult task of sustainability is *precisely* the problem that faces Kerala (and, to some extent, West Bengal and also Sri Lanka), regions of low growth performance, which used to be cited by the critics of reforms as the great 'alternative' example for us to follow. And sustainability inevitably required us to think of growth, a *sine qua non* of an anti-poverty strategy for reasons I set out earlier in this address.

So, as new members of the educated citizenry who must use their education to think, reflect and challenge, you must reject the argument that we have been guilty of neglecting poverty because we did not *value* its removal. The debate must focus instead on what was wrong in our *policies*.

And let me say that, once you do that, the conclusion is inescapable: the economic reforms, which today require a forceful accentuation of the policy changes spearheaded by Dr. Manmohan Singh, are the way to go if India is finally to fulfil its ambition to reduce massively its poverty and destitution. Let me explain this since it is easy to fall prey to the notion that markets, globalisation, privatisation and other such 'neoliberal' reforms are for the likes of us, not for the poor.

First, central to our economic strategy of alleviating poverty was the acceleration of growth and the creation of jobs for the poor. This requires, of course, that our policies promote growth, else the expected benefits in alleviating poverty will not materialise. But, as I argued in the 1960s when I was almost alone (except for my co-authors Padma Desai and later T.N. Srinivasan) and as nearly all except a few diehards now agree, the growth strategy itself was undermined because of our policy framework.

The Indian experience has been that our policies produced an annual growth rate of nearly 3.5 per cent for almost a quarter of a century up to the early 1980s. The economist Raj Krishna described this as the Hindu growth rate, implying perhaps that deep cultural factors destined us to such an unfortunate outcome when the star performers in the Far East had delivered growth rates at almost double digit levels over the same period, transforming in astonishing ways their economies and their standards of living. I doubt this characterisation of Raj Krishna's, believing that we can transcend cultural factors: indeed, the irony is that if the Vajpayee government of the BJP succeeds in cementing the growth-friendly reforms, it will be a Hindu party – the BJP is popularly described in the Western press, interestingly without refutation by the government, as the Hindu Nationalist Party even though BJP translates as the Indian People's Party – that will have finally killed the Hindu rate of growth !

These abysmally low growth rates, it is now agreed among all thoughtful observers who are not wedded to ideology and hence cannot learn from experience, were a result of four sets of policies:

- anti-globalisation policies that meant that India failed to take advantage of the opportunities provided by the growing world economy regarding trade and inward flows of direct foreign investment;
- off-the-charts reliance on public sector enterprises which, afflicted by inevitable overstaffing and lack of incentives, steadily led to losses that meant serious inefficiencies and also a serious strain on our revenues;
- defence of capital-intensive choice of techniques that led to a tolerance of the huge white elephants in the public sector that intensified the sorry performance of these enterprises; and
- an overwhelming expansion of direct controls to a Kafkaesque level that also made India a template, a model, of what not to do in order to grow your way to sustained development.

I must urge you to learn to be sceptical of claims to the contrary even when they come from eminent economists and politicians, especially as we are what sociologists call an ascriptive society (i.e., one where ascribed status matters most) and therefore there is a tendency to think that if successful politicians and economists tell you something it must be true. The next time you hear any of them talk about poverty, and how we have fallen short, just ask them: where were you on these four issues during the nearly three decades that we lost altogether to bad growth and inevitably to worse outcomes on poverty alleviation? And also ask them: where are you *now*, as dedicated and informed reformers are trying desperately to purge the system of these unproductive, indeed counterproductive, policies?

But let me also assure you that the proponents of growth as an effective and necessary instrument for attacking poverty have always been aware of necessary nuances. Thus, growth can certainly *by-pass* some segments of the poor: if you are in a tribal area which has little connection through economic interdependence or labour mobility outwards to the mainland, growth in the latter will not help the poor tribals. So, you need supplemental policies: who denies that?

Again, growth may actually *hurt* certain groups, including the poor. In 1958, I even produced an analysis of the paradox of Immiserising Growth that fortuitously made me known worldwide: it established the conditions under which growth, say in Bangladesh, of additional jute for export would drive down world prices of jute so much that the decline in what economists call Bangladesh's 'terms of trade' (i.e., in what exports will fetch by way of imports) would entail a loss that more than offset the gains from the added production. But the answer again is *not* to oppose growth but to use an appropriate policy of diversification that, in tandem with the growth policy, ensures that immiseration does not occur.

Think again of the mega-debate that growth with Green Revolution would harm the poor by introducing a new divide between the rich and the poor, the former using and the latter unable or unwilling to use the new seeds: many feared, and some hoped, that the Green Revolution would then usher in the Red Revolution! This did not transpire: the Green Revolution increased the demand for labour and worked benignly with regard to workers' wages.

What we need to remember, and this is a point that we knew from the earliest days, is that growth requires *complementary policies* where necessary to *prevent* hurtful outcomes or, better still since it is often difficult to foresee where problems may arise, to *offset* them as and when they materialise. We see the wisdom of the latter way of doing things when we see how we damaged growth by shielding the small-scale sector through a policy that constrained investment and production in the large-scale sector in industries such as textiles and soap. Does anyone seriously think that our planners were not foolish in assuming that the growth of the large-scale sector would necessarily hurt the small-scale sector? Is the soap or khadi made in the small-scale sector a real substitute for the soap and textiles that come out of modern factories? Cannot both co-exist and expand simultaneously? And is it not more sensible to let the large-scale sector expand without restraints and to have an adjustment programme in place that is activated *only* if and when problems arise for the small-scale sector?

Then again, we might ask: has growth, once achieved, managed to improve poverty levels in India? In the 1980s, we changed to a higher growth rate of roughly 5.5 per cent annually; but most analysts agree that it was based on unsustainable borrowing and spending policies. In fact, these policies, along with continuing lack of real reforms, produced the 1990-91 crisis. After 1991, we have had similar growth rates, even higher ones, and these are more sustainable and do reflect the ongoing reforms (though the current Bangalore-led Information Technology Revolution promises yet higher growth rates, and impact on the poor, in ways that I cannot explain here).

Doubtless you know from the newspapers that there has been a big statistical debate whether poverty has declined during the period of higher growth rates. It is clear now that it has. The necessary corrections to the data confirm this. Also, regional disaggregation confirms that the more rapidly growing states have had better impact on poverty. As I tell non-economists among my friends: sometimes economics and common sense do go together!

But let me also emphasise to you that it is not only poverty that will fall with sustained growth but also we will improve literacy and health, even other social agendas. Why? Partly, it is because a growing economy will generate resources, at given tax rates, for the government to spend on schools and public health. Without such revenues, you can profess, but not deliver on, your good intentions. Thus, when our distinguished President Narayanan told us on Republic day that we must build bridges to the poor, my reaction was mixed. Indeed, I said to myself: how true. But then I also recalled that every politician since Independence (and indeed for decades before then, as I reminded you) had said little else. The real problem, which I have been talking to you about today, has been, to use the President's metaphor, to find the resources with which to buy the cement and mortar to build the bridges. And, there, I am afraid that our distinguished President disregards, or underemphasises, the role of the reforms that have engaged the energies of our governments. And, in so doing, he accentuates from his high office the very poverty that he deplores.

Then again, let me just indicate how growth can aid the advancement of social agendas. To get literacy up, we have to build the schools and pay teachers better salaries, which requires both a commitment and the resources which only a growing economy can provide. But we also need incentives for the poor to send the children to school, in face of the compulsion felt to send them to work instead to augment their poor incomes. This is what economists call 'supply response'. Is there any doubt that in a stagnant economy, with few new economic opportunities materialising, impoverished parents are most unlikely to make the choice in favour of sending their children to schools instead of putting them to work? Again, if you have social legislation that says that you cannot beat your wife, that helps as a norm. But unless the wife can walk out on her husband and support herself with a job, something that is greatly aided by a rapidly growing economy, how is the legislation going to be truly effective? The cute phrase 'empowerment' which the World Bank has discovered works best when the minorities have economic alternatives which can come, in the end, only from expanding economic opportunities, (albeit interacting with a political democracy where effective universal suffrage gives all a vote and hence a voice).[1]

In short, sometimes all good things do go together: growth improves incomes, pulls up people out of poverty, improves literacy, helps spend more on public health, and does much more along these lines. And economic reforms, aimed at a reversal of the anti-globalisation, anti-market, pro-public-enterprise attitudes and policies that produced our dismal growth performance, are therefore the most important thing that we need to do.

And, in conclusion, let me urge you, not just to think on a bigger canvas about reforms and their favourable impact on poverty and social agendas, but to think *concretely* and at a level of personal experience about them and ask: how does each of the reforms work out for the common man? I would venture the thought that the reforms will come out smelling like roses once you do that. Let me just quote to you what I said in reviewing a recent book by two distinguished economists (whom I shall not name because of diplomacy on this solemn occasion but which I urge you to avoid in public debate where no reputation must be a shield against error and cant). These economists had made the following astonishing, backward-looking, observation on Indian reforms:

> "Debates on such questions as the details of tax concessions to multinationals, or whether Indians should drink Coca Cola, or whether the private sector should be allowed to operate city buses, tend to 'crowd out' the time that is left to discuss the abysmal situation of basic education and elementary health care, or the persistence of debilitating social inequalities, or other issues that have a crucial bearing on the well-being and freedom of the population".

Mindful of the damage that such attitudes have done to the cause of poverty reduction in India over decades, I was moved to remark in my review:

> "Much is wrong here. No one can seriously argue that there is a crowding out when the articulation of Indians is manifest in multiplying newspapers, magazines and books and the expression of a whole spectrum of views on economics and politics; this reviewer has noticed no particular shyness in discussing social issues, including inequality and poverty in India... But more important, the put-down of attention to multinationals misses the point that India's economic reforms require precisely that India join the Global Age and that India's inward direct investments were ridiculously small in 1991, around $ 100 million, and that this was an important deficiency that had to be fixed. The reference to Coca Cola is no better, serving as a cheap shot against multinational investment; but it also betrays the assumption that Coca Cola is drunk by the elite or the Westernised middle class, not by the truly poor. It is more likely, however, that the rich derive their caffeine from espresso coffee as well whereas the rich are the ones who must depend on coke instead!"

Indeed, the contemptuous reference to the privatisation of bus transportation in the cities could come only from elite economists who travel by private car and are unaware that the common people travel by buses where efficiency needs to be improved by privatisation (accompanied by necessary regulation). Again, let these economists reflect on the fact that when state-run electricity generation and distribution has led to long-accumulating problems that result in continual breakdowns of supply, whom does that hurt? Not the elites of Delhi who, perhaps like the ones in Chandigarh, have their own private generators so they continue sleeping in airconditioned comfort; but the common man who sleeps on the coir cot, with an Usha fan that can no longer function when electricity supply has broken down.[2]

In short, these economists are like the politicians who espouse the cause of the poor but are themselves the unwitting cause of the perpetuation of that poverty. This is not just ironic; it is tragic. The true heroes in India, I urge you, then are not those who go around talking about development with a 'human face', or noting with a touch of moral fervour the need to eliminate 'abysmal poverty' in India. Rather, they are those who, like your alumnus Dr. Manmohan Singh, have vigorously worked for the reformed policies which alone can translate these time-worn sentiments into concrete reality.

I urge you then to join forces with these men and women. After all, you are the young generation that must carry this task forward. It is in your own hands to achieve the ideals of our great leaders, Gandhiji and Panditji. Let me assure you, as an economist who began his career in India's Planning Commission some 40 years ago by addressing this very problem and has worked on these issues ever since, that victory is within your grasp if you only turn your backs with contempt on the populist and beguiling rhetoric and reach out for the prize by standing on the shoulders of the reformers today.

Notes

1. See my Rajiv Gandhi Memorial Lecture on 'Democracy and Development', 1994, reprinted in my collection of public-policy essays, *A Stream of Windows: Unsettling Reflections on Trade, Immigration and Democracy*, MIT Press, 1998; Indian edition by Oxford University Press, 1999.
2. Perhaps I can speak from my own experience as, for nearly 18 months, when I was a young professor at Delhi School of Economics, my life was characterised by the absence of a private generator and the presence of a coir cot and an Usha fan!

Convocation Address at Punjab University, Chandigarh, December 2000.

8

Economic Reforms and Their Macro-Economic Impact

NAGESH KUMAR

After pursuing an inward-looking development strategy with the state assuming an important role for more than four decades, India decided to take a historic step of changing tracks in 1991. It embarked on a comprehensive reform of the economy to widen and deepen its integration with the world economy as a part of structural adjustment. There seems to be a general consensus on the desirability of reforms to dismantle the bureaucratic regulatory apparatus evolved over the years that may have outlived its utility. However, there has been considerable debate on the contents of the reform package, their sequencing and the pace, their implementation and their impact. The debate has become a highly polarised one between two camps of scholars. One group of analysts hail the achievements of reform and seek faster implementation of the remaining issues on the reform agenda. Prominent contributions in this tradition are Bhagwati (1994), Srinivasan (1998), Joshi and Little (1996), Ahluwalia and Little (1998), Parikh (1999), Mohan (1999), among others. The other school is more critical of the approach to the reforms. It focuses on the adverse effects on the society especially the vulnerable groups, questions the sustainability of growth and the reforms themselves. Hence, they seek rethinking on the coverage, sequencing and pace of implementation of reforms. Prominent contributors in this tradition are Nayyar (1996), Ghosh (1997), Nagaraj (1997), Patnaik and Chandrasekhar (1997), among many others.

Reforms are a means to achieve the ultimate goal of economic development of the country and the wellbeing of its people. In the words of the 1998 World Bank Report on India as cited in Srinivasan (1999) "Reform is not needed for its own sake but for the sake of India's poor and in the interest of having them both contribute to the growth process and benefit from it". Against that background, this paper reviews the performance of the Indian economy in terms of certain broad macro-economic indicators over the past 7-8 years of the 1990s for which data are now available. Section I of this paper will provide a brief contour of the reform package and Section II will discuss the macroeconomic performance of the economy in the 1990s. Section III offers some implications for the second generation of reforms.

I

BACKGROUND AND NATURE OF REFORMS

After a period of relatively robust economic performance in the late 1980s, the Indian economy entered into a period of unprecedented liquidity crisis during 1990-91. This crisis was a combined effect of a number of events coinciding. These included collapse of the Soviet Union that had emerged as India's major trading partner. The Gulf War that erupted in January 1991 worsened the balance of payments crisis not only with rising oil prices but also by causing a virtual stop-page of remittances from Indian workers in the Gulf. These events coupled with political uncertainty prevailing in the country led international credit rating agencies to lower India's rating both for short- and long-term borrowings. The erosion of international confidence in the Indian economy not only made borrowings in international markets difficult but also led to outflow of deposits of non-resident Indians with Indian banks. These developments together brought the country to the verge of default with respect to external payments liability which could be averted by resorting to borrowings from the IMF under the stand-by arrangements and CCF and by mortgaging gold to the Bank of England. This was complemented by emergency measures to restrict imports.

In June 1991, a new government came to power following the elections. This government initiated a programme of macroeconomic stabilisation and structural adjustment with the support of the IMF and the World Bank. The structural adjustment programme adopted by India has been in the mould of orthodox package of reform that has come to be referred to as the Washington Consensus. The implementation of the agenda of the reforms over the eight years has covered the following, among others.

Trade Policy Reforms: A major reform of trade policy regime has been effected since 1991. The import licensing system has been dismantled. All non-tariff barriers (NTBs) have been phased out from all tradables except consumer goods. The peak tariff rates have been brought down to maximum 50 per cent from up to 355 per cent. Table 1 shows the progressive decline in the average tariff rates applicable to imports confirming a major reform of the trade regime. Besides India has also undertaken a major commitment to liberalise its trade regime under WTO Agreement. India had agreed to bind tariff rates to lower levels than those prevailing at the time of signing of the Agreement (viz, 1994) for a large number of commodities. Tariff rates on most of the commodities have been brought well below the bound rates by 1998-99 except for 40 commodities [Mehta 1999]. The NTBs on the remaining items are being phased out by March 2001 although the earlier plan was for phase out by 2003. Besides this, India is liberalising her trade with south Asia on a faster

Table – 1

Tariff Rates of India

	Maximum Tariff Rate	Average Weighted Tariff Rate
1990-91	355	87
1993-94	85	47
1995-96	50	25
1996-97	52	25
1998-99	50.8	20

Source: WTO (1998): Trade Policy Review: India (WT/TPR/S/33) World Trade Organisation, Geneva; and Indian Planning Commission.

track than all trade. India has unilaterally removed all quantitative restrictions on imports of around 2,300 items from SAARC countries in 1998. Negotiations on exchange of trade preferences have been undertaken with SAARC trade partners under three rounds of SAPTA.

Industrial Policy Reforms: Although some liberalisation and streamlining of the industrial policy had been effected in the mid-1980s, the New Industrial Policy (NIP) announced on July 24, 1991 and subsequent amendments brought far-reaching changes in the policy regime governing industrial investments. The NIP dismantled the industrial licensing (or approval) system that regulated the industrial investments in the country by abolishing the requirement of obtaining an industrial licence from the government in all except 14 specified industries. These specified industries need to be regulated in view of environmental hazards, national security or social well-being considerations.

NIP has thrown open new industries and services to private including foreign private sector by pruning the list of 'Industries Reserved for the Public Sector'. Only six industries, which are now reserved for exclusive development by public sector, include those considered sensitive from national security point of view. Thus a large number of industries and services including infrastructure such as telecommunication, roads, ports, power generation, petroleum refining have become accessible to the private sector. NIP accords a much more liberal attitude to foreign direct investments (FDI) than ever in post-independence India. The policy allows automatic approval system for priority industries by the Reserve Bank of India within two weeks subject to their fulfilling specified equity norms. Three slabs of foreign ownerships have been defined for automatic approvals. Up to 50 per cent foreign ownership is permitted in six mineral industries listed in the Annexure III Part A of NIP. Up to 51 per cent ownership is allowed in 35 priority industries specified in Annexure III and in 14 additional industries specified in Annexure III Part B of NIP. Foreign ownership of up to 74 per cent is allowed in select high priority infrastructure sectors and other priority industries specified in Annexure III-C of NIP. Recently, the government has decided to permit up to 100 per cent foreign ownership on automatic basis to investment proposals in ports and roads. A more favourable treatment is also accorded to non-resident Indian (NRI) investors who are allowed up to 100 per cent ownership priority industries.

A Foreign Investment Promotion Board (FIPB) has been set up to consider all other proposals that do not qualify for automatic clearance. However, to bring transparency into the working of FIPB, elaborate guidelines and time frame of six weeks in normal cases are also specified. FIPB is authorised to negotiate with foreign investors in person to expedite the clearances. FIPB is empowered to approve up to 100 per cent foreign ownership in cases involving transfer of high technology, projects producing pre-dominantly for exports, energy and infrastructural projects, consultancy or trading companies. The restrictions on investments by large industrial houses and foreign controlled companies under the MRTP Act were also abolished.

A phased programme of disinvestment of public ownership in public sector corporations has been launched. A Disinvestment Commission has been set up to make recommendations on the phasing of the disinvestments.

The outward investments by Indian enterprises were also liberalised and proposals fulfilling certain norms could now be granted automatic approval.

Exchange Rate Reforms: The rupee was devalued twice in July 1991 leading to a 20 per cent depreciation in its value. The partial convertibility of rupee on the trade account was announced in the 1992-93 budget that was subsequently broadened to full convertibility on current account by August 1994.

Capital Market: The Capital Issues Control Act was repealed and the Securities and Exchange Board of India (SEBI) was set up as a watchdog for regulating the functioning of the capital market. SEBI has focused on regulatory reform of the capital market as well as on market modernisation. Online trading and dematerialised trading have been introduced. Companies have been allowed to buy back their own shares subject to the regulations laid down by SEBI.

In September 1992, the government announced guidelines for investments by foreign institutional investors (FIIs) in the Indian capital market. FIIs were now welcome to invest in all types of securities traded on the primary and secondary market with full repatriation benefits and without restrictions on either volume of trading or lock-in-period.

Financial sector: In January 1993 a package of financial sector reforms was announced that included permission to new private sector banks including foreign joint ventures. The government has also established a policy regime for functioning of private non-banking finance companies (NBFCs) and agencies for rating their credit worthiness.

The above discussion thus shows that the government since 1991 has undertaken a comprehensive reform of the economy. In addition to the above measures there has been an emphasis in the government budget-making to restricting budget deficits, on lowering tax rates in tune with the tenets of Washington consensus.

II

MACROECONOMIC IMPACT OF REFORMS

As indicated earlier, seven to eight years is not a long period to evaluate the impact of reforms that involve structural changes of the type summarised above. Therefore, the following analysis should be taken as indicative and not definitive.

Growth and Its Sustainability

Table 2 summarises the growth rate of India's GNP at factor cost at constant prices. The compound rate of growth for the second half of 1980s was 5.8 per cent per annum. Compared to that for the post-reform period excluding 1991-92 as year of exceptional crisis, the average for 1992-98 comes to 6.5 per cent per annum. The average rate for the 1993-94 to 1998-99 period (based on the new series of GDP) comes to 6.8 per cent. Similarly, the trend rate for the post-reform period estimated at 6.9 per cent is higher than 5.5 per cent applicable for the 1980s. The post-reform growth, therefore, has been at least 1.1 percentage points higher than the average rate achieved during the pre-reform period. The average rates reflect the robust growth performance recorded by the Indian economy during the first five years after the initiation of reforms. The growth rate of the Indian economy has considerably decelerated in 1997-98 to 5.1 per cent from 8.1 per cent recorded in the previous year. The rate of growth in 1998-99 has been estimated at 6.0 per cent by CSO. To some extent the recent slow down could be on account of the contagion effect of the east Asian crisis on India indirectly and economic sanctions imposed on India in May 1998 following Pokhran II by major industrial countries. In large part the recent slow down reflects the effect of industrial recession that started in the year 1996-97. Hence, the sustainability of average growth rates recorded in future has to be evaluated in terms of the trends with respect to revival of industrial growth.

Table – 2

Annual Growth Rate of Gross National Product at Factor Cost

Year	Old Series at 1980-81 Prices	New Series at 1993-94 Prices
1980-81	7.3	
1981-82	5.8	
1982-83	2.6	
1983-84	7.9	
1984-85	3.8	
1985-86	4.1	
1986-87	4.0	
1987-88	4.1	
1988-89	10.2	
1989-90	6.9	
1990-91	5.2	
1991-92	0.5	
1992-93	5.2	
1993-94	6.2	
1994-95	7.8	7.7
1995-96	7.4	7.8
1996-97	7.7	8.1
1997-98		5.1@
1998-99		6.0#
	Annual Average Growth Rates	Trend Growth Rates
1980-91	5.8	5.5
1992-98	6.5	6.9
1993-99	6.8	6.9

Notes: @ Quick estimates # revised estimates.

Source: Economic Survey 1998-99, Appendix Tables, 1.1; and RBI, Report on Currency and Finance 1998-99, Appendix Table NI.3.

Sectoral Performance: The sectoral rates of growth have been summarised in Table 3. After excluding 1991-92, the year of adjustment, the average annual rates of growth for the post-reform period exceed those of the pre-reform period in the case of industry and services. In services in particular, the average rate in the post-reform period shows an increase of 1.5 percentage points. The growth rates of the primary sector are largely governed by external factors because of Indian agriculture's high dependence on rates of rainfall. The average growth rate of industry in the post-reform period at 8.1 per cent is only marginally higher from 7.94 per cent averaged during the second half of the 1980s. Actually, the industrial growth rate has shown a healthy accelerating trend over the 1992-93 to 1995-96 period with growth rates rising steadily from 4.4 per cent for 1992-93, to 6.9, 9.3 and 12.7 per cent in the subsequent years. However, since 1996 growth rates of the secondary sector have decelerated during the subsequent years to 6.0 per cent in 1996-97 and to 6.2 per cent in 1997-98. The estimated growth rate for industry in 1998-99 was even lower at 4.6 per cent. It is clear that the Indian industry entered into a recessionary phase since 1996 that has been worsening over the 1996-99 period. The recovery of the GDP growth rate to 6.0 per cent in 1998-99 is actually on account of a healthy 7.6 per cent growth recorded by the primary sector up from - 0.7 per cent during the previous year. Industry recorded only 4.6 per cent rate of growth during 1998-99 compared to 6.2 per cent in the previous year. The service sectors' growth performance has also decelerated since 1995-96. The key reason for a slow down in industrial growth has been the significant fall in public investment levels that have occurred during the 1990s especially since 1995 as seen later.

Signs of Industrial Revival: Recent trends and surveys do indicate that the industry may finally be coming out of the recession in the second half of 1999-2000. The growth of industrial production during April-September 1999 has been 6.4 per cent compared to 4.1 per cent for the corresponding period in 1998 [RBI 1999]. Similarly, the growth rates of basic, intermediate and capital goods industries picked up in the first 6 months of the year 1999-2000 which again might be suggestive of the impending recovery of industrial growth (Table 4). A survey conducted by

Table – 3

Annual Rates of Growth of Real GDP at Factor Cost by Broad Sectors

Years	Agriculture, Forestry & Logging, Fishing and Mining	Manufacturing, Construction, Electricity Gas, Water Supply	Transport, Communication and Trade	Banking and Insurance, Real Estate, and Business Services	Public Administration, Defence and Other Services
1986-87	-1.0	6.9	6.3	8.2	9.2
1987-88	0.5	6.6	5.8	6.0	6.6
1988-89	16.3	8.7	7.0	9.2	6.1
1989-90	2.0	10.5	8.2	10.8	8.3
1990-91	4.2	7.0	5.2	6.4	4.3
1991-92	-2.0	-1.7	2.3	10.5	4.1
1992-93	5.8	4.4	6.2	4.6	5.0
1993-94	3.6	6.9	12.5	5.6	3.9
1994-95	5.7	9.3	12.8	5.6	3.4
1995-96	0.8	12.7	11.5	8.3	7.8
1996-97	8.7	6.5	8.6	7.9	6.7
1997-98	-0.7	6.2	5.7	8.4	13.3
1998-99	7.6	4.6	6.7	6.2	5.4
	Agriculture and Allied	**Industry**	**Services**		
Average Growth Rates					
1980-91	4.5	7.2	6.2		
1992-98	3.0	8.1	7.7		
1993-99	4.3	8.2	7.8		
Trend Growth Rates					
1980-91	3.1	7.6	6.5		
1992-98	2.4	9.3	8.4		
1993-99	4.0	8.3	7.9		

Note: Average of rates of growth for the period 1992-94 at 1980-81 prices and for 1994-99 at 1993-94 prices. Quick estimates for 1997-98; revised estimates for 1998-99.

Source: Compiled from the Economic Survey 1998-99, Appendix Table 1.6; and RBI; Report on Currency and Finance 1998-99, Appendix Table NI.3.

CII also finds that 46 out of 84 segments show a 10 per cent or higher growth during April-November 1999 led by strong recovery of transport equipment sector (Economic Times, January 14, 2000). Another indication of future growth of industrial production can be had from the trends in growth of a composite index of infrastructure sectors comprising electricity, coal, saleable steel, cement, crude, and petroleum refinery products. This index registered a growth rate of 6.7 per cent during April-September 1999 compared to 3.4 per cent during the corresponding period in the previous year [RBI 1999]. The stock market also started to rise in the second half of the 1999-2000 with Bombay Stock Exchange sensitive index crossing the level of 5,000 points for the first time and staying there. All these indicators do suggest that the industry may finally be coming out of recession that it has faced in the past three years. However, one has to wait and watch if these trends are sustained and the Indian economy is firmly on a higher growth trajectory.

Industrial Restructuring, Productivity and Innovation: Liberalisation is expected to bring efficiency and productivity gains in the industry. The accompanying paper by Basant observes that liberalisation has provoked a trend of corporate restructuring and consolidation through mergers and acquisitions (M and As). Foreign technology purchases have also expanded considerably. Has the restructuring, consolidation and technology import contributed to the improvement of efficiency and productivity of the industry? The evidence available so far does not indicate any significant productivity improvement. Das (1999) who examined the productivity performance of Indian industries in the pre- and post-reform periods finds that productivity performance of Indian industries worsened in the 1990s as against the 1980s. Hence, the contribution of total factor productivity growth to output growth is negligible. The result holds good for analysis conducted both at 3-digit and 2-digit levels. Furthermore, Mani and Bhaskar (1998), and Goldar and Ranganathan (1998) find evidence of declining trend in inhouse R and D in the corporate sector in 1990s. Basant also reports R and D to sales ratios in the Indian corporate sector either stagnating or declining. Neglect of R and D is a matter of concern because R and D activity is an important determinant of long-term productivity growth, competitiveness and hence sustainability of growth of industry.

Table – 4

Index Numbers of Industrial Production

Year	General Index	Mining and Quarrying	Manu-facturing	Electri-city	Use-Based Classification: Basic Industries	Capital Goods Industries	Intermediate Goods Industries	Consumer Goods Industries: All	Durables	Non-Durables
1993-94	100	100	100	100	100	100	100	100	100	100
1994-95	108.4	107.6	108.5	108.5	108.9	105.7	105.3	111.8	116.2	110.8
1995-96	122.3	117.9	123.5	117.3	120.6	110	125.4	125.6	146.2	121.1
1996-97	129.1	115.6	131.8	122	124.3	120.2	135.5	132.1	153	127.5
	(5.6)	(-1.9)	(6.7)	(4.0)	(3.0)	(9.3)	(8.1)	(5.2)	(4.6)	(5.3)
1997-98	137.6	122.4	140.5	130	132.4	126.4	146.5	139.6	164.9	134.1
	(6.6)	(5.9)	(6.7)	(6.6)	(6.5)	(5.3)	(8.1)	(5.7)	(7.8)	(5.2)
1998-99*	143.1	120.3	146.7	138.4	134.4	142.4	155.1	144.0	172.6	136.5
	(4.0)	(-1.8)	(4.4)	(6.4)	(1.5)	(12.7)	(5.9)	(2.4)	(4.7)	(1.8)
1999-2000	146.4	115.7	150.4	146.7	na	na	na	na	na	na
(Apr-Sept)*	(6.4)	(0.4)	(6.8)	(7.7)	(5.1)	(9.2)	(9.1)	(4.0)	(12.8)	(1.6)

Note: * provisional. Figures in parentheses indicate rate of change over the previous year.

Source: RBI, Report on Currency and Finance 1997-98, Bombay.

FDI Inflows: Liberalisation of FDI policy regime was an important aspect of the reforms. The approvals of FDI inflows since the liberalisation of policy in 1991 reveal a dramatic jump. Compared to approvals of FDI totalling $ 200 million in 1991, US $ 14.6 billion worth of FDI inflows have been approved in the year 1997. In 1998, however, the magnitude of approvals declined to US $ 7.8 billion, partly on account of the east Asian crisis. The approvals, however, have been slow in materialising into actual inflows and are still much lower than FDI inflows. Actual inflows in 1997 amounted to $3.2 billion declining to $ 2.3 billion in 1998. However, all the expansion in the magnitude of FDI inflows could not be attributed to the reforms alone. Kumar (1998a) has found that policy liberalisation has not yet helped India improve her share in FDI outflows from major European countries or the US. Hence, the recent expansion of FDI inflows in part reflects the dramatic expansion in the global FDI flows to developing countries from about $35 billion per year on average during 1987-92 to $166 billion in 1998.

The bulk of the approved inflows in the 1990s have been directed to non-manufacturing sectors bringing the share of manufacturing down from 85 per cent in the stock of FDI in 1990 to just 35 per cent in cumulative approvals. Infrastructural sectors such as energy (29 per cent) and telecommunication services (20 per cent) account for the bulk of the approvals as is clear from Table 5. These sectors had not been open to FDI inflows before and hence, the inflows directed to them could be attributed to policy liberalisation.

Another change brought about by liberalisation is the policy barriers that were neutralising the internalisation advantages of foreign investors to the country have been removed. Hence, a greater proportion of technology transactions of Indian enterprises take place through internal or FDI mode. The proportion of foreign collaborations that are internalised through FDI in total approved has gone up from just over 16 per cent in the 1970s to nearly 58 per cent during the 1990. Therefore, liberalisation has shifted the balance between FDI and licensing in favour of FDI. Furthermore, majority foreign ownership which was restricted to certain exceptional cases during the 1970s and 1980s because of regulations is becoming more popular again. Majority of approvals over the 1990s have been in the 50-100 per cent foreign ownership range with a third accounted for by wholly foreign owned subsidiaries. A number of MNEs have taken advantage of new rules to increase their stake in their existing affiliates in the country. The importance of joint venture mode of operations has declined with liberalisation [Kumar 1998a]. As Basant has also noted in the accompanying paper, acquisition of existing enterprises has become an increasingly popular entry mode for MNEs in India in the recent years.

Table – 5

Sectoral Distribution of Stock of FDI in India

(Million rupees)

Industry Group	FDI Stock as in March 1980		FDI Stock as in March 1990		Approvals 1991-97	
	Value	Per Cent	Value	Per Cent	Value	Per Cent
I Plantations and horticulture	385	4.1	2560	9.5	4901	0.33
II Mining	78	0.8	80	0.3	15576	1.06
III Petroleum and power	368	3.9	30	0.1	423905	28.91
IV Manufacturing	8116	86.9	22980	84.9	545135	37.18
Food & beverages	391	4.2	1620	6.0	75748	5.17
Textiles	320	3.4	920	3.4	23700	1.62
Machinery & machine tools	710	7.6	3540	13.1	32830	2.24
Transport equipment	515	5.5	2820	10.4	71082	4.84
Metal & metal products	1187	12.7	1410	5.2	73225	6.00
Electricals & electronics	975	10.4	2950	10.9	79702	5.44
Chemicals & allied products	3018	32.3	7690	28.4	100759	6.88
Miscellaneous manufacturing	1000	10.7	2030	7.5	88089	6.01
V Services	385	4.1	1400	5.2	459086	31.31
Telecommunications	0	0	0	0	296271	20.21
Finance and banking	na	na	na	na	63012	4.30
Hotels and tourism	na	na	na	na	29720	2.03
Air and sea transport	na	na	na	na	19954	1.36
Consultancy	na	na	na	na	10068	0.69
Other services	na	na	na	na	40061	2.73
Total	**9332**	**100.0**	**2,7050**	**100.0**	**1466218**	**100.0**

Note: Percentages might not add up to 100 because of rounding off errors.

Sources: Kumar (1998a).

While the magnitudes of inflows have recorded impressive growth, they are still at a small level compared to the country's potential. Furthermore, one of the objectives of the current reforms of policies is to remove impediments for export-oriented manufacture in general and to attract MNEs to locate efficiency-seeking FDI in the country. These investments could help India in expanding manufactured exports by using her as an export platform. The majority of the recent approvals of FDI, however, aim to exploit India's sizeable and expanding domestic market. The efficiency seeking or export-oriented FDI have yet to start flowing to the country in a considerable manner.

Fiscal Adjustment and Stabilisation

A key aspect of the structural adjustment programmes is to restrict the fiscal deficits of the governments. Table 6 summarises the trends in budget deficit of the central government in the late 1980s and 1990s. In the second half of 1980s, the fiscal imbalance worsened with average fiscal deficit rising to 8.2 per cent of GDP compared to 6.3 per cent in the early 1980s (*Economic Survey, 1992-93*). Compared to this, the average fiscal deficit in the post-reform period has been 5.7 per cent of GDP. This suggests that the government has succeeded in managing the fiscal situation quite well. The extent of fiscal deficits tends to mask the method adopted by the government to balance the budget and its implications. In fact the revenue deficit which represents the gap between revenue receipts and revenue expenditure has increased in the post-reform period (at 2.9 per cent) on average compared to an average of 2.6 during the second half of 1980s. This implies that the government has been unable to contain its current expenditure. Therefore, fiscal deficit has been contained either by reducing capital investment or by raising capital receipts such as borrowings or disinvestment of public sector holdings of the government. A rising level of revenue deficit has thus been sustained with government borrowings of the scale of the revenue deficit to finance its consumption expenditure rather than producing a revenue surplus to finance capital expenditure in social sectors (and defence) which do not yield a future income flow to the exchequer. Nayyar (1996:37), among other analysts, has argued that such a fiscal regime "is not sustainable in medium-term for it is bound to fuel inflationary pressures or strain the balance of payments, and thus disrupt the process of growth".

Table – 6

Trends in Central Government Deficit

As percentage of GDP

Year	Revenue Deficit	Fiscal Deficit
1985-86	2.2	8.3
1986-87	2.7	9.0
1987-88	2.7	8.1
1988-89	2.7	7.8
1989-90	2.6	7.8
1990-91	3.5	8.4
1991-92	2.6	5.9
1992-93	2.6	5.7
1993-94	3.7	6.9
1994-95	3.0	5.6
1995-96	2.4	4.9
1996-97	2.3	4.7
1997-98	3.0	5.7
1998-99(RE)	3.4	5.9
Averages		
1985-86	2.6	8.2
1992-99	2.9	5.7

Source: Economic Survey 1992-93 and RBI (1999).

Fiscal adjustment has been achieved by squeezing public investment rather than government consumption. Capital expenditure as a proportion of total government expenditure has declined steadily from 30.18 per cent in 1990-91 to 21.8 per cent in 1998-99 (Table 7). As a proportion of GDP, capital expenditure has come down from 5.5 per cent to 3.6 per cent during the same period. The sharp decline in government capital investment especially since 1995 has been held responsible for industrial recession. Concerns have been raised about the decline in budget support for key infrastructure sectors such as energy, transport and communications not only in terms of proportion of GDP but even in nominal terms [Nayyar 1996:38-39]. The relative neglect of infrastructure sectors has resulted in a widening gap between demand and supply of infrastructural services which may adversely affect future growth prospects. Private investment can at best be a complement to and not a substitute for public investment in physical and social infrastructures. As Mohan (1999:7) argues "private sector investment would itself be crowded in by greater and more efficient public investment".

Table – 7

Receipts and Expenditure of Central Government

Years	Capital Expenditure	Total Expenditure	Capital Expenditure as Per cent of Total	Capital Expenditure as Per Cent of GDP	Total Expenditure as Per Cent of GDP
1985-86	21477	53112	40.4	8.2	21.5
1990-91	31782	105298	30.2	5.5	18.1
1994-95	38627	160739	24.0	3.7	15.5
1995-96	38414	178275	21.5	3.2	14.6
1996-97	42073	201007	20.9	3	14.3
1997-98	51718	235245	22.3	3.3	14.8
1998-99(RE)	63773	281912	21.8	3.6	16.0
1999-2000(BE)	46895	283882	16.5	2.3	14.2

Source: Economic Survey 1998-99 and RBI (1999).

Finally, it has been shown that the burden of adjustment has been unequal in that it has led to declining expenditures on social sectors such as education, health and poverty alleviation. In the accompanying papers, Panchamukhi and Mahendra Dev observe a decline in social sector spending especially during the early post-reform period. Hence, concerns have been raised regarding the levels of human development. The analysis of NSSO data by, among others, Srinivasan (1999), Datt (1999), as by Mahendra Dev in the accompanying paper suggests that the process of decline in levels of poverty was arrested during the 1990s. Hence, the decade of 1990s can be termed as a 'decade of lost opportunity' as far as poverty alleviation is concerned [Datt 1999]. Mahendra Dev also observes that inequalities between rich and poor states have increased during the 1990s.

Prices: An important focus of the stabilisation programme is to bring the rate of inflation under check. The rate of change in wholesale and consumer prices in Table 8 and the accompanying Figure suggest that the overall trend in prices has been one of decline since 1992. One striking trend noticeable from Table 8 and the Figure is the growing divergence between the rate of inflation based on wholesale prices and that for consumer price index since 1993-94. Until 1993-94 the two rates generally converged. Since 1995-96, the consumer price index based rate of inflation has exceeded that based on wholesale prices by a wide margin. The diverging trend in the wholesale and consumer prices has been explained in terms of the change in the weighting scheme for the two indices. The consumer price index has a 57.0 per cent weight of the food group compared to just 27.5 per cent in WPI [RBI 1999]. The divergence between the two indices therefore, reflects substantial increases in food prices in the 1990s. Besides, a spurt in prices of housing, medical care and personal care has also contributed to the rise in CPI. The rise in food prices and other goods of mass consumption at a faster rate than prices of other goods also indicates that sharing of burden of adjustment by different sections of society has been uneven and weaker sections may have been affected more.

Table – 8

Inflation in India

Years	Index No of WP	Annual Change	Index No of CP (General)	Annual Change
1986-87	132.7		137	
1987-88	143.6	8.21	149	8.76
1988-89	154.3	7.45	163	9.40
1989-90	165.7	7.39	173	6.13
1990-91	182.7	10.26	193	11.56
1991-92	207.8	13.74	219	13.47
1992-93	228.7	10.06	240	9.59
1993-94	247.8	8.35	258	7.50
1994-95	274.7	10.86	279	8.14
1995-96	295.8	7.68	313	12.19
1996-97	314.6	6.36	342	9.27
1997-98	329.8	4.83	366	7.02
1998-99	352-5	6.9	414	13.1
1999-2000up to Oct		2.9		7.5

Notes: Base: 1981-82 =100.
WP = Wholesale prices, all commodities, average of weeks;
CP = Consumer prices for urban industrial workers general index (average of months).

Figure: Rate of Inflation

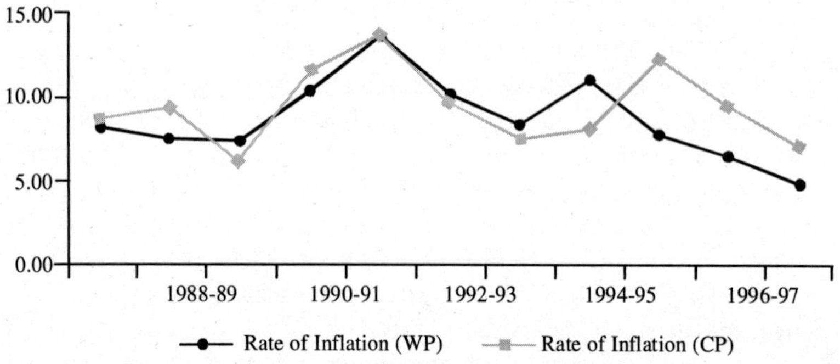

Source: Computed from Economic Survey 1998-99 and RBI (1999).

External Sector

Trade Performance: Liberalisation of the trade regime since 1991 has led to the proportion of trade in GNP going up steadily from 14.1 per cent in 1990-91 to 18.2 per cent in 1998-99 (Table 9). Indian Economy, therefore, is more deeply integrated with the world economy today than it was in 1991 as a result of high rates of growth of both exports and imports in the first half of the 1990s.

In the early post-reform period, there was a considerable buoyancy in exports during 1993-94 to 1995-96 period when the annual growth rate of exports averaged at nearly 20 per cent in US dollar terms. However, export growth rate has slowed down considerably since 1996-97. Indian exports recorded just 5.3 and 4.6 per cent growth in 1996-97 and 1997-98 respectively. In the 1998-99, exports actually declined by 3.9 per cent. Yet the average growth rate of exports in US dollar terms during 1992-93 to 1998-99 at 9.8 per cent is higher compared to 8.2 per cent achieved in the 1980s.

The average annual growth rate of 20 per cent in dollar terms that India's exports witnessed during the mid-1990s has received a lot of attention in the literature. Most of the analysts have attributed it to the growth of world trade and sharp depreciation of the exchange rate following the reforms [Brahmbhatt et al 1996; Marjit and Ray Chaudhuri 1997; Srinivasan 1998, among others]. The recent decline in the growth rate of exports is on account of a combination of factors. The decline in the growth of world trade since 1996 is one such factor. The East Asian crisis has also put a strain on India's exports not only by shrinking demand in the affected countries but also by adversely affecting international competitiveness of India's exports due to sharp depreciation of east Asian currencies [Kumar 1998b]. Furthermore, India's competitiveness may have been affected by the tendency of the rupee to appreciate in real terms in the mid-1990s following the switchover to a unified market determined exchange rate management in March 1993.

Table – 9

Major Indicators of India's Foreign Trade

Year	Exports	Imports	Trade Balance	Growth Rate of Exports	Exports GDP Ratio	Import GDP Ratio	Export Import Ratio
1980-81	8485	15867	-7382	7.0	4.9	9.2	53.5
1981-82	8704	15173	-6468	2.6	4.9	8.5	57.4
1982-83	9108	14787	-5679	4.6	4.9	8.0	61.6
1983-84	9449	15311	-5862	3.8	4.7	7.6	61.7
1984-85	9878	14412	-4534	4.5	5.1	7.4	68.5
1985-86	8905	16067	-7162	-9.9	4.2	7.5	55.4
1986-87	9745	15727	-5982	9.4	4.3	6.9	62.0
1987-88	12089	17156	-5067	24.1	4.7	6.7	70.0
1988-89	13970	19497	-5527	15.6	5.1	7.1	71.7
1989-90	16613	21219	-4607	18.9	6.1	7.7	78.3
1990-91	18145	24073	-5927	9.2	6.1	8.1	75.4
1991-92	17865	19411	-1545	-1.5	7.1	7.8	92.0
1992-93	18537	21882	-3344	3.8	7.6	9.0	84.7
1993-94	22238	23306	-1068	20.0	8.0	8.3	95.4
1994-95	26331	28654	-2324	18.4	8.0	8.7	91.9
1995-96	31795	36675	-4880	20.8	8.7	10.1	86.7
1996-97	33470	39132	-5663	5.3	8.4	9.9	85.5
1997-98	35006	41485	-6478	4.6	8.3	9.9	84.4
1998-99P	33659	41858	-8199	-3.9	8.1	10.0	80.4
Average							
1980-81 to 1990-91				8.2	5.0	7.7	65.1
1992-93 to 1995-96				15.7	8.1	9.0	89.7
1996-97 to 1998-99				2.0	8.3	9.9	83.4
1992-93 to 1998-99				9.8	8.2	9.4	87.0

Note: P : Provisional.

Source: RBI Report on Currency and Finance, 1998-99, Appendix Table TR1.

Finally, India's competitiveness has also been adversely affected by the failure to diversify the commodity composition of her exports. Apparently, the commodity concentration of India's exports has increased with a 9 per cent rise in the share of top six commodity groups of exports in total exports between 1987-88 and 1998-99 [RBI 1999]. India's inability to diversify her export structure has also been observed by Sinha-Roy (1998) and Ganesh-Kumar et al (1999).

The robust export growth during the first half of 1990s has helped narrow the trade deficit from 2.7 per cent of GDP on average during the 1980s to just 0.9 per cent during the 1992-93 to 1995-96 period. However, with the recent slackening of exports growth, the trade deficit has again widened to1.6 per cent during the 1996-97 to 1998-99 period. Hence, the export growth has to be revived if the trade deficit is not to climb back to the 1980s levels. It becomes all the more urgent in view of the recent announcement that all the remaining non-tariff barriers will be phased out by April 2000, i e, two years ahead of the original schedule. This may lead to rapid expansion of consumer goods and cause further widening of trade deficit. The indications are that exports growth is picking up in the year 1999-2000 as the estimated export growth during the April-November period has been 12.7 per cent (Economic Times, January 27, 2000).

Invisibles Trade: The surplus on invisibles trade has improved during the 1990s on account of growing service exports. This has been reflected in the increasing private transfers by Indians working abroad. These transfers amounted to 2.5 per cent of GDP during the period 1993-94 to 1998-99 compared to just 1 per cent in the late 1980s (Table 10). The invisible receipts have also risen on account of booming exports of software especially since 1993-94 which now account for 0.6 per cent of GDP. The invisible payments especially investment income have been kept under check by the increasing reliance on the non-debt capital flows and by reducing the dependence on short-term borrowings. The private transfers and software exports have kept rising even during the second half of the 1990s when the merchandise exports stagnated. The rising surplus in invisibles trade has helped to reduce the current account deficit to manageable levels. The current account deficit came down to just 1 per cent of GDP in 1998-99 compared to 2.3 per cent on average during the late 1980s.

Table – 10

Some Indicators of India's Balance of Payments

(As per cent of GDP)

Item	1985-90 (Average)	1990-91	1991-92	1992-93	1993-94	1994-95	1995-96	1996-97	1997-98	1998-99
1	2	3	4	5	6	7	8	9	10	11
Current Account										
Exports	5.1	6.2	7.3	7.8	8.1	8.1	8.9	8.6	8.5	8.2
Imports	8.2	9.4	8.3	10.2	9.6	10.9	12.0	12.3	12.2	11.4
Invisible receipts	2.8	2.5	3.8	3.8	4.0	4.7	4.9	5.4	5.5	6.2
of which Private Transfers	1.0	0.7	1.5	1.6	1.9	2.5	2.4	3.1	2.8	2.5
Invisible Payments	2.0	2.6	3.1	3.2	3.0	3.0	3.4	2.8	3.2	4.0
of which Investment Income	0.8	1.4	1.6	1.6	1.3	1.3	1.3	1.1	1.2	1.3
Invisible net	0.8	-0.1	0.7	0.6	1.0	1.7	1.5	2.6	2.4	2.2
Current account deficit	2.3	3.2	0.4	1.8	0.4	1.0	1.6	1.2	1.3	1.0
Capital Account										
Foreign investment	0.1	0.03	0.1	0.2	1.5	1.5	1.3	1.5	1.3	0.6

(Contd...)

1	2	3	4	5	6	7	8	9	10	11
of which										
Direct	0.1	0.03	0.1	0.1	0.2	0.4	0.6	0.7	0.9	0.6
Portfolio	0.0	0.0	0.0	0.1	1.3	1.1	0.7	0.8	0.4	0.0
Debt flows	2.0	2.0	1.3	0.7	0.7	0.6	0.7	1.9	1.2	1.3
of which Commercial borrowings	0.6	0.8	0.6	-0.2	0.2	0.3	0.4	0.7	0.9	1.1
Total capital account surplus	2.3	2.4	1.5	1.7	3.5	2.8	1.3	2.9	2.4	2.0
Overall Balance Reserves and External Debt (end-period) Foreign exchange reserves (US$ million)	5616	5834	9220	9832	19254	25186	21687	26423	29367	32490
Import cover of foreign exchange reserves										
(No of months)	3.4	2.5	5.3	4.9	8.6	8.4	6.0	6.5	6.9	8.2
Total external debt (US $ million)	-	83801	85285	90023	92695	99008	93730	93470	94320	98231
Short-term debt (as per cent of reserves)	-	146.5	76.7	64.5	18.8	16.9	23.2	25.5	17.2	13.3
Debt/GDP ratio (per cent)	-	30.4	41.0	39.8	33.1	30.0	26.3	23.8	23.8	23.7
Debt Service Ratio (per cent)	-	35.3	30.2	27.5	25.6	26.2	24.3	21.2	19.1	18.0

Note: - not available.

Source: RBI Report on Currency and Finance, 1998-99, Appendix Table IF1.

On the capital account, the inflows of non-debt resources, viz, FDI and portfolio investments have steadily increased over the 1990s thus bringing down the relative reliance on external commercial borrowings and short-term credit. A healthy development on the capital account has been the ability of prominent Indian companies to raise capital at the western stock exchange through GDRs and ADRs. Encouraged by the successes of Indian issues abroad, the government has recently done away with the need for approvals for issue of GDRs/ADRs. The total surplus on the capital account has been of the order of about 2.5 per cent of GDP over the 1996-97 to 1998-99 period, i e, more than adequate to neutralise the current account deficit. Hence, the foreign exchange reserves of India have accumulated. On March 31, 1999, the foreign exchange reserves stood at $ 32.5 billion, that is, covering 8.2 months of imports. By January 1, 2000 the foreign exchange reserves had climbed to a $ 35 billion level (*Economic Times*, January 27, 2000).

The improvement in balance of payments situation is also indicated by the decline in debt/GDP ratio from 41 per cent to 23.7 per cent from 1991-92 to 1998-99 and in debt service ratio from 30 per cent to 18 per cent. The foreign exchange reserves at $ 35 billion may appear sizeable. However, there is as yet no room for complacency as the bulk (i.e., 61 per cent) of these reserves comprise of short-term debt and portfolio investments (such as FII's investments on the stock market). As the recent east Asian crisis shows these resources are highly volatile in nature.

III

THOUGHTS FOR SECOND GENERATION OF REFORMS

The balance sheet of the adoption of economic reforms in India in the 1990s that emerges from the analysis of this and the accompanying papers is mixed. The overall post-reform growth rate of output has been robust at an average of 6.8 per cent. The observed growth rate for the 1990s is not only significantly higher than that recorded during the 1980s but it is also more sustainable in terms of parameters of fiscal and current account. Although industry has faced a recession since the 1996, there are signs that it is coming out of it. Deregulation and liberalisation of trade and investment regimes has provoked widespread restructuring and consolidation of Indian industry. Indian industry has also relied more on technology imports and affiliations with outside multinational companies and less on in-house R and D activity. Increased dependence on imported technology and industrial consolidation, however, have not yet resulted in any measurable productivity improvement. The neglect of inhouse R and D is a matter of concern for sustaining industrial growth and competitiveness as the access to technology is becoming increasingly crucial to industrial success in the knowledge economy.

The fiscal imbalance that had widened during the 1980s has been contained and inflationary tendency has been curbed. However, the fiscal adjustment has been achieved by pruning capital expenditure rather than by containing current expenditure of the government. The decline in public investment in physical and social infrastructure raises a question about the sustainability of growth. Concerns have been raised on the impact of declining social sector outlays on levels of human development and hence on long-term sustainability of growth.

The prices of goods of consumption of the masses such as food have risen faster than those of other goods. Inequalities between rich and poor states, as between rural and urban populations and between affluent and poor households seem to have widened. The process of poverty alleviation particularly in rural India has suffered a setback. It would appear, therefore, that the sharing of burden of adjustment between different sections of society has been unequal and weaker sections have been affected more adversely.

Robust export growth during the mid-1990s has helped to narrow the trade deficit. The growing surplus on invisibles trade has been made possible by rising remittances by Indian workers abroad and booming software exports. The composition of capital flows has changed in favour of non-debt creating flows such as FDI and foreign portfolio investments thus helping to contain external debt to more manageable levels. The increasing balance of payments surplus has augmented the foreign exchange reserve to healthier levels. However, there is no room for complacency on the balance of payments front especially in view of further liberalisation of trade regime contemplated with the phasing out of the remaining non-tariff barriers in the year 2000-01. Rising oil prices are also likely to strain India's trade balance. India's exports profile needs to be broadened to cover more products and increase value addition and take advantage of the liberalising world economy.

In the light of the above observations and experience gathered during the past decade, one may now draw implications for the second generation of reforms.

***Social and Physical Infrastructure*:** It has become clear that government will have to continue to play a key role in providing social and physical infrastructure to sustain high rates of economic and social development. Efficiently organised public investment in these sectors will crowd in more private sector investment to complement it. In particular, education and health deserve to receive their due place in public spending. While the goal of provision of universal primary education is important and should be achieved, it should not be at the cost of higher education. The emphasis on quality of higher education in the past decades has been responsible for enabling India to participate in the ongoing knowledge and information revolution. The 21st century will be even more intensively driven by knowledge and availability of highly trained and skilled manpower will be a key factor in determining India's place in international division of labour. The quality of higher education seems to have suffered from the budgetary squeeze in the past decade. Universities and institutions of higher education should be allowed time to become financially more independent through raising endowments from their alumni, and adopting more rational fee structures. Adopting a fee structure based on the ability to pay is one option. There should be incentives for faculty members, institutions and universities to pursue excellence. There is a general feeling that standards of academic excellence in Indian institutions, barring a few exceptions, have declined. Indeed lack of funds is not the only reason for that. There is also an immediate need to reform and re-engineer the educational system in the country, to bring it in line with the changed requirements to avoid skills mismatch. On the one hand colleges and universities are producing conventional science and social science graduates who cannot find adequate job opportunities. On the other hand there is a serious scarcity of computer-trained manpower. Computer education should be integrated in school and college curricula and other traditional disciplines, e g, fine arts which could feed the growing needs of CAD personnel [see Kumar 2000 for more details].

Similarly, investments in physical infrastructure have lagged behind in the past few years. Major projects involving private participation (including foreign involvement) have been sanctioned in power, expressways, bridges, ports, etc. They have been slow in getting off the ground. While such projects should be promoted and encouraged, they should not be at the cost of public investments in infrastructure and maintenance of existing infrastructure.

Social Safety Nets and Social Security Schemes: The industrial restructuring provoked by liberalisation has led to job losses and increasing casualisation of employment in the corporate sector [Panchamukhi and Das 1999]. There is therefore, need to provide social safety nets to guard vulnerable workers from the threat of job losses and the need for a framework for social security cover to contract workers and those in the informal sector in the industry.

Regional Disparities: After dismantling of the industrial licensing system, there is no mechanism left with the government to channel industrial investment to relatively less developed regions. This might explain the increase in interstate disparities that has been observed during the post-reform period. The government might create a regional development fund which is built up with a cess imposed on the units set up in more developed states and subsidises the investments in poorer states, among other measures, to bring about regional balance.

Privatisation: The privatisation of public enterprises is an important aspect of the reform process. However, privatisation, like the reform process itself, is a means rather than an end by itself. The privatisation process should be driven by the aim of achieving efficiency and securing long-term interests of the enterprises rather than as a means to reduce budget deficits. The proceeds of privatisation could be exclusively used to retire public debt or to fund infrastructure investments. Furthermore, the method of privatisation could be different according to the objective and the strategic element involved. For instance, in the case of enterprises which represent nation's technological capability in strategic industries, viz, 'national champions', privatisation could take the form of sale of non-controlling stake through initial public offerings (IPOs) to the public at large. In other cases controlling stake could be sold to a strategic partner bidding highest in a public auction.

FDI Policy: In a developing country such as India that seeks FDI as a development resource, the focus of the FDI policy should be on maximisation of its contribution to India's development rather than on maximisation of the magnitude of inflows by itself. One respect where substantial potential remains to be exploited in terms of MNEs' contribution to India's development is expansion of her exports. MNEs have so far come to India primarily for exploiting her large domestic market and their contribution to India's exports is negligible. In contrast, MNEs account for nearly 40 per cent of China's manufactured exports. The evidence also suggests that export-oriented FDIs bring to the host country best practice technology and also cause beneficial information spillovers on the export opportunities and hence could facilitate exporting activity of domestic enterprises as well [Kumar and Siddharthan 1997 for evidence].

Furthermore, the FDI policy needs to have a strategic perspective particularly in relation to the strategic sectors identified as a part of the industrial competitiveness policy for building local capability. It should be pursued in such a manner that foreign entry does not threaten the existence of national champions in an unfair manner [Kumar 1999 for details].

Competition Policy: The recent consolidation and restructuring of industry has raised the importance of competition policy to ensure the delicate balance between competitiveness and market competition. While corporate consolidation is important for strengthening the international competitiveness of enterprises, some competitive pressure is also necessary for them to sharpen their efficiency and to prompt them to pursue innovation based rivalry. Another aspect of competition policies is to provide a level playing field for local enterprises vis-a-vis subsidiaries of MNEs which enjoy access to their parent's brand and trade names besides a number of other intangible assets especially in the context of liberalisation of national economies to MNEs. An affiliation with established global chains of companies having a wide range of products and services lends a formidable edge to MNE affiliates over the national firms in the host markets. A competition policy, to promote a healthy competition between local firms and MNE affiliates, could either offset the monopoly power of MNE affiliation and foreign brands through fiscal measures or assist national firms to build their own brands and technological capability.

Enterprise Level R and D: In the globalising world economy, technological competence is a key to the competitiveness of enterprises. In-house R and D is increasingly becoming critical with rising knowledge content of economic activities. In that context the neglect of in-house R and D by Indian enterprises in the post-reform period is an issue of concern. This trend needs to be reversed by providing a policy package to encourage R and D. In view of the liberal policy on technology imports, enterprises feel less inclined to invest in a rather uncertain activity like in-house R and D and prefer to meet their technological needs through imports. The imported technology has several commercial attractions over the locally developed alternatives. Hence, indigenous innovative effort will need some protection from technology imports. Because of substantial spillovers of domestic R and D most of the developed countries promote it through a variety of policy incentives and subsidies [Kumar and Siddharthan 1997: chapter 2 for details]. Technology imports could continue to be governed by liberal policy such as automatic approvals as in force currently, because restricting them could possibly lead to technological obsolescence. However, the landed cost of technology imports could be increased through levies imposed on technological payments [Kumar 1990]. These levies could be returned to the domestic enterprises conducting R and D. Further incentives in the form of subsidies for approved R and D projects of domestic enterprises could be provided. Furthermore, products based on indigenously developed technology could be extended excise concessions (such as those extended to products of small scale industry) and income tax concessions (such as those enjoyed by export turnover). R and D subsidies up to 50 per cent do not contravene WTO obligations and are widely used by most of the industrialised countries.

These are some of the issues that could be considered while drawing up an agenda for the second generation or second phase of reforms, among many other initiatives that are needed to keep the economy moving upwards.

[An earlier version of this paper was presented at the International Conference on Economies of Transition at the Turn of the Century: Panel on India, organised by the IEEM in Macau, April 6-9, 1999. The author wishes to thank Maria do Ceu Esteves for her invitation to prepare the paper and to co-ordinate the Panel on India.]

References

Ahluwalia, Isher Judge and IMD Little (eds) (1998): *India's Economic Reforms and Development: Essays for Manmohan Singh*, Oxford University Press, Delhi.

Bhagwati, Jagdish (1994): *India in Transition: Freeing The Economy*, Oxford University Press, Delhi.

Brahmbhatt, M, T G Srinivasan and K Murrel (1996): 'India in the Global Economy', Policy Research Working Paper No 1681, World Bank, Washington DC, November.

Das, Debkusum (1999): 'Productivity Growth in Indian Manufacturing: An Application of Domer Aggregation', paper presented at the Workshop on Measurement of Productivity in India, New Delhi, July 9-10, Institute for Human Development.

Datt, Gaurav (1999): 'Has Poverty Declined since Economic Reforms?: Statistical Data Analysis', *Economic and Political Weekly*, December 11, 3516-18.

Ganesh-Kumar, A, Kunal Sen and Rajendra Vaidya (1999): 'India's Export Competitiveness and Finance' in Parikh (ed) op cit.

Ghosh, Jayati (1997): 'India's Structural Adjustment: An Assessment in Comparative Asian Context,' *Economic and Political Weekly*, May 17-24.

Golder, R N and V S Ranganathan (1998): 'Economic Reforms and R and D Expenditure in Industrial Firms in India', *The Indian Economic Journal*, Vol 46, No 2, 60-75.

Joshi, Vijay and I M D Little (1996): *India's Economic Reforms 1991-2001*, Oxford University Press, Delhi.

Kumar, Nagesh (1990): 'Cost of Imported and Local Technologies: Implications for Technology Policy', *Economic and Political Weekly,* 25(January 13): 103-06.

——— (1998a): 'Liberalisation and Changing Patterns of Foreign Direct Investments: Has India's Relative Attractiveness as a Host of FDI Improved'?, *Economic and Political Weekly*, Vol XXXIII, No 22, May 30.

——— (1998b): 'East Asian Economic Crisis and South Asian Growth Prospects: A Note', *RIS Digest*, Vol 14, September.

——— (1999): 'Host Country Policies, WTO Regime and the Global Patterns of FDI Inflows: Implications of Recent Quantitative Studies for India', paper presented at National Seminar on Economy, Society and Polity in South Asia, Delhi, November 16-17, organised by Institute of Economic Growth.

——— (2000): 'New technology based small service enterprises and employment: The case of software and related services industry', paper for the National Workshop on Strategic Approach to Job Creation, ILO, Surajkund, February 17-19.

Kumar, Nagesh and N S Siddharthan (1997): *Technology, Market Structure and Internationalisation: Issues and Policies for Developing Countries,* Routledge, London and New York.

Mani, Sunil and M Vijaya Bhaskar (1998): 'A Curmudgeon's Guide to Economic Reforms in India's Manufacturing Sector', *Economic and Political Weekly*, December 19.

Marjit, S and A Ray Chaudhuri (1997): *India's Exports*, Oxford University Press, Delhi.

Mehta, Rajesh (1999): *Tariff and Non-Tariff Barriers of Indian Economy* A Profile, RIS, New Delhi.

Mohan, Rakesh (1999): 'Economic Reforms: The Next Wave', Lalit Doshi Memorial Lecture, Mumbai, August 30.

Nagaraj, R (1997): 'What Has Happened since 1991? Assessment of India's Economic Reforms', *Economic and Political Weekly*, November 8.

Nayyar, Deepak (1996): *Economic Liberalisation in India: Analytics, Experience and Lessons*, R C Dutt Lectures,Orient Longman, New Delhi, Centre for Studies in Social Sciences.

Panchamukhi, V R and Ram Upendra Das (1999): *Economic Reforms, Regional Integration and Labour Markets in the SAARC Region*, ILO-SAAT, New Delhi.

Panda, Manoj, Gangadhar Darbha and Kirit S Parikh, (1999): 'Macroeconomic Development and Prospects' in Parikh K (ed), *India Development Report, 1999-2000*, Oxford University Press, Delhi, pp 35-47.

Parikh, Kirit (ed) (1999): *India Development Report, 1999-2000*, Oxford University Press, Delhi.

Patnaik, Prabhat and C P Chandrasekhar (1995): 'Indian Economy Under Structural Adjustment', *Economic and Political Weekly* November 25.

Reserve Bank of India (RBI) (1999): *Report on Currency and Finance*, 1998-99, RBI, Bombay.

Sinha-Roy, Saikat (1998): 'Post-Reforms Export Growth: Exploration into the Issue of Disparity in Structures', mimeo, RIS, New Delhi.

Srinivasan, T N (1998): 'India's Export Performance: A Comparative Analysis' in I J Ahluwalia and I M D Little (eds) op cit.

——— (1999): 'Poverty and Reforms in India', paper presented at NBER-NCAER Conference on Reforms, Neemrana, December 14-15.

WTO (1998): '*Trade Policy Review*', WT/TPR/S/33, World Trade Organisation, Geneva.

EPW, March, 2000.

9

Economic Reforms : Strategy for the Next Decade

RAJA J. CHELLIAH

Although the need for changes in the structure and elements of economic policies that were being followed since the beginning of the Second Plan had been recognised in the eighties, only mild reforms had been introduced till the end of that decade in the form of some reduction in the rigour of controls and of allowing the market a little more play. Some little liberalisation of imports had also taken place. There was no general willingness to give up or alter in any substantial way the philosophy that was the foundation of the economic policy framework. Then, in the midst of the grave balance of payments (BoP) crisis of 1990-91, the decision was taken in 1991 by the government of Narasimha Rao to give up the old paradigm. It initiated far-reaching reforms that would transform India from a controlled, closed economy to a fairly open economy in which not only would the private sector have a much enhanced role, but the market would be given the prime role in the allocation of resources. Further, there would be a gradual opening up of the economy so that the economy would become linked to the world economy to a substantial extent.

That changes in these directions were necessary and indeed inevitable was tacitly accepted by a large section of industry, business, political parties and economists, but it would be wrong to say that there was a general consensus among the political parties or intellectuals. Opposition came notably from the vested interests that were adversely affected, from those who could not or would not change their ideology and also from many who had genuine fears about the possible negative impact on the poor and on our sovereignty.

But fortunately, the major reforms carried out in the years 1991-92 to 1994-95 had, by and large, very favourable effects on the economy. In the years immediately following the start of the structural adjustment programme (SAP), or later, India did not suffer any drop in total GDP, high inflation or sizeable increase in unemployment unlike in many other developing countries which carried out SAP with or without stabilisation measures. In my view the stabilisation programme had some negative effect because of the compression of imports and of government expenditure. The SAP had, on the whole, a positive impact.

In the nineties the growth rate of GDP could reach the level of 7 per cent per annum (Table–1). After three years of high growth, the economy entered a period of downswing and deceleration in growth with the onset of political instability and the east Asian crisis. Still, the rate of growth of GDP hovers around 5 per cent. The average rate of growth in the nineties up to 1996-97 (including the early years affected by the BoP crisis of 1990-91 and the stabilisation attempt) is not much higher than that of the eighties. But there is a significant difference. This rate has been achieved in the context of a slowdown in the world economy and has been sustained along with a remarkable build-up of our foreign exchange reserves. Indeed in the external sector there is a remarkable transformation. Three significant developments may be noted: (a) a tremendous increase in foreign investment; (b) a very large flow of remittances with a realistic exchange rate; and (c) remarkable growth in exports until the beginning of the world economic slowdown and no balance of payment problem after 1991-92.

The most significant gain from the reforms so far carried out is the capacity to grow at a fairly high rate without running into BoP problems, provided of course reasonably sound fiscal policies are followed. As Bimal Jalan has pointed out, in 30 of the 36 years preceding 1990-91, we had some BoP problem or the other [Jalan 1992]. Now it can be said that we have achieved self-reliance in one important respect. Ironically, the extreme left is saying that we have come under the dominance of IMF and the World Bank, whereas the fact is, unlike in the past, we do not need to go to the IMF at all, and can carry on even without World Bank loans.

During the next decade, to sustain a high rate of growth, we need, among other things, to maintain a high growth of exports and obtain large and growing remittances and sizeable foreign investment. For this purpose, we have to have a fairly open economy with a realistic exchange rate and the efficiency of our economy has to be further increased. Therefore, there is no doubt that the major reforms carried out from 1991-92 to 1996-97 were in the right direction. In the subsequent two years some more reforms have been carried out, but owing to political instability and quick changes of government, the reform initiatives have not been quite consistent and in some areas the action has not been carried out on a sustained or consistent basis.

Considerations for Determining the Directions of Reforms

As we near the end of this decade and century, it seems opportune to look back, review the developments that have occurred in the Indian and the world economies and examine what lessons we can learn from our experience with reforms in the context of world developments. In the light of these lessons, we can determine the kind and pace of reforms that should be pursued during the coming decade.

While undoubtedly the major structural changes have benefited the economy, we must recognise that there is some genuine fear in some sections of the population that the direction of reform – greater role for the market, vastly reducing the importance and role of public enterprises and opening up the economy to foreign investment and MNCs – would adversely affect the vulnerable sections of the population and even erode the substance of our national sovereignty. We should examine the grounds for these fears in the light of our and other countries' experiences. I know that some groups like the extreme left are repeating old arguments on ideological grounds or to please their special constituencies.

However, it would be quite useful to consider if a re-orientation of the economic reforms is needed to minimise their adverse economic, social and political effects.

The ratio of population below the poverty line is subject to a secular trend but is also influenced by fluctuations in output in particular years. It is seen that according to official figures, the poverty proportion in India (the so-called head-count ratio) fell from 38.5 per cent in 1987-88 to 35 per cent in 1993-94. (In between there was a slight rise in the ratio in one year according to calculations based on a smaller sample.) The reforms have not reversed or altered the trend of steady fall in the head-count ratio since 1973-74 [Chelliah and Sudarshan 1999:5, Table–1.1]. Also, it is seen that the economically better off states (in terms of higher per capita incomes)such as Kerala, Punjab, Haryana and Gujarat have lower poverty ratios. (In Kerala, the per capita income is distinctively higher than per capita SDP.)

Table – 1

Growth of Gross Domestic Product
(At constant prices, 1990-91 to 1996-97)

Years	Rs. Crore	Per Cent
1990-91	2,12,253	5.36
1991-92	2,13,983	0.82
1992-93	2,25,240	5.26
1993-94	2,39,145	6.17
1994-95	2,57,700	7.76
1995-96	2,76,132	7.15
1996-97Q	2,96,845	7.50

Annual average rate of growth, 1980-81 to 1989-90 = 5.69.
Annual average rate of growth, 1990-91 to 1996-97 = 5.75.
Q - Quick Estimates.

Fast growth is thus essential for reducing poverty and it does reduce poverty. However, the economic reforms that accelerate growth could adversely affect some poorer sections in the short run. Also, when substantial changes take place, there are gainers and losers. Hence the society (government) has to provide a safety net for those affected and also slow down or modify the reforms to safeguard the interests of the vulnerable sections. We need to look back and examine whether during the decade we have imposed undue hardships on some sections of the population and how similar effects can be avoided or mitigated.

In considering the directions of reforms in the next decade we must also keep in mind the fact that India, which has been criticised by strongly pro-reform economists (westerners as well as Indians) as being too tardy and too slow in carrying out structural reforms, was not affected by a financial crisis such as those suffered by the south-east Asian nations or Mexico. Furthermore, we survived, fairly unscathed, the severe impact on the world economy of the crisis that overtook the Asian economies. From this experience we might perhaps legitimately draw the conclusion that there is a trade-off between stability and growth in efficiency and productivity. Hence, in the pursuit of efficiency we should not expose ourselves to excessive instability by proceeding too fast with reforms in some directions. In my view, this is an important lesson we have learnt (or should learn) from the events of the last three or four years.

It is also to be kept in mind that the relatively small size of the external sector in India, in terms of the ratios of imports/ exports to GDP, is a factor that helps ensure that the economy is relatively less affected by fluctuations in the world economy. This of course does not mean that the degree of openness should not be increased; indeed exports as a percentage of GDP must grow from its present level (8.5 per cent). But the extent of increase needed could be moderated or reduced by maintaining near self-sufficiency in basic foodgrains and increasing the efficiency and productivity of industries in several key sectors so that the need for greater imports also would be moderated. For maintaining near self-sufficiency in basic foodgrains we need to invest more in agriculture and further increase agricultural productivity and also drastically curtail the growth of population so as to bring about the state of zero population growth within the next 10 years.

At this juncture, with a fractured polity, it is difficult to bring about a general consensus, embracing at least the major parties, on the nature and pace of economic reforms to be carried further without some compromises. The compromises cannot be such that the growth rate of the economy will be significantly affected. I would say that a minimum 6 per cent rate of growth should be achieved and maintained. And improvement in resource allocation and increase in efficiency should continue to be given high importance. But the increase in efficiency needed to maintain a fairly high rate of growth could be attained even if some moderate compromises are made in areas where trade-offs are involved the choice among which is partly dependent on value judgements or differences in perception. In this context, I would urge that economists should clearly distinguish their value judgements from the positive economic propositions they are propounding on the basis of their empirical observations and scientific analysis.

Given that there are important trade-offs, there are bound to be differences in the relative weights attached to various objectives by different individuals, hence economic advisors have to work out certain compromise packages. In other words, we as advisors should give priority to reforms which are essential and most beneficial and agree to slow down or postpone reforms in some areas which would not cause any significant slowdown in growth. We need not accept all the advice that western economists might give.

The three basic objectives that we should set before ourselves for the next decade are: (a) 6 to 6.5 per cent annual rate of growth of GDP; (b) considerable emphasis on human development such that there is at least 20 per cent point improvement in social development indices such as rate of literacy, rate of infant mortality, expectancy of life at birth, extent of malnutrition and incidence of infectious diseases; and (c) reversing the trend of worsening regional disparities by initiating a trend of reduction in the gap between the per capita SDP of the poorest states and the highest per capita SDP; and also reducing the disparities in the state of infrastructural development.

The economic reform strategy for the next decade will be dictated and determined by these objectives. For achieving the objective of maintaining an average rate of growth of 6 per cent (from now on the figure of 6 per cent growth rate is used to stand for 6 per cent or slightly higher than 6 per cent) we will continue to need a high rate of domestic savings of around 24 per cent, foreign investment amounting to around 2 per cent of GDP (implying a current account deficit of the same magnitude), a fairly high rate of growth of exports (10 per cent), sustained further improvement in efficiency through competition, better resource allocation and beneficial changes in laws and procedures. There have also to be conscious efforts to considerably improve the infrastructure and performance of the backward states. For this purpose, there would be need to divert more investible resources as well as resources for human development to the backward regions. It is for this reasons that the suggestion has been made that we should aim at around 6 per cent rate of growth although if resources are not to be consciously diverted to the backward areas and investment is concentrated in areas where the immediate rate of return will be quite high, we might be able to achieve even a 6 to 7.5 per cent rate of growth.

We should concentrate on carrying forward, or initiating those reforms which are essential for, or would be helpful in, achieving the objectives mentioned above. Considered in this perspective, I believe that it is not necessary to make any preparations for moving towards full capital account convertibility. Some relaxation in regulations regarding flows on capital account could and should be made, but past experience shows that for maintaining a 6 per cent rate of growth and attracting a fairly sizeable flow of foreign investment into India full capital account convertibility is not necessary. On the other hand, maintenance of stability is greatly helped by the kind of controls we have on movements of capital.

International Aspects

There is difference of opinion among political parties on the degree of opening up of our economy to foreign trade and foreign investment. As regards foreign trade, we are members of WTO and as such we are bound to fulfil all the obligations entailed by that membership. It could be argued that developing countries could have obtained WTO rules more favourable to them in some important respects. It is now too late to go into that question. Anyhow, taking all the provisions together, India definitely stands to gain by the coming into operation of all the agreements. If we lose something in the area of pharmaceuticals and agrochemicals, we stand to gain in the field of textiles, etc.

Membership of WTO also requires that we should abide by

the agreement on TRIPS. Out of the eight categories of intellectual property for which standards of protection are incorporated in the TRIPS agreement, our existing and proposed laws and regulations in respect of six categories of intellectual property are largely in consonance with the required standards. Our concerns with respect to TRIPS agreement are limited to granting product patent to pharmaceuticals and agrochemicals, patenting of micro-organisms or life forms and establishing an effective *sui generis* system for the protection of new plant varieties, i.e., plant breeders' rights [Ganesan 1999: vi].

To take the first category, namely, granting of product patents to pharmaceuticals and agrochemicals, the fear in the minds of many is that prices of new products will go up considerably after the product patent regime comes into effect by 2005. In the interim, that is until India introduces the product patent regime by January 1, 2005, we have to grant exclusive marketing rights (EMR) to products for which patent obligations were filed in India and elsewhere on or after January 1, 1995. A number of people have misgivings about granting EMR. This fear is not warranted because, as A V Ganesan points out, EMR will be extinguished by the end of 2004 and between now and that date probably 10 or less products will seek EMR. The reason is that it generally takes eight to 10 years for a new patented product to come into the world market from the date of filing the patent application [Ganesan 1999: v].

As regards product patents for pharmaceuticals, while it is true that the prices of new products will be higher than what they would otherwise have been, we must recognise that the inventors' rights have to be protected and piracy should not be rewarded. Perhaps, if the representatives of developing countries had understood the implications better and had insisted during the negotiations on conditions that would have been beneficial and could have been obtained with pressure, we could have had a regime more favourable to developing countries. For example, the developing countries should not have agreed to a uniform period of protection of 20 years for all commodities. In respect of patents, for which applications are filed after 2005, the period could have been cut down to 10 to 15 years – 10 for pharmaceuticals and 15 for other products. But now we have to make the best of the existing situation.

We must remember that many developing countries have already enacted legislation granting product patents. Apart from that, since we have the capacity to conduct research and produce new pharmaceutical products, in course of time we would greatly benefit by product patents in this area. We should encourage R and D in the pharmaceutical field and at the same time the government should effect improvements in the working of the patent office and in procedures relating to the grant of patents.

The Uruguay Round of Multilateral Trade Negotiation was concluded in 1993 and the results of the negotiations were embodied in the Final Act or the international treaty that was signed by the ministers of the member countries in 1994. Apart from TRIPS, the Uruguay Round led to agreements in a wide area covering agriculture, textiles, tariffs, trade rules, services and trade related investment measures. All of these agreements are such as to promote more competition, liberalisation and fair play while affording protection to the rights of 'inventors'. It is the developed countries which pushed for greater competition, liberalisation and protection. Hence there is grave apprehension among several people in India which defines itself as a developing country.

There are fears that our agriculture and food security will be severely affected, that the agreements on trade related investment measures (TRIMS) will force us to accept foreign investment in all areas with majority participation and that our service industry will be totally submerged by large foreign service providers. Many of these apprehensions are not well founded. However, we certainly should be on our guard and in all future negotiations ensure that our gains will be at least as much as the gains of the developed countries. At the moment, we must concentrate on strategies to be adopted to maximise to the gains from, and to minimise the adverse effects of, the agreements. Generally, speaking, we should adopt a conservative approach and take full advantage of the transition periods granted for the different agreements to be fully implemented. We should be prepared to be tough in the negotiations on opening up the field of services.

We are quite well placed as far as agriculture is concerned. Except for one or two commodities, our minimum support prices for different agricultural products are far below the prevailing international prices. Our public distribution system and the system of buffer stocks will not be affected. Our policies should aim at maximising our benefits from the agreement on agriculture [for detailed discussion, see Debroy 1998: pp 13-20].

As already pointed out, the agreement on TRIMS does not require a member country to grant unrestricted entry to foreign investment or to grant majority equity stake in all cases. It does not also prohibit export obligations. We have plenty of elbow room to formulate our policies regarding foreign investment to suit our needs and ensure that our long-term interests are not affected. My own view is that we need not go overboard in attracting foreign investment. Even with the restriction of majority foreign equity participation to some important industries where high technology is needed, to power generation and to construction of important infrastructure projects such as roads and ports, we can attract high volumes of foreign direct investment. The present rules regarding direct foreign investment go beyond this [see Government of India 1999: Annexure III] and 100 per cent equity can be granted to the foreign party by the Foreign Investment Promotion Board (FIPB). It is said that FIPB is becoming the main channel through which FDI is flowing. Under the present policy 74 per cent foreign equity is allowed in some areas which seems unwarranted. And in any case FIPB can give the nod to 100 per cent equity. There are some sections which are solidly opposed to all majority foreign equity. Here is an area where a compromise can be effected without losing the advantages of foreign investment. We certainly need to take a second look at the rules regarding FDI.

Another important area where we have to formulate a proper strategy is international trade. On the imports side, we have to shift from QR to tariff control of imports - except for food crops (this is part of WTO obligation) and we have to gradually reduce the level of import duties. The gradual reduction of import duties must keep pace with the increase in the degree of general efficiency of the economy and the increase in the productivity of our industries. We must assiduously promote these two goals. And we must draw up a calendar for the phased reduction of import duties in consultation with industry groups. Such a policy will cause the least instability and give time to the affected industries to make the necessary adjustments. Domestic trade tax reform is also essential as cascading taxes place domestic producers at a disadvantage in the home market as well as in the world market. Instead of speeding up the reform of domestic trade taxes – especially the cascading taxes at the state and local government levels – the government of India has imposed a special additional duty on imports to counteract the cascading effect of the domestic taxes.

I have already underlined the importance of the growth of exports. A high growth rate of the economy cannot be sustained without a corresponding high growth of exports. This is because imports will grow *pari passu* with the growth of GDP and in order to maintain the viability of our balance of payments, we need sufficient growth of exports whose proceeds can pay for the cost of a high proportion of imports. In that case the deficit in the balance of trade can be kept down to manageable limits. However, we should not aim to transform ourselves into what may be called an export-oriented economy. The limited degree of openness shields us to a good extent from fluctuations and cyclical crises in the world economy. The large share of agriculture in GDP is also a cushioning factor.

The rate of growth of exports that I have suggested as a target is a modest one, and within our reach if we pursue the right policies and bring about the necessary changes in the economy and governance. With a 6 per cent growth rate, imports are likely to grow at about 9 per cent, if we base the calculation on the buoyancy of imports in the period 1993-94 to 1997-98. With remittances continuing at the same rate (as per cent of GDP) and a current account deficit of 2 per cent of GDP to be met largely by foreign investment, we should have a comfortable balance of payments situation. However, at the end of the decade (i.e., by 2010) the ratio of exports to GDP would be only around 12.5 per cent.

In order that our exports may grow at an average rate of 10 per cent per annum in dollar terms and also in order to be able at the same time to bring down gradually import duty levels, in most cases, to the levels prevailing in the Asian developing countries, we need to effect quickly other changes/reforms needed to bring about higher productivity and efficiency in all sectors of the economy – industry, infrastructure, the transport system, the financial system, governmental laws and procedures and tax administration.

There will be general agreement about the need for bringing about improvement in the legal system and governmental procedures and the steps to be taken for that purpose. But there are obstacles to reforms in other areas or there are some ideological differences about how to proceed.

Public Sector Reform

One sphere where reforms are absolutely necessary is the sector of public enterprises (we exclude the railways and the electricity boards for the time being). There is no doubt that more than half of the public enterprises of the centre and the states taken together cast a heavy burden on the economy. There are a very large number of loss-making unviable public enterprises. Even among public enterprises that are making profits, many are inefficiently run, are overstaffed and are subject to political interference and patronage.

Several public sector banks have sizeable NPAs. Some are making losses, almost all are overstaffed. With a few notable exceptions, the general level of efficiency of public enterprises cannot be said to be satisfactorily high. Hence the reform of public enterprises is absolutely necessary.

One extreme view is that there should be complete privatisation and the government should get out of the production of all private goods except for atomic energy and military related industries. This view is naturally opposed by socialists and trade unions and also those who do not wish to rely completely on private enterprises. The view that the government sector should concern itself only with the production of public goods and some part of merit goods (except for some highly sophisticated weaponry and military goods) is generally held among western economists and policy-makers. In their economies governments do not play a direct developmental role through investment. Their private enterprises are large, efficient and multinational in scope. This is not the case in India. It could be legitimately argued that here in some important areas public enterprises should continue to exist at least till the private enterprises come of age.

Moreover, it would seem that public enterprises impart a measure of stability to the economy because of the reason that public investment is not so sensitive to market signals. When profit expectations are reduced and as a result private investment falls, government could induce the public enterprises to maintain their investment levels which at least to some extent would counteract the deflationary impact of reduced private investment. One of the reasons for the relative stability of the Indian economy in the midst of Asian crisis may be the existence of relatively large public enterprises.

Whatever may be ultimately decided upon, for the coming decade we need to place emphasis only on substantially reducing the burden that the functioning of the public enterprises is imposing on the government and the economy. For this purpose, we do not need complete privatisation. Here again it is possible to effect a compromise. Instead of debating the question whether there should be wholesale privatisation, we could agree on certain specific steps to increase the efficiency and reduce the financial burden on the governments. I would suggest the following :

(a) Sell or close down loss-making public enterprises producing all non-strategic private goods in a phased manner. One-tenth of the total number of such public enterprises should be closed down each year. In this way, we can avoid causing hardship to a very large number of employees within a short period. It would be easier to take care of a limited number of people/labourers affected in any one year. The labourers who would lose their jobs should be given generous compensation and also priority for appointment to fill vacancies that arise in the government of other public enterprises (other things being equal). No attempt should be made to revive these enterprises as, in any case, the governments are not to spend their energies on producing such private goods as cement, textiles, sugar, cables and leather goods.

(b) Private shareholding should be brought into profit-making public enterprises in all areas except railways, atomic energy and most defence related industries. Among them we can distinguish three categories: (i) those which are to be sold off to the private sector; (ii) those in which the government need only to have 49 per cent of equity, so that the enterprises can become truly autonomous; and (iii) those in which for policy purposes or because of the importance of the industry concerned, the government would like to have majority shareholding.

(i) Enterprises to be sold off: public enterprises engaged in producing consumer goods and services or some minor producer goods.

(ii) In many public enterprises which are not producing basic or strategic goods (but only goods such as chemicals, petrochemicals, drugs) or are running hotels or engaged in transport services, the government should hold only 49 per cent of equity.

(iii) In public enterprises in the areas of basic goods, aeronautics, banking, development finance, petroleum exploration and refinery, etc, if they are profit-making and reasonably efficient, the government should retain 51 to 74 per cent equity. Where important policy decisions are involved it may be necessary for the government to hold 74 per cent equity. This is also necessary if a foreign private partner is involved. In banking, government equity could be brought down to 51 per cent.

It is an accepted proposition that except for railways, atomic energy and strategic defence related areas (e.g., missile development), public enterprises should not be monopolies. Public enterprises in both categories (ii) and (iii) should be subjected to competition. Such competition has been allowed now in many sectors, though in some areas, e.g., airways, it is still limited. There must be good exposure to private sector competition in all areas. There should be some private sector equity participation (through the issue of new shares) in LIC and GIC. Apart from that Indian private sector companies should be allowed into the insurance business, but initially only a few of them may be licensed. Private sector insurance companies may be allowed foreign partners holding up to only 26 per cent equity. Pension business should be allowed to be carried on only by public trusts. I am saying this in the light of the experience of the developed countries with private pension funds.

I have been talking about bringing private sector equity into public enterprises and reducing the government's stake. This involves disinvestment as well as issue of new equity. As of now, funds from disinvestment are used to cover government sector deficit. In my view, this is a totally wrong policy. Government should fix the permissible level of deficit by determining the amount of borrowing that could be considered prudent and proper from the macro-economic point of view, and then keep the deficit down to that level by adjusting the level of expenditure, given the amount of revenues that are contemplated to be raised. The funds from disinvestment should not be brought into the budget to cover the deficit.

I would suggest that there should be a separate extra-budgetary fund into which the proceeds of disinvestment in public enterprises should be put. This fund could be used to subscribe to the capital of infrastructure finance companies, to lend to enterprises to finance the construction of roads, ports and other such facilities, to pick up the rights shares issued by public enterprises, etc. In other words, government should use the proceeds so as to maintain the level of its assets.

As regards railways, their monopoly position has to be maintained and with all its disadvantages the control of the railways by the government has also to remain. However, the railways should concentrate on providing services and leave largely to the private sector the production of wagons, engines and other equipment so that their own surpluses could be used mainly for expanding the railway network or to effect improvement in tracks, signalling equipment, etc.

We then come to the state electricity boards (SEBs). Along with the closure of loss-making public enterprises, the reform of SEBs should be taken up on a priority basis. The extremely unsatisfactory state of the electricity boards in terms of both efficiency of operations and of financial results is too well known to be detailed here. With only one or two exceptions, the SEBs are incurring large commercial losses. Most of them owe sizeable dues to the central public undertakings from which they are buying power or material or services. There are large transmission losses (to a sizeable extent accounted for by pilferage) and the plant load factor, although it has improved during the nineties, is still low on an average (for details see Table–2). Given their financial condition, they are in no position to generate funds either to add substantially to capacity or to spend on renovation or modernisation. Since the SEBs are state government enterprises, they cannot act independently to set adequate tariff or to reduce their staff size to a reasonable level or enforce discipline. There could be no reform of the power sector until the SEBs are effectively taken out of the control of the state governments. There are two steps involved in the reform. First, the operations of the SEBs should be 'unbundled', i.e., generation, transmission and distribution should be separated and be put in the charge of different entities. The private sector should be brought into generation as well as into distribution. The SEBs can gradually get out of the business of distribution. Transmission should be in charge of one corporation in which the government may hold 30 to 40 per cent stake. There should be effective competition in the sectors of generation and distribution. The tariff and the wheeling charges will be set by an independent State Tariff Regulatory Authority. Reform along these lines has already been started in the states of Orissa, Andhra Pradesh and Haryana. If we wish to maintain a reasonably high growth rate during the coming decade, the state governments should be pressurised to bring about reform of their power sector along the lines indicated as quickly as possible. Nothing stands in the way of such a reform except short-sighted political considerations. One hopes that the major political parties in each state would arrive at a consensus on this issue in the long-term interest of the people of the state concerned.

State Level Reforms

The state governments do not seem to realise what a great handicap the state of their roads is to industry and trade and what delay and consequent increase in costs is caused by the various hindrances to the quick and free movement of goods, which exist because of the state governments' own policies and procedures.

Table – 2

Data on Poor Performance of SEBs 1997-98

(1)	Commercial losses	Rs. 10,164.9 crore (without subsidy)		
		Rs. 7,218.7 crore (with subsidy)		
(2)	Sales revenue as ratio of cost	80.5 (average)		
(3)	Outstanding dues payable to central sector power corporations	Rs. 16,807 crore with surcharge (as on 30.9.1998)		
(4)	Plant load factor (thermal)	Average	64.4	1996-97
		Lowest (Bihar)	15.3	1996-97
		Highest (Andhra Pradesh)	78.3	1996-97
(5)	Transmission and distribution losses (per cent) (leaving out J and K)	Average	20.6	
		Highest (Orissa)	34.8	
		Lowest (Maharashtra)	14.8	

Source: Government of India, Ministry of Power (1998).

Even our major highways cannot stand comparison with those in any developed country or even the roads in China's developed provinces. The unsatisfactory condition of the roads and the checks and stops to which the traffic is subjected significantly increase the costs of production in the economy. Take this example: today it takes a truck an average of 6-7 days to carry goods from Mumbai to Calcutta. It must traverse no less than 15 checkpoints/octroi stations during the trip, where approximately two days are lost in waiting. The average speed on the existing roads is only 40 kms per hour. Trips between Mumbai and Calcutta, or Delhi and Chennai, should not take more than two days at safe average speeds of about 60-80 kms per hour on a reasonably good roadway system. With such a system, the savings in fuel costs and better transport turnaround times would be significant (TELCO Annual Report, 1999, p vi). The layout of the present roadways is inadequate and dangerous for the density of commercial vehicles, passenger cars and other local forms of transport that ply these roads. Roadway deaths have become an issue of national concern.

The urgent need to improve the road traffic system is well recognised. Investment of huge amounts of money is required.

Hence the private sector has to be brought in. This is also recognised. But the movement has been slow. And no worthwhile attention has been paid to the removal of hurdles to the free flow of traffic. The state governments have to consider this area as one priority area for reform along with the power sector.

Indeed during the coming decade, most of the pressing reforms have to be carried out at the level of the state governments. No great ideological issues are involved in these reforms except perhaps in the case of reform of the power sector.

The major reforms and the policy changes to be effected at the state level during the coming decade are :

(a) power sector reform:

(b) improvement in the roads and extension of road network;

(c) removal of hindrances to a maximum possible extent to the free movement of goods;

(d) closing down or sale of loss-making public enterprises;

(e) reduction in subsidies in respect of consumption of power by the agricultural and domestic sectors along with other reforms in the power sector;

(f) at least partial privatisation of the road transport (passenger) services; and

(g) higher outlay on primary and secondary education, health and family planning and significant improvement in the standards of these services.

The obstacles to reform are to some extent lack of understanding, short-term political considerations, and lack of financial resources. Understanding of issues is growing, but there seems to be no improvement in the financial conditions of the state governments.

Though I mention it last, improvement of the fiscal situation of the state governments is a precondition for several reforms. The reform of the power sector would significantly aid the governments in improving their financial position. However, given the extremely weak financial position of most state governments, structural reform of the budget including tax reform, expenditure control and public debt management are called for. While the reform of state-level public enterprises would help to some extent, it is absolutely necessary to raise the ratio of revenues to state domestic product (SDP) by at least 1 to 1.5 percentage points. Correspondingly, on the other side, administrative expenditure and the size of the administrative staff would have to be drastically reduced. All in all the ratio of government's revenue expenditure to SDP should be brought down by about 1 percentage point. These changes would ensure that the revenue deficits of the state governments would be wiped out and that all their borrowings could be used for capital formation. Most of the capital formation can be for infrastructure development and for human development, with public enterprises not requiring any investment because most of them would be gradually phased out.

Conclusions

It would be seen that many of the reforms sketched above would help rather than adversely affect the poor. However, it is necessary not only to moderate the growth-promoting reforms to safeguard the interests of the poor and the vulnerable sections (such as only gradually phasing out loss-making public enterprises), but also to formulate special policies designed to protect those sections. Small fishermen operating near the coast with non-mechanised boats, handloom weavers, and tribals dependent on the forests are examples of sections of the population to protect whom special schemes are needed, even though there would be some loss in efficiency. Every government should announce publicly what schemes it has formulated in this regard, and the legislatures should discuss and monitor their progress. These schemes are to be apart from the traditional poverty alleviation programmes.

But the major succour to the poor will come from growth and progress in human development. In the coming decade, the decline in the ratio of expenditure on human development to total government expenditure should be reversed. The proportion of expenditure on administration, unwarranted subsidies and interest payments should be brought down to make the former possible.

As I had emphasised earlier, we should ensure that proportionately more resources are diverted to the backward states.

To begin with, a special development programme must be prepared for Bihar (other backward states can be taken up in turn). This development programme should be geared to flood control, irrigation, agricultural development, land reforms and infrastructure development. This programme should be developed in consultation with the state government jointly by the Planning Commission and a team of experts with assistance from IDA. Most of it will be implemented by the central government or under its supervision with the state government being associated with the Supervisory Committee. That is to say, there will be turnkey projects undertaken under the supervision of the centre. This programme will be in addition to the normal plan of the state and central assistance to the plan. There would be an incentive for the state to accept this programme because it will gain enormously in terms of additional investment (say, around Rs. 15,000 to 20,000 crore). I am suggesting that the programme for Bihar should be largely concentrated on agriculture and infrastructure development (roads and power) because Bihar can become a large and efficient producer of rice. With the WTO obligations in agriculture coming into force and the large subsidies given by the developed countries gradually being reduced, there will be a world market for rice from Bihar. The consequent agricultural prosperity will trigger industrial development in Bihar. This is one other important change in development strategy that I am advocating.

If the matter is left to the politicians alone, the reforms will not come up to the desired level. Of course, we must lobby with the political parties for the adoption of a reform agenda on the lines detailed in this paper. That would not be enough. Intellectuals, professionals or housewives, industry associations, NGOs and in fact the entire middle class should constantly apply pressure on the governments to do what is good for the people in the long run. Without the active participation of the intelligent and informed electorate in public affairs, through NGOs or otherwise, progress is likely to be much less than the country is capable of achieving.

References

Chelliah, Raja J and R Sudarshan (1999): *Income-Poverty and Beyond Human Development in India*, Social Science Press, New Delhi.

Debroy, Bibek (1998): 'Intellectual Property Rights', Rajiv Gandhi Institute for Contemporary Studies, New Delhi.

Ganesan, A V (1999): 'The Implications of the Patents (Amendment) Ordinance, 1999', Indian Council for Research on International Economic Relations, New Delhi.

Jalan, Bimal (1992): *The Indian Economy*, Penguin Books India, New Delhi.

Government of India (1999): *Manual on Industrial Policy and Procedures in India*, New Delhi.

Government of India, Ministry of Power (1998): Chief Ministers' Conference on Power, Background Papers (Annexures), New Delhi.

Dr. Waheeduddin Khan Memorial Lecture delivered at Centre for Economic and Social Studies, Hyderabad, August 9, 1999.

10

India's Decade of Economic Transformation

Impact Analysis of Unilateral & Global Changes in Trade Policy[1]

RAJESH CHADHA

INTRODUCTION

The last decade of the 20th century has had immense significance for India's economy in the context of the unilateral as well as the global changes in trade policy. Apart from the impact of various unilateral economic reforms undertaken since 1991, the economy also had to reorient itself to the changing multilateral trade discipline within the newly written GATT/WTO framework. The unilateral trade policy measures have encompassed exchange-rate policy, foreign investment, external borrowing, import licensing, custom tariffs and export subsidies. The multilateral aspect of India's trade policy refers to India's WTO commitments with regard to trade in goods and services, trade related investment measures, and intellectual property rights. The multilateral trade liberalisation under the auspices of the Uruguay-Round Agreement and the forthcoming WTO negotiations is aimed at reducing tariff and non-tariff barriers on international trade.

The author is extremely thankful to Professor Robert M. Stern for having provided very useful comments on an earlier draft of this paper. Besides, my discussions with Prof. Alan V. Deardorff have immensely benefited this work.

The purpose of this paper is to provide a summary of India's unilateral trade policy changes along with the impact on India of the changing global trade scenario. Some indicative results of the computational analysis of the impact of such changes on the economic welfare, trade, and the intersectoral allocation of resources in India and its major trading partners are also discussed. Finally, I spend some time on India's export performance during the 1990s.

The paper is organised as follows. Section II discusses the relevance of changing global trade policies for developing countries. Section III outlines the trade policy reforms undertaken by India during the 1990s. Section IV deals with India's role in the context of the WTO. In Section V, I present the results of computational analysis of the impact on India of the Uruguay Round negotiations and the prospective WTO negotiations that are presently underway and that will continue in the next few years pending a consensus on the negotiating agenda. Conclusions and policy implications are discussed in Section VI.

I

RELEVANCE OF CHANGING GLOBAL TRADE POLICIES FOR DEVELOPING COUNTRIES[2]

The Uruguay Round

The Uruguay Round (UR) was the eighth round of multilateral trade negotiations (MTN) concluded under the auspices of the General Agreement on Tariffs and Trade (GATT). The negotiations were completed in 1993 and agreements signed in 1994. The earlier rounds of multilateral trade negotiations had not received active participation from the developing countries. The developed countries could manage to leave the sectors of greatest interest to the developing countries, such as agriculture, textiles and clothing, out of the negotiations. Both the developing and the developed countries shared active participation in the UR. The developing countries have now taken on the full rights and obligations embedded in the World Trade Organisation, which was officially initiated in January 1995. The main features of the UR negotiations are summarised in Annexure-1. Agriculture and textiles and clothing have been brought within the GATT fold. The system of multilateral rules was extended to include intellectual property rights and services. While certain agreements, like TRIPS, may involve some short-run costs for the developing countries, these are likely to be more than offset by the effects of inclusion of agriculture and textiles and clothing under the GATT umbrella. Further, the WTO embodies a much stronger enforcement / dispute settlement mechanism than what existed under GATT. However, the Uruguay Round did little to liberalise trade in agriculture and services.

A comprehensive overview of the expected achievements and failures of the Uruguay Round is provided in Srinivasan (1998a). The three major areas with regard to market access for goods include liberalisation of trade of manufactured goods, agriculture and textiles and clothing. Both developed as well as developing countries have declared bound tariffs on a large number of manufactured goods along with lowering of the tariff rates. In the case of the UR agreement on agriculture, there is a clear emphasis on the objective of increased market orientation in agricultural trade. The trade-distorting domestic support measures in agriculture have been discouraged. The non-tariff barriers on trade are to be replaced by their tariff equivalents (tariffication) and then reduced by an average of 36 per cent over a period of six years by developed countries and by 24 per cent over a period of 10 years by developing countries. One of the major accomplishments of the UR agreement is the Agreement on Textiles and Clothing (ATC) which stipulates that the multifibre arrangement (MFA) is to be phased out in three stages over a period of 10 years commencing January 1, 1995. This would integrate trade in textiles and clothing into the GATT.

Various studies have estimated the potential welfare gains from the multilateral liberalisation efforts of the UR of negotiations. These include Francois et al. (1996), Harrison et al (1996) and Hertel *et al.* (1996) with a summary provided in Srinivasan (1998a). These studies are based on the GTAP database (release 3) for 1992. Separate results for India are, however, not reported in these studies. Chadha et al. (1999b) and Martin and Hertel

(1999) have used the GTAP database-Release-4 (McDougall et al., 1998) to analyse the developing country interests in liberalising manufactures trade. The welfare gain results for India have also been reported in these studies.

Multilateral Negotiations Since the Uruguay Round

There have been some significant multilateral initiatives following the conclusion of the UR and creation of the WTO. The first WTO Ministerial Conference was held in Singapore in December 1996. The main agenda items and results of the Singapore Ministerial Conference (SMC) are summarised in Annexure-2. The second Ministerial Conference held in Geneva in May 1998 carried forward the results of SMC (1996) and established a work program to examine trade-related issues involving global electronic commerce. Attention was paid towards preparations for the negotiations mandated under the UR-built in agenda. There was an ongoing interaction among the WTO members as a follow-up of the two ministerial meetings and for the preparation for the third Ministerial Conference to be held in Seattle from November 30 to December 3, 1999. This conference was expected to launch a new round of multilateral trade negotiations to begin in 2000 (Millennium Round). This new round was to be devoted to items on the UR built-in agenda together with new issues to be decided upon.

The third Ministerial Conference ended in a failure with the members of the WTO not being able to agree on an agenda for the Millennium Round. There were a number of reasons for the failure of the Seattle Ministerial to launch a new round (Chadha et al., 2000). Domestic US politics played a key role. There were strong differences between the European Union and the United States on the issues relating to agricultural liberalisation. Developing countries were unwilling to accept inclusion of labour standards and environmental issues within the purview of the new round. Small countries were left completely in the cold.

II

INDIA'S REFORMS IN TRADE POLICY[3]

In the summer of 1991, India found itself in one of its worst balance of payments crisis since 1947. That there was a crisis in the making during the second half of 1980s had been evident for a long time. The inflow of foreign borrowing had increased at a rapid rate during the late 1980s. This was due to the excess of domestic expenditure over income - the fiscal deficit of the Centre and the states soared to over 11 per cent in 1991 - and the political need to undertake large-scale maintenance imports was financed by short-term borrowings. During this period total public debt as a proportion of GNP doubled to nearly 60 per cent and foreign currency reserves were depleted rapidly. Matters were made worse by an accompanying double-digit inflation in 1990-91. The oil price increase resulting from Iraq's invasion of Kuwait in August 1990 reinforced the crisis-like situation in India, which was made all the worse by the new finance minister's statement that the "coffers were empty".

India's credit rating got downgraded as, for the first time in its history, it was on the verge of defaulting on its international commitments and was denied access to external commercial credit markets. A net outflow of Non Resident Indian (NRI) deposits commenced in October 1990 and continued during 1991. The only way left for India was to borrow against the security of its gold reserves transported abroad.

But out of all terrible things, some good emerges and from the BOP crisis of 1991, these emerged long overdue economic reform. Apart from an immediate programme of macroeconomic stabilisation, structural reforms were also introduced in the industrial and trade policy regimes with a view to improving the efficiency, productivity and international competitiveness of India's economy.

The overvalued exchange rate was corrected by devaluation in 1991, followed by partial convertibility of the rupee in 1992-93 and then making the rupee fully convertible on trade account in 1993-94. Tariffs were also cut steeply to open Indian industry to foreign competition[4]. The focus of import liberalisation has primarily been on intermediate and capital goods industries with the imports of consumer goods remaining, by and large, regulated.

Unilateral reforms have been undertaken with regard to exchange-rate policy, foreign investment, external borrowing, import licensing, custom tariffs and export subsidies.

Exchange Rate

The macroeconomic stabilisation and structural adjustment programme initiated in mid-1991 commenced with adjustment in the external value of rupee, which was determined on the basis of a weighted basket of currencies of India's major trading partners. The rupee had been overvalued for most of the period prior to 1991, thus adversely affecting exports. It has been estimated that the rupee was overvalued by about 30 per cent during the eighties (Gulati and Pursell, 1995). The rupee was devalued from Rs.21 to Rs.23.12 per U.S. dollar on July 1, 1991 and to Rs.25.95 per U.S. dollar on July 3, 1991, amounting to a cumulative devaluation of about 19 per cent. This exchange rate continued till March 1992.

An explicit dual exchange rate system was introduced in March 1992 on a temporary basis to facilitate the shift to a more liberal exchange-rate regime. The newly introduced Liberalised Exchange Rate Management System (LERMS) consisted of a free market rate along with an official rate set by the Reserve Bank of India (RBI) in U.S. dollars. Forty per cent of current account receipts from exports of goods and services were to be surrendered at the official exchange rate while the remaining 60 per cent could be converted at the market exchange rate. Import transactions undertaken through the official rate included crude and diesel oil, kerosene, certain fertilisers, raw materials for fertilisers, life-saving drugs and imports by government departments. All other imports were to be undertaken at the free market rate. All capital account transactions, except IMF transactions, were undertaken at the free-market rate. The RBI could intervene by entering the free market at its discretion to level excessive and erratic movements as well as to offset seasonal fluctuations in the exchange rate.

The exchange rate was unified in March 1993. The rupee was floated and the exchange rate was henceforth to be determined by demand and supply in the foreign exchange market. At that time, the rupee's value was set close to the previous free market rate of about Rs.31 per U.S. dollar.

The RBI administers the foreign exchange controls in consultation with the Ministry of Finance in accordance with the Foreign Exchange Regulation Act, 1973, as amended periodically. Transactions on trade account were freed from foreign exchange controls along with unification of exchange rates in March 1993. It was in March 1994 and again in August 1994 that various types of current-account transactions were liberalised from exchange-control regulations with some indicative limits, which could be relaxed. With these steps towards current account liberalisation, India became the ninety-eighth country to acquire Article VIII status (Sections 2,3, and 4) of the IMF Articles of Agreement.

Foreign Investment

Foreign investment had played a very limited role in India's economy prior to 1991. It was permitted in industries where foreign technology was deemed necessary for economic growth. Foreign equity participation was tightly regulated normally to a limit of 40 per cent of total equity capital. A higher foreign equity was, however, considered in priority industries if the required technology was sophisticated and not available in the country or if the venture was largely export intensive. FDI policy was relatively more liberal in free-trade zones and export-oriented industrial units, where permission for foreign equity participation up to 100 per cent could be granted. The restrictions on equity participation, the technology requirements and the then existing industrial licensing regime tended to dampen the climate for FDI.

The new industrial policy announced in July 1991 liberalised the existing industrial policy regime. This led to liberalisation of foreign direct investment, foreign technology agreements and compulsory industrial licensing. Automatic approval was permitted for investment up to 51 per cent equity in 34 industries. The Foreign Investment Approval Board (FIPB) was set up to process applications for cases not covered by automatic approval[5]. Several additional measures were undertaken during 1992-93 to encourage investment flows including foreign direct investment, portfolio investment, NRI investment and deposits, and investment in global depository receipts (GDRs).

Foreign Direct Investment

The policy towards foreign investment was liberalised in 1991 to permit automatic approval for foreign investment up to 51 per cent of equity in 34 priority sectors, which has now been extended to 48 sectors. The limit is up to 50 per cent in the mining sectors, and up to 74 per cent in nine specified sectors[6]. Non-resident Indians (NRIs) and overseas corporate bodies (OCBs) in which NRIs hold at least 60 per cent of the equity, can invest up to 100 per cent in these sectors through the automatic route. No approval is required for FDI inflow up to 24 per cent of the equity in any Indian firm and up to 20 per cent in any new private bank (40 per cent for NRIs). The investment limit for telecommunications services (basic, cellular and paging) is 49 per cent; domestic air taxi operations or airlines is 40 per cent (100 per cent for NRIs); and the bulk drugs producing pharmaceutical sector is 51 per cent. Items for which approval for foreign direct investment is not covered by automatic route include: items reserved for the small-scale sector; items, which require industrial licence under the existing policy; all items for aerospace and defence equipment whether specifically mentioned or not; and all items relating to production and use of atomic energy.

Portfolio Investment

Policies relating to Inflow of investment by foreign institutional investors (FIIs) and through Global Depository Receipts (GDRs) have undergone various changes since 1991. Indian companies were permitted to raise capital through Euro-market issues of Global Depository Receipts (GDRs) and Foreign Currency Convertible Bonds (FCCBs). Indian companies have been allowed to access international capital markets since February 1992. Reputed FIIs including pension funds, mutual funds, asset management companies, investment trusts, nominee companies and incorporated or institutional portfolio managers have been allowed to invest in the Indian capital market since September 1992. The investing FIIs need to be registered institutions within their respective home countries or countries of origin and also registered with the Securities and Exchange Board of India (SEBI). A single FII can invest up to 10 per cent while a group of FIIs can invest up to 30 per cent of share capital of listed companies. Investments by FIIs can also be put in non-listed companies. However, this is subject to the approval of limit by the Board of Directors and a special resolution passed by the general body. FIIs can hold up to 100 per cent of the equity in debt-funds, as well as in government securities. The profits from portfolio investment can be repatriated freely subject to India's foreign exchange regulations.

International Investment Agreements

India is a member of the Multilateral Investment Guarantee Agency (MIGA). Full subscription and membership rights became operational in January 1994. All foreign investment approvals granted by the Government are insured by MIGA against expropriation and nationalisation. India also has bilateral treaties for promotion and protection of FDI with a number of countries, including Denmark, Germany, Italy, France, the Netherlands and the United Kingdom.

External Borrowing

The strategy for balance of payments management includes substantial support in the form of external financial flows including external assistance and external borrowings including fast-disbursing assistance from official multilateral and bilateral sources and also through new schemes to attract funds from non-residents, their corporate bodies and foreign banks.

External Assistance

The share of external assistance in aggregate net foreign capital inflows went down during the 1980s from 61 per cent in 1980-81 to 31 per cent in 1990-91. It went up sharply in 1991-92 to 80 per cent and came down to 63 per cent in 1992-93. This was due to the large availability of exceptional finance during these years to meet the balance-of-payments crisis. The share has been going down during the 1990s and was below 10 per cent level during 1996-97 and 1998-99.

External Commercial Borrowings

External Commercial Borrowings (ECBs) provide an additional

source of funds to Indian companies to augment domestically available resources while also taking advantage of lower interest rates prevailing in the international markets. ECBs are permitted within an annual ceiling that is consistent with prudent debt management, keeping in view the balance-of-payments position. Infrastructure and exports continue to be accorded high priority in ECB allocation. The limit under US$ 3 million scheme has been raised to US$ 5 million in 1998-99. Small borrowers can now avail of a higher borrowing limit than before. The government has delegated ECB sanctioning power to RBI up to U.S.$ 10 million under all ECB schemes. The net inflow of ECB in 1997-98 turned out to be U.S.$ 4 billion, much higher than the 2.8 billion in 1997-98 due to relatively low repayments.

Import Licensing

India's trade policy regime was quite complex until the beginning of 1990s. There were various categories of importers, import licenses and ways of importing. The regimenting details were contained in 19 Appendices and spanned over 200 pages[7].

The Import and Export policy (1990-93) was replaced by Export and Import policy (1992-97) with effect from April 1, 1992. The change in colour of the cover page from red to green apparently symbolises emphasis on the green channel. The content was substantially reduced into 20 crisp pages, thus making matters simpler for exporters and importers. The new EXIM policy 1992-97 contained Negative List imports subject to licensing[8]. Almost all consumer goods remained subject to import licensing[9].

The first stage of India's reforms since 1991 continued to focus on manufacturing while agriculture was largely ignored. The share of value added in the manufacturing sector, protected by QRs, declined from 90 to 47 per cent by May 1992 and further down to 36 per cent by May 1995 (Pursell 1996: 5). The corresponding decline was much less in agriculture, from 94 to 93 per cent by May 1992 and further to 84 per cent by May 1995. The tradable GDP protected by QRs was still at 66 per cent as of May 1995.

A recent study estimates that only one-third of the value of India's import in 1998-99 was subject to some type of NTBs (Mehta, 1998: 35-36). After the EXIM Policy (April 1998) announcement, about thirty per cent of the 10-digit tariff lines (3068 out of 10281) under harmonised system of India's trade classification (HS-ITC) were subject to NTBs (prohibited, restricted or canalised, i.e. controlled by the state)[10]. The 3068 restricted tariff lines include 1379 lines for consumer goods. The import value of these consumer goods is only 0.2 per cent of India's total imports, thus reflecting the degree of restrictions. The import of 40 per cent of agricultural products is still restricted since these are classified as consumer goods.

The import of some restricted items has been liberalised through freely transferable Special Import Licenses (SILs). Apart from being used as a step towards liberalisation, the SIL regime also provides incentives to exporters. SILs are granted to: large established exporters; exporters of electronic and telecommunication equipment, diamonds, gems and jewellery, deemed exports; and manufacturers who have acquired prescribed quality certification.

The coverage of tariff lines has gradually expanded since their introduction in 1992-93. Tariff lines have typically moved from the restricted list to the SIL list, and thereafter to the free list. SILs are concentrated in industrial products with nearly 55.8 per cent of the HS eight-digit tariff lines under SIL as of April 1, 1997. The corresponding coverage was 29.6 per cent for textile and clothing products and 14.6 per cent for agricultural products including fisheries (WTO, TPR-India, 1998: 66). The SIL coverage has been extended significantly since April 1999 freeing various items from restricted list to SIL list and from SIL list to OGL list. Various items have also been de-canalised.

The balance-of-payments excuse for using QRs had become unconvincing given that there was a strong current account, substantial capital inflows and large foreign exchange reserves during the years following the devaluation of 1991. India's unrestrained use of QRs was strongly challenged in the WTO balance-of-payments committee by the United States, European Union and other developed countries in December 1995[11]. India has lost the case and it is clear now that it shall have to do away with its QR regime by 2001.

The EXIM policy amendments of March 31, 2000 are directed towards India's commitments to the WTO rules. The announcement regarding the removal of QRs on 714 tariff lines is as expected and is in line with the WTO administration. There was no other choice left. Prior to this announcement, 1429 tariff lines, using an 8-digit harmonised classification system, were under QRs. These included 685 lines/items under special import licences (SILs), 700 restricted and 44 canalised lines. India does not yet have WTO-bound rates on 863 of the 1429 items under QRs. Of the remaining 566 items, bound rates exceed applied rates for 362 items. The Minister did not have a complete choice on which items to move to Open General Licence with effect from April 2000. An existing agreement with India's trading partners like the European Union, Switzerland, Canada and Japan had pre-determined shifting 204 items to OGL. Out of the remaining 510 items shifted to OGL, the majority belongs to the then existing SIL category. The remaining SIL items can be used for one more year. Many sensitive items including automobiles and items reserved for small-scale sector (SSI) have been kept pending for OGL after one year. Only 58 less-significant SSI items have been moved to OGL. Thus, there has been a cautious movement towards OGL and the Minister himself remarked that this year's removal of QRs would not have much impact on producers or consumers. The announcement that all SILs shall be abolished after March 31, 2001 is only a corollary to the above discussion.[12]

Tariffs

Prior to 1991, India's import tariff structure was among the highest in the world. The Chelliah Committee (1992) proposed that the import-weighted average duty rate should go down from 87 per cent in 1989-90 to 45 per cent in 1995-96 and further to 25 per cent by 1998-99 (Govt of India, Tax Reforms Committee, 1991 and 1993). The Chelliah Committee recommended seven different rates of custom tariff, namely 5, 10, 15, 20, 25, 30 and 50 per cent to be achieved by 1997-98 (Govt. of India, Chelliah Committee, 1993). It was further suggested that additional or special protection might be given for a limited period to new industries, new products, or new technologies. The 5 per rate was to apply to inputs for fertiliser and newsprint, 10 and 15 per cent to other basic inputs, 20 per cent to capital goods, and 25 per cent to chemicals and intermediates. Other final products (excluding inessential consumer goods) would be charged 30 per cent duty. Inessential consumer goods, if permitted for import, would have a duty rate of 50 per cent.

While the multiple suggested tariff rates can be used to achieve the Committee's philosophy of systematic escalation according to the degree of processing, this provides scope for effective protection rates that are much higher than the nominal tariffs on finished goods. When QRs on consumer goods are removed, a 50 per cent duty on imports of consumer goods combined with 25 per cent or less duty on tradable inputs would lead to a high effective rate of protection close to 100 per cent on consumer goods (Joshi and Little, 1994: 76). The tariff escalation has been prevalent in India's economy throughout the 1990s (Table 1). Whereas the simple average tariff on processed goods was 37 per cent in 1997-98, that on unprocessed goods (primary products) had an average tariff of 25 per cent only. Significant tariff escalation is displayed in paper and paper products; printing and publishing; wood and wood products; and food, beverages and tobacco (WTO, 1998: 19).

India has lowered its average applied tariff rate from 125 per cent in 1990-91 to 71 per cent in 1993-94, 41 per cent in 1995-96 and to 35 per cent in 1997-98 (Table 2). The corresponding reduction in the import weighted-average has gone down from 87 per cent in 1990-91 to 47 per cent in 1993-94, 25 per cent in 1995-96 and to 20 per cent in 1997-98, thus moving ahead of Chelliah Committee's recommendations. It may be observed that the simple average applied tariff is substantially higher in manufacturing than in agriculture and mining.

The peak rate of duty has declined from 355 per cent in 1990-91 to 45 per cent in 1997-98 and to 40 per cent in 1999-2000. It has been reduced to 35 per cent in 2000-01 but has been subjected to a 10 per cent surcharge thus making it 38.5 per cent.

The World Bank estimates of changes in tariffs on consumer, intermediate and capital goods are given in Table 3. Though the average import-weighted tariff rate on consumer goods was reduced from 153 per cent in 1990-91 to 25 per cent in 1997-98, a large portion of this category still remains protected by QRs.

Export Subsidies

India does not provide direct subsidies to exporters. Subsidies are provided indirectly through duty and tax concessions, export finance, export insurance and guarantee, and export promotion and marketing assistance. Export subsidies were considered important to increase exports during the period 1980-81 to 1990-91 since it has been estimated that the trade policy – induced rupee overvaluation was about 30 per cent. This was no match to the ratio of value of the principal export incentives to their fob value, estimated at 8 per cent (Gulati and Pursell, 1995). However, this incentive ratio does not allow for the very considerable transaction costs, delays and corruption involved in using various schemes.

The emphasis of the export-incentive system has been considerably changed and modified since 1991 (Pursell, 1996: 25). The cash compensatory scheme (CCS) was abolished in July 1991. This contributed to reduction in fiscal deficit and saved Indian exporters from a potential threat of countervailing duties and anti-dumping measures, which could be imposed by the importing countries. The Exim Scrip scheme was abolished with the introduction of the dual exchange-rate scheme for importing countries. The replenishment (REP) import licences were replaced by EXIM Scrips, which allowed imports of a much wider range of intermediate products than was possible under REP licences. The Exim Scrip regime was abolished with the introduction of the dual exchange-rate scheme for exporters in February 1992.

The role of duty-free import licences (for exporters) has been enhanced since 1991 through expanding the lists of products with published physical input-output norms to facilitate computation of values of duty-free import licences. A new class of value-based, duty-exempt import licences was introduced in which the exporter could import materials of his choice, rather than pre-defined, precise values of certain categories of import, up to the permitted foreign exchange value of the licence. A special scheme known as Export Promotion Capital Goods (EPCG), originally introduced in 1990 was liberalised in April 1992 to encourage imports of capital goods. The concessional import duty was reduced from 25 to 15 per cent. Finally, export income is exempt from income taxes.

The efficacy of the complex structure of export subsidies to enhance exports is not very clear. The Handbook of Procedures (two volumes), which accompanies the EXIM Policy document, continues to remain a complicated reference manual. Though there have been some efforts since 1991 to reduce administrative problems and delays in implementation of various export incentives, the sharp growth of exports during 1993-96 cannot be attributed to changes in export incentives. More effective measures were rupee devaluation, removal of industrial licensing and other controls over industry and opening up imports of intermediate and capital goods.

Despite various steps towards liberalising trade, the economy continued to remain protected by QRs on consumer goods and tariffs continue to remain high in comparison with many other developing countries. This created incentives for misuse of export subsidies since rent-seeking behaviour continues to be an attractive option. India does not provide direct subsidies to exporters but relies on a wide range of indirect subsidies, including duty and tax concessions, export finance, export insurance and guarantee, and export promotion and marketing assistance. The WTO consistency of the income tax exemption has recently been questioned within the WTO Trade Policy Review Mechanism (TRPM) forum (WTO, 1998: x).

Some of the EXIM Policy amendments (March 31, 2000) deal with rationalisation of the existing export-promotion schemes. The Export Promotion Capital Goods (EPCG) Scheme has been extended uniformly to all sectors, including capital goods, without any threshold limits, on payment of 5 per cent custom duty. The 10 per cent countervailing duty on imports under the EPCG scheme has been withdrawn. The schemes for neutralising duties paid on inputs for the export products have been rationalised. Non-transferable advance licences shall be available for physical exports, deemed exports and for intermediate supplies. This advance licence will be exempt from all kinds of duties except in the case of deemed exports, in which the imports will be exempt only from the basic custom duty. Otherwise, exporters can opt for a post-export duty-free replenishment certificate, which would enable them to import inputs used in the exports as per the standard input-output norms. The duty entitlement passbook scheme (DEPB) will end after March 31, 2002 and will be subsumed into one Drawback Scheme. In the meantime, the threshold limit of Rs.200 million for fixing new DEPB rates has been removed, and hence the scheme will now be more widely available during the two-year interim period. However, the Minister outlines the difficulties in the way of simplification of the duty-neutralisation mechanism until a single value-added tax (VAT) structure is introduced.

III

INDIA AND THE WTO

India is a founding member of the GATT (1947) as well as the WTO, which came into effect from January 1, 1995. By virtue of its WTO membership, India automatically is availed of Most Favoured Nation Treatment (MFN) and National Treatment (NT) from all WTO members for its exports and vice versa. Its participation in this increasingly rule-based system is aimed towards ensuring more stability and predictability in its international trade. India has agreed for the following commitments in the WTO:

Tariffs

The Uruguay Round has resulted in increased tariff-binding commitments by developing countries. India has bound 67 per cent of its tariff lines compared to 6 per cent prior to this round. All agricultural tariff lines and nearly 62 per cent of the tariff lines of industrial goods are now bound. The unbound lines include some consumer goods and some industrial items. Ceiling bindings for industrial goods are generally at 40 per cent ad valorem for finished goods and 25 per cent on intermediate goods, machinery and equipment. The phased reduction to these bound levels is to be achieved during the 10-year period commencing in 1995. Tariff rates on equipment covered under the Information Technology Agreement and software shall be brought down to zero by 2005. The only exception is in textiles in which India has kept the option of reverting to the 1990 tariff levels in case the Agreement on Textiles and Clothing does not fully materialise by 2005. It may be observed from Table 4, that applied tariff rates in India are below the Uruguay Round bound levels. The differential is the maximum in the case of agriculture and also in unprocessed primary goods categories. The bound rates do not show tariff escalation by stage of processing; in fact, the reverse seems to be true, which is also equally undesirable.

Quantitative Restrictions

As mentioned earlier, India has to remove QRs on imports by March 31, 2001. Most of these are consumer goods, including agricultural products. These products shall be protected with the peak rate of tariff at 35 per cent plus 10 per cent surcharge, except for a few items like capital goods.

TRIPS

The Agreement on Trade Related Intellectual Property Rights (TRIPS) establishes certain minimum standards concerning the availability, scope, use and enforcement of IPRs and extends the basic principles of non-discrimination and transparency to these spheres[13]. A transition period up to January 1, 2000 for implementing these obligations is available, except in the case of provisions relating to MFN and National Treatment. In addition, for areas of technology, where product patents is not currently available, a further period of up to January 1, 2005 is available. However, in the latter case, means to achieve product patent applications in the field of pharmaceuticals and agricultural chemical products and grant of Exclusive Marketing Rights on fulfilment of certain conditions need to be provided from entry into the force of the WTO Agreement, i.e., 1995. India has agreed to amend its domestic laws in line with these obligations by April 19, 1999. From the point of view of India, TRIPS has been one of the most debated agreements. Though India's Copyrights and Trademark laws are considered to be in conformity with the WTO agreements, patents and geographical indications are the areas needing immediate attention. India has to change its Patent Act in conformity with WTO by extending product patents. In the case of the pharmaceutical sector, it is feared that the shift to product patents would increase drug prices and adversely affect Indian pharmaceutical industry. However, this fear has been termed as 'myth' by some economists (Prasad, 1999: 22-28).

TRIMS

Under the Trade Related Investment Measures (TRIMS), India has already notified the TRIMs maintained by it. These have to be eliminated by January 1, 2000. Under the Information Technology Agreement (ITA), tariffs have to be brought down to zero on 95 HS-6 digit tariff lines by the year 2000, on 4 more tariff lines by 2003, on 2 more tariff lines by 2004 and on the balance of 116 tariff lines in the year 2005. India is also committed, under the Agreement on Technical Barriers to Trade and Sanitary and Phytosanitary Measures, to establishing and administering national standards and technical regulations, keeping in view the basic precepts of MFN, National Treatment and Transparency.

GATS

The "General Agreement on Trade in Services" (GATS) has a "positive list" approach, thereby allowing WTO members to take on obligations in the sector of their choice. India has made commitments in 33 activities, as compared to an average of 23 activities for developing countries. India's objective in service negotiations has been to offer entry to foreign service-providers in which entry was considered to be most advantageous in terms of capital inflows, technology and employment

Notwithstanding the recent liberalisation of the foreign direct investment regime, restrictions on these investments continue to impede market access in the services sectors. Foreign equity is limited to 49 per cent in some of the major components of telecommunications (including basic cellular, mobile, paging and other wireless services). The corresponding limit is 20 per cent in the banking sector.

Other service areas such as shipping, roads, ports, and air are beginning to open up, but foreign participation remains low. Railways remain one of the six areas reserved for the public sector, although some private-sector participation is encouraged in some off-line activities. The insurance sector has only recently been opened for private investors. Opening up of the services sectors to international competition under GATS is expected to make these sectors more efficient, which, in turn, would lead to gain in

GDP of India's economy.

Trade and Labour Standards

The increased competition from low-cost imports from developing countries allegedly imposes an adjustment cost in terms of declines in output, wages, employment and working conditions in the developed import-competing countries. Consequently, many developed countries have been demanding the formal inclusion of a "social" clause in the mandate of the WTO that would allow restrictions to be placed on imports of products originating in countries not complying with a specified set of minimum standards, particularly labour standards. Unsuccessful efforts were made at the December 1996 World Trade Organisation (WTO) Ministerial Meeting in Singapore to extend the WTO to include rules governing trade- related labour standards. Such a demand by the developed countries with an implicit threat of trade sanctions is seen by the developing countries as loaded with trade protection motives (Srinivasan, 1998a: 71-79).

The view of the developed countries favouring inclusion of labour standards clause in WTO has been considered fallacious (Brown, Deardorff and Stern, 1997: 1-2). They offer the following conclusions. Firstly, there is no convincing case for incorporating labour standards into the WTO and into U.S. trade agreements. Secondly, the surest way to improve labour standards is for the United States and other industrialised countries to maintain open markets and to encourage the growth of their developing country partners. Thirdly, steps should be taken to support the activities of the International Labour Organisation (ILO) to provide inducements and technical assistance to help developing countries raise their labour standards.

Conclusion: India has undertaken the process of liberalisation of its trade policy in relatively much broader sense as compared to the pre-1991 scenario. This is true for both unilateral and multilateral reform commitments. However, much more remains to be done particularly since the tariff barriers continue to remain high compared to many other developing countries. Many of the consumer goods are still under NTBs.

IV

COMPUTATIONAL ANALYSIS OF THE IMPACT ON INDIA OF UNILATERAL AND MULTILATERAL TRADE POLICY REFORMS[14]

The empirical evidence from a number of studies points to a strong and significant effect of openness to trade on growth performance (Srinivasan, 1998). Thus, it is expected that the multilateral liberalisation of trade should benefit countries of the world in general. The impact of trade liberalisation provisions in the Uruguay Round and some possible liberalisation efforts in the forthcoming WTO round of negotiations will be analysed by means of a through computational general equilibrium (CGE) technique. For comparative purposes, we have also analysed hypothetical scenarios when only India undertakes unilateral liberalisation. For this purpose simulation analysis is used to assess the potential economic effects arising from the implementation of the various liberalisation provisions. The simulations are based on a special version of the NCAER-University of Michigan computable general equilibrium (CGE) Model patterned after the Michigan Model of World Production and Trade. The main features of the model are described in Chadha et al. (1999b), and the equations and other details are available on the University of Michigan website: www.umich.spp.edu/rsie/. The country/region and sectoral coverage of the model are noted in Tables 5 and 6.

Computational Scenarios

The main data source for the model is "The GTAP-4 Database" (McDougall et al., 1998), which refers to 1995. For purposes of analysis, we have projected this database from 1995 to 2005. This provides us with an approximate picture of what the world could be expected to look like in 2005 assuming that the Uruguay Round (UR) Agreement reached in 1995 had not existed. We then analyse the impact of the UR-induced changes that may occur during the 10-year implementation period after 1995 with respect to reduction/removal of tariff and non-tariff barriers to trade. The scaled-up database of 2005 is then readjusted to mimic the world as it might look once the UR Agreement had been fully implemented. We then carry out some liberalisation scenarios for WTO negotiations that involve possible reductions in tariffs on agriculture and manufacturing and reductions of barriers to services trade and FDI.

Aggregate Computational Results

The results reported in our research include absolute changes in imports, exports, and equivalent variation (a measure of economic welfare); and percentage changes in the terms of trade, equivalent variation, real wage rate, and the real return to capital.

The effects on the welfare of countries arise from a mixture of these terms-of-trade effects, together with the standard efficiency gains from trade and also from additional benefits due to elements of the New Trade Theory.[15] Thus, we expect on average that the world will gain from multilateral liberalisation, as resources are reallocated to those sectors in each country where there is a comparative advantage. In the absence of terms-of-trade effects, these efficiency gains should raise national welfare (equivalent variation) for every country, although some factory owners within a country may lose. However, it is possible for a particular country whose net imports are concentrated in sectors with the greatest liberalisation to lose overall, if the worsening of its terms of trade swamps these efficiency gains.

On the other hand, although the New Trade Theory is perhaps best known for introducing new reasons why countries may lose from trade, in fact its greatest contribution is to expand the list of reasons for gains from trade. It is these that are the dominant contribution of the New Trade Theory in our model. That is, trade liberalisation permits all countries to expand their export sectors at the same time that all sectors compete more closely with a larger number of competing varieties from abroad. As a result, countries as a whole gain from lower costs due to increasing returns to scale, lower monopoly distortions due to greater competition, and reduced costs and/or increased utility due to greater product variety. All of these effects make it more likely that countries will gain from liberalisation in ways that are shared across the entire population.

In perfectly competitive trade models such as the Heckscher-Ohlin Model, one expects countries as a whole to gain from trade, but the owners of one factor-the "scarce factor" – to lose through the mechanism known as the Stolper-Samuelson Theorem. The additional sources of gain from trade due to increasing returns to scale, competition, and product variety, however, are shared across factors, and we routinely find in our CGE modelling that both labour and capital often gain from liberalisation.[16] That is often the case here.

A final point to note concerns the modelling and role of non-tariff barriers, such as are included here especially in agriculture and textiles and apparel. These are quantitative restrictions, captured in the model by endogenous tariff equivalents that rise and fall with changing supplies and demands for trade. The tariff equivalents generate quota rents that accrue to whatever group is granted the rights to trade under the restriction, which is the case of the MFA in the textiles-and-apparel exporting countries. Liberalisation of these non-tariff barriers reduces or eliminates these quota rents, and this can be costly to those who possessed them disproportionately beforehand. Therefore, it is not the case that exporting countries necessarily benefit from relaxation of these trade barriers, since their loss of quota rents can more than outweigh their gains from increased exports. Indeed, their exports can actually decline, along with their national welfare, if increased exports from other countries displace them in world markets.

Let us turn now to the aggregate results. These include changes in exports and imports in millions of dollars, the changes in terms of trade, real wage rate and real return to capital in percentages, and changes in economic welfare measured by equivalent variation, both in millions of dollars and as percent of country GDP. The terms-of-trade is the world price of a country's exports relative to its imports. The equivalent variation is the amount of money that, if given to the country's consumers at initial prices, would be equivalent in terms of their level of welfare to the effects of the assumed liberalisation. In general, as discussed above, a worsening (fall) in a country's terms of trade has an adverse effect on its consumers' welfare. But this can be outweighed by the other gains from trade due to economic efficiency and the other benefits modelled by the New Trade theory. Due to space constraints, detailed results are not presented for all the model scenarios. The same are available in Chadha et al. (1999).

Elimination of the MFA Quota Constraints

While the removal of the MFA quotas is being phased in over a 10-year period, from 1995-2005, we assume for computational purposes that they are removed all at one time. With increased exports of these goods to world markets, their prices fall and all developing countries in the model except Korea and Singapore suffer a worsening of their terms of trade. Some of these countries also suffer a small loss in economic welfare, but others gain in spite of the terms-of-trade loss, presumably because their exports under the MFA were most restricted. The greatest gainers, as percentages of their GDP, are India, Hong Kong, the Philippines, and the Rest of South Asia group, all of which record gains of more than half of one percent of their GDP. Most of the developed countries also gain from MFA elimination, although neither their gains, nor the losses of the few losers-Australia/New Zealand and Japan-are particularly large.

Interestingly, while trade expands by quite a bit for most countries in this scenario, it does not expand for all. Japan, especially, experiences such a worsening of its terms of trade that it can afford only lower imports in return for somewhat larger exports. Likewise, Singapore, Malaysia, and several non-Asian LDCs experience small reductions in both exports and imports.

Changes in returns to labour and capital are quite small and mostly, but not all, positive. The biggest gainer is labour-factor in Hong Kong and the Philippines, where real wages rise by more than one percent. Otherwise, most of the changes in real factor prices are much less.

Full Uruguay Round Liberalisation

The full effects of the Uruguay Round liberalisation, to the extent that we have been able to model it, show a substantial increase in both exports and imports for all countries, and an improvement in economic welfare for all countries except Mexico (Table 7). Mexico's NAFTA preference margins may have been eroded due to the multilateral reductions in U.S. trade barriers. With liberalisation of both tariffs and non-tariff barriers in all sectors combined, India's welfare increases by 1.1 per cent of GDP, Sri Lanka by 1.7 per cent, and the Rest of South Asia

(RSA) by 3.2 per cent. While the welfare increases for the developed countries are smaller in relative terms, their total absolute gain of $115.5 billion is 72 per cent of the world total of $159.7 billion. Both labour and capital have shares in the overall gains to all the countries except Mexico.

As mentioned earlier, we have used the UR scenario as the basis for updating our database to the year 2005, which is the base for our subsequent scenarios for a new round of liberalisation. Of course, this was actually done using the disaggregated results for percentage changes in output, trade, and employment that are applied to the scaled levels from the GTAP data.

We turn now to the Millennium Round Scenarios.

Agricultural Liberalisation

We begin our analysis of potential future liberalisation with agriculture, since textiles and apparel have already been fully liberalised under the commitments of the Uruguay Round. This scenario therefore starts with the post-Uruguay Round tariffs in agriculture, including the often quite sizeable tariffs that resulted from Uruguay Round tariffication of previous non-tariff barriers. We assume that these tariff-rates are reduced by one-third during the new round of liberalisation.

In this case, as tariff reductions divert demand rather than supply onto world markets, we see relative prices of agricultural goods rise rather than fall, and the terms of trade of agricultural exporters such as the United States, Australia, New Zealand, and Canada all improve. The welfare effects of these changes are quite small, however, and a number of countries, including the United States, are shown as losing a negligible amount of welfare. The reason for this loss is a bit difficult to determine, since it is so small, although we suspect that it results from drawing resources into agriculture and out of sectors where scale economies made them more productive.

The biggest gainers from agricultural liberalisation in this scenario are India, Sri Lanka, and RSA, plus China and South Korea. Their gains are likely the straightforward implications of comparative advantage, combined with their high initial trade barriers.

Tariff Reductions on Minerals and Manufactures

Here again we assume for illustrative purposes that post Uruguay-Round tariffs are reduced by one-third. Even though these tariffs tend to be lower than in agriculture, the gains from their reduction are considerably larger because they apply to so much more of the world economy. Since developed country exports bulk large in these industries, it is the terms of trade of the developed countries that improve most clearly in this scenario. However, even though many of the Asian economies experience worsening of their terms of trade, the model shows them gaining welfare even more than the developed countries, particularly as percentages of their respective GDPs. This, again, is due to their high tariffs and the economic inefficiencies as well as other losses that are associated with them. India's welfare increases by 0.7 per cent of GDP, Sri Lanka's by 2.8 per cent, and of RSA's by 1.8 per cent. As was the case in the Uruguay Round experiments, we see here that, while the relative increases in GDP are smaller for the developed countries, their total absolute gain is $100.9 billion, which is 73 per cent of the world total of $137.8 billion.

Services Liberalisation

Although the Uruguay Round was the first round of multilateral trade negotiations to deal at all with trade in services, it really did not succeed in reducing any barriers to speak of. That is why our Uruguay Round scenarios did not include any services liberalisation. However, the Uruguay Round did set up a framework, in the form of the General Agreement on Trade in Services (GATS), for future negotiations to reduce such barriers, and it is widely presumed that any future negotiations will make progress in this area. Therefore, our third scenario for the Millennium Round focuses on service sectors liberalisation.

To model barriers to trade in services, we treat them simply as tariffs on services trade, even though in fact levying tariffs on trade in services is certainly not done, and is probably not even possible for most services. Nonetheless, by the same reasoning as for the use of tariff equivalents for modelling NTBs, tariffs on trade in services may provide a first approximation to the effects of more complex actual barriers.[17]

More difficult is to determine what the sizes of barriers to trade in services actually are. Here we draw upon Hoekman (1995), who constructed what he acknowledged to be *ad hoc* "guesstimates" of *ad valorem* barriers to trade in services, based largely upon offers that countries tabled during the services negotiations of the Uruguay Round. We use these guesstimates by reducing the model's tariff equivalents on imports of services by one third of these amounts.

Once again, trade of all countries in the model expands, and welfare of all countries improves, this time by noticeably more than in the earlier scenarios. Welfare increases in India by 1.6 per cent of GDP, Sri Lanka by 2.8 per cent, and RSA by 1.9 per cent. The largest percentage gains accrue to Hong Kong, Thailand, and Singapore. The potential welfare benefits from the liberalisation of service-sectors' barriers are five times greater in total than from the liberalisation of minerals and manufactures. While the developed countries gain of $550.8 billion is 80 per cent of the $687.9 billion total, the absolute gains for the developing are nonetheless quite large. This is indicative of the importance to both developed and developing countries of pursuing services liberalisation in the forthcoming WTO negotiations.[18]

Combined Effects of the Three Millennium Round Scenarios

Our final multilateral scenario here combines the 33 per cent reductions in barriers for all sectors: agriculture; mining and manufactures; and services (Table 8).

Not surprisingly, both the welfare and the terms-of-trade effects are similar to those in scenario under service-sectors' liberalisation, since the services liberalisation turns out to dominate the liberalisation in the other sectors. Trade expands by quite a bit more here than under service-sectors' liberalisation, since the other sectors include a larger amount of trade being liberalised. But because the initial barriers themselves are so high, the welfare effects of service-sectors' liberalisation appear to be the most important for the well being of the countries involved. Of course, this conclusion is critically dependent on the large size of Hoekman's guesstimates of barriers, as well as on the assumption that they can be significantly reduced through negotiations.

Sectoral Impact of Trade Liberalisation on India

A major contribution that this sort of CGE modelling can make is to identify those sectors that will expand and those that will contract as a result of various patterns of trade liberalisation, as well as the sizes of these changes. Given our assumption that expenditure adjusts within each country to maintain a constant level of total employment, it is necessarily the case that each country experiences a mixture of expansions and contractions at the industry level. This must be true of employment, and it is likely to be true as well for industry output. Detailed sectoral results are available for all the countries/regions included in the model and are available on request. We shall now concentrate on the sectoral results for India.

It is expected that trade liberalisation will stimulate production of labour-intensive sectors in India. Productive resources would then get allocated more efficiently as compared to the pre-liberalisation situation as India would specialise in the sectors where it has comparative advantage. There may of course be transitional costs due to intersectoral movement of factors of production. Beyond such welfare gains, trade liberalisation is also expected to have a "pro-competitive" effect on domestic firms, resulting in additional gains from the realisation of economies of large-scale production. When firms get protection from foreign competition through tariff and non-tariff barriers, they may take advantage of their market power by raising their prices and reducing their domestic sales. The result is that the protected firms may produce below their minimum-cost, efficient plant size. Trade liberalisation should then bring about competitive pressures on the formerly protected firms and induce them to raise production and productivity and also to achieve more efficient plant size and lower per unit costs. Thus, gains in economic welfare are expected to come from improved allocation of resources, lower prices to consumers and business firms, and availability of more varieties to consumers and firms. The realisation of economies of scale in manufacturing also reinforces the welfare enhancing effect.

It may be observed from Table 9 that the wearing apparel is the single largest gaining sector, with increased output of 28.9 per cent under Uruguay Round liberalisation and an additional

10.7 per cent under the MR liberalisation. Other output-gaining sectors under the MR liberalisation include mining and quarrying (4.1 per cent); leather, wood, paper and their products (2.3 per cent); textiles (1.8 per cent); food, beverages, and tobacco (0.3 per cent); non-metallic mineral products (0.3 per cent); and manufactures including electronics equipment (10.7 per cent). Output declines in other manufacturing sectors as well as in agriculture.

The change in number of firms is indicated for all the ten manufacturing sectors that are modelled as monopolistically competitive. These changes are consistent with the changes in output. The scale effect, which is the percent change in the output per firm, is positive in all the manufacturing sectors.[19]

The changes in sectoral exports and imports under the MR liberalisation indicate that the largest export-gaining manufacturing sectors, in percentage terms, include: wearing apparel; (16.6 per cent); textiles (9.7 per cent); and leather, wood, paper and their products (9.4 per cent). The highest import gaining manufacturing sectors, in percentage terms, include: wearing apparel (23.2 per cent); textiles (19.2 per cent); food, beverages, and tobacco (18.9 per cent); manufactures, including electronics equipment (17.8 per cent); and non-metallic mineral products (13.2 per cent). While exports of agriculture increase by 9.1 per cent, imports increase by 8.2 per cent. Trade in the service sectors increases markedly in proportional terms.

Unilateral Liberalisation by India

In earlier work by Chadha et al. (1998a,b), the impacts of India's unilateral, post-1991 economic reforms were analysed, using a stand-alone model of the Indian economy in which the rest-of-the-world was assumed not to undertake any liberalisation. It is interesting in this light to consider how India would be affected by multilateral liberalisation in the forthcoming WTO negotiations as compared to what it might undertake unilaterally. For this purpose, we repeated the MR experiments for India on a unilateral basis. The results indicate that India would gain if it undertook unilateral liberalisation (Table 10). But the increases in welfare and the returns to labour and capital are noticeably higher with the assumed multilateral scenarios.

V

CONCLUDING REMARKS

There has been substantial liberalisation of trade related policies in India since 1991. However, these policies had remained generally confined to intermediate and capital goods in the manufactured goods sector. Agriculture remains a sector least touched by the trade policy reform. As protection on manufactured goods is reduced and agro-exports simultaneously opened up, the domestic terms of trade are expected to move in favour of agriculture. Consumer goods, which have a major overlap with agricultural goods, also remain restricted for imports. Under WTO negotiations, India is already committed to remove all QRs on import of consumer goods by 2001.

India's exports could have been much higher had the country not kept exports of most of the agricultural products under controls. Though some export regulations were removed in 1991 on the export of tea, coffee, spices, tobacco, oil meals, hides and skins, jute, fish, fruits and vegetables, yet many of the restrictions still remain and their exports are still regulated by respective commodity boards. The other important set of agro-products in terms of production, employment and domestic consumption includes foodgrains, sugar, oilseeds and cotton. Exports of all these have generally been controlled by parastatal agencies / canalising agencies and this basic policy was not changed in 1991 (Sharma, 1999).

The Uruguay Round commitments in the area of agriculture fall under three main categories, namely market-access, domestic support and export competition. The agreement calls for converting all types of non-tariff barriers into tariff barriers and reduce these tariffs, open domestic market to imports, reduce domestic and export subsidies under a time bound programme in a phased manner (Sharma, 1999: 167). However, India has missed the opportunity for having used the Uruguay Round negotiations to intensify its efforts towards unilateral liberalisation of agricultural trade policies. India continues to use QRs for balance of payments reasons. The bound tariff rates are very high in certain agricultural commodities.

Trade in services is yet another missed opportunity (Chadha 2000a). Opening up the service sectors to international competition under GATS is expected to make these sectors more efficient, which in turn, would lead to gain in India's GDP by providing a more efficient environment to primary and secondary sectors through their mutual linkages.[20]

The best policy for India is to identify its major areas of slack, which hinder its export competitiveness. The merchandise imports and exports need to be further liberalised with reduction in tariffs on imports and QRs on exports. Opening up of the service sectors to foreign investment and competition can go a long way in making the domestic exports more competitive. Infrastructure bottlenecks need to be removed rapidly. While exchange rate should be left to market forces, except under abnormal variations, a gradual move towards capital account convertibility should be continued. Small-scale reservations and outdated exit policies need immediate review for reform.

The failure of the Third WTO Ministerial meeting in Seattle has led to a temporary setback to the launch of a new round of multilateral trade negotiations. Despite the consequent uncertainties, the built-in agenda from the Uruguay Round has been mandated for negotiations on agricultural and services liberalization to commence in the year 2000. In this paper, we have provided computational estimates of the economic effects that might be realized from trade liberalization for India and other major trading countries/regions in the Uruguay Round and in a new negotiating round.

An important message that emerges is that multilateral liberalization enhances the economic welfare of the major trading countries/regions. The expected welfare gain of the world is close to 0.5 per cent over the extrapolated 2005 GTAP database that incorporates the implementation of the Uruguay Round negotiations. There are significant additional gains from the assumed Millennium Round liberalization.

India's welfare gain is 1.1 per cent ($4.7 billion over its 2005 GDP)) when the UR scenarios get fully implemented. India's additional welfare gain amounts to 2.7 per cent ($11.4 billion) when the assumed Millennium Round multilateral trade liberalization is completed. Resources in India are allocated towards labor-intensive sectors such as textiles, wearing apparel, leather and leather products, and food, beverages, and tobacco. Real returns to both labor and capital increase. The scale effect (percent change in output per firm) is positive for all the ten sectors of manufacturing. Finally, it pays even if India were to undertake unilateral trade liberalization of the order indicated in the multilateral scenarios, with other countries not undertaking any further liberalization.

The gains from the liberalization scenarios that have been noted should of course be interpreted in the light of the assumptions of our modeling structure. In particular, our computational model abstracts from the effects of macroeconomic changes and policies, and we do not capture the effects of dynamic changes in efficiency and economic growth. We have also not analyzed the effects of possible changes in inflows of foreign direct investment. Finally, the analysis of intersectoral employment shifts makes no allowance for the constraining effects of India's sectoral exit barriers and its domestic labor laws.

ANNEXURE–1

OVERVIEW OF RESULTS OF THE URUGUAY ROUND NEGOTIATIONS

- The agricultural agreement was important for developing a set of rules as a basis for future liberalization, but actual liberalization was limited by the way that non-tariff barriers were converted into tariffs. This slippage, however, reduces the risk of adverse effects on net food importing countries.
- Substantial liberalization was achieved in manufactures trade, both in the area of tariffs and through the phaseout of non-tariff barriers such as VERs and the quotas imposed under the MFA.
- Cuts in protection on merchandise trade are estimated to increase real incomes in developing countries by between

US $60 and 100 billion at 1992 prices despite the cautious commitments made by many developing countries.

- GATS is a landmark in terms of creating trade disciplines in virgin territory, but achieved little in terms of immediate liberalization.
- The TRIPS agreement will increase the protection of IPRs worldwide-but may entail short-term costs for developing countries.
- The establishment of the WTO, with its responsibilities for goods, services and intellectual property, stronger dispute settlement procedures, permanent policy review mechanism, and greater ministerial involvement, is necessary for the successful implementation of the Round, and seems likely to contribute to a much-needed strengthening of the trading system.
- In terms of policy implications for developing countries we find that the countries that liberalize their own trade policies are predicted to be the greatest gainers.
- The WTO agreement provides legally binding minimum standards for reform and liberalization, not economically optimal ones. Weak disciplines on antidumping, and the high tariff bindings chosen by many countries, allow very costly protection measures to be maintained or introduced.
- There remain substantial gains from liberalization beyond that undertaken in the Round-particularly in areas such as agriculture and services, where multilateral disciplines are new.
- Over the next few years, developing country members of the WTO need to participate in critical decisions on the future of the trading system, including whether or not to include labor and environmental standards, and investment and competition policies."

Source: Martin and Winters (1996, pp. 1-2).

ANNEXURE–2

SUMMARY AGENDA AND RESULTS OF THE DECEMBER 1996 SINGAPORE MINISTERIAL CONFERENCE

Uruguay Round Implementation

- Numerous reporting requirements for far-reaching and technically complex disciplines have made it difficult for many countries to comply both administratively as well as substantively with the up to 22 agreements that comprise the Uruguay Round Agreements (URA). The ministers' foremost priority at Singapore was to review the considerable backlog of notifications and consider what improvements could be made to help existing URA mechanisms work better to ensure full compliance with current obligations.

Built in Agenda

- Services negotiations continued after the Dec. 1993 Uruguay Round conclusion in the areas of financial services, movement of natural persons, basic telecommunications, and maritime transport, and were scheduled to conclude respectively by June 1995, April 1996, and June 1996. These sectoral negotiations have been extended for the most part due to inadequate concessions in the never-before-negotiated area of services. Ministers hoped that the SMC would reinvigorate these talks, especially those on basic telecommunications rescheduled to conclude in February 1997.
- In addition, the current URA contain provisions that already call for either new negotiations at specified future dates (agriculture, services by 2000) or for periodic reviews at various times of virtually every major agreement (e.g. textiles, subsidies, antidumping, intellectual property, dispute settlement, the U.S. "Jones" Act) that set in motion implementation discussions that in effect amount to much the same thing.

- The Committee on Trade and Environment, established by the April 1994 Marrakesh Ministerial Conference, presented its initial findings to the SMC.

Tariff Initiatives

- Australia and Canada proposed that the SMC act as catalyst to liberalize market access over and above that in the existing URA and "built-in" agenda negotiations, both calling formally for tariff cuts on industrial products to be put on the WTO agenda.
- The EU and the United States advanced sectoral tariff elimination in pharmaceuticals and information technology — the latter leading to the Information Technology Agreement (ITA) presently set to enter into force on July 1, 1997 for completion by 2000.

Least Developed Countries

- Least developed countries (LLDCs) have not integrated themselves into the world economy over the past decade to the degree that developing countries have. Studies by the World Bank and others have concluded that some reforms in the URA could result in a worsening of the terms of trade for LLDCs. The WTO Director-General and several key developed country participants urged that the SMC highlight the plight of such countries and adopt measures to address this problem.

New Issues

- Proposals for launching additional WTO work on "new" issues were put forward by various participants, with intense discussions of possible new issues for WTO consideration held before the SMC. Mentions of labor standards, regionalism, competition policy[1], investment, and government procurement reached the final declaration, whereas other issues were also discussed such as a review of WTO rules in light of the spread of regional trading blocs and the increased "globalization" of the world economy.

Source: USITC (1997, p. 16).

Table – 1

Tariff by Processing Stage, 1990-98 (Per cent)

	1990/91[a] Effe.[e]	1993/94[b] Effe.[e]	1995/96 Effe.[e]	1996/97[c] Effe.[e]	1997/98[d] Effe.[e]
Average Unweighted by stage of processing					
Unprocessed	107	50	27	25	25
Semi-processed	122	75	44	38	35
Processed	130	73	43	42	37

a) Prior to reform package of July 1991. Includes auxiliary duty mostly at 45 per cent.

b) The auxiliary duty was merged with the basic customs duty in the 1993/94 budget.

c) Includes special rate of 2 per cent.

d) Includes special rate of 5 per cent.

e) Effective m.f.n. rate, i.e. actual rates applied where basic rates have been reduced by exempt rates. However, many exempt rates cannot be incorporated such as where the exempt rate applies to only a part of the HS six digit tariff line. The effective rate also excludes specific exemptions.

Note: Tariff averages consider only those tariff lines with ad valorem rates. Year beginning 1 April.

Source: Trade Policy Review: India 1998 (p48).
WTO Secretariat

Table – 2

Tariff Structure of India, 1990/91 to 1997/98 (Per cent)

	1990/91[a] Effe.[e]	1993/94[b] Effe.[e]	1995/96 Effe.[e]	1996/97[c] Effe.[e]	1997/98[d] Effe.[e]
Average Unweighted					
Agriculture	113	43	27	26	26
Mining	100	70	30	26	25
Manufacturing	126	73	42	40	36
Whole economy	125	71	41	39	35
Index of dispersion[f]	32	42	47	49	42
	1990/91	**1993/94**	**1995/96**	**1996/97**	**1997/98**
Maximum tariff rate[g]	355	85	50	52	45
Average Weighted[h]	87	47	25	22	20

a) Prior to reform package of July 1991. Includes auxiliary duty mostly at 45 per cent.

b) The auxiliary duty was merged with the basic customs duty in the 1993/94 budget.

c) Includes special rate of 2 per cent.

d) Includes special rate of 5 per cent.

e) Effective m.f.n. rate i.e. actual rates applied where basic rates have been reduced by exempt rates. However, many exempt rates cannot be incorporated such as where the exempt rate applies to only a part of the HS six digit tariff line. The effective rate also excludes specific exemptions.

f) Index of dispersion for the whole economy as measured by the coefficient of variation, percentage points.

g) Higher than the so-called maximum rate is applied to a few items; in 1997/98, 0.4 percent of tariff lines.

h) Weighted by 1992/93 import values.

Note: Tariff averages consider only those tariff lines with ad valorem rates. Year beginning 1 April. Classifications used is based on the International Standard Industrial Classifications(ISIC): Agriculture = ISIC, Mining = ISIC 2, Manufacturing = ISIC 3, including food processing.

Source: Trade Policy Review : India 1998 (p46).
WTO Secretariat calculations based on Academy of Business Studies (1997), Easy Reference Customs Tariff 1997/98; World Bank (1997a), India 1997 Economic Update: Sustaining Rapid Growth; and data Provided by the world bank

Table – 3

Tariff by products, average import-weighted rates, 1990-98 (Per cent)

	1990/91	1992/93	1993/94	1994/95	1995/96	1996/97	1997/98
Consumer Goods	153	131	86	48	36	33	25
Intermediate Goods	77	55	42	31	22	19	18
Capital Goods	97	74	50	37	29	29	24

Note : Year beginning April 1.

Sources : Trade Policy Review: India 1998 (p49). World Bank (1977a), India 1997 Economics Update: Sustaining Rapid Growth. Annex Table 10.

Table – 4

Bound tariff rates and effective rates of duty (Per cent)

	Bound rate of duty[a] by year 2005	Effective rate by duty[b] 1997/98
Average unweighted tariff (per cent)		
Agriculture (ISIC 1)	94	26
Mining (ISIC 2)	36	25
Manufacturing (ISIC 3, includes food processing)	52	36
Whole economy	54	35
Average unweighted tariff by stage processing (per cent)		
Unprocessed	74	25
Semi-processed	44	35
Processed	56	37

a) Includes only items bound during the Uruguay Round. The bound rates do not include the commitments under the Information Technology Agreement.

b) Effective m.f.n. rate, i.e. actual rates applied where basic rates have been reduced by exempt rates. However, many exempt rates cannot be incorporated such as where the exempt rate applies to only a part of the HS six digit tariff line. The effective rate also excludes specific exemptions.

Note: Tariff averages consider only those tariff lines with *ad valorem* rates, Year beginning April 1.

Source: Trade Policy Review: India 1998 (p54). WTO Secretariat.

Table – 5

Countries/Regions of the Model

COUNTRIES/REGIONS	CODE
(1)	(2)
1. Developed	
Australia & New Zealand	ANZ
Canada	CAN
EUN and EFTA	EUF
Japan	JPN
USA	USA
2. Developing	
2.a Asian	
India	IND
Sri Lanka	LKA
Rest of South Asia	RSA
China	CHN
Hongkong	HKG
Korea	KOR
Singapore	SGP
Indonesia	IDN
Malaysia	MYS
Philippines	PHL
Thailand	THA
2.b Other	
Mexico	MEX
Turkey	TUR
Central European Associates	CEA
Central and South America and Associates	A_N

Table – 6

Sectors of Production

SN	COMMODITY	CODE
1	Agriculture	AGR
2	Mining and Quarrying	MIN
3	Food Beverage and Tobacco	FBT
4	Textiles	TEX
5	Wearing Apparels	WAP
6	Leather, Wood and Paper & Products	LWP
7	Chemicals, Rubber, Plastic and Petroleum Products	CRP
8	Non-Metallic Mineral Products	NMM
9	Metal and Metal Products	MMP
10	Transport and Machinery Equipments & Parts	TEM
11	Manufactures including Electronics Equip.	OMF
12	Electricity, Gas Manufacture and Water	EGW
13	Construction	CNS
14	Trade and Transport	T_T
15	Finance, Business and Recreational Services	OSP
16	Public Administration, Defense, Education and Health & Dwellings	RSR

Table – 7

UR - Elimination of MFA Quota Constraints, Agricultural Liberalisation, and Liberalisation of Minerals and Manufactures

COUNTRIES/REGIONS	CODE	IMPORTS Million Dollars	EXPORTS Million Dollars	TERMS OF TRADE Percent Change	EQUIVALENT Percent Change	VARIATION Million Dollars	WAGE RATE Percent Change	RETURN TO CAPITAL Percent Change
(1)	(2)	(3)	(4)	(5)	(6)	(7)	(8)	(9)
1. **Developed**		**83792**	**77989**	—	**0.4**	**115546**	—	—
Australia & New Zealand	ANZ	3960	3436	0.5	0.6	3214	0.4	0.6
Canada	CAN	2748	2624	0.1	0.3	2271	0.2	0.3
EUN and EFTA	EUF	31410	27870	0.4	0.4	48037	0.2	0.2
Japan	JPN	13326	11563	0.4	0.3	21357	0.1	0.2
USA	USA	32347	32497	-0.2	0.4	40667	0.3	0.4
2. **Developing**		**64157**	**69914**	—	**0.8**	**44143**	—	—
2.a Asian		**51209**	**57160**	—	**1.3**	**37123**	—	—
India	IND	4522	6012	-3.0	1.1	4738	0.5	0.7
Sri Lanka	LKA	212	297	-1.7	1.7	286	1.1	1.4
Rest of South Asia	RSA	3994	5473	-8.3	3.2	3749	1.9	2.2
China	CHN	22091	25809	-1.3	1.5	13330	1.0	0.9
Hong Kong	HKG	3150	2646	0.5	1.3	1700	1.8	0.7
Korea	KOR	4392	3702	0.4	0.8	4741	0.4	0.4
Singapore	SGP	2794	2243	0.3	1.6	1221	2.0	2.3
Indonesia	IDN	1346	1287	0.1	0.5	1194	0.5	0.2
Malaysia	MYS	1888	2174	-0.2	1.1	1310	1.6	1.4
Philippines	PHL	5112	6050	-3.0	3.3	2913	3.6	1.7
Thailand	THA	1707	1467	0.2	0.9	1941	1.0	0.3
2.b Other		**12948**	**12753**	—	**0.3**	**7020**	—	—
Mexico	MEX	324	460	-0.0	-0.2	-795	0.2	-0.2
Turkey	TUR	477	318	0.3	0.5	1007	0.1	0.2
Central European Associates	CEA	2581	2248	0.2	0.5	1814	0.3	0.3
Central, South America etc	A_N	9565	9727	-0.2	0.3	4994	0.1	-0.0
3. **World Total**		**147949**	**147903**	—	**0.5**	**159689**	—	—

Table – 8

MR - 33 Percent Bilateral Tariff Reductions in All Sectors Combined (MR1, MR2 and MR3)

COUNTRIES/REGIONS	CODE	IMPORTS Million Dollars	EXPORTS Million Dollars	TERMS OF TRADE Percent Change	EQUIVALENT Percent Change	VARIATION Million Dollars	WAGE RATE Percent Change	RETURN TO CAPITAL Percent Change
(1)	(2)	(3)	(4)	(5)	(6)	(7)	(8)	(9)
1. **Developed**		**254179**	**249532**	—	**2.4**	**656028**	—	—
Australia & New Zealand	ANZ	11903	11874	-0.0	3.4	17320	1.1	1.1
Canada	CAN	11855	12176	-0.1	3.1	22648	0.9	1.0
EUN and EFTA	EUF	92436	93657	-0.0	2.3	253381	0.5	0.5
Japan	JPN	57153	58871	-0.2	2.5	165669	0.5	0.7
USA	USA	80831	72955	0.7	2.2	197009	0.6	0.5
2. **Developing**		**151772**	**157692**	—	**3.2**	**179748**	—	—
2.a Asian		**106939**	**111191**	—	**3.6**	**105191**	—	—
India	IND	5438	6340	-1.6	2.7	11412	0.6	1.0
Sri Lanka	LKA	930	1074	-2.6	6.0	1010	3.3	3.9
Rest of South Asia	RSA	2910	3074	-0.8	4.4	5065	1.1	1.7
China	CHN	26078	29791	-1.2	2.2	20193	1.4	1.3
Hong Kong	HKG	18076	15763	2.2	9.6	12277	7.2	7.1
Korea	KOR	19297	20367	-0.6	3.9	22018	1.8	1.7
Singapore	SGP	6735	4834	1.2	5.2	3897	8.6	6.9
Indonesia	IDN	4595	4609	0.0	3.1	7859	1.1	0.8
Malaysia	MYS	5587	5913	-0.3	3.8	4598	3.3	3.2
Philippines	PHL	6564	7411	-2.2	7.0	6153	4.7	4.3
Thailand	THA	10727	12016	-1.5	5.2	10708	6.1	4.2
2.b Other		**44833**	**46501**	—	**2.8**	**74558**	—	—
Mexico	MEX	5144	5312	-0.2	3.4	12081	1.0	1.0
Turkey	TUR	6024	5188	1.9	4.5	9432	1.3	2.2
Central European Associates	CEA	12499	12743	-0.2	3.1	11363	1.9	1.8
Central, South America etc	A_N	21167	23257	-1.2	2.4	41682	0.5	0.4
3. **World Total**		**405951**	**407224**	—	**2.5**	**835776**	—	—

Table – 9

MR - Sectoral Effect on Exports, Imports, Output, Number of Firms, and Change in Employment in India

SN	COMMODITY	CODE	EXPORTS	IMPORTS	OUTPUT	No. of FIRMS	SCALE EFFECT	CAPITAL	EMPLOYMENT PERCENT	EMPLOYMENT TOTAL
1	Agriculture	AGR	9.1	8.2	-0.1	—	—	0.2	-0.1	-229492
2	Mining and Quarrying	MIN	7.5	-3.2	4.1	3.0	1.1	3.3	3.4	100167
3	Food, Beverages, and Tobacco	FBT	7.3	18.9	0.3	-0.2	0.5	-0.2	0.3	25475
4	Textiles	TEX	9.7	19.5	1.8	1.1	0.8	1.2	1.6	166091
5	Wearing Apparel	WAP	16.6	23.3	10.7	9.9	0.8	10.1	10.6	76751
6	Leather, Wood, and Paper & Products	LWP	9.4	4.6	2.3	1.5	0.8	1.6	2.1	155858
7	Chemicals, Rubber, Plastic & Petr. Prod.	CRP	7.1	7.9	-0.3	-1.1	0.8	-0.9	-0.4	-7014
8	Non-Metallic Mineral Products	NMM	7.9	13.2	0.3	-0.6	0.8	-0.8	-0.4	-11246
9	Metal and Metal Products	MMP	5.9	9.9	-1.8	-2.6	0.8	-2.5	-2.0	-62549
10	Transport and Machinery Equipment & Parts	TEM	6.0	9.4	-2.1	-3.3	1.2	-3.6	-3.1	-104192
11	Manufactures, including Electronic Equip.	OMF	5.5	17.8	0.1	-0.9	1.0	-0.9	-0.5	-23092
12	Electricity, Gas, and Water	EGW	64.6	50.1	0.7	—	—	0.1	0.5	7881
13	Construction	CNS	21.3	19.2	-0.1	—	—	-0.3	0.2	20648
14	Trade and Transport	T_T	41.5	41.8	-0.6	—	—	-1.3	-0.7	-297355
15	Finance, Business, and Recreational Services	OSP	23.5	25.0	0.0	—	—	-0.4	0.1	1701
16	Public Admn, Defense, Edn, Health & Dwellings	RSR	21.9	17.0	0.7	—	—	-0.1	0.4	144329
	All Sectors		11.4	9.9	0.4	-0.2	—	—	0.0	0

Note: All figures are in percent unless specified

Table – 10

Impact of Multilateral and Unilateral Trade Liberalization for India

	MR1	MR2	MR3	MR4
Multilateral				
Equivalent Variation				
Percent	0.4	0.7	1.6	2.7
Million US dollars	1541	3031	6840	11412
Returns to Factors, % change				
Wage Rate	0.0	0.3	0.3	0.6
Returns to Capital	0.0	0.5	0.4	1.0
Trade				
Imports (million US dollars)	249	3161	2028	5438
Exports (million US dollars)	253	3934	2152	6340
Unilateral				
Equivalent Variation				
Percent	0.4	0.3	1.3	2.0
Million US dollars	1709	1317	5350	8376
Returns to Factors, % change				
Wage Rate	0.0	0.2	0.0	0.2
Returns to Capital	0.1	0.5	0.3	0.8
Trade				
Imports (million US dollars)	134	2086	1070	3290
Exports (million US dollars)	197	3264	1599	5060

Multilateral

MR1: 33 percent bilateral reduction in post-Uruguay round tariffs on agricultural products

MR2: 33 percent bilateral reduction in post-Uruguay round tariffs on minerals and manufactures

MR3: 33 percent bilateral reduction in tariff equivalents of barriers to trade in services

MR4: 33 percent bilateral tariffs reduction in all sectors combined (MR1, MR2 and MR3)

Unilateral

India's unilateral :

UNIMR1 : 33 percent reduction in post-Uruguay round tariffs on agricultural products

UNIMR2 : 33 percent reduction in post-Uruguay round tariffs on minerals and manufactures

UNIMR3 : 33 percent reduction in tariff equivalent of barriers to trade in services

UNIMR4: 33 percent tariff reduction in all sectors combined (UNIMR1, UNIMR2 and UNIMR3)

References

Bhagwati, Jagdish and Padma Desai 1970. "India: Planning For Industrialisation," Oxford University Press, Oxford.

Bhagwati, Jagdish and T.N. Srinivasan 1975. "Foreign Trade Regimes and Economic Development-India," National Bureau of Economic Research, New York.

Bhagwati, Jagdish N. 1984. "Splintering and Disembodiment of Services and Developing Nations", *World Economy* 7(2), 133-44.

Bhagwati, Jagdish and T.N. Srinivasan 1993. "India's Economic Reforms," Paper prepared for the Ministry of Finance, Government of India.

Brown, Drusilla K. and Robert M. Stern. 1999. "Measurement and Modeling of the Economic Effects of Trade and Investment Barriers in Services," presented at the World Services Congress, Atlanta, GA, November 1-3.

Brown, Drusilla, Alan V. Deardorff, and Robert M. Stern. 1993. "Protection of Real Wages: Old and New Trade Theories and their Empirical Counterparts," Discussion Paper 331, Research Forum for International Economics, *Institute of Public Policy Studies*, University of Michigan.

Brown, Drusilla K., Alan V. Deardorff, Alan Fox, and Robert M. Stern. 1996. "The Liberalization of Services Trade: Potential Impacts of the Aftermath of the Uruguay Round," in Will Martin and L. Alan Winters (eds.), *The Uruguay Round and the Developing Countries*. Cambridge: Cambridge University Press, Cambridge.

Brown, Drusilla K, Alan V. Deardorff and Robert M. Stern 1996. "Computational Analysis of Economic Effects of an East Asian Preferential Trading Bloc", *Journal of Japanese and International Economies* (10), 37-70.

Brown, Drusilla K, Alan V. Deardorff and Robert M. Stern. 1997. "Trade and Labor Standards", Mimeo, University of Michigan, Ann Arbor.

Chadha, Rajesh 1998. "India's Export performance: A Comparison With East Asian Countries", paper published in *Indian Economy in Transition: Environmental and Development Issues*, Manmohan Agarwal et al (eds.), Har Anand, New Delhi.

Chadha, Rajesh. 1999. "Trade and Balance of Payments," *NCAER-ADB Workshop*, December, New Delhi.

Chadha, Rajesh. 2000a. "GATS and Developing Countries: A Case Study of India," forthcoming in Robert M. Stern (ed.), *Services in the International Economy: Measurement and Modeling, Sectoral and Country Studies, and Issues in the WTO Services Negotiations*. University of Michigan Press.

Chadha, Rajesh. 2000b. "The Impact of Changing Global Trade Policies on India", *ICRIER-SANEI-World Bank Project,* NCAER, New Delhi.

Chadha, Rajesh, Sanjib Pohit, Alan V. Deardorff, and Robert M. Stern. 1998a. "Analysis of India's Policy Reforms," *World Economy* 21:235-59.

Chadha, Rajesh, Sanjib Pohit, Alan V. Deardorff and Robert M. Stern. 1998b. "The Impact of Trade and Domestic Policy Reforms in India: A CGE Modeling Approach," University of Michigan Press, Ann Arbor.

Chadha, Rajesh and Sanjib Pohit. 1998c. "Rationalising Tariff and Non-Tariff Barriers on Trade: Sectoral Impact on Indian Economy," paper prepared for the Tariff Commission, Government of India.

Chadha, Rajesh, Sanjib Pohit, Alan V. Deardorff, and Robert M. Stern. 1999a. "Phasing Out the Multi-Fibre Arrangement: Implications for India," paper presented at the *Second Annual Conference on Global Economic Analysis,* June, Copenhagen.

Chadha, Rajesh, Drusilla K. Brown, Alan V. Deardorff, and Robert M. Stern. 1999b. "Computational Analysis of Impact on India of the Uruguay Round and the Forthcoming WTO Trade Negotiations," *NCAER-World Bank WTO 2000: South Asia Workshop*, December, New Delhi..

Chadha et al. 2000. "Introduction", *WTO Special Issue: World Economy*, April.

Desai, Ashok 1993. "My Economic Affair," Wiley Eastern, New Delhi.

Dixit, Avinash K. and Joseph E. Stiglitz. 1977. "Monopolistic Competition and Optimum Product Diversity", *American Economic Review*, 67.

ESCAP, United Nations. 1995. "Review and Analysis of Intraregional Trade Flows in Asia and the Pacific" New York.

Francois, Joseph, Bradley McDonald and Hakan Nordstrom (1996) "The Uruguay Round: A numerically Based Qualitative Assessment" in Will Martin and L. Alan Winters, eds, *The Uruguay Round and the Developing Countries,* Cambridge University Press, Cambridge.

Francois, Joseph and Anna Strutt. 1999. "Post Uruguay Round Tariff Vectors for GTAP Version 4," Mimeo, Faculty of Economics, Erasmus University, Rotterdam, Netherlands.

General Agreement on Tariffs and Trade 1993. "India: Trade Policy Review," Vol. I and II, GATT, Geneva.

Government of India (various issues) *Export and Import Policy documents.* Ministry of Commerce.

Government of India (various issues) *Economic Survey,* Ministry of Finance.

Government of India 1991. "Tax Reforms Committee: Interim Report," Chairman: Raja J. Chelliah, Ministry of Finance.

Government of India 1992. "Tax Reforms Committee: Final Report Part I," Chairman: Raja J. Chelliah, Ministry of Finance.

Government of India 1993. "Tax Reforms Committee: Final Report Part II," Chairman: Raja J. Chelliah, Ministry of Finance.

Gulati, Ashok and Rajesh Chadha 1995. "India Poised for Take-off Reforms in Trade, Industry and Agriculture: Stock-Taking and Future Challenges," article published in *Understanding India's Economic Reforms: The Past, The Present, and The Future*!, Vol.5, eds. Raj Kapila and Uma Kapila, Academic Foundation, Delhi.

Gulati, Ashok and Garry Pursell 1996. "Trade Policy Incentives and Resource Allocation in Indian Agriculture," The World Bank, Washington, D.C.

Harrison, Glenn, Thomas Rutherford and David G. Tarr (1996) "Quantifying the Uruguay Round" in Will Martin and L. Alan Winters, eds, *The Uruguay Round and the Developing Countries,* Cambridge University Press, Cambridge.

Helpman, Elhanan and Paul R. Krugman 1985. "Market Structure and Foreign Trade: Increasing Returns," *Imperfect Competition and*

International Economy, Cambridge, MA: MIT Press.

Hertel, Thomas W., Will Martin, Koji Yanagishima and Betina Dimaranan (1996) "Liberalizing Manufactured Trade in a Changing World Economy", in Will Martin and L. Alan Winters, eds, *The Uruguay Round and the Developing Countries,* Cambridge University Press, Cambridge.

Hindlley, B. and A. Smith 1984. "Comparative Advantage and Trade in Services", *World Economy* 7(4), 369-90.

Hoekman, Bernard. 1995. "Tentative First Steps: An Assessment of the Uruguay Round Agreement on Services," *Centre for Economic Policy Research,* London.

Hoekman, Bernard 1996. "Assessing the General Agreement on Trade in Services" Will Martin and L. Alan Winters (eds.) *The Uruguay Round and Beyond.* Cambridge: Cambridge University Press.

Hoekman, Bernard and Carlos A. Primo Braga 1997. "Protection and Trade in Services A Survey" *Open Economies Review.*

Hoekman, Bernard and Simeon Djankov 1997. "Towards A Free Trade Agreement with the European Union: Issues and Policy Options for Egypt", in A Galal and Bernard Hoekman (eds) *Regional Partners in Global Markets.* London: CEPR.

Hussain, Abid 1997. "Report of the Expert Committee on Small Enterprises," Ministry of Industry, Government of India.

International Monetary Fund 1998. "Balance of Payments Statistics Year Book", Washington, D.C

Joshi, Vijay and I.M.D. Little 1994. "India: Macroeconomics and Political Economy 1964-1991," The World Bank, Washington, D.C.

Joshi, Vijay and I.M.D. Little 1996. "India's Economic Reforms: 1991-2001," Oxford University Press, Delhi.

Kathuria, Sanjay 1995. "Competitiveness of Indian Industry", chapter in *Indian Industry:Policies and Performance*, ed. Dilip Mookherjee, Oxford University Press, New Delhi.

Low, Patrick 1995. "Impact of the Uruguay Round on Asia: Trade in Services and Trade-Related Investment Measures," unpublished manuscript.

Martin, Will and Alan Winters. 1996. "Uruguay Round: A Milestone for the Developing Countries", in Will Martin and L. Alan Winters (eds.), *The Uruguay Round and the Developing Countries.* Cambridge: Cambridge University Press, Cambridge.

Martin, Will and Thomas W. Hertel. 1999. "Developing Country Interests in Liberalising Manufactures Trade", paper presented at the *Second Annual Conference on Global Economic Analysis*, June, Copenhagen.

Matto, Aaditya 1999. "Developing Countries in the New Round of GATS Negotiations: From a Defensive to a Pro-Active Role", *The WTO/World Bank Conference on Developing Countries and the Millennium Round,* Geneva, September.

Mattoo, Aaditya and Arvind Subramanian. 1999. "South Asia in the Next Round of WTO Negotiations from a Defensive to a Pro-Active Role", *NCAER-World Bank WTO 2000: South Asia Workshop*, December, New Delhi..

McDougall, Robert et al. 1998. "Global Trade, Assistance and Protection:

GTAP-4 Database," Purdue University.

Mehta, Rajesh. 1998. "Tariff and Non-Tariff Barriers of the Indian Economy: A Profile," Study Report submitted to the Tariff Commission, Government of India.

Mohan, Rakesh. 1996. "Expert Group on Infrastructure India Infrastructure Report," NCAER, New Delhi.

NCAER 1998. "Protection in Indian Industry," Mimeograph.

NASSCOM 1999. "The Software Industry in India: A Strategic Review, NASSCOM," New Delhi (www.nasscom.org).

Panagriya, Arvind 1999a. "Trade Policy in South Asia: Recent Liberalisation and Future Agenda," *World Economy* 22 (3): 353-78.

Panagriya, Arvind 1999b. "The WTO Trade Policy Review of India, 1998" *World Economy* 22 (6): 719-24.

Prasad, H.A.C. 1999. "WTO Negotiations: Some Important Issues and Strategies for India", Commonwealth, New Delhi.

Pursell, Gary. 1996. "Indian Trade Policies Since the 1991/92 Reforms," Mimeo, World Bank.

Reserve Bank of India, RBI 1999. "Report on the Currency and Finance," 1998-99.

Sampson, P. Gary and Richard H. Snape 1985. "Identifying the Issues in Trade in Services" *World Economy* 8(2): 171-82.

Sauvant, Karl P. 1990. "The Tradability of Services" *Services in the World Economy*, The World Bank.

Singh, Manmohan 1964. "India's Export Trends," Clarendon Press, Oxford.

Sharma, Anil 1999. "Indian Agricultural Trade Liberalisation Under Uruguay Round Agreement", paper in *Implications of the Uruguay Round for South Asia: The Case Sturdy of Agriculture,* The World Bank-Allied Publishers, New Delhi.

Srinivasan, T. N. 1998a. "Developing Countries and the Multilateral Trading System." Westview Press.

Srinivasan, T.N. 1998b. "India's Economic Performance: A comparative Analysis", paper in *India's Economic Reforms and Development: Essays for Manmohan Singh,* eds. Isher Judge Ahluwalia and I.M.D. Little, Oxford University Press, Delhi.

Stern, Robert M., Drusilla K. Brown, Dilip K. Das, and Alan V. Deardorff. 2000. "The Stakes for the Asian Economies in the Forthcoming WTO Negotiations," a study prepared for the Asian Development Bank, in process.

United Nations, 1989. "International Trade Statistics Yearbook", 1991, 1993, 1996.

UNCTAD-World Bank 1994. "Liberalizing International Transactions in Services: A Handbook," United Nations.

WTO 1995. *The Results of the Uruguay Round of Multilateral Trade Negotiations: The Legal Texts,* Geneva.

WTO. 1998. *Trade Policy Review: India.* Bernan Associates, Geneva.

World Bank. 1998. *World Development Report,* 1998/99, Washington, DC.

End Notes

1 This paper is based on an ongoing collaborative programme of computable general equilibrium (CGE) modelling research beginning in 1994 between the National Council of Applied Economic Research (NCAER), New Delhi, and the University of Michigan, Ann Arbor. In this connection, see Chadha, Pohit, Deardorff and Stern (1998a,b) and Chadha and Pohit (1998), Chadha, Brown, Deardorff and Stern (1999) and Chadha (1999, 2000). The authors of this collaborative effort would like to express their gratitude to S.L. Rao and Rakesh Mohan for active and sustained support of the NCAER-UM collaborative research effort. Special thanks are due to Shashanka Bhide, K.L. Krishna, Arvind Panagariya, V.N. Pandit and T.N. Srinivasan for having provided valuable comments on our earlier work. Devender Pratap, Bikram Prakas Ghosh and Praveen Sachdeva of the NCAER and Alan Fox and Soraphol Tulayasathien of the University of Michigan provided excellent research assistance.

2 Discussion in this section draws upon Chadha, Rajesh (2000b), "The Impact of Changing Global Trade Policies on India", Mimeo, ICRIER-SANEI-World Bank Study.

3 The discussion in this section is based on WTO (1998), Chadha (1999) and Panagariya (1999b).

4 Severe import controls instituted in 1990-91 were kept in place during 1991-92 and their relaxation commenced only during 1992-93 through export and Import Policy: 1992-1997.

5 The Foreign Investment Promotion Board (FIPB) and the Secretariat for Industrial Approvals (SIA) were established to examine FDI project proposals that involved more than 51 per cent of foreign equity holding in priority industries and all other industries. In case of foreign investment applications that do not conform to the requirements for automatic RBI approval, they are referred to the FIPB and the SIA for approval. These proposals are examined on a case-by-case basis. The approval is generally granted up to 100 per cent foreign equity in cases where a foreign company has been unable to find a suitable Indian partner for a joint venture, subject to the condition that the foreign investor would disinvest at least 26 per cent of equity to Indian companies within three to five years; where a holding company is to be established and all downstream investments need prior approval; where proprietary technology is sought; where at least 50 per cent of the production is exported; and for consultancy services and projects in the power, roadways, ports and industrial towns and estates sectors.

6 These include mining services, basic metal and alloy industries, other manufacturing industries (including NIC categories 380, 381 and 388), electric generation and transmission, non-conventional energy generation and distribution, construction, land transport, water transport, and storage and warehousing facilities.

7 Prior to the announcement of Export and Import Policy (1992-97), all imports unless specifically exempted required a license or a customs clearance permit. All imports were classified under one of four main licensing types, namely restricted items, banned items, and limited permissible items and open general licenses (OGL). The items falling

under OGL were only nominally unrestricted. In practice, many OGL imports required government approval and most remained subject to actual user conditions. The system was made more complicated by applying different import and approval procedures between license types and frequently shifting products across licensing categories.

8 Other goods under licensing precious, semi-precious and other stones; safety, security and related items; seeds plants and animals; insecticides and pesticides; drugs and pharmaceuticals; chemicals and allied items; items relating to small scale sector; and miscellaneous and special categories.

9 It was declared that consumer goods, howsoever described, of industrial, agricultural, mineral or animal origin whether in SKD/CKD condition or ready to assemble sets or in finished form will remain under import licensing.

10 India implemented the Harmonized Commodity Description and Coding System (HS) for classifying imports and exports in February 1986. Although the Indian Customs Tariff Schedule is sub-divided into 5,134 standard HS six-digit codes (as of April 1, 1997), India uses a 10-digit HS classification for import licensing purposes.

11 India obtained the right to use QRs from GATT in 1949 for balance of payments reasons and had retained it ever since then till the mid-1990s. This right was reasserted in its Uruguay Round submissions.

12 See Chadha, Rajesh. 2000. "What is in a name: Let's do it right this time", Economic and Political Weekly, April 15, 2000.

13 The TRIPS agreement, which includes seven types of IPRs, namely patents copyrights, trademarks, geographical indications, industrial designs, layout designs, integrated circuits and undisclosed information.

14 This section draws upon Chadha et al. (1999b).

15 It is useful to review the features of the model that serve to identify the various economic effects that are being captured in the different scenarios. Although the model includes the imperfect-competition features of the New Trade Theory, it remains the case that markets respond to trade liberalisation in much the same way that they would with perfect competition. That is, when tariffs or other trade barriers are reduced in a sector, domestic buyers (both final and intermediate) substitute toward imports and the domestic-competing industry contracts production while foreign exporters expand. With multilateral liberalisation reducing tariffs and other trade barriers simultaneously in most sectors and countries, each country's industries share in both of these effects, expanding or contracting depending primarily on whether their protection is reduced more or less than in other sectors and countries. At the same time, countries with larger average tariff reductions than their trading partners tend to experience a real depreciation of their currencies in order to maintain a constant trade balance, so that all countries therefore experience mixtures of both expanding and contracting sectors.

16 For details, see Brown et al. (1993). In the real world, all of these effects occur over time, some of these occur rapidly while others slowly. Our model is however static, based upon a single set of equilibrium conditions rather than relationships that vary over time. Our results

therefore refer to a time horizon that is somewhat uncertain, depending on the assumptions that have been made about which variables do and do not adjust to changing market conditions, and on the short- or long-run nature of these adjustments. Because our elasticities of supply and demand reflect relatively long-run adjustments and because we assume that markets for both labour and capital clear within countries, our results are appropriate for a relatively long time horizon of several years - perhaps two or three at a minimum. On the other hand, our model does not allow for the very long-run adjustments that could occur through capital accumulation, population growth, and technological change. Our results should therefore be thought of as being superimposed upon longer-run growth paths of the economies involved. To the extent that these growth paths themselves may be influenced by trade liberalisation, therefore, our model does not capture that.

17 See Brown and Stern (1999) for a CGE analysis in which the services barriers are modeled in terms of raising the cost of providing services through foreign direct investment.

18 A similar conclusion was reached in earlier work by Brown et al. (1996).

19 Scale effects were not calculated for the services sectors because of the lack of data on numbers of firms.

20 A recent study conducted on behalf of the Tariff Commission of India indicates that opening up of India's merchandise imports through reducing the tariff rate to 10 per cent in all sectors (where the existing tariff rate is above 10 per cent) leads to 1 per cent gain in GDP. The gain in GDP increases to 2.8 per cent in case there is an efficiency gain of 5 per cent in the service sectors, namely, utilities, transport, storage, communications, finance and insurance (Chadha et al., 1998c: p10).

Paper presented at the conference to honour Prof. K.L. Krishna, *Industrialisation in a Reforming Economy: A Quantitative Assessment,* December 20-21, 2000, Delhi School of Economics, Delhi.

11

World Trade Organisation: DOHA Round

MURASOLI MARAN

Our intention at DOHA (WTO) was to protect our national interest and I have achieved that goal. I am happy with what we have been able to get.

It is a question of fixing the text of the declaration which runs into 10 pages. There was a text on 13th November which was suddenly altered in the late hours without our knowing and a new text was presented on the 14th. There were three earlier drafts and you know we rejected all of them. We could have avoided all this and the unpleasantness it entailed if we had avoided sudden surprises and had a draft that incorporated the concerns of all member countries. The WTO process was not transparent and was not democratic. Developing countries had no role to play in the agenda setting. If this continues the institution will be greatly harmed. That is why the negotiations became so long-drawn at Doha. We finally secured a draft that meets our concerns. That text was suddenly withdrawn and another text was presented.

WTO is WTO. The real thing is that market power talks. Those who are powerful call the shots. The reality is that a majority of the members are from the developing world, but we are not united. If we stand together and work together no one can harm us.

We wanted to give priority to implementation issues. We did not oppose or support a "new round". My concern was with issues.

What issues will be on the agenda. There we have ensured that the issues which we do not want on the agenda are not yet there.

The position after Doha is the same as after Singapore. I have taken the issue back to the Singapore Declaration; we have not added anything at all at Doha. It is precisely on this issue that we held up the entire proceedings for 18 hours. India alone stood in the way and I made it very clear that I am willing to return home without signing any declaration if my point of view is not incorporated. The declaration has made it clear that there will have to be an "explicit consensus" among all member countries before these issues are brought into any negotiating agenda. They will be studied for the next two years, that is what was decided at Singapore. So there is no progress beyond this point. I have prevented the declaration from regarding these issues as available for negotiations.

We were not alone. Many developing countries openly supported our views.

India is committed to clean environment. Our Supreme Court is actively defending environmental causes. Environment as a subject is already in and there are already multilateral environment agreements (MEA). But we opposed this text which EU was very keen on and finally agreed to give and take.

Trophies for India

International trade negotiations are not a one shot affair. It is a continuous process of give and take. We tried to pursue a win-win approach in which all countries are satisfied. I believe I have been able to defend our national interest very well at Doha and to that extent the meeting was a success. I have come back from Doha with many trophies. First, we got the declaration on TRIPs and public health. India and Brazil were at the forefront of this campaign which will benefit people all over the world, especially in sub-Saharan Africa. This is the biggest trophy we got. It will also benefit the Indian pharmaceutical companies.

My second trophy was securing recognition of implementation issues which are today explicitly recognised in the declaration. The third trophy was the declaration on agriculture where we have been able to address our food security interests, created the basis for a 'development box' and ensured better market access in developed country markets. My fourth trophy is the agreement relating to textiles. In textiles, the real challenge for us is internal, to be able to make use of the market opportunities coming our way. Finally, we have been able to bring the issue of geographical indications back onto the agenda for the future. Most important, the issues pertaining to special and differential treatment have also been incorporated in the way we would have liked them to be. No critic can show that anything we have agreed to will harm India.

Let us not be oversensitive to negotiations on environment. India is anyway committed to preventing environmental degradation. Every high court in India has a green bench, we follow Euro-II standards for automobile emission in Delhi, the Supreme Court has ordered the use of CNG to fuel buses and we even have a time-bound programme for cleaning up Yamuna. Our only worry is that environment should not be used as a Trojan horse for protection and hurt exports from developing countries. The current development will not lead to any such hassle. We have only agreed to certain studies on the relationship between environment and trade.

In a way, it is political acknowledgement of the importance of environment. The study will not affect us or harm our market access. We have already signed global agreements to preserve the ozone layer and prevention of trade in endangered species. I remember Mrs. Indira Gandhi saying poverty is the biggest polluter. We will plead on these lines and seek poverty alleviation as a strategy for checking environmental degradation. There is no negative outcome for India from the Doha declaration. The limited agenda on environment had to be conceded in order to obtain a commitment for reduction of domestic support and export subsidies for farm goods. In view of the pressure from green parties, the European Union (EU) wanted negotiations on environment in return for a commitment to phase out agricultural subsidies.

In my view, the declaration on Trips and public health is the biggest trophy for India. WTO has unequivocally accepted that patents will not stand in the way of public health. When it comes to crunch, public health first, patents later. Under the Uruguay agreement, this facility was available only for pandemics and the provision was useful only in the fight against Aids/HIV. Now, patents can be overlooked in the case of epidemics like tuberculosis and malaria. This is important for India. National governments can now decide if a particular situation is an emergency that warrants sidelining of patents.

The concession on Trips materialised due to staunch efforts by India, Brazil and 55 African countries. The myth that India was isolated at WTO was broken. India participated actively in the drafting despite accusations that India was pushing for the amendment since its pharmaceutical companies would benefit along with those from Brazil and China. People were overlooking the fact that a handful of developed nations were the beneficiaries from patents.

The rent paid by the developing world to the industrialised nations on account of Trips is estimated at $8.3 billion for just four countries. Of this, the US alone account for $5.3 billion, according to a study by Yale University professors. Therefore, the pharmaceutical companies of the US and EU were mounting pressure on negotiators. The major benefit from the amendment is that WTO now has a human face. Access to affordable drugs is a human right which has been restored to erase the stigma of WTO allowing multinationals to fleece developing countries.

Textiles was never the central issue. Yes, we were seeking a better deal on the growth-on-growth factor which would have given us higher quota allocation. We were only using it as a bargaining chip. However, we have succeeded in stalling back-to-back anti-dumping investigations with the statement on implementation issues saying that there should be a gap of at least one year between two investigation on the same product.

The acknowledgement of the need to resolve implementation issues is another feather in India's cap. We had to highlight these issues since the industrialised world was misusing and misinterpreting rules much to the detriment of the developing countries. In view of our consistent emphasis on these issues and concerns, a time-bound programme has now been cleared to resolve all implementation issues. Some of these issues will be directly taken up for negotiation while others have been referred to subsidiary bodies for their report by the end of 2002. Many of these issues concern least developed countries (LDC) and we had thrown our lot with them.

India is a sovereign, independent, democratic republic. Our views are independent. What we do at negotiations is a matter of strategy. We negotiated for safeguarding our national interests. There is no question of losing when it comes to national interests. We can accept only a win or a win-win situation. Secret deals are not in the interest of multilateral trade policies. We already have regional trade agreements where bilateral pacts make all the difference.

We have very little experience in dealing with competition laws. Therefore, we are not in a position to take up obligations now. Is it possible to give national treatment if, for example, Coke and Pepsi, transnational giants with a turnover of billions of dollars, come together? Under Indian laws, it is possible to treat such unusual situations differently. All argument in favour of investment, competition and transparency in government procurement is valid in an ideal world. Unfortunately, we are not living in an ideal world. Is the WTO in a position to take up all these issues? *It will crumble under its own weight if we try to convert WTO into a global government.*

We know that we have to ultimately reform, open up and lower tariffs for our own good. But do not coerce us, let us do it on our own. If we rush with provisions like transparency in government procurement, developing countries may have to close down a number of public sector undertakings. Our tendering norms are already on par with global standards. Look at the problems we face: whenever there is a scam, we now go to Parliament or the Supreme Court. If new issues are taken on board the WTO, we may have to go to Geneva every time to face dispute settlement. For the time being, let us study these issues. Once the study is completed, we can reach conclusions.

Trade facilitation looks simple but is fraught with complexities. First of all, what is the aim of the agreement: who will it facilitate? The industrialised world exports 80 per cent of the goods imported by developing countries? We have to first build our capacity to facilitate trade and then go in for such agreements. We do not even know how many crores it will take to build the necessary infrastructure. If we get into such an agreement, somebody will drag us to the dispute settlement body if a computer in, say Kanpur or Surat, does not function. We are not in a position to face such situations now.

That is the reason why we decided to opt out of concensus, withdrawing our support to the ministerial declaration. The clarification from the chairman, Qatar's finance, economy and trade minister Youssef Hussain Kamal, states clearly that every WTO member will have the veto power against negotiations on new issues. It is part of the official text. Only after this we rejoined concensus to clear the ministerial declaration.

From statements made by the Commerce Minister, Shri Murasoli Maran.

12

WTO Ministerial Declaration at DOHA

Ministers from 144 countries agreed on Wednesday, the 14th November, 2001, to launch a broad series of trade liberalisation talks. The following are the excerpts of the approved ministerial declaration.*

We hereby agree to undertake the broad and balanced work programme set out below. This incorporates both an expanded negotiating agenda and other important decisions and activities necessary to address the challenges facing the multilateral trading system.

WORK PROGRAMME

Implementation-Related Issues and Concerns

We attach the utmost importance to the implementation-related issues and concerns raised by members and are determined to find appropriate solutions to them. In this connection, and having regard to the General Council Decisions of May 3 and December 15, 2000, we further adopt the decision on implementation-related issues and concerns in document WT/MIN(01)/W/10 to address a number of implementation problems faced by the members. We agree that negotiations on outstanding implementation issues shall be an integral part of the Work Programme we are establishing, and that agreements reached at an early stage in these negotiations

* Reuters

shall be treated in accordance with the provisions in this document. In this regard, we shall proceed as follows: (a) where we provide a specific negotiating mandate in this Declaration, the relevant implementation issues shall be addressed under that mandate; (b) the other outstanding implementation issues shall be addressed as a matter of priority by the relevant WTO bodies, which shall report to the Trade Negotiations Committee by the end of 2002 for appropriate action.

Agriculture

We recognise the work already undertaken in the negotiations initiated in early 2000 under Article 20 of the Agreement on Agriculture, including the large number of negotiating proposals submitted on behalf of a total of 121 members. We recall the long-term objective referred to in the Agreement to establish a fair and market-oriented trading system through a programme of fundamental reform encompassing strengthened rules and specific commitments on support and protection in order to correct and prevent restrictions and distortions in world agricultural markets. We reconfirm our commitment to this programme. Building on the work carried out to date and without prejudging the outcome of the negotiations we commit ourselves to comprehensive negotiations aimed at: substantial improvement in market access; reductions of, with a view to phasing out, all forms of export subsidies; and substantial reductions in trade-distorting domestic support. We agree that special and differential treatment for developing countries shall be an integral part of all elements of the negotiations and shall be embodied in the schedules of concessions and commitments and as appropriate in the rules and disciplines to be negotiated, so as to be operationally effective and to enable developing countries to effectively take account of their development needs, including food security and rural development. We take note of the non-trade concerns reflected in the negotiating proposals submitted by members and confirm that non-trade concerns will be taken into account in the negotiations as provided for in the Agreement On Agriculture.

Modalities for the further commitments, including provisions for special and differential treatment, shall be established no later than March 31, 2003. Participants shall submit their comprehensive draft schedules based on these modalities no later than the date of the Fifth Session of the Ministerial Conference. The negotiations, including with respect to rules and disciplines and related legal texts, shall be concluded as part and at the date of conclusion of the negotiating agenda as whole.

Services

The negotiations on trade in services shall be conducted with a view to promoting the economic growth of all trading partners and the development of developing and least-developed countries. We recognise the work already undertaken in the negotiations, initiated in January 2000 under Article XIX of the General Agreement on Trade in Services, and the large number proposals submitted by Members on a wide range of sectors and several horizontal issues, as well as on movement of natural persons. We reaffirm the Guidelines and Procedures for the Negotiations adopted by the Council for Trade in Services on March 28, 2001 as the basis for continuing the negotiations, with a view to achieving the objectives of the General Agreement on Trade in Services, as stipulated in the Preamble, Article IV and Article XIX of that Agreement. Participants shall submit initial requests for specific commitments by June 30, 2002 and initial offers by March 31, 2003.

Market Access for Non-Agricultural Products

We agree to negotiations which shall aim, by modalities to be agreed, to reduce or as appropriate eliminate tariffs, including the reduction or elimination of tariff peaks, high tariffs and tariff escalation, as well as non-tariff barriers, in particular on products of export interest to developing countries. Product coverage shall be comprehensive and without "a priori" exclusions. The negotiations shall take fully into account the special needs and interests of developing and least-developed country participants, including through less than full reciprocity in reduction commitments, in accordance with the relevant provisions of Article XXVIII "bis" of GATT 1994 and the provisions cited below. To this end, the modalities to be agreed will include appropriate studies and capacity-building measures to assist least-developed countries to participate effectively in the negotiations.

Trade-Related Aspects of Intellectual Property Rights

We stress the importance we attach to implementation and interpretation of the Agreement on Trade Related Aspects of Intellectual Property Rights (TRIPS Agreement) in a manner supportive of public health, by promoting both access to existing medicines and research and development into new medicines and, in this connection, are adopting a separate Declaration.

With a view to completing the work started in the Council for Trade-Related Aspects of Intellectual Property Rights (Council for TRIPS) on the implementation of Article 23.4, we agree to negotiate the establishment of a multilateral system of notification and registration of geographical indications for wines and spirits by the Fifth Session of the Ministerial Conference. We note that issues related to the extension of the protection of geographical indications provided for in Article 23 to products other than wines and spirits will be addressed in the Council for TRIPS pursuant to paragraph 12 of the Declaration.

We instruct the Council for TRIPS, in pursuing its work programme including under the review of Article 27.3(b), the review of the implementation of the TRIPS Agreement under Article 71.1 and the work foreseen pursuant of this Declaration, to examine "inter alia", the relationship between the TRIPS Agreement and the Convention on Biological Diversity, the protection of traditional knowledge and folklore, and other relevant new developments raised by Members pursuant to Article 71.1. In undertaking this work, the TRIPS Council shall be guided by the objectives and principles set out in Articles 7 and 8 of the TRIPS Agreement and shall take fully into account the development dimension.

Relationship Between Trade and Investment

Recognising the case for a multilateral framework to secure transparent stable and predictable conditions for long-term cross-border investment, particularly foreign direct investment, that will contribute to the expansion of trade, and the need for enhanced technical assistance and capacity-building in this area, we agree that negotiations will take place after the Fifth Session of the Ministerial Conference on the basis of a decision to be taken, by explicit consensus, at that session on modalities of negotiations.

We recognise the needs of developing and least-developed countries for enhanced support for technical assistance and capacity building in this area, including policy analysis and development so that they may better evaluate the implications of closer multilateral cooperation for their development policies and objectives, and human and institutional development. To this end, we shall work in cooperation with other relevant Intergovernmental organisations, including UNCTAD, and through appropriate regional and bilateral channels, to provide strengthened and adequately resourced assistance to respond to these needs.

In the period until the Fifth Session, further work in the Working Group on the Relationship Between Trade and Investment will focus on the clarification of: scope and definition; transparency: non-discrimination; modalities for pre-establishment commitments based on a GATS-type, positive list approach; development provisions; exceptions and balance-of-payments safeguards; consultation and the settlement of disputes between members. Any framework should reflect in a balanced manner the interests of home and host countries, and take due account of the development policies and objectives of host governments as well as their right to regulate in the public interest. The special development, trade and financial needs of developing and least-developed countries should be taken into account as an integral part of any framework, which should enable members to undertake obligations and commitments commensurate with their individual needs and circumstances. Due regard should be paid to other relevant WTO provisions. Account should be taken, as appropriate, of existing bilateral and regional arrangements on investment.

Interaction Between Trade and Competition Policy

Recognising the case for a multilateral framework to enhance the contribution of competition policy to international trade and development, and the need for enhanced technical assistance and capacity-building in this area, we agree that negotiations will take place after the Fifth Session of the Ministerial Conference on the basis of a decision to be taken, by explicit consensus, at that Session on modalities of negotiations.

We recognise the needs of developing and least-developed countries for enhanced support for technical assistance and capacity-building in this area, including policy analysis and development so that they may better evaluate the implications of closer multilateral cooperation for their development policies and objectives, and human and institutional development. To this end, we shall work in cooperation with other relevant intergovernmental organisations, including UNCTAD, and through appropriate regional and bilateral channels, to provide strengthened and adequately resourced assistance to respond to these needs.

In the period until the Fifth Session, further work in the Working Group and the Interaction between Trade and Competition Policy will focus on the clarification of: core principles, including transparency, non-discrimination and procedural fairness, and provisions on hardcore cartels; modalities for voluntary cooperation; and support for progressive reinforcement of competition institution in developing countries through capacity building. Full account shall be taken of the needs of developing and least-developed country participants and appropriate flexibility provided to address them.

Transparency in Government Procurement

Recognising the case for a multilateral agreement on transparency in government procurement and the need for enhanced technical assistance and capacity building in this area, we agree that negotiations will take place after the Fifth Session of the Ministerial Conference on the basis of a decision to be taken, by explicit consensus, at that session on modalities of negotiations. These negotiations will build on the progress made in the Working Group on Transparency in Government Procurement by that time and take into account participants' development priorities, especially those of least-developed country participants. Negotiations shall be limited to the transparency aspects and therefore will not restrict the scope for countries to give preferences to domestic supplies and suppliers. We commit ourselves to ensuring adequate technical assistance and support for capacity building both during the negotiations and after their conclusion.

Trade Facilitation

Recognising the case for further expediting the movement, release and clearance of goods, including goods in transit, and the need for enhanced technical assistance and capacity building in this area, we agree that negotiations will take place after the Fifth Session of the Ministerial Conference on the basis of a decision to be taken, by explicit consensus, at that session on modalities of negotiations. In the period until the Fifth Session, the Council for Trade in Goods shall review and as appropriate, clarify and improve relevant aspects of Articles V, VIII and X of the GATT 1994 and identify the trade facilitation needs and priorities of Members, in particular developing and least-developed countries. We commit ourselves to ensuring adequate technical assistance and support for capacity building in this area.

WTO Rules

In the light of experience and of the increasing application of these instruments by Members, we agree to negotiations aimed at clarifying and improving disciplines under the Agreements on Implementation of Article VI of the GATT 1994 and on Subsidies and Countervailing Measures, while preserving the basic concepts, principles and effectiveness of these agreements and their instruments and objectives, and taking into account the needs of developing and least-developed participants. In the initial phase of the negotiations, participants will indicate the provisions, including disciplines on trade distorting practices, that they seek to clarify and improve in the subsequent phase. In the context of these negotiations, participants shall also aim to clarify and improve WTO disciplines on fisheries subsidies, taking into account the importance of this sector to developing countries.

We also agree to negotiations aimed at clarifying and improving disciplines and procedures under the existing WTO provisions applying to regional trade agreements. The negotiations shall take into account the developmental aspects of regional trade agreements.

Dispute Settlement Understanding

We agree to negotiations on improvements and clarifications

of the Dispute Settlement Understanding. The negotiations should be based on the work done thus far as well as any additional proposals by Members, and aim to agree on improvements and clarifications not later than May 2003, at which time we will take steps to ensure that the results enter into force as soon as possible thereafter.

Trade and Environment

With a view to enhancing the mutual supportiveness of trade and environment, we agree to negotiations, without prejudging their outcome, on:

(i) the relationship between existing WTO rules and specific trade obligations set out in multilateral environmental agreements (MEAs). The negotiations shall be limited in scope to the applicability of such existing WTO rules as among parties to the MEA in question. The negotiations shall not prejudice the WTO rights of any Member that is not a party to the MEA in question;

(ii) procedures for regular information exchange between MEA Secretariats and the relevant WTO committees, and the criteria for the granting of observer status;

(iii) the reduction or, as appropriate, elimination of tariff and non-tariff barriers to environmental goods and services.

We note that fisheries subsidies form part of the negotiations.

We instruct the Committee on Trade and Environment, in pursuing work on all items on its agenda within its current terms of reference, to give particular attention to.

(i) the effect of environmental measures on market access, especially in relation to developing countries, in particular the least-developed among them, and those situations in which the elimination or reduction of trade restrictions and distortions would benefit trade, the environment and development;

(ii) the relevant provisions of the Agreement on Trade-Related Aspects of Intellectual Property Rights; and

(iii) labelling requirements for environmental purposes.

Work on these issues should include the identification of any need to clarify relevant WTO rules. The Committee shall report to the Fifth Session of the Ministerial Conference, and make recommendations, where appropriate, with respect to future action, including the desirability of negotiations. The outcome of this work as well as the negotiations carried out under paragraph 31 (i) and (ii) shall be compatible with the open and non-discriminatory nature of the multilateral trading system, shall not add to or diminish the rights and obligations of members under existing WTO agreements, in particular the Agreement on the Application of Sanitary and Phytosanitary Measures, nor alter the balance of these rights and obligations, and will take into account the needs of developing and least-developed countries.

We recognise the importance of technical assistance and capacity building in the field of trade and environment to developing countries, in particular the least-developed among them. We also encourage that expertise and experience be shared with members wishing to perform environmental reviews at the national level. A report shall be prepared on these activities for the Fifth Session.

Electronic Commerce

We take note of the work which has been done in the General Council and other relevant bodies since the Ministerial Declaration of May 20, 1998 and agree to continue the Work Programme on Electronic Commerce. The work to date demonstrates that electronic commerce creates new challenges and opportunities for trade for members at all stages of development, and we recognise the importance of creating and maintaining an environment which is favourable to the future development of electronic commerce. We instruct the General Council to consider the most appropriate institutional arrangements for handling the Work Programme, and to report on further progress to the Fifth Session of the Ministerial Conference. We declare that members will maintain their current practice of not imposing customs duties on electronic transmissions until the Fifth Session.

Small Economies

We agree to a work programme, under the auspices of the General Council, to examine issues relating to the trade of small economics. The objective of this work is to frame responses to the trade-related issues identified for the fuller integration of small, vulnerable economies into the multilateral trading system, and not to create a sub-category of WTO Members. The General Council shall review the work programmes and make recommendations for action to the Fifth Session of the Ministerial Conference.

Trade, Debt and Finance

We agree to an examination, in a Working Group under the auspices of the General Council, of the relationship between trade, debt and finance, and of any possible recommendations on steps that might be taken within the mandate and competence of the WTO to enhance the capacity of the multilateral trading system to contribute to a durable solution to the problem of external indebtedness of developing and least-developed countries, and to strengthen the coherence of international trade and financial policies, with a view to safeguarding the multilateral trading system from the effects of financial and monetary instability. The General Council shall report to the Fifth Session of the Ministerial Conference on progress in the examination.

Trade and Transfer of Technology

We agree to an examination, in a Working Group under the auspices of the General Council, of the relationship between trade and transfer of technology, and of any possible recommendations on steps that might be taken within the mandate of the WTO to increase flows of technology to developing countries. The General Council shall report to the Fifth Session of the Ministerial Conference on progress in the examination.

Technical Cooperation and Capacity Building

We confirm that technical cooperation and capacity building are core elements of the development dimension of the multilateral trading system, and we welcome and endorse the New Strategy for WTO Technical Cooperation for Capacity Building, Growth and Integration. We instruct the Secretariat, in coordination with other relevant agencies, to support domestic efforts for mainstreaming trade into national plans for economic development and strategies for poverty reduction. The delivery of WTO technical assistance shall be designed to assist developing and least-developed countries and low-income countries in transition to adjust to WTO rules and disciplines, implement obligations and exercise the rights of membership, including drawing on the benefits of an open, rules-based multilateral trading system. Priority shall also be accorded to small, vulnerable, and transition economics, as well as to members and observers without representation in Geneva. We reaffirm our support for the valuable work of the International Trade Centre, which should be enhanced.

We underscore, the urgent necessity for the effective coordinated delivery of technical assistance with bilateral donors, in the OECD Development Assistance Committee and relevant international and regional intergovernmental institutions, with in a coherent policy framework and timetable. In the coordinated delivery of technical assistance, we instruct the Director-General to consult with the relevant agencies, bilateral donors and beneficiaries, to identify ways of enhancing and rationalising the Integrated Framework for Trade-Related Technical Assistance to Least-Developed Countries and the Joint Integrated Technical Assistance Programme (JITAP).

We agree that there is a need for technical assistance to benefit from secure and predictable funding. We therefore instruct the Committee on Budget, Finance and Administration to develop a plan for adoption by the General Council in December 2001 that will ensure long-term funding for WTO technical assistance at an overall level no lower than that of the current year and commensurate with the activities outlines above.

We have established firm commitments on technical cooperation and capacity building in various paragraphs in this Ministerial Declaration. We instruct the Director-General to report to the Fifth Session of the Ministerial Conference, with an interim report to the General Council in December 2002 on the implementation and adequacy of these commitments in the identified paragraphs.

Least-Developed Countries

We acknowledge the seriousness of the concerns expressed by the least-developed countries (LDCs) in the Zanzibar Declaration adopted by their ministers in July 2001. We recognise that the integration of the LDCs into the multilateral trading system requires meaningful market access, support for the diversification of their production and export base, and trade-related technical assistance and capacity building. We agree that the meaningful integration of LDCs into the trading system and the global economy will involve efforts by all WTO members. We commit ourselves to the objective of duty-free, quota-free market access for products originating from LDCs. In this regard, we welcome the significant market access improvements by WTO members in advance of the Third UN Conference on LDCs (LDC-III), in Brussels, May 2001. We further commit ourselves to consider additional measures for progressive improvements in market access for LDCs. Accession of LDCs remains a priority for the membership. We agree to work to facilitate and accelerate negotiations with acceding LDCs. We instruct the secretariat to reflect the priority we attach to LDCs' accession in the annual plans for technical assistance. We reaffirm the commitments we undertook at LDC-III, and agree that the WTO should take into account, in designing its work programme for LDC, the trade-related elements of the Brussels Declaration and Programme of Action, consistent with the WTO's mandate, adopted at LDC-III. We instruct the Sub-Committee for Least-Developed Countries to design such a work programme and to report on the agreed work programme to the General Council at its first meeting in 2002.

We endorse the Integrated Framework for Trade-Related Technical Assistance to Least-Developed Countries (IF) as a viable model for LDCs' trade development. We urge development partners to significantly increase contributions to the IF Trust Fund and WTO extra-budgetary trust funds in favour of LDCs. We urge the core agencies, in coordination with development partners, to explore the enhancement of the IF with a view to addressing the supply-side constraints of LDCs and the extension of the model to all LDCs, following the review of the IF and the appraisal of the ongoing Pilot Scheme in selected LDCs. We request the Director-General, following coordination with heads of the other agencies, to provide an interim report to the General Council in December 2002 and a full report to the Fifth Session of the Ministerial Conference on all issues affecting LDCs.

Special and Differential Treatment

We reaffirm that provisions for special and differential treatment are an integral part of the WTO Agreements. We note the concerns expressed regarding their operation in addressing specific constraints faced by developing countries, particularly least-developed countries. In that connection, we also note that some members have proposed a Framework Agreement on Special and Differential Treatment (WT/GC/W/442). We therefore agree that all special and differential treatment provisions shall be reviewed with a view to strengthening them and making them more precise, effective and operational. In this connection, we endorse the work programme on special and differential treatment set out in the Decision on Implementation-Related Issues and Concerns.

Organisation and Management of the Work Programme

The negotiations to be pursued under the terms of this Declaration shall be concluded not later than 1 January 2005. The Fifth Session of the Ministerial Conference will take stock of progress in the negotiations, provide any necessary political guidance, and take decisions as necessary. When the results of the negotiations in all areas have been established, a Special Session of the Ministerial Conference will be held to take decisions regarding the adoption and implementation of those results.

The overall conduct of the negotiations shall be supervised by a Trade Negotiations Committee under the authority of the General Council. The Trade Negotiations Committee shall hold its first meeting not later than 31 January 2002. It shall establish appropriate negotiating mechanisms as required and supervise the progress of the negotiations.

With the exception of the improvements and clarifications of the Dispute Settlement Understanding, the conduct, conclusion and entry into force of the outcome of the negotiations shall be treated as parts of a single undertaking. However, agreements reached at an early stage may be implemented on a provisional or a definitive basis. Early agreements shall be taken into account in assessing the overall balance of the negotiations.

Negotiations shall be open to:

(i) all Members of the WTO; and

(ii) States and separate customs territories currently in the process of accession and those that inform Members, at a regular meeting of the General Council, of their intention to negotiate the terms of their membership and for whom an accession working party is established.

Decisions on the outcomes of the negotiations shall be taken only by WTO Members.

The negotiations shall be conducted in a transparent manner among participants, in order to facilitate the effective participation of all. They shall be conducted with a view to ensuring benefits to all participants and to achieving an overall balance in the outcome of the negotiations.

Th negotiations and the other aspects of the Work Programme shall take fully into account the principle of special and differential treatment for developing and least-developed countries embodied in: Part IV of the GATT 1994; the Decisions of 28 November 1979 on Differential and More Favourable Treatment, Reciprocity and Fuller Participation of Developing Countries; the Uruguay Round Decision on Measures in Favour of Least-Developed Countries; and all other relevant WTO provisions.

The Committee on Trade and Development and the Committee on Trade and Environment shall, within their respective mandates, each act as a forum to identify and debate developmental and environmental aspects of the negotiations, in order to help achieve the objective of having sustainable development appropriately reflected.

Those elements of the Work Programme which do not involve negotiations are also accorded a high priority. They shall be pursued under the overall supervision of the General Council, which shall report on progress to the Fifth Session of the Ministerial Conference.

13

Shifts in Industrial Policy Paradigm

C. RANGARAJAN

Given the historical developments world over, it is not surprising that growth was identified with industrialization in all the developing economies. The Indian planners went a step further and talked of industrialization with an emphasis on heavy industries. It was, no doubt, recognized that for the process of industrialization to start, there has to be a transfer of resources from agriculture. That inadequate agricultural growth and insufficient availability of wage goods including foodgrains could act as a restraint on industrial growth was realised only later. The industry-agriculture relationship was mainly seen in terms of agriculture making available the required raw materials. Once again, the recognition of the importance of agricultural growth and rural incomes as a source of demand for industrial goods, thereby fueling industrial growth, came later.

The process of industrialization in India in the first four decades was governed by two considerations – import substitution and industrial licensing. Import substitution constituted a major plank of India's foreign trade policy and, therefore, of industrialization. Planners, more or less, chose to ignore the option of foreign trade as an engine of India's economic growth. This was primarily due to the highly pessimistic view taken on the potential for export earnings. A further impetus to the inward orientation was provided by the existence of a vast domestic market. In retrospect, it is clear that the policy makers not only under-estimated the export possibilities but also the import intensity of the import substitution process itself. As a consequence, India's share of total world exports declined from 1.91 per cent in 1950 to about 0.53 per cent in 1992.

The inward looking industrialization process did result in high rates of industrial growth between 1956 and 1966. However, several weaknesses of such a process of industrialization soon became evident, as inefficiencies crept into the system and the economy turned into an increasingly 'high-cost' one. Over a period of time, this led to a 'technological lag' and also resulted in poor export performance.

Foreign trade policy issues became the subject of intensive discussion in early eighties. It came to be realised that a scheme of import licensing under which imports were permitted only to the extent that domestic production fell short of domestic demand irrespective of differences in cost and prices, could only lead to inefficiency. The view gained ground that a more liberal policy of imports of capital goods and technology would enable India to reap the benefits of international division of labour. The attempt, therefore, was to move away from import substitution *per se* towards efficient import substitution, so that considerations relating to cost and efficiency were incorporated in the overall policy framework. It also became increasingly clear that production for export could not be isolated from production for the home market.

Another important element in the process of industrialization was a system of industrial licensing under which a license was required before setting up any large unit. This practice had roots in the belief that resources could be best allocated only by a planning authority and that licensing was the best way to manage limited resources. While the industrial licensing system underwent some changes in terms of threshold levels and types of products, it formed an essential part of Government policy until the end of the 80s.

Commenting on the process of industrialization until the end of 80s, Prof. K.L. Krishna wrote: "Since independence, industrial policy in India has stressed rapid industrial growth with diversification of the industrial structure as one of the important objectives of industrialization. There is general agreement that while India has achieved a very diversified industrial structure, her growth performance leaves much to be desired, both with regard to the magnitude of the growth rate and its stability over time. Three phases of growth have been distinguished: a phase of rapid growth from the early 1950s to the mid-1960s; a phase of deceleration from the mid-1960s to late 1970s; and a phase of revival in the late 1970s followed by rapid growth in the 1980s".

The year 1991 is an important landmark in the economic history of post Independent India. The country went through a severe economic crisis triggered by a serious balance of payments situation. The crisis was converted into an opportunity to introduce some fundamental changes in the content and approach to economic policy. The response to the crisis was to put in place a set of policies aimed at stabilization and structural reform. While the stabilisation policies were aimed at correcting the weaknesses that had developed on the fiscal and the balance of payments fronts, the structural reforms sought to remove the rigidities that had entered into the various segments of the Indian economy. The structural reforms introduced in the early Nineties broadly covered the areas of industrial licensing, foreign trade, foreign investment, exchange rate management and the financial sector. From the point of view of industrialization, changes in the areas of licensing and foreign trade and investment had important implications. Even before the onset of reforms the problems associated with industrial licensing were well recognised. The approach document of the Eighth Plan submitted in May, 1990 had remarked: "A return to the regime of direct, indiscriminate and detailed controls in industry is clearly out of question. Past experience has shown that such control system is not effective in achieving the desired objective. Also the system is widely abused and leads to corruption, delays and insufficiency". One early step that was undertaken as part of the structural reform process was to dispense with licensing. Changes in foreign trade policy focussed on reducing the tariff rates and dismantling quantitative controls over imports. The tariff rates have been brought down in stages. Some caution in this regard becomes necessary to enable the Indian industries set up behind high protective tariff walls to adjust to the changed situation. The policy towards foreign investment underwent a significant change with foreign investors given the freedom to own majority share holding over a wide spectrum of industries.

Without going into details, the common thread running through the various policy measures introduced since 1991 has been the improvement of the efficiency of the system. The regulatory mechanism involving multitudes of controls had fragmented capacity and reduced competition even in the private sector. The thrust of the New Economic Policy has been towards creating a more competitive environment in the economy as a means to improving the productivity and efficiency of the system. This is to be achieved by removing the barriers to entry and the restrictions on the growth of firms. While the Industrial Policy seeks to bring about a greater competitive environment domestically, the Trade Policy seeks to improve the international competitiveness subject to the degree of protection offered by the tariffs. Private sector is being given a larger space to operate in as much as some of the areas reserved exclusively earlier for the public sector are now allowed to private sector. In these areas, the public sector will have to compete with the private sector, even though the public sector may continue to play the dominant role. What is sought to be achieved is an improvement in the functioning of the various entities, whether they be in the private or public sector.

Judged by the standard criteria of growth rates in national income and per capita income, the Indian economy has done well since liberalisation. Between 1992-93 and 1998-99 the average annual growth rate was 6.55 per cent. This is even higher than the previous high of 6.04 per cent achieved between 1985-86 and 1989-90. Between 1992-93 and 1999-2000, there is no year in which the growth rate has been less than five per cent. The coefficient of variation of growth rate has been lower than in the 80s. The average annual per capita income growth rate between 1992-93 and 1998-99 has been 4.7 per cent as compared with a growth rate of 3.4 per cent in the eighties. There has, thus, been a significant step up in terms of the per capita income growth rate. The current account deficit has remained low and averaged only 1.3 per cent of GDP, since 1992-93.

The average growth rate of industrial production since 1992-93 has been 6.4 per cent. This is lower than the growth rate of 7.5

per cent in industrial production in the 80s. However, in terms of value added in industry, the growth rate in the 90s works-out to 6.62 per cent which is a shade higher than the growth rate of 6.55 per cent in the 80s. The distinctively higher growth rate in GDP in the 90s has been because of the sharp increase in the growth rate of services. The share of the services sector in the gross domestic product has increased by 7 percentage points in the Nineties to reach 47.10 per cent in 1999-2000.

The liberalisation process has come in for criticism from two opposite ends. There are those who feel that the process has been slow and not sufficiently comprehensive. At the other end, there are critics who view the reform process as misconceived, ignoring the basic requirements of the people. While it is accepted that the growth rate in the post reform period has generally been higher, some concerns have been expressed about the slower growth rate in agriculture, lesser impact on poverty, reduction in capital expenditures of Government, lack of adequate investment in social infrastructure and growing disparities in growth rates among States. Some of these criticisms have a validity and some others do not. Some are related to the liberalisation process. Others are not. Obviously the reform process must take into account these criticisms. Reforms have not reduced the role of the state. In some areas, the role has expanded and some others, it has contracted. As has been, somewhat paradoxically, remarked "More market does not mean less government but only different government". The need for expanded state intervention in areas of education, health and sanitation cannot be underestimated. But it is only an efficient economy which will generate the necessary surplus which will enable the state to fulfil its socio-economic obligations. Efficiency and equity should not be posed as opposing considerations.

Changes in the foreign trade and foreign investment policies have altered the environment in which Indian industries have to operate. The path of transition is, no doubt, difficult. A greater integration of the Indian economy with the rest of the world is unavoidable. We must recognise that there are many countries which are knocking on the doors of the WTO to enter. It is important that the Indian industry be forward looking and get organised to compete with the rest of the world at levels of tariff comparable to those of other developing countries. Obviously, the Indian Government should be alert to ensure that Indian industries are not the victims of unfair trade practices. The safeguards available in the WTO agreement must be fully utilised to protect the interests of Indian industries. India must take a proactive stand in the next round of trade negotiations and articulate its own demands, focussing on what it wants from the global trading system, such as prohibition of unilateral trade action, establishing symmetry between the movement of capital and natural persons and zero tariffs in industrialized countries on labour intensive exports of developing countries.

There have been some concerns on the slackening of the growth of the industrial production particularly in the current year. The growth rate is still reasonable because of the utilisation of the higher capacities created earlier. The three years beginning 1994-95 were marked by high rates of growth of industrial production. This was also the period during which the investment rate remained high. In 1998-99, which is the latest year for which data on savings and investment are available, the gross domestic savings rate had declined by 2.4 percentage points. With current account deficit as percentage of GDP remaining more or less at the same level, there has been a decline in the aggregate investment rate as well. The decline in the savings rate is highest in relation to public sector. The savings rate of the public sector which comprises of both Government administration and public sector enterprises is estimated at zero. In the final analysis, investment is the major driving force of growth. All investment decisions are, however, based on future prospects. Continuity of economic policy thus becomes key to sustaining expectations in the right direction. This can happen only, if there is a consensus on the core elements of the economic policy among the political parties and policy makers. Such a consensus will pave the way for the economy to achieve higher levels of investment and growth.

Inaugural address at the Conference to honour Prof. K.L. Krishna, Industrialization in a Reforming Economy: A Quantitative Assessment, December 20, 2000, Delhi School of Economics, Delhi.

14

Economic Reforms and Indian Agriculture

Long Term Issues and Recent Experience

V. S. VYAS • V. RATNA REDDY

I

INTRODUCTION

Liberalization has brought about a change in the basic orientation of development policies in the country by placing greater reliance on the markets for allocations of resources, emphasizing private initiative and encouraging domestic and global competition. Since the early nineties a package of economic reforms were introduced to set the stage for gradual liberalization and globalization, to reinvigorate the economy and to reap the benefits of world wide moves in these directions. These reforms were introduced, first as a part of stabilization policy and later to bring in structural adjustment. Stabilization of the economy was important to correct the distortions in key economic areas, but more far reaching results could come only from structural reforms in the economy. These reforms were directed more or less in a sequential order: first to industrial, then foreign trade and financial sectors.

Advisedly, the reforms in the agricultural sector have been slow and cautious for several reasons. Majority of the agricultural producers cultivate marginal and sub marginal holdings. Their dependence on the market for procurement of inputs and the sale of output is insubstantial. The strategic objectives related to these sections of rural population are the expansion of their meager production base, raising productivity of their existing resources, providing them with alternative sources of livelihood and protecting them from risks and uncertainties. Markets have a limited role to play in meeting these objectives. For the medium and the large farmers non-price factors, particularly technological and organizational factors, are more important to augment their production and fetch higher values for their produce. In any event, because of the economic and political power enjoyed by the medium and the large agricultural producers on the one hand, and the competitive, multi-party nature of our polity on the other, it is not easy to introduce reforms which may hurt the interests of this section.

For a large and poor country such as India food security considerations weigh heavily in determining agricultural policies. Comprehensive reforms which may jeopardize the prospects of food security for the rural and urban poor even in the short-run will not be accepted very easily. Besides, some of the major policy induced handicaps faced by agricultural producers were attended to even before the beginning of the reforms. For example, Indian agriculture was much less severely 'taxed' compared to several other developing countries. Agriculture's terms of trade vis-a-vis non-agricultural sector, though still adverse, were progressively improving (Nadkarni, 1993). Apart from these reasons, there was no urgency felt by the policy makers to institute reforms in the agricultural sector due to the complacency about agricultural growth prospects with ten successive good monsoons.

With the beginning of the current phase of reforms, changes in agricultural policies related mainly to agricultural trade and these too reflected rather short sighted and ad hoc considerations. For example, the 1995-96 Economic survey reported, "Rice and wheat are emerging as major export products. Quantitative ceiling and minimum export price in respect of rice have been abolished. To further enhance exports Food Corporation of India has been permitted to export/ sell for export 3 million tonnes of fine/ superfine varieties of rice. Export of wheat up to 2.5 million tonnes in case of non-durum wheat and 0.5 million tonnes in case of durum wheat has also been permitted." (Govt. of India, 1996, p. 41) . But the volatility of Indian agriculture was aptly reflected when the country instead of exporting food grains had to import 2 million tonnes of wheat by the end of 1996 itself. The story of over optimism and subsequent frustration is repeated, year after year, in the case of cotton, sugar and other agricultural commodities.

Due to the complacent attitude of the policy makers reinforced by the objective of reducing fiscal deficit as a part of the reform package, there has been a continuous decline in the public investment for capital formation in agriculture, as well as in the share of the priority sector lending by the public sector banks during the 90s (Mujumdar, 1999). These trends coupled with the ad hoc measures aimed at cutting down input subsidies, raising procurement prices and reducing the food subsidies, had serious, intended or unintended, consequences for agriculture sector in terms of changes in cropping pattern, input usage and commercialization of agriculture. It is necessary to understand the direction of these changes and their long term impact on the economy, especially in the light of the recent east and south east Asian experience (or the Asian crisis) which reemphasized the importance of food security and consequently of the agricultural sector.

This paper is an attempt to address some of the above questions. Firstly, we examine the impact of liberalization policies on agriculture. Next, an attempt is made to understand the likely impact of Asian Crisis on Indian agriculture. Finally, we try to draw lessons to reach the avowed goals of agricultural development.

II

ECONOMIC REFORMS AND AGRICULTURE

Exclusion of agriculture in any serious discussion on structural reforms in the developing countries is indefensible. It is the largest private sector in the developing economies; it produces tradable goods; as it is now well established, agricultural producers respond positively to economic signals. Yet, there is very little discussion on the implications of Structural Adjustment Policies (SAP) on agriculture in specific country context. Focus of reforms in the countries undergoing structural adjustment, as noted earlier, is mainly on industry and financial sectors. In this section we examine direction of macro as well as sectoral reforms in agriculture.

The Macro Scene

Economic reforms in India began in the early 1980s with progressive relaxation of controls on investment and capacity utilization in industry, liberalization of imports and, support to capital markets. It also comprised fiscal reforms, reforms in the public financial institutions and, realignment of external value of the rupee by gradual devaluation. However, the premises on which earlier policies were based, i.e., emphasis on self sufficiency, "commanding heights" for the parastatals, controls on the allocation and use of resources, regulations of markets, and the like, were not challenged. The reforms which were introduced from July 1991 and continuing since then, are qualitatively different. The underlying principles informing the current policies are: greater reliance on the markets for allocation of resources, emphasis on private initiative and, encouragement to domestic and global competition.

The economic reforms introduced in the country as a part of the stabilization policy and those to achieve structural adjustment are more or less on the expected lines. These measures have proved to be reasonably successful. India could tide over its balance of payments crisis swiftly and smoothly. The fiscal deficit in the central budget has come down from about 8 percent (of GDP) during 1990-91 to about 5 percent by the year 1995-96,but has become rigid thereafter. This resulted in high inflation rates in the initial years of reforms, though inflation seems to be under control in recent years. However, the cost of living index of the agricultural and rural workers increased much faster during these years indicating a disproportionately high burden of adjustment on the poor.

The reforms introduced in industrial, foreign trade and financial sectors have made a good beginning. Industrial licensing, quotas, and permits are gradually being abandoned. A liberalized foreign trade regime is being introduced, with closer links established between exports and imports; import duties are progressively lowered; rupee has been made partially convertible. Major changes have been effected in the financial sector by encouraging inflow of foreign capital, restructuring interest rates, greater autonomy to the financial institutions and strengthening their capital base. It goes to the credit of the reform policies in India that initial destabilization effects of the reforms such as a steep decline in GNP, upsurge in unemployment, major shifts in commodity prices, etc., could be largely contained. Process of deepening of the reforms in these sectors is continuing. Although it should be noted that the real and tougher issues like privatization of loss making public sector enterprises, or reforms in growth inhibiting labor policies, are yet to be tackled

Agricultural Policies

As in other developing countries – in fact, more so in developed countries – in India also, Government interventions in agricultural sector are quite extensive. The principal agricultural crops are subjected to a variety of administered price regimes (minimum prices, support prices, levy prices, issue prices, etc.). There are formal or informal restrictions on the movement of crops. Government agencies play an important role in marketing of agricultural inputs. Credit delivery is regulated as a part of overall financial controls. External trade in agricultural commodities is restricted or canalized through the parastatal organizations. At the same time, huge subsidies are expended to bring down the real prices of inputs for the agricultural producers.

In these and certain other areas, need for policy reforms has been felt since long. It has become more insistent with the adoption of the New Economic Policy in 1991. The types of policy changes advocated, and implemented to an extent, include removing restrictions on the movement of agricultural commodities (i.e., dezoning), reforms in domestic trade and stocking policies, reforms in the policies of administered prices, liberalization of trade in agricultural commodities – abolition of the quantitative restrictions and substitution, wherever necessary, by export and import tariffs

– revamping public distribution system and, gradual removal of input subsidies. However, in practice several measures reflect political compulsions rather than a part of well thought out, long term, growth strategy. The "stop-go" policies on cotton and rice exports and sugar imports are typical examples of the short term, ad hoc, approach.

Even though most of the policies are formulated at the central level their countrywide adoption depends on the cooperation from the state governments. As a result, although there is consensus on reducing input subsidies at the central level, so far the government could tinker with only fertilizer subsidies as most of the other major subsidies, such as subsidies on irrigation, power, etc., are in the purview of the state governments. Most of the state governments are not prepared to reduce these subsidies for political reasons. For example, Government of India has recommended that agricultural power tariff should be raised to Rs. 0.50 per unit, but very few states have implemented this recommendation. Similarly, irrigation subsidies are vertually untouched in most of the states, despite repeated suggestions for cost recovery through increase in water charges. True, privatization of some of the services in agricultural sector has been carried out in recent years. The areas of privatization include seed production, veterinary services, de-licensing of retail input supply, demonstrations and survey work. The focus of the reforms at the states level is to enlarge the scope of privatization. There is very little evidence to ensure cost recovery for inputs and services provided by the state.

Impact of Policy Changes

The policy changes at the macro level and those instituted at the sectoral level seem to have made some impact on agricultural growth, but more importantly on the dynamics of production relations. The impact may be discussed at two levels. Firstly, the impact of macro policy reforms especially the attempts to curtail budgetary deficits and realign the value of domestic currencies on agricultural sector could be looked into. Secondly, we may examine the impact of sectoral policies addressed to agriculture. Latter would include agricultural price policies, subsidy policies, trade policies, credit policies, etc. These two sets of impacts are overlapping. Our main attention however, is on second aspect of economic policies, i.e. the sectoral policies in Agriculture. As a backdrop we review the overall growth of agriculture sector, its contribution to GDP and plan allocation and capital formation in agriculture.

Sectoral Performance

Indian agriculture was characterized by low and stagnant growth performance till the mid sixties. The performance improved from then on till the end of eighties (Table–1).

Table – 1

Average Compound Growth Rates of GDP and by Sectors During 1980s and 90s.

Year	GDP	Agriculture	Industry	Manufacturing	Services	Per capita GNP
1980-90	5.8	3.1	7.1	7.4	6.7	3.4*
1990-96	5.8	3.1	6.8	7.5	7.0	4.9#

Note : GDP= Gross domestic Product.

* Per capita Gross National Product (GNP) is the average of Sixth (1980-85) and Seventh (1985-90).

\# Per Capita GNP pertains to Eighth Plan (1992-97).

Source : CMIE, Agriculture, 1996; Economic Survey, 1996-97.

The nineties have seen a deceleration of the rate of growth in agricultural output. Agriculture maintained a rate of growth of 3.1 percent during the 80s as well as in the 90s. Though the other sectors have recorded high growth rates in the 80s as well as the 90s, in their case also there was no significant difference in performance over two decades. A distinguishing feature in the case of agricultural output is sharp year to year fluctuations. These high variations imply unpredictable nature of agriculture in India and the precariousness of our food security position.

The share of agriculture in GDP is declining steadily, still it continues to contribute nearly thirty percent of the GDP (Table–2). It is interesting to note that agriculture's share in work force is not declining despite its declining importance in GDP (Table–3). This indicates that more and more people are depending on agricultural activities. It also suggests low absorption capacity of the secondary and tertiary sectors. Figures of employment in the rural areas in general, and agriculture in particular, should be interpreted with caution, due to the short interval between two estimates cited in the above table. However, the fact remains that agriculture still employs nearly two thirds of the country's work force. This coupled with declining share of agriculture in GDP

Table – 2

Macro Economic Indicators Relating to Indian Agriculture

Year	GDP Value (in Rs. crores)*	GDP growth rate	Agricultural GDP*	Agricultural GDP growth rate	Share of agriculture in GDP	Capital formation in agriculture (% of GDP)	% of agriculture in Total outlay
1989-90	201453	6.89	67064	1.99	33.29	25.0	5.6
1990-91	212253	5.36	69860	4.17	32.91	27.7	5.5
1991-92	213983	0.82	68480	–1.98	32.00	23.4	6.2
1992-93	225240	5.26	72421	5.75	32.15	23.9	5.8
1993-94	799077	—	262140	—	32.80	22.4	4.8
1994-95	861064	7.76	277033	5.68	32.17	25.4	5.5
1995-96	926412	7.59	279204	0.78	30.14	25.8	4.7
1996-97	998978	7.83	303572	8.72	30.39	25.7	4.9
1997-98	1049191	5.03	301436	-0.70	28.73	24.8	4.5
1998-99	—	—	—	—	—	—	3.7

Note: * GDP figures till 1992-93 are based on old series with 1980-81 base and from 1993-94 are based on new series with 1993-94 base.

Source: Economic Survey of Various years, Government of India.

Table – 3

Shares of Workforce by Agriculture and Non-agriculture.

Sector	Rural		Urban		Total	
	1989-90	1992	1989-90	1992	1989-90	1992
1. Agriculture	75.1	79.4	13.0	13.2	62.1	65.5
2. Non-agriculture	24.9	20.7	87.0	86.8	37.9	34.5
of Which						
Secondary	12.2	9.5	31.5	33.7	16.2	14.6
Tertiary	12.7	11.1	55.4	53.1	21.7	19.6

Source: Natarajan and Patnaik (1999).

indicates low labour productivity and or adverse terms of trade faced by the sector. The sector's adverse position is also reflected in the rise in the percentage of rural population below poverty line between 1990-91 and 1993-94. The rural population below poverty line was at 34.4 percent in 1988-89, which went up to 44 percent in 1991-92 and came down to 37.5 percent during 1993-94 (Natarajan and Patnaik, 1999).

The plan outlays for agriculture are also showing a downward slide in the recent years. Although capital formation in agriculture as a percentage of GDP has remained stable, at about 25 percent, over the years, the share of public capital formation is on the decline. It has come down from 38.1 percent in 1980-81 to 25.1 percent in 1990-91 and to 21 percent in 1997-98 (Table–4). The decline in public investment in agriculture is causing serious concern as reflected in the recent discussions on the subject. (Dhawan, 1998).This is because, as a recent study has shown, state level growth rates in agriculture are positively and significantly correlated to the level of Government expenditure in that sector (Rao, Shand and Kalirajan, 1999).

Table – 4

Gross Capital Formation in Agriculture and the Shares of Public and Private Capital Formation.

Year	Gross Capital Formation (Rs. '000' Crores)	Share of Public Capital formation	Share of Private Capital formation
1980-81	4636	38.1	61.3
1990-91	4594	25.1	74.9
1991-92	4729	21.2	78.8
1992-93	5372	19.7	80.3
1993-94	5031	22.9	77.1
1994-95	6256	21.0	79.0
1995-96	6961	18.2	81.8
1996-97	6999	16.2	83.8
1997-98	—	21.0	79.0

Source: Economic Survey, 1998-99.

During the last decade two significant changes have taken place in Indian agriculture. These are, (i) significant growth in irrigated farming and, (ii) shifts in the cropping pattern. Net area under irrigation has gone up from 28 percent in 1980 to 35 percent during 1993 (Table–5). Cropping intensity has gone up by 5 percent, from 125 to 130, during the same period. More importantly, distribution of area by source of irrigation (canals and wells) has undergone significant changes between 1981-82 and 1992-93 (Table–6). During the 90s the share of well irrigation has increased while the share of canal and tank irrigation has declined. This has had important distributional repercussions.

Table – 5

Changes in Cropping Pattern

Cropping Pattern		1980-81	1992-93
Gross Cropped Area		172630	185487
Net Cropped Area		140002	142509
Food Crops as Percentage of GCA	Total	73.37	66.39
	Rice	23.27	22.52
	Wheat	12.90	13.25
	Coarse Cereals	24.20	18.55
	Pulses	13.01	12.59
Non-food Crops as Percentage of GCA	Total	26.63	33.61
	Oilseeds	10.19	13.60
	Cotton	16.43	20.01

Source: CMIE, Agriculture, September1999.

Table – 6

Percentage Area Irrigated by Different Sources

Sources	1980-81	1985-86	1990-91	1992-93	1995-96
Total Irrigated Area (Percentage share of canals, tanks, wells, and other sources)	38720	41865	48023	50296	53510
Canal (Government Canals, Private Canals)	15292	16180	17453	16986	17142
Tank	3182	2765	2944	3179	3111
Well (Tube Wells, Other Wells)	17695	20418	24694	26920	29797
Other Sources	2551	2502	2932	3211	3460
Percentage of Net Area Irrigated	27.66	29.71	33.61	35.29	37.63
Irrigation Cropping Intensity	128	130	131	132	133

Source: CMIE, Agriculture, September1999.

It was generally accepted that irrigation distribution in India favours small holdings, i.e., smaller holdings have higher proportion of area under irrigation. Of late, this assumption has been questioned and it is argued that irrigation development in India is, in fact, iniquitous (Sampath, 1992). However, this argument does not appear to be true with regard to public irrigation though it is true in case of private irrigation (Sagar and Reddy, 1995). The shift in favor of well irrigation clearly reflects the increase in private investment, presumably by the large farmers, in irrigation development. In other words, the growth of private investment in irrigation development is resulting in a bias in favour of large farmers (This is not to argue that private investment in ground water development, would lead to inequitous distribution of water per se. In fact, it was observed by Shah (1994) that water markets would help in equitable distribution of ground water. However, the possibility for water markets to emerge in extreme scarcity conditions is remote. This is mainly due to the decline in public investment in agriculture. While this looks like the fallout of the macro policies which aim at compressing public outlay, at the root of the problem lies the sectoral policies reflecting a bias in favor of major projects and high subsidies for canal irrigation. A large chunk of public investment in agriculture has gone for major irrigation projects which are, generally, located in better endowed regions.

Despite the fact that farmers in the canal-irrigated regions have been reaping large benefits due to irrigation, they are not contributing even to the operational and maintenance costs through user charges. The reforms have, so far, failed to address this issue. On the other hand the backward regions, i.e. the arid and semi-arid tracts, have to rely more on private investment (i.e. on well irrigation). This has not only aggravated inter-regional inequalities but also widened intra regional inequalities. The high capital intensive nature of well irrigation has made access to water privy to well-to-do farmers. The poorer farmers in the disadvantaged region are the real losers as their savings are meager and access to credit is limited. On the top of it, the cost of energy to lift water is sought to be raised.

As far as cropping pattern is concerned, the 1980s have seen a significant shift in cropped area towards non-food crops. The major gainers were the oilseed crops which have gained in area at the cost of coarse grains. Superior cereals like wheat and rice have also showed slight improvement in area. Oilseeds have recorded highest growth rate in area as well as output between 1990-91 and 1997-98. All other crops have recorded lower growth rates in output during the post-reforms period, compared to their performance in the 1980s (Table–7).

Table – 7

Compound Growth Rates of output for Selected Agricultural Products (Triennium ending)

Crop	1980-81 to 1989-90	1990-91 to 1997-98
1. Rice	4.29	1.53
2. Wheat	4.24	3.67
3. Pulses	–0.54	0.76
4. Coarse Grains	0.74	–0.49
5. Total Cereals	3.63	1.84
6. All Food Grains	3.54	1.66
7. Oil seeds	—	4.93

Source: Economic Survey 1998-99.

The export thrust of the new economic policies has also accelerated the cropping pattern shifts. (The decline in area under foodgrain crops in favour of exportable or import substitute crops during the post reform period in our country is similar to the pattern observed in China). As a result, the growth in foodgrain production has fallen short of population growth for the first time since 1975 (Natarajan and Patnaik, 1999). The benefits from the export-oriented policies do not seem to have reached all sections of the farming community. While the large farmers are reaping the benefits of the policies, small and marginal farmers are languishing for want of resources such as water, and limited access to capital. A case in point is the distressed cotton growers in Andhra Pradesh, Karnataka and Maharashtra; or for that matter the case of oilseeds growers in the states like Rajasthan (Reddy, 1996).

In dry regions, unless access to water is made equitable through some institutional mechanisms there is no way the small and marginal farmers can reap the benefits of market oriented agriculture. Though small and marginal farmers are very adaptive to crop technologies, lack of resources (especially credit) makes them non- participants. Ignoring this fact, it is sometimes argued that the non-viable farmers should be allowed to leave cultivation and join the labour force. This would only lead to their pauperization. This argument fails to recognize the legitimate right of these farmers to share the available water resources . Besides, it also fails to reckon the impact on real wages if these farmers also join the already surplus labour force in agriculture. From what sources they be able to get even the subsistence level income? Can the industrial sector absorb the additional labour force? The recent evidence, as shown earlier, does not support such optimism.

The preceding discussion brings out some interesting aspects of recent policy changes. The main macro policy impact on agriculture is the shift in terms of trade in favour of agriculture. It has also resulted in the enhanced market sensitiveness of the producers. However, absence of continuity in policies (especially pertaining to agricultural trade) has increased the market induced risk and uncertainty. The recent suicides of the cotton growers in some of the states is attributed to sharp price fluctuations. Government keeps lifting and imposing the ban on cotton exports to appease certain sections. The small and marginal farmers are lured by market signals, but they do not have the strength to deal with the market risks. Their problems are aggravated with declining public investment in agriculture.

The small and marginal farmers, who do not possess the wherewithal i.e. access to capital and hence other resources including water, to face the market, have to fend for themselves. The plight of the small and marginal farmers is becoming increasingly serious in the arid and semi arid regions, which had been even previously neglected by the state. Agricultural producers in these neglected regions are now faced with degraded environment, poor resource base and unfriendly institutional environment. Under these conditions market penetration in the recent yeas has increased the concentration of scarce resources in fewer hands leading not only to increasing inequalities but also pushing the poor farmers to the edge.

While the shrinking state involvement in agricultural sector may have some justification in the light of increasing financial constraints, the failure of the state in mobilizing the resources from within the sector (through user charges) reflects the myopic nature of the politicians and policy makers. However, of late there appears to be some change in the attitude of some state government in this regard. States like Andhra Pradesh and Madhya Pradesh are pushing institutional reforms, which are prerequisites for market reforms, at the grass roots level. These include strengthening local institutions like water user associations and the panchayati raj institution. These institutional reforms are crucial not only for creating unbiased, market-friendly environment but also for sustaining the growth impetus. The institutional reforms have assumed greater prominence in the recent years with the Asian crisis, which is attributed mainly to institutional failure, though at a different level, i.e. financial and macro. This aspect is taken up in the next section.

The changes discussed in the context of sectoral policies, i.e. expansion of ground water irrigation and shift in cropping patterns towards non-foodgrains, are not the direct fall-out of the recent policy changes but the policy changes have certainly accentuated these tendencies. These processes are likely to perpetuate, if not accelerate in the coming years. In rural environment water is the main source of change and agent for growth. The viability of farming depends to a large measure on the access to irrigation. Equitable distribution of water resources ensures equity in the distribution of gains from it. But the recent trend in expansion of irrigation facilities indicates that access to irrigation is moving in favour of the large farmers due to large scale private investment in this area. Some of the important indicators point towards the likely aggravation of 'large farmer' bias in this regard. While at the macro level investment in irrigation is vital for sustaining agricultural growth (Rao and Gulati, 1995: Parikh, et al, 1995), public investment in irrigation is necessary to address the equity issue. In fact, in fragile eco systems public investments is necessary not only in irrigation and water conservation but also in dry farming technologies like watershed development.

While the recent policy changes repeatedly point to resource constraints for public investments, they are conspicuously silent on resource generation. One neglected area in this regard is user charges, especially for irrigation. Unless future developmental programs are funded internally through user charges, feasibility of these programs will be at stake. Provided there is political will and administrative acumen cost recovery is not a difficult proposition. It has been shown that farmers willingness to pay for improved irrigation facilities is significantly above the present rate structure (Reddy, 1998). This is also demonstrated in the case of reduction in fertilizer subsidy. When the subsidy was removed, in 1991, fertilizer use did not decline, in majority of regions, especially in high fertilizer intensive regions; in fact, it increased in few cases (Reddy and Deshpande, 1992).

III

ASIAN CRISIS AND ITS IMPACT ON INDIAN AGRICULTURE

The structural adjustment, with liberalization and globalization policies was seen as panacea for development till the east and south-east Asian economies faced their recent crisis. These economies were viewed as miracle economies before the onset of the crisis in 1997. Since then serious questions have been posed on the efficacy of liberalization policies and their institutional underpinning. These economies witnessed export-led high growth rates for over a decade. They had low budget deficit, sufficient forex reserves, and other positive features. More importantly, these countries could effectively solve the problem of poverty. They were set as examples for other developing countries to follow. Till the crisis occurred in July 1997 neither economists nor policy makers had any inkling of the danger lurking around the corner.

Genesis of the Crisis

Six countries of south east Asia and east Asia have been affected by the crisis, of which four (Thailand, South Korea, Indonesia and Malaysia) are severely and two (Philippines and Hong Kong) are moderately affected (Rao, 1998a and 1998b) . There are number of explanations for the crisis, (CJE, 1998, JDS,1998, IDS Bulletin, 1999). The factors leading to crisis which might have acted singly or in conjunction can be grouped under three principal categories. These are: a) structural aspects, b) macro-economic imbalances, and c) financial failures. However, financial factors are often identified as the main cause of the crisis. In these countries financial systems were poorly regulated, which allowed speculative and unproductive investment on large scale. After reviewing various explanations Bhalla and Nachane concluded that, "volatility of capital inflows and launching of financial liberalization without adequate preparation were the main causes of the financial panic" (p. 2362). The situation was identified as 'crony capitalism' by perceptive commentators (Wade, 1998). An additional factor contributing to the crisis was the artificially fixed exchange rates; which were pegged to dollar. This led to the appreciation of the real effective exchange rates of the local currencies especially, during 1994 to 1997 (Cliff, 1999).

The main impact of this crisis has fallen on the urban poor through loss of jobs and rising food prices. The crisis has reversed the impressive record of poverty alleviation achieved during the previous 20 years. For instance, in Indonesia percentage of population living below poverty line almost doubled (from 13 to 25 percent) after the crisis (Cliff, 1999). This is attributed to the fact that the poverty alleviation achieved in these economies was a result of " trickle down" effect of growth, and not an outcome of redistribution. It is argued that the south east Asian economies had achieved substantial reduction in absolute poverty because of high rate of economic growth, but their strategy was not effective in reducing income inequalities (Rao, 1999). While traditional social security systems were eroded, no modern systems were put in place during the high growth period (Cliff, 1999). This proved to be a costly mistake and resulted in social unrest and political instability in countries, more particularly in Indonesia. The policy of providing social services through private sector proved undependable. The erosion of livelihoods rendered the private systems unaffordable and hence increased the pressure on public services. In the process the private services remained under-utilized and became non-viable. People had to resort to illegal means of survival such as smuggling, prostitution, etc.

India's Economic Relations With South-East Asia

The recent discussions on Asian crisis have, by and large, sidelined the impact on agriculture in the countries which faced the crisis. This may be due to the (wrong) notion, that agriculture sectors in these countries are neither responsible nor affected by the crisis. In the same way, impact of the crisis on Indian agriculture has gone largely unnoticed. This was because of the fact that the immediate impact of the crisis on Indian agriculture was not as conspicuous as in the case of activities, such as stock market operations or foreign capital flows.

The impact of Asian crisis on Indian economy could be assessed at three levels. One, the direct and indirect trade impact due to the downturn in the Asian markets; two, decline in the foreign capital inflow; and, three, slow down in the domestic reforms as a reaction to the crisis. These impacts were blurred due to Pokhran nuclear tests and the consequent economic sanctions by USA, other developed countries and multilateral aid agencies. The vulnerability indicators analyzed by Bhalla and Nachane (1998) do not bring out any possibility of contagion effect (Table–8). According to their assessment "reasonable grounds do exist for supposing that India will whether the crisis". India's high fiscal deficit seems to have had a far greater impact on the net foreign capital inflows as the foreign direct investment (FDI) declined between 1995-96 and 1996-97 i.e. before the onset of Asian crisis. However, foreign portfolio investors turned net sellers of Indian stocks to make up for their losses in Asian markets (The Banker, March, 1998, as quoted in Bhalla and Nachane, 1998).

Table – 8

India's Ranking on Crisis Indicators vis-a-vis Asian Economies

Indicator	India	Thailand	Korea	Philippines	Malaysia	Indonesia
1. Govt. budget Balance (percent of GDP)	6	1	5	4	3	2
2. External debt/GDP ratio	1	2	na	5	3	4
3. External debt service (percent of Exports)	2	3	na	na	1	4
4. External debt service (percent of GDP)	1	2	na	na	3	4
5. Current account/ GDP ratio	1	5	2	na	4	3
6. External liabilities of Banks (percent of GDP)	1	4	5	3	1	6
	2	4	5	3	1	6

Note: The ratings represent an ascending order of vulnerability, viz, rank 1 corresponds to the least vulnerable country on that criterion and so on. Source: Bhalla and Nachane (1998).

Another area where the impact of the Asian crisis was likely to be felt strongly is the external trade. The direct outcome was due to depreciation of Asian currencies. The effect was compounded due to slow down in world economy, growth declining from 4 percent to 3.5 percent. This had, naturally, a negative impact on India's exports and consequently on Indian Economy. For our current discussion the trade linkages with the four most severely affected south- east Asian countries, Indonesia, Malaysia, South Korea and Thailand, are more important. Malaysia accounts for 28.9 percent of our exports to these countries, followed by Indonesia (26.1 percent), South Korea (24.7 percent) and, Thailand (20.3 Percent). Thus, structure of India's exports to these countries is not biased in favor of any one country. Growth of India's trade with these countries slowed down during the post- crisis period, i.e., after 1996-97 (Table–9). South- East Asian countries' share in India's exports was 6.2 percent during 1996-97, It came down to 5.4 percent in the following year. Though the magnitude of our exports to these countries is small, given

Table – 9

India's Exports to South-East Asian Economies

(percentage of total exports)

Country	1991-92	1992-93	1993-94	1994-95	1995-96	1996-97	1997-98	Share of Selected Countries (1997-98)
1. Indonesia	0.8	0.7 (9.6)	1.1 (83.7)	1.1 (18.3)	2.1 (154.1)	1.8 (-6.3)	1.8 (-23.0)	26.1
2. Malaysia	1.1	1.0 (10.2)	1.1 (41.1)	1.1 (16.0)	1.2 (46.2)	1.6 (41.6)	1.4 (-5.1)	28.9
3. South Korea	1.4	0.9 (-17.4)	0.9 (27.8)	1.3 (61.2)	1.4 (43.6)	1.5 (18.4)	1.2 (-16.9)	24.7
4. Thailand	1.1	1.4 (50.1)	1.6 (52.2)	1.5 (14.2)	1.5 (23.9)	1.3 (-0.3)	1.0 (-20.9)	20.3
5. Total	4.4	4.0 ((11.4)	4.7 (49.6)	5.0 (24.8)	6.2 (61.6)	6.2 (10.2)	5.4 (-16.5)	100
6. World	100	100 (21.9)	100 (29.9)	100 (18.5)	100 (28.6)	100 (10.5)	100 (6.3)	100

Note: Figures in brackets are rate of growth over previous year. Source: CMIE, Foreign Trade, 1998.

our precarious balance of payments position even the small changes will have serious consequences. Indian exports to these countries had recorded high growth rates during the pre-crisis period, indicating that India had benefited from these booming economies. Since the onset of 'crisis' exports have recorded negative growth in case of all the four countries, and this trend is likely to continue till these economies recover. Thus, the "crisis" has adversely affected Indian economy with a decline in exports to these countries.

Imports from these countries were consistently increasing in recent years. This trend was not much affected by the crisis, which may be due to the cheapening of imports from these countries consequent to the depreciation of their currencies (Table–10). The rate of growth in imports from these countries was higher than India's imports from 'world' as a whole, indicating the strengthening of trade linkages and economic integration between India and the countries of the south-east Asia. But, crisis

Table – 10

India's Imports from South-East Asian Economies

(percentage of total exports)

Country	1991-92	1992-93	1993-94	1994-95	1995-96	1996-97	1997-98	Share of Imports from the Selected Countries
1. Indonesia	0.3	0.3 (5.3)	0.5 (116.1)	1.1 (169.6)	1.3 (52.5)	1.6 (38.2)	1.8 (27.6)	23.2
2. Malaysia	2.0	1.9 (22.5)	1.1 (-33.4)	1.7 (96.7)	2.5 (96.2)	2.6 (19.5)	2.9 (19.2)	37.7
3. South Korea	1.6	1.6 (30.7)	2.4 (72.1)	2.2 (11.6)	2.2 (39.7)	2.2 (7.8)	2.2 (6.2)	31.9
4. Thailand	0.2	0.3 (41.3)	0.2 (6.2)	0.6 (200.3)	0.5 (5.3)	0.5 (23.0)	0.6 (22.3)	7.2
5. Total	4.1	4.1 (25.4)	4.2 (22.0)	5.6 (63.0)	6.5 (55.8)	6.9 (19.3)	7.5 (17.0)	100
6. World	100	100 (32.4)	100 (15.3)	100 (23.1)	100 (36.4)	100 (11.5)	100 (9.1)	100

Note: Figures in brackets are rate of growth over previous year. Source: CMIE, Foreign Trade, 1998.

seems to have had an adverse impact on growth in imports which slowed down during the year 1997-98. Among the four countries, India's share of Imports is the highest from Malaysia (37.7 percent), followed by south Korea (31.9 percent), Indonesia (23.2 percent) and, Thailand (7.2 percent). Unlike the case of exports, the share of imports is not evenly balanced among these countries.

Impact on Agriculture

The likely impact of the Asian crisis on Indian agriculture becomes clear if we look at the composition of India's exports and imports to these countries (Tables–10 and 11). More than a third of India's exports to these countries consist of agriculture and allied products, while India imports agricultural commodities to the tune of about fifteen percent in it's total imports from these countries (in 1997-98). These countries were net importers of agricultural goods from India. In the trade with these countries agriculture exports are the second largest category after manufactured goods (Table–11). It is clear, therefore, the trade-related impact of the Asian crisis on Indian agriculture could not be insubstantial and one can not remain complacent about the

Table – 11

Composition of India's Exports to South-East Asian Economies in 1997-98

(percentages)

Commodity	Indonesia	Malaysia	S. Korea	Thailand	Total
All Commodities	100	100	100	100	100
1. Agriculture and Allied products	46.21	33.16	28.59	27.1	33.8
2. Ores and Minerals	5.99	1.92	5.62	1.7	3.8
3. Manufactured goods	45.12	63.12	64.54	68.5	60.3
3.1. Leather & Leather manufactures	0.45	1.03	0.99	0.6	0.8
3.2. Chemicals & Related Products	11.79	8.98	19.41	14.1	13.6
3.3. Engineering Goods	26.57	39.15	11.93	18.4	24.0
3.4. Textiles (Excluding RMG)	4.66	8.38	29.2	5.1	11.8
3.5. Readymade Garments	0.17	2.05	0.93	0.5	0.9
3.6. Other Manufactured goods	1.49	3.53	2.09	29.7	9.2
4. Other commodities	2.68	1.81	1.26	2.7	2.1

Source: CMIE, Foreign Trade, August, 1998.

likely impact of Asian crisis on Indian agriculture. Apart from this direct trade impact, Indian agriculture may loose in terms of competition for its products in the international markets due to the depreciation of the currencies of the crisis hit countries.

If we look at the important countries we are competing with for various commodities, it would appear that about 40 percent of our exports are vulnerable to the crisis (Sathe, 1998). Of this, about 10 percent of the commodities are agricultural commodities (e.g. rice, cashew, spices, floriculture, tea, etc.) while another 45 percent of the commodities (textiles and ready-made garments) are agro-based and would be indirectly affected by competition from these countries (Table–12).Though it is too early to understand the clear impact of the Asian crisis on Indian agriculture, some of the adverse effects could be noticed at the regional level, as they may not figured out at the national level . For instance, recent reports in newspapers suggest growing problems of rubber and coconut growers in Kerala due to the crash in the international prices with cheapening of these products from 'crisis' countries. Similarly, the cotton crisis in Andhra and Maharashtra could also be attributed to price fluctuations initiated by the Asian crisis. However, the clear picture will emerge only after a few years, assuming that the crisis will continue.

Table - 12

Areas Where Indian Exports Compete with South-East Asian Exports

Product		Competitor Economies
1. Jewellery, Gems (14%)	:	Thailand, Indonesia, UAE, Malaysia.
2. Marine products (3%)	:	China, Japan, US, Thailand, Indonesia, Malaysia
3. Spices (1%)	:	China, Iran, Pakistan, Indonesia.
4. Ready made garments (9%)	:	China, Indonesia, Bangladesh, South Korea.
5. Textiles (9%)	:	South Korea, Indonesia, Thailand
6. Foot wear (<1%)	:	US, Denmark, Italy, Colombia, Kenya, Thailand.
7. Floriculture (<1%)	:	Indonesia
8. Rice (1%)	:	Pakistan, US, Thailand.
9. Cashew (1%)	:	Indonesia, Vietnam, Mozambique
10. Tea, Coffee	:	Indonesia
11. Leather, Handicrafts	:	No competitors from South-East Asia.

Note: Figures in brackets indicate share in total exports.
Source: Sathe (1998).

Lessons of Asian Crisis

The East Asian crisis drives the point clear that growth oriented development is not the panacea for all economic and social ills. Equity or distributional aspects need to be given equal weight in the process of economic development. The neglect of distributional aspects in the East-Asian countries made the poor bear disproportionately high incidence of recession. The issue of income inequalities in these countries came to the centre stage once the recession set in (Rao, 1999). In the Indian context also it is clear that distributional aspects are taking back seat as the reward systems dictated by the market tend to dominate the thinking.

Failure to create an effective social security system is another reason for aggravation of Asian crisis. The export oriented growth failed to ensure food security in these countries for the bottom 20 percent of their populations (FAO, 1998). The main victims of the crisis are the urban poor in these countries. In India too the new economic policies do not lay out any specific agenda for creating appropriate social security system. On the contrary, the existing social security systems are being weakened for want of resources. This may prove disastrous in the event of any crisis situation similar to that of east-Asian one. More importantly, in India distress will not be limited to urban areas as agriculture, the main occupation of the rural work force, has continued to remain vulnerable. Though the key economic indicators do not warrant any such situation in the near future, some necessary steps are to be taken in order to protect the economy from a crisis triggered either by internal developments or due to contagious effect of neighboring countries. The most important among them are the curtailing of the fiscal deficit, injecting efficiency into financial institutions, exercising regulatory measures with regard to foreign investment as well as capital inflows through financial institutions, above all, strengthening the food security of the vulnerable sections.

Given the magnitude of the agricultural sector and its share in the national economy, some hard policy measures, and institutional innovations and strengthening are necessary in this sector also. A number of authors have commented on the macro policy measures. Similar attention is not given to the reforms in agricultural sector. Some of the important issues include: price policies, policies on subsidies, and trade policies. Besides, the issue of Food Security deserves special attention in our context. These issues are briefly discussed in the following paragraphs.

IV

POLICY REFORMS IN AGRICULTURAL SECTOR

Long term goals of economic development as much as the short term considerations suggest the need for clarity of the policy objectives. In our context agricultural policies have to address three principal objectives. As the primary sector, agriculture has to generate surpluses for financing economic growth. Secondly, it has to ensure productive employment and adequate incomes to the large number of households directly dependent on this sector. Finally, in a poor country where a substantial number of people spend significant proportion of their income on food, agriculture has the pivotal role in ensuring Food Security. Non- price, non-market, measures such as institutional arrangements, voluntary cooperation and good governance have important role to play in meeting these objectives. However, economic policies can materially affect the outcome of public efforts as well as private initiatives. We will briefly comment on some of the major policy interventions in agriculture in our country.

Price Policies

By now India has accumulated vast experience in agricultural price formulation and implementation. However, contribution of such interventions in enhancing productivity or ensuring equity is questionable. This is mainly due to the following reasons: a) there is no link between price policies and other policies like subsidy policies and trade policies; b) there is no consistency in the policies and hence they fail to give any clear signals to the producers. (For example, subsidies are being reduced with the objective of restoring economic efficiency, but farmers are not allowed to reap the benefit of market determined prices as government intervention continues in the output market) ; c) as a reaction to the situation obtaining at a point of time, ad hoc decisions are taken in terms of export restrictions, imposition of import quotas, restrictions on the movement of produce, etc.; d) price policies do not take into consideration the equity aspects i.e., which section of producers benefits from these policies. e) with policy interventions in terms of the minimum support price, price induced uncertainty is reduced to some extent. But with the progressive globalization of agriculture the trade induced price fluctuations are becoming a norm. Policy measures to correct violent fluctuations in widely traded commodities are not in place.

In order to fulfill the basic objectives of enhancing productivity and equity in agricultural sector, serious consideration may be given to the following: i) the objectives of the price policy need to be carefully defined and its scope delimited, ii) large measure of flexibility should be imparted in the formulation and administration of price policy, iii) measures such as open market operations should be resorted to in cooperation with the producers and consumers organizations, iv) restrictive practices such as movement on regulation, and compulsory levy or procurement should be abolished, iv) there should be much closer coordination among different types of policy interventions, particularly between the trade policy and the price policy, and v) price policy should not be dictated by the border prices, but use of border prices as one of the important considerations in the formulation of price policy should be recognized (V.S. Vyas 1994).

Policies on Subsidies

The burden of subsidies is one of the important factors contributing to the large fiscal deficit. Though the growing fiscal deficit calls for a drastic cut in subsidies, there is need for prioritizing the subsidies rather than imposing an 'across the board' cut. The subsidy regime was introduced mainly to implement a policy of 'low input low output' (Acharya 1996). However, the justification of the input subsidies even in this context would be their contribution to increase productivity. As far as input subsidies are concerned, studies have shown that a majority of the implicit or explicit subsidies are unproductive or redundant. In the case of explicit subsidies while the more productive subsidy on fertilizers is sought to be pruned, the major (in terms of outlay) and less productive subsidies on water and power are more or less untouched. Cutting down these subsidies would not only lighten the financial burden but would also lead to efficient allocation of scarce resources. It is important to aim at an orderly withdrawal of subsidies. There is need for a flexible and non-doctrinaire approach. While considering progressive elimination of input subsidies, repercussion on agricultural production, regional imbalances and incentive structure of the 'late users' should be taken into account. The economic reforms, if properly implemented, may create an environment in which the case for the removal of input subsidies would be further strengthened.

On the other hand, there is a strong case for continuing food subsidies for quite some time to come, especially after the recent experience of south-east and east Asian countries. These subsidies should be used as a social security net. In the present context where a sizable number of people are suffering from malnutrition – and periodically from hunger – and when opportunities for gainful employment are inadequate, it is difficult to justify any drastic cut in the food subsidy for the poor. Eliminating this (only) safety device for the poor may prove a recipe for disaster in the event of any economic upheaval. In this context, the recent price hike in the commodities covered by the public distribution is difficult to justify. In fact, an efficient Public Distribution System (PDS) should be a precondition for globalizing agriculture. Though, India has a well designed PDS, it has many detractors. True, efficiency of PDS can be improved through reducing cost of storage and handling, and better targeting of the poor. But it should be recognized that no viable alternative to PDS is available for a country like ours.

Trade Policy

Traditionally, a two pronged approach was followed in agricultural trade policy. Keeping food security a primary goal, import substitution policies were favoured in the case of foodgrains, while non-food 'commercial crops' were identified for export promotion. This approach seems to be justifiable given the volatile nature of agriculture in India and primary concern of food security. The Asian crisis has amply demonstrated that it is not wise to abandon the goal of food self-sufficiency for large to medium size developing countries. For, any large- scale imports of foodgrains will have serious repercussions on income and employment prospects of agricultural producers and workers. The existing favorable price ratios may disappear once a large country like India enters the market. This could easily create food shortages. At the same time, the scope for exports of the major foodgrains commodities, especially cereals, is limited. An aggressive policy on food exports initiated in the recent years has so far proved unsuccessful (Mujumdar, 1999). A desirable policy would be to divert resources from foodgrains to non-food crops or even non-agricultural enterprises once the prospects of genuine surplus in foodgrains emerge.

The criteria by which we should judge the export potential of an agricultural commodity should be: a) the place of the commodity in the consumption basket of the people, especially the poorer sections; b) supply and price elasticities; c) the ratio of the import price and the domestic price; and d) future demand/supply prospects in the international markets. What it implies in terms of trade strategy is an order of priority in export promotion, with high priority accorded to processed agricultural goods, to be followed by non-food agricultural commodities, and some special varieties of foodgrains, e.g., basmati or superfine rice, duram wheat, etc.

Summing Up

Our long term goals as well as contemporary developments, more specifically the experience of the Asian Crisis, suggest a cautious approach to reforms in agriculture without loosing sight of distributional aspects within the sector and vis-a-vis other sectors of the economy. Agriculture will continue to be a primary sector in the true sense of the term. Sequencing of policy reforms should be in such a way that the adverse impact on poor, both urban and rural, could be avoided. In order to achieve the objective of a dynamic surplus generating agriculture, ensure equitable distribution and, provide safety nets for the vulnerable sections, the role of the non-price factors, especially the institutional factors, is important. There is need for building and strengthening delivery systems and local initiatives. Institutions such as water user's associations or joint forest committees, not only help in sustainable resource management but also ensure equitable distribution of the gains. Panchayati Raj institutions provide valuable opportunity for participatory growth and more transparent distribution of the benefits of the state subsidies, including the benefits of PDS. This is not to deny the importance of macro economic policies. India has an opportunity to take a lead in agricultural reforms and avoid pitfalls which the fast growing countries of Asia could not avoid.

References

Acharya S.S. (1996) Marketing Environment for Farm Products: Emerging Issues and Challenges, Visions in Agricultural Marketing. (1987-1996). Vol.1.pp 147-148, Indian Society of Agricultural Marketing

Bagchi Amiyakumar(1998), "Growth Miracle and its Unravelling in East and South-East Asia: Unregulated Competitiveness and Denouement of Manipulation by International Financial Community", Economic and Political Weekly, Vol. 33, No. 18, May 2-8.

Bhalla Ajit. S and Dilip M. Nachane, " Asian Eclipse: India and China in the Penumbra", Economic and Political Weekly, Vol. 33, Nos. 36 & 37, September 5-7.

CJE (1998), "Special Issue on The Asian Crisis", Cambridge Journal of Economics, Vol. 22, No. 6, November. Clift, Charles (1999), "East Asia Crisis Seminar: Summary of Discussion", IDS Bulletin, Vol. 30, No.1, January.

Dhawan B. D (1998), Studies in Agricultural Investments and Rural Savings, Commonwealth Publishers, New Delhi.

FAO (1998), Poverty Alleviation and Food Security in Asia: Lessons and Challenges, Food and Agricultural Organisation of the United Nations Regional Office for Asia and the Pacific, Bangkok, December. Institute of Development Studies, Jaipur, IDS Bulletin, 1999.

JDS (1998), " Special Issue on East Asian Development: New Perspective" The Journal of Development Studies, Vol. 34, No. 6, August.

Mujumdar, N.A. (1999), Investment in Agriculture and the Globalization Syndrome", Economic and Political Weekly, Vol. 34, No. 14, April 3.

Natarajan Sriram and Utsa Patnaik (1999), "Post Reform Trends in Crop Area, Output and Employment in China and India", Paper presented at the International Seminar on Economic Reforms in India and China, Department of Economics, University of Hyderabad, Hyderabad, March 10-12.

Nadkarni M.V. (1998) " Crisis of Increasing Costs in Agriculture, is there a Way Out?" Economic and Political Weekly, Vol.23, No.39, September 24.

Parikh, Kirit, S., N.S.S. Narayana, Manoj Panda, A. Ganesh Kumar (1995) "Strategies for Agricultural Liberalisation – Consequences for Growth, Welfare and Distribution", Economic and Political Weekly, Vol. XXIX, No. 39, September 30.

Rao M. Govinda; R. T. Shand and K. P. Kalirajan (1999), "Convergence of Incomes Across Indian States: A Divergent View" Economic and Political Weekly, Vol. 34, No. 13, March 27.

Rao V. V. Bhanoji (1998a), "East Asian Economies: Growth Within an International Context", Economic and Political Weekly, Vol. 33, No. 6, February 7.

Rao V. V. Bhanoji (1998b), "East Asian Economies: The Crisis of 1997-98", Economic and Political Weekly, Vol. 33, No. 23, June 6.

Rao V. V. Bhanoji (1999), "East Asian Economies: Trends in Poverty and Income Inequality", Economic and Political Weekly, Vol. 34, No. 18, May 1.

Reddy, V. Ratna (1995) Willingness and Ability to Pay for Water: A Study of Rajasthan, Project Report, Institute of Development Studies, Jaipur.

Reddy V. Ratna (1996), "Liberalisation and the Poor: A Study of Rajasthan", Paper presented at the International Seminar on Liberalization and the Poor: Impact, Barriers and Opportunities, Indo-Dutch Program on Alternatives of Development (IDPAD), March 7-9.

Reddy V. Ratna (1998), "Institutional Imperatives and Coproduction Strategies for Large Irrigation Systems in India", Indian Journal of Agricultural Economics, Vol. 53, No. 3, July-September.

Reddy, V. Ratna and R.S. Deshpande (1992) "Input Subsidies: Whither the Direction of Policy Changes", Indian Journal of Agricultural Economics, Vol. XLVII, No. 3, July-September.

Sagar, Vidya and V. Ratna Reddy (1995) "Irrigation Development in India", Working Paper, Institute of Development Studies, Jaipur.

Sampath, R.K. [1992] "Farm Size-wise Analysis of Irrigation in Indian Agriculture", Journal of Development Studies, Vol. 29, No. 1, October.

Sathe Dhanmanjari (1998), "Asian Currency Crisis and the Indian Economy", Economic and Political Weekly, Vol. 33, No. 18, May 2.

Vyas V. S (1994), "Agricultural Price Policy: Need for Reformulation" in G. S. Bhalla (ed.), Economic Liberalisation and Indian Agriculture, Institute for Studies in Industrial Development, New Delhi.

Vyas V.S. (1996) " Agricultural Trade Policy for the Nineties: Issues and Approaches", Economic and Political Weekly, Vol.29, No.26, pp. A-54-64.

Vyas V.S. (1990) "Food Policy and Food Security in Asia with Particular Reference to South Asia", Increasing Access to Food: An Asian Experience (ed. D.S. Tyagi and V.S.Vyas), Sage Publication India Pvt. Ltd, New Delhi.

Vyas V.S. and kruse-Rodenacker, A.(1974) Cooperative of Agricultural Products, Food and Agriculture Organization of the United Nations, Rome.

15

Restructuring of Public Finances and Macro-Economic Stability

Y. V. REDDY

New Realities

With increasing integration between the Indian and world economy, in terms of trade and financial flows and especially private external capital flows, we have to recognise the need for some sort of convergence of macro-economic stability parameters. Most critical are, fiscal deficit and within it revenue deficit and especially monetised deficit, inflation and of course interest rates. So, we should consider world trends in say, inflation and fiscal deficit, public sector savings and compare our performance in this respect to judge how competitive we stand in terms of stability and efficiency indicators. While we may afford to be out of alignment temporarily, or marginally, or with reference to one or two of the parameters, we will find it difficult to maintain macro stability if we are too far away on most of them, especially, on the inflation and fiscal deficit front. Today, fiscal and monetary options are no longer driven by domestic compulsions alone; they have to broadly conform to certain internationally acceptable norms of what constitutes the sound fundamentals of an open and competitive economy. I do not think we have much option to

Dr. Reddy is grateful to the officials of the Department of Economic Analysis and Policy and the Internal Debt Management Cell of the Reserve Bank of India for their valuable assistance.

deviate from these standards in the medium to long-run.

The challenges for fiscal restructuring also stem from several domestic factors. Reforming the financial sector to augment efficiency in financial intermediation is inevitable. Further intensification of financial sector reforms means development of a well-organised and efficient debt market, which cannot be realised without strengthening fiscal consolidation and addressing legal, institutional and technology issues. Hence, limiting the fiscal deficit of Centre and States to a sustainable level is critical for further progress in financial sector reform. This will facilitate further liberalisation of regulation relating to banks' investment in government securities and promotion of a more orderly growth of debt market. Fiscal discipline is a precondition for successful financial sector reform. Incidentally, the concept of public sector deficit which includes government deficit including those of public-enterprises', loses, technically, its significance when many enterprises get into diversified (government and public) ownership patterns or being privatised, and when they start operating purely on commercial lines. However, there is an implicit government guarantee in respect of borrowings by any public enterprise, and thus the magnitude of public sector deficit also needs to be reckoned.

There is now an increasing realisation about the importance of monetary policy, and the autonomy in conduct of monetary policy as well as efficiency in monetary transmission mechanism and these require drastic reduction in the currently ruling high level of government borrowing – which again has a significant bearing on fiscal and revenue deficits.

Economic reform in a broader sense would also encompass realigning of relative functions of Centre and States towards achieving economic prosperity and improving the quality of life. In our context, it means greater emphasis on development of social infrastructure and physical infrastructure. Most of the social, and a significant part of physical infrastructure lies in the domain of States compared to Centre. Expenditure responsibility of States is likely to grow in social sectors; particularly education, health, sanitation and nutrition, even after reckoning with some unbundling as also scope for private provision. Economic reform is not sustainable if expenditure of State Governments is not buoyant in desired directions and this has a bearing on vertical distribution of resources.

On the inter-state plane, the new reality is greater role for market based resources for development of a State. So, while States need to be encouraged to compete for resources in the market, there should exist mechanisms in transfer of resources which would differentiate between ability-consistent efforts and the ability–enhancing efforts. By this I mean States which already have a reasonably developed institutional support base and strong fiscal position can garner resources from market and consequently reduce their dependence on central transfers. In States where institutional setting is underdeveloped, public policies may have to address the issue of improving their ability to access financial markets, while at the same time augmenting their resource base through transfers to help prepare them towards a greater degree of self-sufficiency. This has greater relevance now than before due to market orientation and has a bearing on equity/horizontal distribution.

Against the backdrop of new constitutional provisions relating to giving financial autonomy and responsibilities to local bodies and its inclusion as terms of reference for the first time for Eleventh Finance Commission, the issues of inter-state and intra-state transfers have assumed a new dimension. In this context, there is an increasing reference to Municipal bonds as a means of financing urban infrastructure, especially against the backdrop of recommendations of the Rakesh Mohan Committee. To the extent these proposals involve guarantees by State Governments, they affect State finances and provide expediency to state level reforms, and to the extent there is a demand for counting them as approved securities for SLR, it has a bearing on interest rate structure and monetary and debt management policies. Our objective is to reduce statutory preemptions. The Central and State enterprises should, therefore, be encouraged to access market on the basis of financial strength and viability rather than through sops like tax benefits and SLR routes which distorts the interest rate structure and hampers market efficiency.

On fiscal deficit situation, we have to be concerned about the total liabilities of governments, rather than marketable debt alone, since this has dynamic and spiraling consequences for fiscal policy and its future sustainability, involves a signaling effect for the market, and is important from the view point of the focus of rating agencies. While market liabilities would include public debt and contingent liabilities due to guarantees, total liabilities would include, for example, provident fund, small savings, etc.

Against the backdrop of Asian crisis, a new reality in the sphere of management of financial risk for the economy is the need to recognise and monitor off-balance sheet liabilities, whether these are due to banks or Governments. In this context, the guarantees given by the State Governments and Central Government, will have to be assessed and monitored. The focus on such guarantees has increased recently in the context of attracting private sector and foreign investment in infrastructure, especially when cost recovery systems are not fully in place. Managing these guarantees can pose difficult problems at a time when exchange rate is fluctuating and the guaranteed amount is pushing up the external liabilities, as for example, in the case of power projects. Another non-transparent way of assuming liability by the Government is to issue letters of comfort which do have the same effect as guarantees for the rating purpose and for the sustainability of government finances, though such letters of comfort may not be reported in the budget documents.

We have to be also aware of new realities in the Government borrowing programme. Let me draw attention to two critical issues in the government market borrowing programme. One is the increasing cost of Government borrowings, and the other, the shortening of maturities. Both affect the debt management and monetary policy objectives. While the former is related to the size of the borrowing and hence the fiscal deficit, the latter is influenced by the future policy uncertainties, particularly relating to fiscal policy, and consequently the market preference for short-term government papers to ward off long-term interest rate risk. What is therefore important is a dynamically consistent fiscal policy with emphasis on low fiscal deficit. Another source of high cost fund for the Government is borrowing through the tax-favoured instruments such as small savings and relief bonds, apart from public sector undertaking bonds, which not only affect the overall cost to Government but operate as wrong benchmarks for other markets. These schemes may need a thorough review if we have to move away from dependence on captive borrowing sources towards retailing of Government securities to a larger investor class.

Abolition of *ad hoc* treasury bills and introduction of the scheme of Ways and Means Advances for the Centre is a major development, impinging on both development of Government securities market and fiscal discipline, including quality of cash and debt management. Adherence to budget assumptions on borrowing programme and to the extent possible, subject to monetary policy considerations, adherence to pre-announced extent of monetisation of government debt by RBI would be essential if credibility in the new system is to be reinforced.

Finally, in consonance with the Narasimham Committee–II recommendations, we have introduced risk weights for Government securities for the purpose of assessing capital requirement for the banking system and provisioning norms for unhonoured guarantees as essential measures to promote soundness of financial sector. This could imply greater caution on the part of banks in supporting Government borrowing or granting advances against guarantees. Incidentally, the share of banks in total financial intermediation, and that of public sector banks in total banking system are likely to come down in the medium term. Hence, the extent of what may be called captive investors for Government securities, could be proportionately less in both formal and informal terms. This has implications for the interest rate in funding a high level of fiscal deficit of centre and states.

As part of economic reform, substantial restructuring of public enterprises has been taking place both at Centre and States and this is likely to be intensified in future. Such restructuring has often meant some immediate financial costs, especially when there is large scale rescheduling of debt, and conversion of debt into equity. These measures amount to impact of not several hundreds but several thousands of crore. There is a potential for serious erosion of quality of assets. This aspect requires intensive analysis for designing a suitable approach to restructuring and it is as important as an approach to privatisation in terms of its dynamic impact on government finances.

MACRO-ECONOMIC ISSUES

In the light of the new realities described, revenue and expenditure assessments by the commission should reflect the broad macro-economic concerns of reducing the revenue and fiscal deficit of the combined Government sector. This may require working towards a consensus on the desirable path of fiscal deficit of Centre and States.

While fixing the target levels of fiscal deficits for the combined Government sector, some redistribution of revenue deficits and perhaps even creation of revenue surplus would be needed. This poses a critical task of devising a balancing mechanism by the Eleventh Finance Commission. The major element here would be the incentive system, which needs to be built into the devolution mechanism for transfer of resources. Tenth Finance Commission provided a weight of ten per cent for tax effort in its devolution formula. This may need some review. Also, a revisit to the issue of unutilised tax potential in the States, tax capacities etc. may be worthwhile. Given the importance of cost recovery of expenditure, an analysis could be made to see if we could build some reasonable incentives for promoting fiscal performance of states.

A 'totality' view of fiscal and financial sector interaction is absolutely essential, in the context of new realities that have been described. What we have to keep in mind is the signaling effect that the Commission's fiscal recommendations would have on the financial markets. If there is a clear and credible indication of fiscal consolidation by the Eleventh Finance Commission, it will help smoothening the movements in long-term interest rates. Now, with the growing size of gross and net borrowings of Centre and States, persistent combined revenue deficits, and cut in capital expenditures, borrowing costs to Government remain high and sticky. The Eleventh Finance Commission's recommendations can help change the market expectations through the adoption of a more credible approach to fiscal restructuring.

While the Finance Commission deals basically with horizontal and vertical equity in resource sharing arrangement, incentives for tax-effort, and perhaps even cost-recovery issues, one can raise the question of incentive framework in expenditure allocations also. If education and health are critical for reform, and if the assignment of resources is based on the assumption of increased outlays to such sectors, how do we ensure that the assumption is realised? How should we devise transfer mechanisms that ensure allocation and performance in these sectors? In a way, this is stretching the point, but it is worth exploring to confront the reality.

RBI'S INITIATIVES

RBI has been taking initiatives, in multiple capacities, viz., as monetary authority, as debt-manager of Centre and States, and as banker to Centre and States. There is an overlap, and for that matter even conflict, in discharge of these three functions. Hence, it is difficult to pigeonhole RBI's initiatives. For the present purpose, let me allude to some of the efforts we have taken to improve the quality of information, analysis, and operations relating to government finances.

RBI has been expressing its views in its Annual Reports on the issue of government borrowings. A specific proposal on putting a ceiling on public debt has also been suggested in a technical paper on the subject published in the RBI Bulletin (December, 1997).

Initiatives have been taken to bring about reconciliation between interests of some well managed States and others in imparting market orientation to State borrowings, in the absence of progress on State Funding Corporation earlier advocated by the RBI. Currently, a State has an option to access market borrowings outside the tranche of all States, to the extent of 5 to 35 per cent of annual borrowing programme.

A scheme for consolidated Sinking Fund has been designed by the RBI as a mechanism to ensure orderly retirement of market debt, although only a few States have responded favourably.

In recognition of the emerging problems relating to guarantees, we have constituted a Working Group whose Report is due soon. Similarly, we had constituted an informal Committee to review Ways and Means Advance System of States. The recommendations of this committee are under study.

RBI is, separately, studying the implications of management

of public account for finances of governments.

RBI has been taking active interest in developing Government securities market, in terms of policy (elimination of *ad hoc* Treasury Bills), instruments (Treasury Bills of varying maturities and innovative instruments in dated securities), institutional development (Primary Dealers and Satellite Dealers), technology (screen based) and legal changes (Public Debt Act, SCR Act, Stamp Duty, etc.).

RBI is constantly improving interactions with Governments, as for example, through recently constituted Cash and Debt Management Group with the Central Government, and two meetings with State Finance Secretaries conducted recently. The interaction is also continuing through *ad hoc* groups.

RBI publishes data and analysis in its weekly and monthly Bulletins, which are available at website on an adequate and regular basis. The Report on Currency and Finance and the Annual Report provide the Bank's analysis of government finances and the policy priorities in this sector. There is an annual study of State Finances published in the RBI Bulletin, which carries a wealth of information on State Finances.

RBI has been conducting policy intensive research studies on fiscal and other macro-economic issues through its Development Research Group (DRG) wing and through the medium of its research journal, viz.; Occasional Papers, which are available for wider public dissemination. Moreover, the bank provides active research support to Government, Planning Commission and other national institutions on public finance issues. Recently, we have initiated a DRG study on the implications of fiscal deficit for macro-economic stability which should be of use to the Eleventh Finance Commission. As requested by the Commission, we will take up analysis of specific subjects in this study and make it available to the Commission in view of the Eleventh Finance Commission's appreciation of research capabilities available in the RBI.

COMMENTS ON SPECIFIC ISSUES

A number of issues have been flagged in this meeting by the eminent economists and economic administrators and I agree with most of what has been said especially on the importance of cost-recovery for commercial services rendered by government, especially in sectors of power, water and road transport. There were strong and somewhat divergent views on the relevance of fiscal deficit, importance of public ownership, advantages of decentralisation, transparency in tax-expenditures and on the issue of insensitivity to market related interest rates. I will briefly give my views on each of these issues.

On the issue of fiscal deficit, what level of fiscal deficit is sustainable is contextual – depends entirely on the context, including in particular, the level of domestic savings, especially financial savings of households, the level of Current Account deficit, the acceptable level of inflation and, of course, the rate of economic growth. More than size, what is important is how fiscal deficit is financed and for what purposes it is used. If it is financed by large order of monetisation, it has adverse implications for inflation with a lag. This has been an empirical fact for us. Dr. C. Rangarajan, our former Governor, has made research based observations on this phenomenon in our country. As regards use, to the extent it is used for financing revenue deficit, there would be no return directly attributable to such expenditures. Further, there is an addition to stock of liabilities without corresponding addition to stock of assets, impinging on future cash flows. On the other hand, if the deficit is used to finance capital expenditures, there is addition to both stock of assets and liabilities, but even then such a deficit will have negative impact as long as the direct financial return to Government on addition to stock of assets is less than cost of servicing of additional liabilities. If such expenditures directly compete with private investment and if productivity in public sector is demonstrably lower than that of private sector in the same activity, there would be a further negative impact. To the extent there is funding of public investment out of such a deficit with clear complementarity to private investments, it is possible that deficiency in direct return is made up by increase in indirect returns. One aspect often ignored by economists advocating large fiscal deficits to fund public investment is the expectations on the part of potential creditors, domestic or foreign, that borrowed funds are indeed used for genuinely productive purpose. It is not merely the advocacy or promise of productive use of funds but expectations of creditors about such productive use that becomes important if 'preemption' is reduced. The sustainable or defensible level of fiscal deficit should be viewed in the current context of mode of financing and use of funds in Centre and States. Sometimes, it is argued that increased fiscal deficit would help stimulate demand and should not be eschewed. But the issue really is whether this is a sustainable course to follow in the medium to long term. Year-to-year variations may be desirable from the view point of counter-cyclical objectives of fiscal policy but only within the objective of medium-term sustainability. The desirability or otherwise cannot, therefore, be settled in abstract terms, but only with reference to context.

On public ownership also, there have been strong views and it cannot be held that public ownership, by itself is inefficient or for that matter relatively more efficient, be it efficiency in technical, allocative or dynamic terms. Contextually, I would suggest, that there are three inter-related approaches. First, if on ideological and strategic grounds, an enterprise has to be a public enterprise, 100 per cent owned or 51 per cent, there can be no debate. On instrumentalist grounds, i.e., as an instrument of non-commercial objective, alternative ownership patterns and optimisation of results could be examined to achieve such non-commercial objectives, provided there is a debate on desirable changes, if any, in market structure also. Third, and in all other cases, a portfolio approach to ownership rather than ideological or instrumentalist needs to be considered. In an investment portfolio approach, it is not material whether a particular public enterprise is currently profit making or loss making or giving high or low returns. For all predominantly commercial activities, where entry of private enterprise is permitted, portfolio approach appears logical. In a portfolio approach, we can project future cash flows, both with plans for restructuring and without to obtain the Net Present Value. If the present value of anticipated proceeds from privatisation appear to exceed the net asset value, with or without restructuring, then privatisation is warranted. The portfolio approach can factor-in degrees of public ownership and control since restructuring option includes consideration of degrees of autonomy also. Such a framework can be applied for public enterprise in both Centre and States. The real issue is a credible threat of privatisation, which in itself will help improve the efficiency of public enterprise in as much as management and workforce would be motivated to improve their performance toward change of ownership. As a result, it is inevitable that a large public enterprise sector will remain, but with greater dynamism. I agree with the view that, a large segment of public enterprise sector will continue to exist for quite some time because of sheer size of public enterprise now. It could also be as a consequence of costly restructuring to avoid privatisation resulting in continued fiscal burden. In my view, effective threat of privatisation is useful, resulting in some actual privatisation combined with increased level of efficiency in the public enterprise sector, thus reducing the fiscal burden.

On the issue of decentralisation, either a conceptual approach or a pragmatic approach is possible. Conceptually, the case for decentralisation in Government can be made when an optimal distribution of powers and functions between various levels is arrived at and a process of decentralisation is warranted to reach the optimum. Further, decentralisation in some aspects or powers could be combined with centralisation in regard to others while meeting optimality criterion.

In the current debate, there is an impressionistic or anecdotal evidence of need for decentralisation. Empirically, it can be established, that where Centre and States are currently performing same functions (Delhi Electricity or Road Transport), States are seen to be less inefficient both in physical and financial parameters. Quantitative analysis of efficiencies, activity-wise, at Centre/district/municipal/panchayat could certainly be attempted. I will not be surprised if the results vary as between States, with a distinct tilt in favour of more decentralisation. However, real decentralisation is not possible unless the staff is squarely brought under the administrative control of relevant level of Government and democratic process is ensured.

Transparency in budget, especially quantifying, to the extent possible, and presenting tax-expenditures is certainly worthwhile. Ideally, the Eleventh Finance Commission should work on quantifying tax-expenditures in the last five years at Centre and State levels, recast their budgets on a proforma basis and consider these as inputs for assessing revenues and expenditures. There are also related issues of tax exemption of municipal bonds which has been advocated by some. It is no doubt a standard practice in many countries. In India however, municipal bonds may not sell without State guarantees, which could imply adverse credit worthiness effects for states themselves. Further, while Centre has been allowing tax exemptions to entities like PSUs for raising resources from the market, no such allowance was made for its own securities, till two years ago. Now, some relief on par with mutual funds is available. One clear way of reducing interest burden and encouraging retailing of Government securities would be to review this issue.

Finally, it has been argued that encouragings borrowing by Government at market related interest rates has not brought about any fiscal discipline since Governments in India are not sensitive to interest rates. Hence, it is argued that we need not pursue this cause. I am afraid I have serious problems with such an approach. At an abstract level, one can argue that accepting over-sensitivity in these matters as a fact helps none except those who are insensitive. Again, at an abstract level, it can be argued that price has both a demand side and supply side. If the whole of borrowing programme is monetised technically, then price is immaterial, especially since seigniorage or interest paid by Government comes back, as dividend from the Reserve Bank to Government of India. But what about costs of monetisation or inflation costs to the economy, which are recognisably high and distorting? Hence, if government does not pay this price, someone else pays it. Even so, ends of transparency of budget operations are not met. We have to separately reckon such other costs of monetisation. Assuming that there is a mix of monetisation and non-monetisation, not charging market related rates on monetised deficit has moral hazard implications. As regards non-monetised part, some cross subsidisation between the Government and the financial sector becomes inevitable if interest rates are not market related. It is true that for this logic to be convincing, markets need be developed, but developing markets and gradually adopting market related rates serve the longer term interests of efficiency and any effort in the meantime, to artificially depress the cost of borrowings to Government will not be desirable.

Presentation at the Eleventh Finance Commission in the meeting of select economists on December 4, 1998, New Delhi. The presentation does not necessarily represent the RBI's views.

16

Fiscal Reforms at State Level

Review and Prospects

Y. V. REDDY

The paper is divided into five parts, viz. role of RBI in the State finances; review of fiscal reform effort; changing role of State Governments; impact of financial sector reforms on State finances; and prospects for and issues in fiscal improvement.

Role of RBI in State Finances

RBI has been the only authentic source of regular information and analysis of State finances on a consolidated and annual basis. These reports are published by RBI and are widely circulated.

Since 1997, RBI had convened seven conferences of State Finance Secretaries, which were also attended by senior officials of central government and Planning Commission. The Conferences have provided a forum for several initiatives by State Finance Secretaries for which RBI provided professional inputs. A report on *State Level Guarantees* was generated which enabled several States to bring about legislation imposing a ceiling on State level guarantees while some other States are considering such a legislation. A *Core Group on Disclosure Norms for State Budgets* helped improve the design and coverage of budget related documents in several States. Many States recently adopted economic and functional classification of budgets with the assistance of RBI. A study on Public Account was sponsored by RBI at the request of State Finance Secretaries which was discussed in the latest Conference. State Governments interactions with credit rating agencies and with Advisory Group on Fiscal Transparency were also facilitated by RBI. In fact, several initiatives with State Governments were made possible with the RBI's role as banker, debt-manager and adviser.

Thus, as banker, RBI has been assisting States in improved cash management to maximise returns on deployment of temporary surpluses. The Ways and Means Arrangement was reviewed and a new system was introduced in 1998 in consultation with States. Arrangements have been made for electronic exchange of information between Central Accounts Section, Nagpur and individual States on daily transactions.

As debt-manager, RBI had devised a scheme for Consolidated Sinking Fund. Seven States have since set up such a Fund while several others have expressed interest. Flexibility has been provided to State Governments, since 1998-99 to directly access the market for borrowings between 5 to 35 per cent of their gross borrowing programme. Seven States have already raised funds through this route and these States appear to have obtained finer terms than otherwise.

As adviser on a variety of issues, RBI has been active in matters impinging on fiscal matters relevant to States. Thus, RBI participated in formulating a scheme for management of the *Calamity Relief Fund*. Help on technical issues was rendered on the proposed *Legislation on Fiscal Responsibility* by Centre. RBI's analysis of State finances has been used extensively by the Eleventh Finance Commission, which has acknowledged the RBI's contribution. In fact, RBI is represented in the Advisory Panel on Fiscal – Monetary Policies set up by the National Commission to Review the Working of the Constitution.

Review of Efforts towards Fiscal Reform

A reading of State budgets and speeches of Finance Ministers for the year 2000-01 helps in understanding the broad directions of the reform effort, though the measures announced do vary from State to State.

The budgets of the States for 2000-01 contain proposals relating to new tax and non-tax measures aimed at strengthening the revenue base, and expenditure management measures to arrest the growth in current expenditures. The finances of States during 2000-01 are budgeted to record an improvement over the deterioration experienced during 1999-2000. The Gross Fiscal Deficit (GFD) of the 26 States as a ratio to GDP is budgeted at 4.1 per cent in 2000-01, as compared to 3.9 per cent budgeted in 1999-2000 and the revised estimates of 4.9 per cent. The States' own taxes are budgeted to record a buoyant rise of 18.9 per cent, with sales tax receipts expected to record a 19.6 per cent increase. Consequently, the States' own resources are expected to finance 54.1 per cent of the revenue expenditure, as compared with 49.8 per cent in 1999-2000.

Complementing the efforts of States' to augment their own resources, the resource flow from the Centre in the form of devolution of taxes is anticipated to be of a higher order. The shareable taxes are estimated to show a rise of 4.3 per cent as compared with the growth of 12.8 per cent in the previous year.

The expenditure control measures initiated by the State Governments are reflected in the deceleration in both revenue and capital expenditures. However, the imbalance in the composition of expenditures would continue, with non-developmental components recording a growth of 13.9 per cent in 2000-01 on top of the growth of 27. 4 per cent in 1999-2000. The rise in the non-developmental component is predominantly due to committed expenditures viz., interest payments, administrative services, and pensions.

The important policy initiatives towards reform as culled out from the Budget Speeches of the State Government Budgets for 2000-01 may be classified broadly into fiscal consolidation, institutional, and sectoral reforms.

Fiscal consolidation measures proposed in the State budgets explore ways of moderation of expenditure and revenue augmentation. Some States have proposed the setting up of Expenditure Reforms Committees. A few States have identified performance indicators to assess the quality of expenditure restructuring. States have also initiated measures for reduction in non-merit subsidies, better targeting of subsidies and reduction of non-productive expenditures as part of expenditure management.

Fiscal restructuring measures through downsizing the Government, have also been proposed. With regard to revenue augmentation, the budget proposals include enhancement and restructuring of sales tax, land revenue rates, vehicle tax, betting tax, introduction of professional tax, etc. The State Governments have through a landmark agreement, decided to implement a harmonized floor rate of sales tax, as a prelude to the introduction of a uniform Value Added Tax (VAT).

The institutional reforms proposed in the State budgets also support the fiscal consolidation process. Many States have announced ways of reducing the cost of administration by proposing a freeze on fresh recruitment as well as reviewing manpower requirements. Some States have adopted decentralisation as the main policy plank through which expenditure moderation is sought while a few are attempting contract-employment. In order to strengthen the administrative machinery, States have also proposed the computerization of their records/departments.

The financial health and management of State level public sector undertakings have been a cause for concern in the last few years. To address this issue, proposals for financial and managerial restructuring include setting up of Board and a comprehensive review of the functioning of the State Public Sector Undertakings, which includes closing down of non-viable undertakings, after providing suitable safety nets to the employees and offering voluntary retirement schemes (VRS). Some of the States propose to set up Infrastructure Development/Investment Funds.

Sectoral reforms are varied and include commissioning Software Technology Parks or setting up Hi-Tech City, or Export Promotion Industrial Parks. In the agricultural sector, initiatives include strengthening horticulture, floriculture, animal husbandry, farm mechanization, expanding irrigation and wasteland development. Industry status is proposed for agriculture. Environmental protection is another important agenda for action proposed by the State Budgets consisting of "Green Goa Fund" and a 'plastic containment fund' through a cess on industries using plastic packing material and plastic mineral water bottles.

Power sector reforms receive a major thrust in the reform

agenda of the State Budgets. Some States have outlined initiatives aimed at restructuring of the power sector through measures relating to private sector entry into power generation; reorganization of power monoliths into separate corporations for generation, transmission and distribution; privatization of assets; and most importantly, statutory steps for establishment of regulatory/tariff authorities.

To sum up, there is a widespread realisation about the need for fiscal stabilisation and reform. Each State has devised its own measures but most of these have a common thread of reform of public enterprises, reduction in subsidies, expenditure containment and revenue augmentation. There are, however, severe limitations in regard to the adjustment effort in view of the large magnitudes of committed expenditures viz. salaries, pensions and interest charges.

Changing Role of State Governments

The changing role of State Governments on account of the reform may be analysed in terms of the vertical balance between Centre and States, horizontal inter-State imbalances and balance within State Governments.

As the reforms progress, it appears that the relative balance between Centre and States tends to tilt in favour of States for a number of reasons.

First, the most important areas for the Central Government's responsibilities are in international trade, financial sector, telecommunications, aviation, and especially banking and corporate law/practices. In most of these areas, factors such as multilateral agreements (say, WTO), globalisation, and recommended best practices of the world, tend to circumscribe, over a period, the discretionary power available in normal times to Central Government.

Second, the capacity of the Centre to reach tax levels as well as tax regimes, very different from international practices (customs, excise, corporate or income tax) also tends to get constrained, over a period, since the free and rapid flow of commodities, skills and finances among the countries would require us to be not too much out of alignment.

Third, major thrust-areas needing expansion of Government are in physical infrastructure such as road, waterworks, power, antisocial infrastructure, such as, schools and hospitals. Whether it is direct or indirect intervention, the regime that governs funding and provision in these areas is to be determined by State Governments. Thus, relative to the Centre, States are currently in the expansionary module in the State-market optimal mix. State Governments currently have more freedom to access resources for financing economic growth from the market both from domestic and in some ways, global sources. Hence, the proportion of net official flows from Centre to State as a proportion of total capital flows to States tend to get reduced.

Fourth, States could also seek advice on growth strategies not only from Planning Commission as in the past, but also from institutions like Asian Development Bank or the World Bank.

The balance, especially, economic balance among States is also likely to be affected to the extent the overall Governments' role in allocation of resources tilts in favour of markets. Thus, first States will be competing more intensely than before, in market place for resources in future and, States may find it somewhat difficult to place a significant responsibility on the Centre for their relative performance.

Second, with growth in communications, especially on economic and financial issues, people will tend to benchmark economic performance of States. There may be a slow beginning but the momentum could pick up, as evidenced by varying capacities (both in terms of amounts and interest rates) to raise financial resources for State level public enterprises, on the basis of their guarantees.

Third, there are a variety of options for managing change, which are adopted by different States. For example, a single Electricity Board for each State was an earlier model for all States, while now each State is looking at its own model of combination of institutional arrangements as well as transition path. There are plenty of opportunities to learn from each other's experiences and make modifications. Thus, inter-State interaction tends to be more intensive, by themselves or through institutional consultants, who may be interacting with several States.

Fourth, there is in this decentralised scenario, a potential for increasing the divergence in levels of income among States or even intra-State. To this extent, there may be pressure from less developed States on the Centre to play a more active role in countering market's possible neglect of less developed States.

Fifth, there could be competition among States to benchmark, perform and excel but, the new balance will have to ensure healthy competition.

The balance between the Ministries representing the combination of political executive and Government bureaucracies *vis-a-vis* exercise of ownership functions as well as regulatory functions may also change somewhat adverse to Ministries. The process of privatisation, diversified ownership and autonomy of public enterprises may erode the discretionary element of the Ministries. Once separate regulatory bodies on statutory basis are established and strengthened, they are meant to be semi-autonomous. Often, their membership need not coincide with political cycles and thus may impart greater stability to regulatory regime. Increasing role of semi-autonomous regulatory bodies tilt the balance away from the Ministries and in favour of more stable policies.

Furthermore, experience at State level in some areas has shown that the preferred route to enlarging the role of, and efficiency in functioning of Government is decentralisation in Government. For example, in primary schools or water management, the approach in some State seems to be through decentralisation or localised water management users' committees or village panchayats. This may also involve emerging new balances between Ministries or departments at State headquarters and local bodies, in favour of the latter.

While regulatory framework would be critical for development of physical infrastructure, social infrastructure would require significant Government funding. No doubt, the traditional water tight division between Government or public and private sector each combining within itself funding and provision may get blurred and larger scope realised for intermingling of the two. Such intermingling may involve non-Governmental organisation as well as local initiatives. These are in a nascent stage but evolution of new balances between public and private sectors is on the horizon. Funding and provision of social infrastructure will, however, remain the primary responsibility of States for a long time.

In brief, the major focus of economic reform in India has to be States. Second, the inter-State issue will have to be the major concern of Governments. Third, the focus of economic-management may shift from Ministries to regulatory bodies. Fourth, the major thrust of reform is to expand what may be called social infrastructure especially drinking water, health and sanitation, elementary schools, roads etc. all of which require large public funding and scope for private funding is extremely limited in the short run – especially among poorer regions. Fifth, the objectives of reform can be attained by fiscal reorientation towards larger responsibilities for States to provide public goods and social services, including anti-poverty programmes, with concomitant rollback of fiscal activism in commercial activities.

Impact of Financial Sector Reform

The financial sector reforms encompassing RBI's funding of fiscal deficit, deregulation of interest rates, regulation of banks and credit delivery through banks have a bearing on the fiscal management at the State level.

(i) The introduction in 1997 of Ways and Means Advance system in respect of the Government of India also implies that the RBI now considers the extent of monetisation at its discretion, taking into account internal debt management policy objectives. In a sense this imposes limitations, if not a precise limit, on expansionary fiscal policy to fund expenditures.

(ii) Combined with automatic monetisation of budget deficits, RBI's contributions to financial institutions also caused significant increases in primary or reserve money. This practice has been gradually discontinued in recent years on the ground that in a liberalised environment, financial institutions should expand the avenues of raising resources from the market and to the extent certain activities require cross-subsidisation, it should rightfully be the primary responsibility of the Government of India. Thus, while discontinuing RBI's support to financial institutions, net transfer of profits of the RBI as dividend has increased.

(iii) Interest rates have been deregulated to a significant degree not only to facilitate more effective monetary policy, but also because the administered interest rate regime proved to be inefficient and costly, without necessarily ensuring flow of credit to the deprived. The RBI's recommended approach, however, does not preclude subsidisation by the Government but, it disfavours in-principle excessive use of banking system to cross subsidise especially as credit seepages are not controllable. RBI favours a financial system that provides incentives to encourage flow of credit and at the same time ensuring servicing of interest and principal, i.e., bankability of schemes. Thus, the RBI has introduced modified interest rate prescriptions, providing concessionality in the case of small borrowers to size of credit limits, rather than to specified sectors or groups of borrowers.

(iv) There are two issues relating to credit delivery on which the RBI's initiative is sought, namely, regional dimension and rural-urban divide. The regional variations or inter-State disparities in credit-deposit ratio existed in the past and continue to persist in the post-reform period also. The variations may be less pronounced in some cases if ratio of credit plus investments to deposits is taken into consideration. RBI has been sensitising banks to ensure flow of credit to all States, while at the same time, urging State Governments to create enabling environment for flow of credit. Progressively, the instruments available with the RBI to 'direct' credit are less in a deregulated environment, especially since financial intermediation through non-banks including mutual funds and NBFCs, is justifiably expanding. In fact, unequal distribution of burden of social obligations between banks and non-banks could undermine the health of the banking system, which is vital to our economy.

Similarly, on the rural-urban divide in flow of bank resources, there are some constraints, as mentioned above, on the policy instruments available. The RBI, therefore, encourages local level financial intermediaries to address this issue. These include expanding the network of urban cooperative banks which are also local, revitalising the Regional Rural Banks (whose banking business in recent years is growing faster than scheduled commercial banking activity), promoting local area banks, apart from efforts to improving the cooperative credit system as a whole.

(v) As part of reform in the financial sector, there have been significant reductions in statutory preemptions, under the Statutory Liquidity Ratio in respect of banks. The share of market of non-public sector banks in the banking system is increasing. There has been diversification of ownership of several large banks. Insurance companies are also coming under competitive pressure, and hence there are limits to what may be termed as involuntary subscriptions to public debt. Under these circumstances, full subscriptions to borrowing programme approved by Government of India in respect of some of the States may not be possible if the banks and other market participants do not volunteer to subscribe. At the same time, some States which are favourably perceived by financial markets do get subscriptions at more favourable rates when they exercise the limited option of approaching the market directly.

(vi) Monetary and credit policy in India thus focusses increasingly on what Dreaze and Sen call "growth mediated security" while "support-led security", often consisting of direct anti-poverty interventions are to be addressed mainly by fiscal and other governmental activities.

In brief, as a result of financial sector reform, there are more stringent overall limits to fiscal expansion, impinging on both

Central and State finances. Second, the non-bankable components of developmental activities are required to be increasingly met by fiscal policies. Third, the commercial components or bankable components of development could be squarely shifted by State Government to financial sector provided they are made commercially viable. Fourth, the administrative, social and economic infrastructure and overall perception of governance influences flow of credit due to diversification of means of financial intermediation, deregulation and competition. Fifth, the perceptions of financial markets including credit rating agencies is relevant in ensuring full subscription to approved market borrowing programme incorporated in the State budgets. In sum, State budgets may have to differentiate between bankable and non-bankable segments, enable, expand and hive off the former while focussing on efficient use of resources for non-bankable components such as anti-poverty programmes, and social services.

Prospects and Issues

Reserve Bank has been in close interactive mode with State Governments in regard to fiscal matters in the recent past and has been of mutual benefit. There is a clear recognition among all concerned that focus of further reform would increasingly be at the State level. The reforms in financial sector have implications for fiscal management at State level and this has been fully appreciated by State Governments. The State Governments are making valiant efforts to meet the fiscal challenges before them.

The overall strategy for fiscal improvement consistent with the reform agenda in general and financial sector reform in particular is three-fold.

First, commercial activities such as power, transport, water for irrigation will have to be fully funded and operated commercially to reduce fiscal burden and also to attract financial resources from financial sector especially banks. To the extent *cross subsidisation* is deemed necessary, it should be self balancing with no burden on either the fisc or banks. This is a valid strategy irrespective of public or mixed or private ownership of the concerned commercial and financial entities. This approach would also be a precondition to adopt other more compelling strategies.

Second, State Governments will have to concentrate their efforts on institutional infrastructure especially relating to law and order and provision or delivery of essential services such as drinking water, sanitation, primary schools and dispensaries, etc. not only to serve the needs of the poor and the underprivileged but also to attract resources from the financial sector for investments in physical infrastructure and also productive activities. Improving the delivery of services should be the priority. Again, this approach is feasible in the current fiscal situation if and only if the cost recovery for commercial activities is total, with self-balancing cross-subsidisation. A word of caution is, however, necessary. To avoid seepage and misuse of concessions, the extent of cross-subsidisation should be limited.

Third, in the light of the above, public investments will have to be enhanced in agriculture to accelerate gainful employment generation and poverty reduction.

There is a broad consensus on the overall strategy but, in terms of managing the fiscal adjustment, the State Finance Secretaries have articulated several issues. The main consensus expressed in the latest (Seventh) Conference can be summarised. The main fiscal problem is structural and, solutions attempted are incremental and consequently their major pre-occupation is how to pay the each day's bills. They argued, that whenever fiscal adjustment is attempted, there is a cut, in non-committed expenditure but not in non-essential one. A predominant part of the budget is committed expenditure, especially interest, pensions, and salaries, which has no flexibility. As a consequence, there is often an atrophy of delivery of services in as much as there may be hospitals manned by doctors and nurses but no medicines, electricity or water supply. Grants to several institutions performing vital services are often postponed or reduced on account of fiscal adjustment. They apprehend that cuts in output tend to be highly disproportional to cuts in expenditure making expenditure cuts of non-committed items highly unproductive, thus undermining the reform process. Some of the Secretaries also questioned the efficacy of increasing social expenditures on the ground that opening of new schools often meant only appointment of new teachers who do not turn up in schools in any case. A few felt that efficacy of social expenditures can be improved by decentralisation while a few others advocated contract employment of teachers instead of life-time employment. There was virtual unanimity among the State Finance Secretaries that the structural problems underlying fiscal situation in the States cannot be solved unless the issue of high committed expenditures is resolved. There was also a consensus that the fiscal problem is not State specific but an all-India phenomenon, often a result of policies of the Central Government such as in pay hikes and, solutions would warrant initiatives by and setting an example by the Union Government.

From RBI's point of view, there are a few issues that are being addressed in the context of fiscal reforms at State level.

First, the Ways and Means Arrangements and Overdraft Scheme is being reviewed by a group of State Finance Secretaries in the light of settled recommendations of the Vithal Committee and those which are yet to be implemented. The Group will finalise its report by the end of December 2000. No doubt, the review will address only temporary mismatches between receipts and expenditures in State budgets, but not structural issues.

Second, recognising the need to ensure full subscription to approved borrowing programme of all States, it has been decided that RBI would prepare a technical paper on the subject, taking into account the needs of special category States. The role of Primary Dealers in Government Securities would also be addressed in the paper. The paper could also consider some institutional arrangement in the form of a State Funding Corporation as suggested in the RBI Annual Report of 1993-94, which could assist the States that happen to be reluctant, under certain circumstances, to approach the markets individually and directly.

Third, there are a few States whose cash and budgetary positions have some linkage with consortium arrangements for food credit. Such State Finance Securities are being associated with the Committee being constituted for such as review, as announced in Governor Jalan's Mid-Term Review of Monetary and Credit Policy for the year 2000-2001.

Let me conclude with an appropriate quote from the latest book from Mr. A. Premchand *Control of Public Money* (Oxford University Press) :

"Experience shows conclusively that a policy deficit, together with a vigilance deficit, has contributed, over the years to a situation, where the fiscal machinery has not been successful in addressing the concerns of the public. Despite repeated efforts at improving the machinery, the institutional recidivism has become quite common. This, in turn, was partly due to the fact that the reforms did not fully address the major concerns, and partly because they were not fully implemented. Moreover, the solutions of one era became the problems of another era. Measures sought to be implemented within the executive wing of the governments were not always matched by corresponding efforts in the external agencies, such as the audit and the legislature. There is a continuing need for a balanced approach towards improvement in the operations of the executive, audit, and the legislature. This is the task of future managers."

Address at "India: States Reform Forum" organised by The World Bank, New Delhi, November 24, 2000.

17

A Decade of Banking and Financial Sector Reforms

The financial system in India has built, over time, a vast net work of financial institutions and markets. A strong and efficient financial system is crucial to the attainment of our objectives of creating a market-driven, productive and competitive economy and to support higher investment levels and accentuate growth. The creation of such a system has been the objective that has inspired the process of financial sector reform since 1992 as part of the broader programme of structural economic reforms.

As part of this process, reform of the banking sector is now under way. The banking system is, by far, the most dominant segment of the financial sector accounting for about two thirds of the assets of the organised financial sector and it is appropriate that reform in this sector has been receiving major emphasis. The reform measures taken in this area have followed the recommendations of the Committee on the Financial System (CFS), which submitted its report in November 1991. The Report had made a number of recommendations aimed at improving the productivity, efficiency and profitability of the banking system on the one hand, and providing it greater operational flexibility and functional autonomy in decision-making, on the other. It covered policy aspects, accounting practices, institutional and structural issues and matters relating to organisational development.

Following the recommendations of the Committee on Financial System (CFS) which reported in 1991 and the second Report of the Narasimham Committee in 1998, a considerable ground has been covered in putting in place a financial system which can meet the requirements of a more competitive and open economy. By and large, financial reforms in India have proceeded in four major directions.

First, setting the policy conditions right and removing the operational constraints of the financial system. What the reform process has tried to achieve is to lower the share of pre-empted resources in the total resources of the banking system through gradual liberalisation of the cash reserve ratio and the statutory liquidity ratio.

The second directional change has been in the area of creating a more competitive environment in financial sector through reform measures such as relaxation of entry and exit norms, reduction in public ownership in banking industry and letting banks access capital market for meeting their fund requirement. The objective is to bring out the best result in terms of pricing and quality of banking services over a period of time.

The third important direction of reform has been the strengthening of market institutions and allowing greater freedom to financial intermediaries. These reforms have taken the form of gradual liberalisation of interest rates, development of money, capital and debt markets and giving operational flexibility to banks in the management of their assets and liabilities subject, of course, to prudential guidelines.

The fourth important element of reform concerns the "safety" aspects of the financial system. This is the core of the challenges facing the financial system at present. When the reform process was started in 1992, there was a massive problem of cleaning the balance sheets of banks which had deteriorated over the years. Successive reform initiatives in this area have been aimed at prescribing certain prudential standards for the financial system and addressing certain structural weaknesses which could minimise their recurrence in future. Measures such as income recognition norms, asset classification, meeting minimum capital adequacy standards through recapitalisation and devising a supervisory framework are steps in the direction of ensuring the safety of the financial system.

The Report of the Narasimham Committee (April 1998)

provides a framework for the current phase of reforms — the second generation of reforms — which could be conveniently looked at in terms of three broad inter-related issues:

(i) Actions that need to be taken to strengthen the foundations of the banking system;

(ii) Related to this, streamlining procedures, upgrading technology and human resource development;

(iii) Structural changes in the system.

These would cover aspects of banking policy, institutional, supervisory and legislative dimensions. *(Chapter I, para 1.32)*

The RBI has already acted on many of the recommendation as per the following report of RBI (Oct., 31, 2001) – action taken on the recommendations of the Committee.

MEASURES TO STRENGTHEN THE BANKING SYSTEM

Capital Adequacy

1. Recommendation: The Committee suggests that pending the emergence of markets in India where market risks can be covered, it would be desirable that capital adequacy requirements take into account market risks in addition to the credit risks. (Chapter III Para 3.10)

Action Taken: Banks are now required to assign capital for market risk. A risk weight of 2.5 per cent for market risk has been introduced on investments in Govt. and other approved securities with effect from the year ending 31st March, 2000. For investments in securities outside SLR, a risk weight of 2.5 per cent for market risk has been introduced with effect from the year ending 31st March, 2001.

(Circulars DBOD.No.BP.BC.103 /21.01.002 /98 dated 31.10.98 and 121/21.04.124/99-2000 dated 3.11.99).

2. Recommendation: In the next three years, the entire portfolio of Government securities should be marked to market and this schedule of adjustment should be announced at the earliest. It would be appropriate that there should be a 5 per cent weight for market risk for Govt. and approved securities. (Chapter III para 3.11)

Action Taken: The percentage of banks' portfolio of Govt. and approved securities which is required to be marked to market has progressively been increased. For the year ending 31st March, 2000, banks were required to mark to market 75 per cent of their investments. In order to align the Indian accounting standards with the international best practices and taking into consideration the evolving international developments, the norms for classification and valuation of investments have been modified with effect from September 30, 2000. The entire investment portfolio of banks is required to be classified under three categories, viz., Held to Maturity, Available for Sale and Held for Trading. While the securities 'Held for Trading' and 'Available for Sale' should be marked to market periodically, the securities 'Held to Maturity', which should not exceed 25 per cent of total investments are carried at acquisition cost unless it is more than the face value, in which case, the premium should be amortised over a period of time. (Circular DBOD. No BP.BC.32/21.04.048/ 2000-2001 dated 16.10.2000.)

3. Recommendation: The risk weight for a Government guaranteed advance should be the same as for other advances. To ensure that banks do not suddenly face difficulties in meeting the capital adequacy requirement, the new prescription on risk weight for Government guaranteed advances should be made prospective from the time the new prescription is put in place. (Chapter III para 3.12)

Action Taken: In cases of Govt. guaranteed advances, where the guarantee has been invoked and the concerned State Govt. has remained in default as on March 31, 2000, a risk weight of 20% on such advances, has been introduced. State Govts. who continue to be in default in respect of such invoked guarantees even after March 31, 2001, a risk weight of 100% is being assigned. (Circular DBOD.NO. BP.BC.103/21.01.002/98 dated 31.10.98)

4. Recommendation: There is an additional capital requirement of 5% of the foreign exchange open position limit. Such risks should be integrated into the calculation of risk weighted assets.

The Committee recommends that the foreign exchange open position limits should carry a 100% risk weight. (Chapter III para 3.13)

Action Taken: Risk weight of 100% has been introduced for foreign exchange open position limits with effect from March 31, 1999. (Circular DBOD.No.BP. BC.103/21.01.002/98 dt.31.10.98)

5. Recommendation: The Committee believes that it would be appropriate to go beyond the earlier norms and set new and higher norms for capital adequacy. The Committee accordingly recommends that the minimum capital to risk assets ratio be increased to 10% from its present level of 8%. It would be appropriate to phase the increase as was done on the previous occasion. Accordingly, the Committee recommends that an intermediate minimum target of 9% be achieved by the year 2000 and the ratio of 10% by 2002. The RBI should also have the authority to raise this further in respect of individual banks if in its judgement the situation with respect to their risk profile warrants such an increase. The issue of individual banks' shortfalls in the CRAR needs to be addressed in much the same way that the discipline of reserve requirements is now applied, viz., of uniformity across weak and strong banks. (Chapter III, para 3.15 - 3.16)

Action Taken: The minimum capital to risk asset ratio (CRAR) for banks has been enhanced to 9% with effect from the year ending March 31, 2000.

(Circular DBOD.No.BP.BC.103/21.01.002/98 dated 31.10.98).

6. Recommendation: In respect of PSBs, the additional capital requirement will have to come from either the Govt. or the market. With the many demands on the budget and the continuing imperative need for fiscal consolidation, subscription to bank capital funds cannot be regarded as a priority claim on budgetary resources. Those banks which are in a position to access the capital market at home or abroad should, therefore, be encouraged to do so. (Chapter III, para 3.17)

Action Taken: Banks are permitted to access the capital market. Till today, 12 banks have already accessed capital market.

Asset Quality, NPAs and Directed Credit:

7. Recommendation: The Committee recommends that an asset be classified as doubtful if it is in the substandard category for 18 months in the first instance and eventually for 12 months and loss if it has been so identified but not written off. These norms, which should be regarded as the minimum, may be brought into force in a phased manner. (Chapter III, para 3.18)

Introduction of the norm of 90 days for income recognition in a phased manner.

Action Taken: Banks have been advised that an asset will be classified as 'doubtful' if it has remained in the substandard category for 18 months instead of 24 months as at present, by March 31, 2001. Banks have been permitted to achieve these norms for additional provisioning in phases, as under : As on 31.3.2001, Provisioning of not less than 50% on the assets which have become doubtful on account of the new norm. As on 31.3.2002, Balance of the provisions not made during the previous year, in addition to the provisions needed as on 31.3.2002.

(Circular DBOD.No.BP. BC.103/ 21.01.002/98 dt.31.10.98)

In the Monetary and Credit Policy announced in April 2001, the banks have been advised to chalk out an appropriate transition path for smoothly moving over to 90 days norm. As a facilitating measure, banks should move over to charging of interest at monthly rests by April 1, 2002. Banks should commence making additional provisions for such loans, starting from the year ending March 31, 2002, which would strengthen their balance sheets and ensure smooth transition to the 90 days norm by March 31, 2004.

8. Recommendation: The Committee has noted that NPA figures do not include advances covered by Government guarantees which have turned sticky and which in the absence of such guarantees would have been classified as NPAs. The Committee is of the view that for the purposes of evaluating the quality of asset portfolio such advances should be treated as NPAs. If, however, for reason of the sovereign guarantee argument such advances are excluded from computation, the Committee would recommend that Government guaranteed advances which otherwise would have been classified as NPAs should be separately shown as an aspect of fuller disclosure and greater transparency of operations. (Chapter III, para 3.21)

Action Taken: Prudential norms in respect of advances guaranteed by State Governments where guarantee has been invoked and has remained in default for more than two quarters has been introduced in respect of advances sanctioned against State Government guarantee with effect from April 1, 2000. Banks have been advised to make provisions for advances guaranteed by State Governments which stood invoked as on March 31, 2000, in phases, during the financial years ending March 31, 2000 to March 31, 2003 with a minimum of 25% each year. (Circular DBOD. No. BP.BC.103/21.01.002/98 dt.31.10.98).

9. Recommendation: Banks and financial institutions should avoid the practice of "evergreening" by making fresh advances to their troubled constituents only with a view to settling interest dues and avoiding classification of the loans in question as NPAs. The Committee notes that the regulatory and supervisory authorities are paying particular attention to such breaches in the adherence to the spirit of the NPA definitions and are taking appropriate corrective action. At the same time, it is necessary to resist the suggestions made from time to time for a relaxation of the definition of NPAs and the norms in this regard (Chapter III, para 3.22)

Action Taken: The RBI has reiterated that banks and financial institutions should adhere to the prudential norms on asset classification, provisioning, etc. and avoid the practice of "evergreening".

(Cir. DBOD. No.BP. BC.103/ 21.01.002/98 dt.31.10.98)

10. Recommendation: The Committee believes that the objective should be to reduce the average level of net NPAs for all banks to below 5% by the year 2000 and to 3% by 2002. For those banks with an international presence the minimum objective should be to reduce gross NPAs to 5% and 3% by the year 2000 and 2002, respectively, and net NPAs to 3% and 0% by these dates. These targets cannot be achieved in the absence of measures to tackle the problem of backlog of NPAs on a one time basis and the implementation of strict prudential norms and management efficiency to prevent the recurrence of this problem. (Chapter III, para 3.26)

Action Taken: This is the long-term objective which RBI wants to pursue. Towards this direction, a number of measures have been taken to arrest the growth of NPAs: banks have been advised to tone up their credit risk management systems; put in place a loan review mechanism to ensure that advances, particularly large advances are monitored on an ongoing basis so that signals of weaknesses are detected and corrective action taken early; enhance credit appraisal skills of their staff, etc. In order to ensure recovery of the stock of NPAs, guidelines for one-time settlement have been issued in July, 2000.

11. Recommendation: The Committee is of the firm view that in any effort at financial restructuring in the form of hiving off the NPA portfolio from the books of the banks or measures to mitigate the impact of a high level of NPAs must go hand in hand with operational restructuring. Cleaning up the balance sheets of banks would thus make sense only if simultaneously steps were taken to prevent or limit the re-emergence of new NPAs which could only come about through a strict application of prudential norms and managerial improvement. (Chapter III, para 3.27)

Action Taken: Banks have been advised to take effective steps for reduction of NPAs and also put in place risk management systems and practices to prevent re-emergence of fresh NPAs. (Cir. DBOD. No. BP. BC. 103 /21.01.002/98 dated 31.10.1998)

12. Recommendation: For banks with a high NPA portfolio, the Committee suggests consideration of two alternative approaches to the problem as an alternative to the ARF proposal made by the earlier CFS. In the first approach, all loan assets in the doubtful and loss categories - which in any case represent bulk of the hard core NPAs in most banks should be identified and their realisable value determined. These assets could be transferred to an Asset Reconstruction Company (ARC) which would issue to the banks NPA Swap Bonds representing the realisable value of the assets transferred, provided the stamp duties are not excessive. The ARC could be set up by one bank or a set of banks or even in the private sector. In case the banks themselves decide to set up an ARC, it would need to be ensured that the staff required by the ARC is made available to it by the banks concerned either on transfer or on deputation basis, so that staff with institutional memory on NPAs is available to ARC and there is also some rationalisation of staff in the banks whose assets are sought to be transferred to the ARC. Funding of such an ARC could be facilitated by treating it on par with venture capital for purpose of tax incentives. Some other banks may be willing to fund such assets in effect by securitising them. This approach would be worthwhile and workable if stamp duty rates are minimal and tax incentives are provided to the banks. (Chapter III, para 3.28)

Action Taken: The proposal to set up an Asset Reconstruction Company (ARC) on a pilot basis to take over the NPAs of the three weak public sector banks, has been announced in the Union Budget for 1999-2000. The modalities for setting up the ARC are being examined.

13. Recommendation: An alternative approach could be to enable the banks in difficulty to issue bonds which could form part of Tier II capital. This will help the banks to bolster capital adequacy which has been eroded because of the provisioning requirements for NPAs. As the banks in difficulty may find it difficult to attract subscribers to bonds. Government will need to guarantee these instruments which would then make them eligible for SLR investments by banks and approve instruments by LIC, GIC and Provident Funds (Chapter III, para 3.29)

Action Taken: Banks are permitted to issue bonds for augmenting their Tier II capital. Guarantee of the Govt. for these bonds is not considered necessary.

14. Recommendation: Directed credit has a proportionately higher share in NPA portfolio of banks and has been one of the factors in erosion in the quality of bank assets. There is continuing need for banks to extend credit to agriculture and small scale sector which are important segments of the national economy, on commercial considerations and on the basis of creditworthiness. In this process, there is scope for correcting the distortions arising out of directed credit and its impact on banks' assets quality. (Chapter III, para 3.31)

Action Taken: The loans to agricultural and SSI sectors are now generally being granted on commercial considerations and on the basis of creditworthiness of the borrower. Further, the concessionality on interest rates for advances has been done away with, except for advances under the DRI Scheme. While advances upto Rs.2 lakh should carry interest rate not exceeding PLR, interest rates on advances of over Rs.2 lakh have been freed.

15. Recommendation: The Committee has noted the reasons why the Government could not accept the recommendation for reducing the scope of directed credit under priority sector from 40% to 10%. The Committee recognises that the small and marginal farmers and the tiny sector of industry and small businesses have problems with regard to obtaining credit and some earmarking may be necessary for this sector. Under the present dispensation, within the priority sector 10% of net bank credit is earmarked for lending to weaker sections. A major portion of this lending is on account of Government sponsored poverty alleviation and employment generation schemes. The Committee recommends that given the special needs of this sector, the current practice may continue. The Branch Managers of banks should, however, be fully responsible for the identification of beneficiaries under the Government sponsored credit linked schemes. The Committee proposes that given the importance and needs of employment oriented sectors like food processing and related service activities in agriculture, fisheries, poultry and dairying, these sectors should also be covered under the scope of priority sector lending. The Committee recommends that the interest subsidy element in credit for the priority sector should be totally eliminated and even interest rates on loans under Rs.2 lakh should be deregulated for scheduled commercial banks as has been done in the case of Regional Rural Banks and co-operative credit institutions. The Committee believes that it is the timely and adequate availability of credit rather than its cost which is material for the intended beneficiaries. The reduction of the pre-empted portion of banks' resources through the SLR and CRR would, in any case, enlarge the ability of banks to dispense credit to these sectors. (Chapter III, para 3.32)

Action Taken: As per the present stipulation, banks are required to lend 10% of net bank credit (NBC) for weaker sections which includes all small and marginal farmers, all IRDP and DRI borrowers, borrowers under SUME etc. The Committee has recommended that the present stipulation may continue.

As recommended by the Committee, some activities like food processing, related service activities in agriculture, fisheries, poultry, dairying have been brought under priority sector. (circular RPCD. NO.Plan. BC. 60/04.09.01/ 98-99 dt.28-1-99).

Under the existing dispensation, Units in sectors like food processing, etc., satisfying either the definition of SSI [the ceiling of investment in plant and machinery (original cost) for a unit being classified under this category has since been enhanced to Rs. 3 crore from Rs.60 lakhs/Rs.75 lakhs for ancillaries and export oriented units] or small business are already covered under priority sector. No further changes are considered necessary, as larger units need not be given any advantage by enlarging the scope of definition of priority sector advances.

As a first step towards deregulation of interest rates on credit limits up to Rs.2 lakh and eliminating interest subsidy element in credit for priority sector, in the Monetary and Credit Policy announced in April, 1998, it has been stipulated that interest rates on loans up to Rs.2 lakh should not exceed PLR as against the earlier stipulation of 'not exceeding 13.5%', for credit limits of Rs.25,000—Rs.2 lakh and 12% for credit limit up to Rs.25,000. Banks are free to decide their PLR subject to their obtaining the prior approval of their Boards therefor. As the PLR differs from bank to bank, depending on their cost of funds and competitive strategies, the measure is a step towards deregulation of interest rates. Thus the recommendation of the Committee has been implemented in spirit. It may be stated that except for loans under DRI there is no subsidisation of interest.

(Cir. MPD.BC.175/07.01.279/97-98 dated 29.4.98)

Prudential Norms and Disclosure Requirements:

16. Recommendation: With regard to income recognition, in India, income stops accruing when interest or instalment of principal is not paid within 180 days. The Committee believes that we should move towards international practices in this regard and recommends the introduction of the norm of 90 days in a phased manner by the year 2002. (Chapter III, para 3.35)

Action Taken: The recommendation of the Committee that

we should move towards international practices in regard to income recognition is accepted in principle. However, tightening of the prudential norms should be made keeping in view the existing legal framework, production and payment cycles, business practices, the predominant share of agriculture in the country's economy, etc. The production and repayment cycles in the industry in the country generally involve a period of not less than from 4 to 6 months. A large number of SSIs also have difficulties in timely realization of their bills drawn on the suppliers. These have to be taken into account while contemplating any change in the norm.

Implementation of the recommendation would have serious implications on the asset portfolio of banks and even good quality borrowers and find it difficult to comply with the norms recommended. There have been representations from banks and financial institutions seeking relaxations in the above instructions by increasing the period to 3-4 quarters. Keeping in view the current industrial scenario, implementation of the recommendation would have serious implications even to healthy borrowers.

Furthermore, interest on advances is calculated by banks at quarterly rests. Keeping in view the large number and volume of accounts, if we have to implement the recommendation, a few preconditions should be met : –

[a] Banks should introduce calculation of interest at monthly rests;

[b] There should be 100% computerization of banks' operations. Unless 100% computerization is made, it may not be feasible to implement the recommendation ;

[c] It is also necessary to tone up the legal machinery for speedy disposal of the collateral taken as security for the advance.

However, considering the need to bring our norms in line with the best international practices, the recommendations made by the Committee would be our long term objective. As the level of gross NPAs of banks come down because of better management practices, the recommendation to introduce the norm of 90 days will be examined.

17. Recommendation: At present, there is no requirement in India for a general provision on standard assets. In the Committee's view a general provision, say, of 1% would be appropriate and RBI should consider its introduction in a phased manner. (Chapter III, para 3.36)

Action Taken: To start with, a general provision on standard assets of a minimum of 0.25% from the year ended March 31, 2000 introduced. (Cir. DBOD. No. BP.BC.103/21.01.002/98 dt.31.10.98)

18. Recommendation: The Committee believes that in the case of future loans, the income recognition and asset classification and provisioning norms should apply even to Government guaranteed advances in the same manner as for any other advance. For existing Government guaranteed advances, RBI, Government and banks may work out a mechanism for a phased rectification of the irregularities in these accounts. (Chapter III, para 3.37)

Action Taken: Please see comments in respect of item No.8 above.

19. Recommendation: There is a need for disclosure, in a phased manner, of the maturity pattern of assets and liabilities, foreign currency assets and liabilities, movements in provision account and NPAs. The RBI should direct banks to publish, in addition to financial statements of independent entities, a consolidated balance sheet to reveal the strength of the group. Full disclosure would also be required of connected lending and lending to sensitive sectors. Furthermore, it should also ask banks to disclose loans given to related companies in the bank's balance sheets. Full disclosure of information should not be only a regulatory requirement. It would be necessary to enable a bank's creditors, investors and rating agencies to get a true picture of its functioning - an important requirement in a market driven financial sector. (Chapter III, para 3.38)

Action Taken: Banks have been advised to disclose the following information, in addition to the existing disclosures, in the 'Notes on Accounts' to the balance sheet from the accounting year ended March 31, 2000.

i. Maturity pattern of loans and advances,

ii. Maturity pattern of investment securities,

iii. Foreign currency assets and liabilities

iv. Movement in NPAs,

v. Maturity pattern of deposits

vi. Maturity pattern of borrowings

vii. Lending to sensitive sectors as defined from time to time

(Cir.DBOD.No.BP.BC.9/21.04.018/99 dt.10.2.99)

20. Recommendation: Banks should also pay greater attention to asset liability management to avoid mismatches and to cover, among others, liquidity and interest rate risks. (Chapter III, para 3.41).

Action Taken: Detailed guidelines issued to banks on asset - liability management. Implementation of these guidelines would enable banks to avoid liquidity mismatches as also to cover, among others, liquidity and interest rate risks. (Circular. DBOD.No.BP.BC.8/21.04.098/99 dated 10th February, 1999).

21. Recommendation: Banks should be encouraged to adopt statistical risk management techniques like Value-at-Risk in respect of balance sheet items which are susceptible to market price fluctuations, forex rate volatility and interest rate changes. While the Reserve Bank may initially, prescribe certain normative models for market risk management, the ultimate objective should be that of banks building up their own models and RBI backtesting them for their validity on a periodical basis.(Chapter III, para 3.41 - 3.42)

Action Taken: Comprehensive guidelines have been issued to enable banks to put in place appropriate risk management systems. Banks have also been advised to adopt statistical risk management techniques like Value-at-Risk (which is a statistical method of assessing the potential maximum loss from a credit or investment exposure, over a definite holding period at a given confidence level) or other models appropriate to their level of business operation. (Circular. DBOD. No. BP.BC 98/21.04.103/99 dated 7.10.99)

Systems and Methods in Banks :

22. Recommendation: Banks should bring out revised Operational Manuals and update them regularly, keeping in view the emerging needs and ensure adherence to the instructions so that these operations are conducted in the best interest of a bank and with a view to promoting good customer service. These should form the basic objective of internal control systems, the major components of which are : (I) Internal Inspection and Audit, including concurrent audit, (2) Submission of Control Returns by branches/controlling offices to higher level offices (3) Visits by controlling officials to the field level offices (4) Risk management systems (5) Simplification of documentation, procedure and of inter office communication channels.(Chapter IV, para 4.3)

Action Taken: Banks have been advised to bring out revised Operative Manuals and update them regularly. Banks have confirmed having brought out revised Manuals. (Circular. DBOD. No.BP.BC.29/21.01.023/98-99 dt.16.4.99)

23. Recommendation: An area requiring close scrutiny in the coming years would be computer audit, in view of large scale usage and reliance on information technology (Chapter IV, para 4.7)

Action Taken: Banks have been advised to set up EDP Audit Cell, as part of their Inspection Department. (circular DBS. No. CO PP.BC.55/11.01.005/ 98-99 dated 19.6.99).

24. Recommendation: There is enough international experience to show the dangers to an institution arising out of inadequate reporting to and checking by the back offices of trading transactions and positions taken. Banks should pay special attention to this aspect (Chapter IV, para 4.8).

Action Taken: RBI had in 1992 emphasised to banks the importance of an effective management reporting system, segregation of the trading and back office functions, etc. The efficacy of the systems put in place by banks is being constantly reviewed by the RBI through periodical inspections. (Circular DBOD. No. FSC. BC. 143A/ 24.48.001/91-92 dt.20.6.92)

25. Recommendation: There is need to institute an independent loan review mechanism especially for large borrowal accounts and systems to identify potential NPAs. It would be desirable that banks evolve a filtering mechanism by stipulating in-house prudential limits beyond which exposures on single/group borrowers are taken keeping in view their risk profile as revealed through credit rating and other relevant factors. Further, in-house limits could be thought of to limit the concentration of large exposures and industry/sector/geographical exposures within the Board approved exposure limits and proper overseeing of these by the senior management/ boards. (Chapter IV, para 4.12 - 4.16)

Action Taken: Banks have been advised to put in place an independent Loan Review Mechanism, as recommended by the Committee. (Cir. DBOD.No.BP.BC.103/21.01.002/98 dated 31.10.98).

26. Recommendation: The Committee feels that the present practice of RBI selection of statutory auditors for banks with Board of Directors having no role in the appointment process, is not conducive to sound corporate governance. We would recommend that the RBI may review the existing practice in this regard. It may also reassess the role and function of the Standing Advisory Committee on Bank Audit in the light of the setting up of the Audit Committee under the aegis of the Board for Financial Supervision. (Chapter IV, para 4.19)

Action Taken: The recommendation was put up before the Audit Sub-Committee of the Board for Financial Supervision which was of the view that the existing practice should continue.

27. Recommendation: The Committee notes that public sector banks and financial institutions have yet to introduce a system of recruiting skilled manpower from the open market. The Committee believes that this delay has had an impact on the competency levels of public sector banks in some areas and they have consequently lost some ground to foreign banks and the newly set up private sector banks. The Committee urges that this aspect be given urgent consideration and in case there are any extant policy driven impediments to introducing this system, appropriate steps be taken by the authorities towards the needed deregulation. Banks have to tone up their skills base by resorting, on an ongoing basis, to lateral induction of experienced and skilled personnel, particularly for quick entry into new activity/areas. The Committee notes that there has been considerable decline in the scale of merit-based recruitment even at the entry level in many banks. The concept of direct recruitment itself has been considerably diluted by many PSBs including the State Bank of India by counting internal promotions to the trainee officers' cadre as direct recruitment. The Committee would strongly urge the managements of public sector banks to take steps to reverse this trend. The CFS had recommended that there was no need for continuing with the Banking Service Recruitment Boards insofar as recruitment of officers was concerned. This Committee, upon examination of the issue, reaffirms that recommendation. As for recruitment in the clerical cadre, the Committee recommends that a beginning be made in this regard by permitting three or four large. well-performing banks, including State Bank of India, to set up their own recruitment machinery for recruiting clerical staff. If the experience under this new arrangement proves satisfactory, it could then pave the way for eventually doing away completely with the Banking Service Recruitment Boards.(Chapter IV, para 4.21 - 4.23)

Action Taken: The public sector banks have been permitted to recruit from the open market or by way of campus recruitment, skilled personnel in areas like information technology, risk management, treasury operations, etc.

As regards the recommendation in regard to discontinuing the practice of recruitment of officers through Banking Services Recruitment Boards, Govt. may furnish comments.

28. Recommendation: It seems apparent that there are varying levels of overmanning in public sector banks. The managements of individual banks must initiate steps to measure what adjustments in the size of their work force is necessary for the banks to remain efficient, competitive and viable. Surplus staff, where identified, would need to be redeployed on new business and activities, where necessary after suitable retraining. It is possible that even after this some of the excess staff may not be suitable for redeployment on grounds of aptitude and mobility. It will, therefore, be necessary to introduce an appropriate Voluntary Retirement Scheme with incentives. The managements of banks would need to initiate dialogue in this area with representatives of labour. (Chapter IV, para 4.5 & 4.24).

Action Taken: While some of the public sector banks have introduced VRS after consultations with Employees' Unions, others are in the process of introducing such schemes.

29. Recommendation: The Committee would urge the managements of Indian banks to review the changing training needs in individual banks keeping in mind their own business environment and to address these urgently. (Chapter IV, para 4.32)

Action Taken: Banks have been advised to review the training needs and give more focus to emerging areas like Credit Management, Treasury Management, Risk Management, Information Technology, etc. (Circular DBOD.No.BP.BC.103/ 21.01.002/98 dated 31.10.1998).

30. Recommendation: Globally, banking and financial systems have undergone fundamental changes because of the ongoing revolution in information and communications technology. Information technology and electronic funds transfer systems have emerged as the twin pillars of modern banking development. This phenomenon has largely bypassed the Indian banking system although most technologies that could be considered suitable for India have been introduced in some diluted form. The Committee feels that requisite success in this area has not been achieved because of the following reasons:

- Inadequate bank automation.
- Not so strong commercially oriented inter-bank platform.
- Lack of a planned, standardised, electronic payment systems backbone.
- Inadequate telecom infrastructure.
- Inadequate marketing effort.
- Lack of clarity and certainty on legal issues and
- Lack of data warehousing network.

The Committee has tried to list out series of implementation steps for achieving rapid induction of information technology in the banking system. Further, information and control systems need to be developed in several areas like

- Better tracking of spreads, costs and NPAs for higher profitability.

- Accurate and timely information for strategic decisions to identify and promote profitable products and customers.
- Risk and Asset-Liability management; and
- Efficient Treasury management.

(Chapter IV, para 4.66 & 4.70)

Action Taken: A Working Group was set up with representation from public sector banks, technology experts, to operationalise and implement the programme of computerisation for banks within a definite time frame. All the recommendations of Group have been accepted for implementation.

In pursuance of the recommendations of the Working Group, the Indian Financial Network (INFINET), a wide area Satellite based network using VSAT technology has been commissioned on 24th June, 1999 at IDRBT, Hyderabad which will connect bank branches and RBI Offices in a phased manner.

The development of the Payment System Generic Architecture Model for both domestic and cross-border payments has been undertaken. A consultant has been appointed to assist in the implementation of the RTGS. Progress is also being made towards developing standards for newer payment instruments such as Smart Cards.

Three standing Committees to review security policies, message formats, software, to examine legal issues on electronic banking and to monitor progress of computerization of branches of banks handling Govt. transactions have been formed. Public Sector Banks have been advised to report technology progress on 20 short-listed action points.

Structural Issues :

31. Recommendation: The Committee has taken note of the twin phenomena of consolidation and convergence which the financial system is now experiencing globally. In India also banks and DFIs are moving closer to each other in the scope of their activities. The Committee is of the view that with such convergence of activities between banks and DFIs, the DFIs should, over a period of time, convert themselves to banks. There would then be only two forms of intermediaries, viz. banking companies and non-banking finance companies. If a DFI does not acquire a banking licence within a stipulated time it would be categorised as a non-banking finance company. A DFI which converts to a bank can be given some time to phase in reserve requirements in respect of its liabilities to bring it on par with the requirements relating to commercial banks. Similarly, as long as a system of directed credit is in vogue a formula should be worked out to extend this to DFIs which have become banks (Chapter V, para 5.6) .

Action Taken: Based on the recommendations of the Khan Working Group on Harmonisation of the Role and Operations of banks and DFIs, RBI had released a Discussion Paper in January, 1999 for wider public debate. The feedback on the discussion paper indicated that while universal banking is desirable from the point of view of efficiency of resource use, there is need for caution in moving towards such a system by banks and DFIs. Major areas requiring attention are the status of financial sector reforms, the state of preparedness of concerned institutions, the evolution of regulatory-regime and above all a viable transition path for institutions which are desirous of moving in the direction of universal banking. The Monetary and Credit Policy for the year 2000 -2001 proposed to adopt the following broad approach for considering proposals in this area :

a. The principle of "Universal Banking" is a desirable goal and some progress has already been made by permitting banks to diversify into investments and long-term financing and the DFIs to lend for working capital, etc. However, banks have certain special characteristics and as such any dilution of RBI's prudential and supervisory norms for conduct of banking business would be inadvisable. Further, any conglomerate, in which a bank is present, should be subject to a consolidated approach to supervision and regulation.

b. Any DFI, which wishes to do so, should have the option to transform into bank (which it can exercise), provided the prudential norms as applicable to banks are fully satisfied. To this end, a DFI would need to prepare a transition path in order to fully comply with the regulatory requirement of a bank. The DFI concerned may consult

RBI for such transition arrangements. Reserve Bank will consider such requests on a case by case basis.

(Circular MPD.BC.196/07.01.279/99-2000 dt. 27.4.2000)

32. Recommendation: Mergers between banks and between banks and DFIs and NBFCs need to be based on synergies and locational and business specific complimentarities of the concerned institutions and must obviously make sound commercial sense. Mergers of public sector banks should emanate from management of banks with Govt. as the common shareholder playing a supportive role. Such mergers, however, can be worthwhile if they lead to rationalisation of workforce and branch network; otherwise the mergers of public sector banks would tie down the managements with operational issues and distract attention from the real issue. It would be necessary to evolve policies aimed at "rightsizing" and redeployment of the surplus staff either by way of retraining them and giving them appropriate alternate employment or by introducing a VRS with appropriate incentives. This would necessitate the co-operation and understanding of the employees and towards this direction, managements should initiate discussions with the representatives of staff and would need to convince their employees about the intrinsic soundness of the idea, the competitive benefits that would accrue and the scope and potential for employees' own professional advancement in a larger institution. Mergers should not be seen as a means of bailing out weak banks. Mergers between strong banks/FIs would make for greater economic and commercial sense and would be a case where the whole is greater than the sum of its parts and have a "force multiplier effect". (Chapter V, para 5.13 - 5.15)

Action Taken: The recommendation has been noted. A non-banking finance company has since been permitted to merge with a bank. Two banks in the private sector have also merged based on synergies and business specific complementarities.

33. Recommendation: A 'weak bank' should be one whose accumulated losses and net NPAs exceed its net worth or one whose operating profits less its income on recapitalisation bonds is negative for three consecutive years. A case by case examination of the weak banks should be undertaken to identify those which are potentially revivable with a programme of financial and operational restructuring. Such banks could be nurtured into healthy units by slowing down on expansion, eschewing high cost funds/borrowings, judicious manpower deployment, recovery initiatives, containment of expenditure etc. The future set up of such banks should also be given due consideration. Merger could be a solution to the problem of weak banks but only after cleaning up their balance sheets. If there is no voluntary response to a take over of these banks, it may be desirable to think in terms of a Restructuring Commission for such public sector banks for considering other options including restructuring, merger amalgamation or failing these closure. Such a Commission could have terms of reference which, inter alia, should include suggestion of measures to safeguard the interest of depositors and employees and to deal with possible negative externalities. Weak banks which on a careful examination are not capable of revival over a period of three years, should be referred to the Commission. (Chapter V, para 5.16 - 5.18)

Action Taken: In addition to the two definitions for identifying 'weak' banks recommended by the Committee, RBI monitors banks to identify 'potential weakness' on the basis of five more parameters (related to solvency, profitability and earnings) as recommended by the Working Group on Restructuring of Weak Public Sector Banks (Chairman : Shri M.S.Verma).

In respect of weak banks, a bank-specific restructuring programme aimed at turning around the bank by reducing their cost of operation, and improving income levels, has been put in place.

The recommendation for setting up of a Restructuring Commission has not been considered. However, the Union Budget for 2000-2001 has proposed setting up of a Financial Restructuring Authority for a weak or potentially weak bank.

34. Recommendation: The policy of licensing new private banks (other than local area banks) may continue. The start up capital requirements of Rs.100 crore were set in 1993 and these may be reviewed. The Committee would recommend that there should be well defined criteria and a transparent mechanism for deciding the ability of promoters to professionally manage the banks and no category should be excluded on a priori grounds. The question of a minimum threshold capital for old private banks also deserves attention and mergers could be one of the options available for reaching the required capital thresholds. The Committee would also, in this connection, suggest that as long as it is laid down (as now) that any particular promoter group cannot hold more than 40% of the equity of a bank, any further restriction of voting rights by limiting it to 10% may be done away with. (Chapter V, para 5.20)

Action Taken: The policy of licensing new banks in the private sector has been reviewed by an in-house Working Group set up by RBI. Based on the recommendations of the Working Group, the licensing policy is being revised.

35. Recommendation: The Committee is of the view that foreign banks may be allowed to set up subsidiaries or joint ventures in India. Such subsidiaries or joint ventures should be treated on par with other private banks and subject to the same conditions with regard to branches and directed credit as these banks (Chapter V, para 5.21).

Action Taken: The recommendation has been examined. It has been felt that branch presence by foreign banks would be better for the reason that the parent bank would stand ready to support the branch in times of distress. Since subsidiaries would be set up as a joint stock companies with limited liability, the parent bank's liability to its subsidiary would be limited to its shareholding. In the case of branches, the parent bank has responsibility both towards capital and management whereas in the case of subsidiaries, the parent bank's responsibility towards capital is limited.

36. Recommendation: All NBFCs are statutorily required to have a minimum net worth of Rs.25 lakhs if they are to be registered. The Committee is of the view that this minimum figure should be progressively enhanced to Rs.2 crores which is permissible now under the statute and that in the first instance it should be raised to Rs.50 lakhs. (Chapter V, para 5.36)

Action Taken: In respect of new NBFCs, which seek registration with the RBI and commence the business on or after April 20,1999 the criteria in regard to minimum net worth has been increased to Rs.2 crore, vide the Monetary and Credit Policy for the year 1999-2000.

(Circular MPD.BC.185/07.01.279/98-99 dated 20th April, 1999).

37. Recommendation: Deposit insurance for NBFCs could blur the distinction between banks, which are much more closely regulated, and the non banks as far as safety of deposit is concerned and consequently lead to a serious moral hazard problem and adverse portfolio selection. The Committee would advise against any insurance of deposits with NBFCs. (Chapter V, para 5.38)

Action Taken: The recommendation on not providing insurance cover for deposits with NBFCs has been noted.

38. Recommendation: RBI should undertake a review of the current entry norms for urban cooperative banks and prescribe revised prudent minimum capital norms for these banks. Though cooperation is a state subject, since UCBs are primarily credit institutions meant to be run on commercial lines, the Committee recommends that this duality in control should be dispensed with. It should be primarily the task of the Board of Financial Supervision to set up regulatory standards for Urban Cooperative Banks and ensure compliance with these standards through the instrumentality of supervision. (Chapter V, para 5.39)

Action Taken: The norms with regard to minimum capital requirements for urban cooperative banks(UCBs) have been revised with effect from 1st April, 1998. Implementation of this recommendation on doing away with duality of control over UCBs would involve amendments to State Cooperative Societies Acts. The Government therefore, has to consider.

39. Recommendation: The Committee is of the view that there is need for a reform of the deposit insurance scheme. In India, deposits are insured upto Rs.1 lakh. There is no need to increase the amount further. There is, however, need to shift away from the 'flat' rate premiums to 'risk based' or 'variable rate' premiums. Under risk based premium system all banks would not be charged a uniform premium. While there can be a minimum flat rate which will have to be paid by all banks on all their customer deposits, institutions which have riskier porfolios or which have lower ratings should pay higher premium. There would thus be a graded premium. As the Reserve Bank is now awarding CAMELS ratings to banks, these ratings could form the basis for charging deposit insurance premium. (Chapter V, para 5.42)

Action Taken: This has been accepted for implementation. The Working Group on Deposit Insurance appointed by RBI has recommended the modalities for switching over to 'risk based' premium for deposit insurance and the recommendations are under examination.

40. Recommendation: The Committee is of the view that the inter-bank call and notice money market and inter-bank term money market should be strictly restricted to banks. The only exception should be the primary dealers who, in a sense, perform a key function of equilibrating the call money market and are formally treated as banks for the purpose of their inter-bank transactions. All the other present non-bank participants in the inter-bank call money market should not be provided access to the inter-bank call money market. These institutions could be provided access to the money market through different segments. (Chapter V, Annexure para A7)

Action Taken: The phasing out of non-bank participants from inter-bank Call/Notice Money market will be synchronized with the development of repo market. Keeping in view this objective, RBI has widened the scope of repo market to include all entities having SGL Account and Current Account in Mumbai, thus increasing the number of eligible non-bank entities to 64. Further, the permission given to non-bank entities to lend in the call/ notice money market by routing their operations through PDs has been extended upto June, 2001. RBI aims to move towards a pure inter-bank(including PDs) call/notice money market. With a view to further deepening the money market and enable banks, PDs and AIFIs to hedge interest rate risk, these entities are allowed to undertake FRA/IRSs as a product for their own balance sheet management and for market making purposes. Mutual Funds, in addition to corporates are also permitted to undertake FRAs/IRSs with these players. This measure is, inter alia, expected to help development of a term money market.

41. Recommendation: There must be clearly defined prudent limits beyond which banks should not be allowed to rely on the call money market. This would reduce the problem of vulnerability of chronic borrowers. Access to the call market should be essentially for meeting unforeseen swings and not as a regular means of financing banks' lending operations (Chapter V, Annexure, para A8).

Action Taken: RBI has advised banks to put in place comprehensive ALM System with effect from 1.4.1999. ALM would effectively put a cap on reliance on call money market. Detailed Risk Management Guidelines have also been issued vide circular DBOD No. BP.BC.98/21.04.103/99 dated 7th Oct. 1999.

42. Recommendation: The RBI support to the market should be through a Liquidity Adjustment Facility under which the RBI would periodically, if necessary daily, reset its Repo and Reverse Repo rates which would in a sense provide a reasonable corridor for market play. While there is much merit in an inter-bank reference rate like a LIBOR, such a reference rate would emerge as banks implement sound liquidity management facilities and the other suggestions made above are implemented. Such a rate cannot be anointed, as it has to earn its position in the market by being a fairly stable rate which signals small discrete interest rate changes to the rest of the system. (Chapter V, Annexure para A8).

Action Taken: The ILAF (Interim Liquidity Adjustment Facility) introduced earlier has served its purpose as a transitional measure for providing reasonable access to liquid funds at set rates of interest. In view of the experience gained in operating the interim scheme last year, an Internal Group was set up by RBI to consider further steps to be taken. Following the recommendation of the Internal Group, it was announced in the Monetary and Credit Policy Measures in April, 2000 to proceed with the implementation of a full-fledged LAF. The new scheme will be introduced progressively in convenient stages in order to ensure smooth transition.

- In the first stage, with effect from June 5, 2000, the Additional CLF and level II support to PDs will be replaced by variable rate repo auctions with same day settlement.
- In the second stage, the effective date for which will be

decided in consultation with banks and PDs, CLF and level I liquidity support will also be replaced by variable rate repo auctions. Some minimum liquidity support to PDs will be continued but at interest rate linked to variable rate in the daily repos auctions as determined by RBI from time to time.

- With full computerisation of Public Debt Office (PDO) and introduction of RTGS expected to be in place by the end of the current year, in the third stage, repo operations through electronic transfers will be introduced. In the final stage, it will be possible to operate LAF at different timings of the same day.

(Cir. MPD.BC. 196/07.01.279/99-2000 dated 27.4.2000)

43. Recommendation: The minimum period of FD be reduced to 15 days and all money market instruments should likewise have a similar reduced minimum duration. (Chapter V, Annexure para A9)

Action Taken: The minimum maturity of CDs has been reduced to 15 days, vide circular DBOD.No. BP.BC. 169/21.01.002/2000 dated 3.5.2000.

44. Recommendation: Foreign institutional investors should be given access to the Treasury Bill market. Broadening the market by increasing the participants would provide depth to the market (Chapter V, Annexure para A 10)

Action Taken: FIIs have been permitted to invest in Treasury Bills, vide Monetary and Credit Policy announced in April 1998. (Cir. MPD.BC. 175/07.01.279/97-98 dated 29.4.98).

45. Recommendation: With the progressive expansion of the forward exchange market, there should be an endeavour to integrate the forward exchange market with the spot forex market by allowing all participants in the spot forex market to participate in the forward market upto their exposures. Furthermore, the forex market, the money market and the securities should be allowed to integrate and the forward premia should reflect the interest rate differential. As instruments move in tandem in these markets the desiderative of a seamless and vibrant financial market would hopefully emerge (Chapter V, Annexure para A 11).

Action Taken: With effect from June 11, 1998 Foreign Institutional investors were permitted to take forward cover from Authorised Dealers to the extent of 15 per cent of their existing investment as on that date. Any incremental investment over the level prevailing on June 11, 1998 was also made eligible for forward cover. The Monetary and Credit Policy for 1999-2000 has further simplified the procedure by linking the above mentioned limits to FIIs' outstanding investments as on March 31, 1999. In other words, 15 per cent of outstanding investment on March 31, 1999 as well as the entire amount - 100 per cent - of any additional investment made after this date will be eligible for forward cover. Further, any FII which has exhausted the limits mentioned above can apply to RBI for additional forward cover for a further 15 per cent of their outstanding investments in India at the end of March 1999.

Rural and Small Industrial Credit :

46. Recommendation: The Committee also recommends that a distinction be made between NPAs arising out of client specific and institution specific reasons and general (agro-climatic and environmental issues) factors. While there should be no concession in treatment of NPAs arising from client specific reasons, any decision to declare a particular crop or product or a particular region to be distress hit should be taken purely on techno-economic consideration by a technical body like NABARD. (Chapter VI, para 6.6)

Action Taken: In the event of adverse agro-climatic and environmental factors, covering all natural calamities, outstanding loans are converted/rescheduled/rephrased suitably. Agricultural advances so rescheduled are provided relief for NPA classification. The decision to declare a particular crop or product or a particular region as distress hit is at present vested in the concerned District Administration Authority and the desirability of consulting NABARD which is the technical body, before taking the decision, would be examined.

47. Recommendation: As a measure of improving the efficiency and imparting a measure of flexibility the committee recommends consideration of the debt securitisation concept within the priority sector. This could enable banks, which are not able to reach the priority sector target to purchase the debt from the institutions, which are able to lend beyond their mandated percentage. (Chapter VI, para 6.8)

Action Taken: The recommendation of the Committee, which basically aims at ensuring that the target for priority sector lending is achieved by each of the banks, has been re-examined. As of March 2000, all public sector banks with the exception of UCO Bank have achieved the priority sector lending target individually and the public sector banks as a Group has exceeded the target at the macro-level. The UCO Bank is short of achievement only marginally. Furthermore, every year the Govt. has been setting up a Rural Infrastructure Development Fund (RIDF) in which all banks which do not achieve the priority sector target contribute the amount of shortfall. Thus all banks, directly or indirectly are able to fulfill the priority sector lending targets. Though the concept of debt securitisation is a novel idea, it will not have any practical application since it will not help in augmenting the flow of credit to the priority sector nor will it help in addressing the question of regional imbalances. It has, therefore, been decided that the recommendation need not be considered for the present.

48. Recommendation: Banking policy should facilitate the evolution and growth of micro credit institutions including LABs which focus on agriculture, tiny and small scale industries promoted by NGOs for meeting the banking needs of the poor. Third-tier banks should be promoted and strengthened to be autonomous, vibrant, effective and competitive in their operations. (Chapter VI, para 6.16)

Action Taken: In principle approval has been granted for setting up of 10 Local Area Banks (LABs). Out of these, on account of non-compliance with the terms and conditions, the 'in principle' approvals given to 4 banks were withdrawn. Of the remaining, 4 LABs have already started functioning after obtaining licences under Section 22 of Banking Regulation Act, 1949.

49. Recommendation: Banks should devise appropriate criteria suited to the small industrial sector and be responsive to its genuine credit needs but this should not be by sacrificing cannons of sound banking. Borrowers also need to accept credit discipline. There is also need to review the present institutional set up of state level financial/industrial development institutions.(Chapter VI, para 6.19).

Action Taken: 48 recommendations of the S.L. Kapur Committee conveyed to banks for implementation. As a further impetus to the flow of credit, banks have been advised that the credit requirement of SSIs having credit limits upto Rs.5 crore, instead of Rs.4 crore, may be assessed on the basis of 20% of the projected annual turnover.

Regulation and Supervision :

50. Recommendation: The Committee recommends that to improve the soundness and stability of the Indian banking system, the regulatory authorities should make it obligatory for banks to take into account risk weights for market risks. The movement towards greater market discipline in a sense would transform the relationship between banks and the regulator. By requiring greater internal controls, transparency and market discipline, the supervisory burden itself would be relatively lighter.(Chapter VII, para 7.13)

Action Taken: Banks are now required to assign capital for market risk. Please see comments against item 1 above. As indicated against item 19 above, the disclosure requirements of banks have been strengthened.

51. Recommendation: There is a need for all market participants to take note of the core principles and to formally announce full accession to these principles and their full and effective implementation.(Chapter VII, para 7.14)

Action Taken: We have endorsed the 'Core Principles for Effective Banking Supervision' and complied with almost all of them. Our compliance with the Core Principles has been rated as satisfactory by IMF Mission.

52. Recommendation: Proprietorial concerns in the case of public sector banks impact on the regulatory function leading to a situation of 'regulatory capture' affecting the quality of regulation.(Chapter VII, para 7.16)

Action Taken: The prudential / regulatory norms stipulated by RBI are applicable to public sector banks, private sector banks and foreign banks uniformly.

53. Recommendation: The Committee recommends that the regulatory and supervisory authorities should take note of the developments taking place elsewhere in the area of devising effective regulatory norms and to apply them in India taking into account the special characteristics but not in any way diluting the rigour of the norms so that the prescriptions match the best practices abroad. It is equally important to recognise that pleas for regulatory forbearance such as waiving adherence to the regulations to enable some (weak) banks more time to overcome their deficiencies could only compound their problems for the future and further emasculate their balance sheets. (Chapter VII, para 7.17)

Action Taken: The Regulatory / Supervisory norms have been formulated taking into account the best international practices. RBI has not waived adherence to the regulatory norms by any individual bank or category of banks.

54. Recommendation: An important aspect of regulatory concern should be ensuring transparency and credibility particularly as we move into a more market driven system where the market should be enabled to form its judgement about the soundness of an institution. There should be punitive penalties both for the inaccurate reporting to the supervisor or inaccurate disclosures to the public and transgressions in spirit of the regulations. (Chapter VII, para 7.19).

Action Taken: We are moving towards greater transparency and Statutory Auditors of banks are now under the obligation to report on the deviations from adherence to the prudential norms prescribed by RBI in their 'Notes to Accounts'. These observations are followed up by the RBI with the concerned banks. In terms of the provisions of Section 47A of the B.R. Act, 1949, as amended in 1994, the RBI can impose a penalty not exceeding Rs. 5 lakh or twice the amount involved in such contravention or default where such amount is quantifiable whichever is more and where such contravention or default is a continuing one, a further penalty which may extent to Rs. 25,000 for every day after the first day when the contravention or default continues.

55. Recommendation: The Committee is of the view that banks should be required to publish half yearly disclosure requirements in two parts. The first should be a general disclosure, providing a summary of performance over a period of time, say 3 years, including the overall performance, capital adequacy, information on the bank's risk management systems, the credit rating and any action by the regulator/supervisor. The disclosure statement should be subject to full external audit and any falsification should invite criminal procedures. The second disclosure, which would be a brief summary aimed at the ordinary depositor/ investor should provide brief information on matters such as capital adequacy ratio, non performing assets and profitability, vis-a-vis, the adherence to the stipulated norms and a comparison with the industry average. This summary should be in a language intelligible to the depositor and be approved by the supervisors before being made fully public when soliciting deposits. Such disclosure, the Committee believes, will help the strong banks to grow faster than the weaker banks and thus lead to systematic improvement.(Chapter VII, para 7.20)

Action Taken: - dbs -

56. Recommendation: The Committee recommends that an integrated system of regulation and supervision be put in place to regulate and supervise the activities of banks, financial institutions and non banking finance companies (NBFCs). The functions of regulation and supervision are organically linked and we propose that this agency be renamed as the Board for Financial Regulation and Supervision (BFRS) to make this combination of functions explicit. An independent regulatory supervisory system which provides for a closely coordinated monetary policy and banking supervision would be the ideal to work towards.(Chapter VII, para 7.24).

Action Taken: BFS needs to be strengthened before regulatory functions are vested with it. It was, therefore, felt that while the Committee's recommendations to set up an agency named Board for Financial Regulation and Supervision (BFRS) to provide an integrated system of regulation and supervision over banks, FIs and NBFCs could be a long term objective. For the time being, BFS may continue with its present mandate.

57. Recommendation: The Board for Financial Regulation and Supervision (BFRS) should be given statutory powers and be reconstituted in such a way as to be composed of professionals.

At present, the professional inputs are largely available in an advisory board which acts as a distinct entity supporting the BFS. Statutory amendment which would give the necessary powers to the BFRS should develop its own autonomous professional character. The Committee, taking note of the formation of BFS, recommends that the process of separating it from the Reserve Bank qua central bank should begin and the Board should be invested with requisite autonomy and armed with necessary powers so as to allow it to develop experience and professional expertise and to function effectively. However, with a view to retain an organic linkage with RBI, the Governor, RBI should be head of the BFRS. The Committee has also set out specific measures to ensure an effective regulatory/supervisory system which are detailed in para 7.27 (Chapter VII, para 7.24)

Action Taken: Please see comments against item 56 above.

Legal and Legislative Framework :

58. Recommendation: With the advent of computerisation there is need for clarity in the law regarding the evidentiary value of computer generated documents. The Shere Committee had made some recommendations in this regard and the Committee notes that the Government is having consultations with public sector banks in this matter. With electronic funds transfer several issues regarding authentication of payment instruments, etc. require to be clarified. The Committee recommends that a group be constituted by the Reserve Bank to work out the detailed proposals in this regard and implement them in a time bound manner. (Chapter VIII, para. 8.15 8.16)

Action Taken: The Group set up by the RBI has submitted its Report and the recommendations are in various stages of implementation.

59. Recommendation: Although there is a provision in our legislation effectively prohibiting loans by banks to companies in which their directors are interested as directors or employees of the latter with liberalisation and the emergence of more banks on the scene and with the induction of private capital through public issue in some of the nationalised banks there is a possibility that the phenomenon of connected lending might reappear even while adhering to the letter of law. It is necessary to have prudential norms which are addressed to this problem by stipulating concentration ratios in terms of which no bank can have more than a specified proportion of its net worth by way of lending to any single industrial concern and a higher percentage in respect of lending to an industrial group. At present, lending to any single concern is limited to 25% of a bank's capital and free reserves. This would seem to be appropriate along with the existing enhanced figure of 50% for group exposure except in the case of specified infrastructure projects. Similarly, concentration ratios would need to be indicated, even if not specifically prescribed, in respect of any bank's exposure to any particular industrial sector so that in the event of cyclical or other changes in the industrial situation, banks have an element of protection from over exposure in that sector. Prudential norms would also need to be set by way of prescription of exposure limits to sectors particularly sensitive to asset price fluctuations such as stock markets and real estate. As it happens, Indian banks do not have much exposure to the real estate sector in the form of lending for property development as distinct from making housing loans. The example of banks in East and South East Asia which had over extended themselves to these two sectors has only confirmed the need for circumspection in this regard. We would leave the precise stipulation of these limits and, if necessary, loan to collateral value ratios to the authorities concerned. The implementation of these exposure limits would need to be carefully monitored to see that they are effectively implemented and not circumvented, as has sometimes happened abroad, in a variety of ways. Another salutary prescription would be to require full disclosure of connected lending and lending to sensitive sectors. (Chapter III, para. 3.40)

Action Taken: As the Committee has noted, Section 20 of the Banking Regulation Act, 1949 prohibits banks from entering into any commitment for granting of any loan or advance to or on behalf of any of its directors, any firm in which any of its directors is interested as partner, manager, employee or guarantor or any company of which any of the directors of the banking company is a director, managing agent, manager, employee, or guarantor or in which he holds substantial interest or, any individual in respect of whom any of its directors is a partner or guarantor.

The RBI has, as noted by the Committee, laid down prudential ceilings on exposures to single / group of borrowers.

Banks on their own, have also prescribed exposure ceilings on single borrower and group of borrowers.

As regards the recommendation that prudential norms be set by way of prescription of exposure limits to sensitive sectors, i.e. those sectors where asset prices are subject to fluctuations, RBI has already put in place a cap on a bank's exposure to share market. The banks on their own have limited their exposure to real estate business. Banks are expected to set norms for lending to any particular industrial sector in their lending policy. Banks have been advised to disclose in 'Notes on Account' to their balance sheets, lending to sensitive sectors, (i.e., advances to sectors such as, capital market, real estate, etc.) and such other sectors to be defined as 'sensitive' by RBI from time to time with effect from the year ended March 31, 2000. (Cir. DBOD.No.BP.BC.9/21.04.018/99 dt.10 February, 1999).

60. Recommendation: The Committee recommends that to improve the soundness and stability of the Indian banking system, the regulatory authorities should make it obligatory for banks to take into account risk weights for market risks. The movement towards greater market discipline in a sense would transform the relationship between banks and the regulator. By requiring greater internal controls, transparency and market discipline, the supervisory burden itself would be relatively lighter. (Chapter VII, para. 7.13)

Action Taken: Please see comments against item 1 above.

61. Recommendation: The Committee recommends that the RBI should totally withdraw from the primary market in 91 days Treasury Bills; the RBI could, of course, have a presence in the secondary market for 91 days Treasury Bills. If the 91 days Treasury Bill rate reflects money market conditions, the money and securities market would develop an integral link. ....The Committee also recommends that foreign institutional investors should be given access to the Treasury Bill market. (Chapter V, Annexure, para. A-10)

Action Taken: The withdrawal of RBI from the primary market in 91 day Treasury Bills is the long term objective. The pace of implementation of the recommendation should depend upon the development and depth of the Govt. securities market. One of the objectives of evolving the system of Primary Dealers is to improve the underwriting and market making capabilities in Government securities market so that RBI could eventually withdraw from primary subscriptions. This will be possible only when Primary Dealers are capable of taking devolvement, if any, to the full extent.

As regards giving access to FIIs to the Treasury Bill market it has been implemented. ((Cir. MPD.BC. 175/07.01.279/97-98 dated 29.4.98).

d) Recommendations on which a view has to be taken by Govt.

(i) So far, a sum of Rs.20,000 crore has been expended for recapitalisation and to the extent to which recapitalisation has enabled banks to write off losses, this is the cost which the Exchequer has had to bear for the bad debts of the banks. Recapitalisation is a costly and, in the long run, not a sustainable option. Recapitalisation involves budgetary commitments and could lead to a large measure of monetisation. The Committee urges that no further recapitalisation of banks be undertaken from the Government budget. As the authorities have already proceeded on the recapitalisation route it is perhaps not necessary to consider de novo the institution of an ARF of the type envisaged by the earlier CFS Report. The situation would perhaps have been different if the recapitalisation exercise had not been undertaken in the manner in which it has been. (Chapter III, para. 3.24 - 3.25)

(ii) As an incentive to banks to make specific provisions, the Committee recommends that consideration be given to making such provisions tax deductible. (Chapter III, para. 3.39)

(iii) It would be appropriate if the management committees are reconstituted to have only whole time functionaries in it, somewhat on the pattern of Central Office Credit Committee constituted in the State Bank of India. All decisions taken by these committees could be put up to the Board of Directors for information. (Chapter IV, para. 4.12-4.16)

(iv) It would be appropriate to induct an additional whole time director on the Board of the banks with an enabling provision for more whole time directors for bigger banks. (Chapter IV, para.4.17)

(v) There are opportunities of outsourcing in other activities like building maintenance, cleaning, security, despatch of mail and more importantly, in computer related areas. The Committee has been informed that in some areas banks are unable to subcontract work because of a notification issued by the Labour Ministry under Contract Labour (Regulation and Abolition) Act, 1970. The Committee would urge that this be looked into by the authorities so that banks are enabled to effect efficiency and productivity improvements. The global trend in the banking and financial sector also reflects an increasing reliance on outsourced services. In an increasingly competitive environment, statutory provisions should not lead to banks having to carry on internally functions and tasks which can be performed more efficiently by outside service provides. (Chapter IV, para. 4.18).

Action Taken: Govt. to reply

(vi) The Committee feels that the issue of remuneration structure at managerial levels prevailing in public sector banks and financial institutions needs to be addressed. There is an urgent need to ensure that public sector banks are given flexibility to determine managerial remuneration levels taking into account market trends. The Committee recommends that the necessary authority in this regard be given to the Boards of the banks initially in the case of profit making public sector banks which have gone public, for they would, in any case, be required to operate with an accountability to the market. The forthcoming wage negotiations provide an opportunity to review the existing pattern of industry-wise negotiations and move over to bank-wise negotiations. (Chapter IV, para. 4.26)

Action Taken: The recent wage settlement of bank staff with Unions has broadly kept this in view and leaving the decision on other perquisites to the potential of individual banks concerned.

Govt. to reply.

(vii) This Committee is of the view that in today's increasingly challenging business environment, a large institution can only be led effectively by a Chief Executive who has a reasonable length of tenure, which the Committee believes should not be less than five years. Since, however, moving over to this tenure may be difficult, we suggest that in the first instance, the minimum tenure should be three years. The Committee feels that there is now a need to delink the pay scales of the Chief Executives of public sector banks and financial institutions from the Civil Service pay scales and that this should be left to be decided by the individual banks, not excluding the possibility of performance based remuneration. The Committee would like to add that these observations and recommendations also apply to the whole time Directors on the Boards of banks and financial institutions appointed by the Government. (Chapter IV, para.4.29 - 4.30)

Action Taken: The recommendation pertaining to reasonable length of tenure for the Chief Executive has been implemented while appointing the new Chairmen of PSBs. As regards the recommendation regarding delinking of pay scales of Chief Executives of public sector banks from that of the Civil Service, this will have to be considered by the Government.

(viii) There may be need to redefine the scope of external vigilance and investigative agencies with regard to banking business. External agencies should have the requisite skill and expertise to take into account the commercial environment in which decisions are taken. The vigilance manual now being used has been designed mainly for use by Government Departments and public sector undertakings. It may be necessary that a separate vigilance manual which captures the special features of banking should be prepared for exercising vigilance supervision over banks. The Committee feels that this is an extremely critical area and arrangements similar to the Advisory Board for Bank Frauds be made for various levels of staff of banks. (Chapter IV, para. 4.35 - 4.37)

Action Taken: A separate chapter capturing special features of banking transactions has been incorporated in the Vigilance Manual.

(ix) The Committee attaches the greatest importance to the issue of functional autonomy with accountability within the framework of purposive, rule bound, non-discretionary prudential regulation and supervision. Autonomy is a prerequisite for operational flexibility and for critical decision making whether in terms of strategy or day to day operations. There is also the question whether full autonomy with accountability is consistent and compatible with public ownership. Given the dynamic context in which the banks are operating and considering the situational experience further capital enhancement would be necessary for the larger Indian banks. Against the background of the need for fiscal consolidation and given the many demands on the budget for investment funds in areas like infrastructure and social services, it cannot be argued that subscription to the equity of public sector banks to meet their enhanced needs for capital should command priority. Public sector banks should be encouraged, therefore, to go to the market to raise capital to enhance their capital. At present, the laws stipulate that not less than 51% of the share capital of public sector banks should be vested with the Government and similarly not less than 55% of the share capital of the State Bank of India should be held by the Reserve Bank of India.

Action Taken: Banks have been given further autonomy in matters relating to their business operations. These relate to greater autonomy to open branches, freedom to charge interest on advances as also on deposits, recruitment of specialist officers and other matters of corporate strategy.

Public sector banks are encouraged to go to the market raise capital to enhance their capital. Eleven public sector banks have since accessed the capital market for raising additional capital.

The recommendation has been accepted. The Bill to bring down the shareholding of the Govt. of India in nationalised banks has been introduced in Parliament.

Recommendation: The current requirement of minimum Government of India/Reserve Bank of India shareholding is likely to become a constraint for raising additional capital from the market by some of the better placed banks unless Government also decides to provide necessary budgetary resources to proportionately subscribe to the additional equity, including the necessary premium on the share price, so as to retain its minimum stipulated shareholding. The Committee believes that these minimum stipulations should be reviewed. It suggests that the minimum shareholding by Government/RBI in the equity of nationalised banks and SBI should be brought down to 33%.

Action Taken: The recommendation in regard to bringing down shareholding of the Govt. of India in nationalized banks to 33% has been accepted. A Bill has been introduced in the Parliament for the purpose.

Recommendation: The Reserve Bank as a regulator of the monetary system should not be also the owner of a bank in view of the potential for possible conflict of interest. It would be necessary for the Government/RBI to divest their stake in these nationalised banks and in the State Bank of India. A reduction in their shares would come about through additional subscription by the market to their enhanced capital. A portion of upto 5 or 10% of the equity of the bank concerned may be reserved for employees of the bank with a provision of some later date for the introduction of stock options. The appointment by the Government of Boards and top executives of banks derives from its majority holding and if, as suggested above, the majority holding itself were to be given up, the appointment of Chairmen and Managing Directors should be left to the Boards of the banks and the Boards themselves left to be elected by shareholders.

Needless to say, with a significant stock holding of not less than 33% Government would have a say in the election of Boards and indirectly of the chief executives without their being seen as administrative appointments. The reduction in the minimum holding of Government below 51% would in itself be a major and clear signal about the restoration to banks and financial institutions of autonomy in their functioning. The Committee makes this recommendation in the firm belief that this is essential for enhancing the effectiveness and efficiency of the system and not on any other consideration. (Chapter V, para 5.27-5.33)

(x) To provide the much needed flexibility in its operations, IDBI should be corporatised and converted into a Joint Stock Company under the Companies Act on the lines of ICICI, IFCI and IDBI. For providing focussed attention to the work of State Financial Corporations, IDBI shareholding in them should be transferred to SIDBI which is currently providing refinance assistance to State Financial Corporations. To give it greater operational autonomy, SIDBI should also be delinked from IDBI

(Chapter V, para 5.34).

(xi) Though cooperation is a state subject, since UCBs are primarily credit institutions meant to be run on commercial lines, the Committee recommends that this duality in control should be dispensed with. It should be primarily the task of the Board for Financial Supervision to set up regulatory standards for Urban Cooperative banks and ensure compliance with these standards through the instrumentality of supervision. (Chapter V, para 5.39)

(xii) The Committee is of the view that the banking system should be in a position to equip itself to identify the eligible clients based on prescribed norms in the Government sponsored programmes so that the full responsibility for all aspects of the credit decision remains with it. This should also help improve the client bank relationship instead of the present system of virtually imposed clientele and build a credit culture and discipline. (Chapter VI, para 6.3)

(xiii) The Committee strongly urges that there should be no recourse to any scheme of debt waiver in view of its serious and deleterious impact on the culture of credit. (Chapter VI, para 6.7)

(xiv) Evolution of a risk management system would provide the needed comfort to the banking system to finance agriculture. At present, under the Income Tax Act, provision for bad and doubtful debts not exceeding 5% of income and 10% of the aggregate average advances made by rural branches of a scheduled or a non scheduled bank are allowed as deduction in computing the income chargeable to tax. Consideration could be given to increasing this to 5% of income and 20% of average aggregate advances of rural branches to provide incentive to banks for lending to rural sectors. (Chapter VI, para 6.10)

Action Taken: Govt. to reply

(xv) The Committee recommends that the RRBs and cooperative banks should reach a minimum of 8% capital to risk weighted assets over a period of five years. A review of the capital structure of RRBs should be undertaken with a view to enlarging public subscription and give the sponsor banks greater ownership and responsibility in the operation of RRBs. While considering the issue of salaries of employees of RRBs the Committee strongly urges that there should be no further dilution of the basic feature of RRBs as low cost credit delivery institutions. Cooperative credit institutions also need to enhance their capital through subscription by their members and not by Government. There should be a delayering of the cooperative credit institutions with a view to reducing the intermediation cost and thus providing the benefit of cheaper NABARD credit to the ultimate borrowers. (Chapter VI, para 6.12)

Action Taken: This recommendation has been accepted in principle. Govt. of India is also contemplating suitable amendments to RRB Act, 1976 to facilitate further restructuring of RRBs involving changes in capital structure, ownership, etc. Pending amendments to RRB Act, sponsor banks have been entrusted with greater powers to guide and monitor the operations of RRBs. As regards the salary structure of employees of RRBs, the S.L. Mahalik Committee appointed by Reserve Bank of India has made certain recommendations on restructuring of the pay scales of RRB employees and these have been forwarded to the Govt. for consideration. As regards delayering of cooperative credit structure, the suggestion would be forwarded to NABARD for detailed examination. Govt. will have to consider amendment to the Cooperative Societies Act.

(xvi) The supervisory function over rural financial institutions has been entrusted to NABARD. While this arrangement may continue for the present, over the longer term, the Committee would suggest that all regulatory and supervisory functions over rural credit institutions should vest with the Board for Financial Regulation and Supervision. (Chapter VI para 6.13)

Action Taken: Govt. to reply since implementation of the recommendation would require amendments to relevant Acts.

(xvii) The present duality of control over the cooperative credit institutions by State Government and RBI/NABARD should be eliminated and all the cooperative banking institutions should come under the discipline of Banking Regulation Act, under the aegis of RBI/NABARD/BFS. Thus would require amendments to the Banking Regulation Act. The control of the Registrar of cooperative sector over cooperatives would then be somewhat on the lines of control that Registrar of Companies has over the Banking Institutions, registered under the Companies Act. (Chapter VI, para 6.14)

Action Taken: Govt. to reply since implementation of the recommendation would require amendments to relevant Acts.

(xviii) A legal framework that clearly defines the rights and liabilities of parties to contracts and provides for speedy resolution of disputes is essential for financial intermediation. The evolution of the legal framework has not kept pace with the changing commercial practices and with the financial sector reforms. The Transfer of Property Act enacted in 1882 is a case in point. (Chapter VIII, para 8.1)

(xix) Given the unsatisfactory state of the law of mortgage, the response has been to vest through special statute the power of sale in certain institutions like Land Development Banks and State Finance Corporations. This approach could be extended to other financial institutions and, if possible, to banks. The other approach is to set up special tribunals for recovery of dues to banks and financial institutions. These Tribunals need to have powers of attachment before judgement, for appointment of receivers and for ordering preservation of property. For this purpose, an amendment to the concerned legislation may be necessary. The Committee would like to emphasise the importance of having in place a dedicated and effective machinery for debt recovery for banks and financial institutions. (Chapter VIII, para 8.2-8.4)

(xx) Securitisation of mortgages is also critically dependent on the ease of enforcement and the costs associated with transfer of mortgages. The power of sale without judicial intervention is not available to any class of mortgages except where the mortgages is the Government or the mortgage agreement so provides and the mortgaged property is situated in Mumbai, Chennai and Calcutta and other towns so notified. Even if the power of sale without judicial intervention were available there would need to be measure to put the buyer in possession. (Chapter VIII, para 8.5-8.6)

(xxi) The question of stamp duties and registration fees also requires review. There is a case for reducing stamp duties and registration fees substantially. (Chapter VIII, para 8.7)

(xxii) In view of the recent amendments to Section 28 of Indian Contract Act, banks have expressed a fear that they can no longer limit their liabilities under bank guarantees to a specified period and that they would have to carry such guarantee commitments for long periods as outstanding obligations. Government departments do not generally return the original guarantee papers even after the purpose is served. This whole issue needs to be re-examined and bank guarantees exempted from the purview of the recent amendment to Section 28 of the Indian Contract Act. The issue of enforcing securities in the form of book debts also calls for review. The Committee also agrees with the proposal to amend the Sick Industrial Companies Act, seeking to trigger off the remedial mechanism on the sight of incipient sickness. (Chapter VIII, para 8.9-8.14)

(xxiii) Certain legislative requirements would also be needed to implement some of the Committee's recommendations regarding the structure of the banking system and matters pertaining to regulation and supervision. The Banking Regulation Act is structured on the premise that bank supervision is essentially a Government function and that the Reserve Bank of India's position is somewhat on the lines of an agent. The Act also provides appellate powers to Government over the decisions of the RBI in this regard. It also provides original powers in certain instances. The Committee feels that these provisions should be reviewed. (Chapter VIII, para 8.17)

(xxiv) With respect to recommendations regarding constitution of a Board for Financial Regulation and Supervision, it would be necessary for amendments in the Banking Regulation Act and Reserve Bank of India Act. Amendments would also be needed in the Bank Nationalisation Acts to enable grant of greater managerial autonomy to public sector banks for lowering the minimum requirements of 51% Government ownership and as regards the constitution of Boards of Directors and of the Management Committees. The provisions relating to prior approval of Government for regulations framed under the Act would also need to be reviewed. In line with the above, amendments would also be needed in the State Bank of India Act with regard to shareholding of the RBI and constitution of its Central Board. (Chapter VIII, para 8.19-8.23)

Action Taken: Govt. to reply

(xxv) These suggestions are not exhaustive and we would recommend that the legal implications with reference to each of these recommendations be examined and detailed legislative steps identified by the Ministry of Finance, Banking Division in consultation with the Ministry of Law. In view or the wide-ranging changes needed in the legal framework the Committee recommends setting up of an expert Committee comprising among others, representatives from the Ministry of Law, Banking Division, Ministry of Finance, RBI and some outside experts to formulate specific legislative proposals to give effect to the suggestions made above. (Chapter VII, para 8.22-8.23)

Action Taken: An Expert Legal Group under the chairmanship of Shri. T.R. Andhyarujina, former Solicitor General, was set up. The Group's report is under examination of the Govt. of India.

18

Economic Reforms: A Medium Term Perspective

Recommendations of Prime Minister's Economic Advisory Council (April 2001)

1. INTRODUCTION

Economic Reform: Objectives, Scope & Rationale

There has been a great deal of discussion in recent years on Economic Reform, but not sufficient clarity about its objectives, rationale or scope. It is important to emphasise that the basic objectives of economic reform remain the same as we have set for ourselves ever since Independence; viz. to achieve rapid economic development to improve the living standards of our people and to eliminate poverty. Economic growth, especially broad based growth encompassing growth in agriculture, is a larger part of the solution to the poverty problem. But it is not enough: it has to be supplemented by some direct measures to alleviate poverty in select pockets which may not be touched even by broad based economic growth. There is no need to change this basic perception of our objectives, though in the light of more recent experience and thinking, we need to add concern for the environment and for a broad definition of human development including participation of excluded groups and protection of human rights as additional objectives.

1.2 Reforms became necessary because the earlier regulatory model of development, which was followed for several decades after Independence, did not deliver results upto expectations. There were important achievements during this period, notably the increase in foodgrain production following the green revolution, development of a broad base for industrial development, increase in life expectancy and the creation of an impressive reservoir of scientific and technical personnel. However, the growth rate of the economy remained much below targets and progress in poverty reduction was very limited. In terms of basic social amenities such as safe drinking water, sanitation facilities and primary education, our achievements were also far from satisfactory.

1.3 Economic policies began to change in the 1980s and a much bolder programme of economic reforms was introduced in 1991 which has been continued by successive governments since then. These reforms are aimed at closing the gap between India's potential and our actual performance. Many developing countries in East Asia, with very different social and economic systems, were able to achieve a rapid rate of economic growth over extended periods and to reduce poverty dramatically. India is capable of no less, and economic reforms can be seen as an effort to achieve this potential.

1.4 The past ten years have given us some indication of what is possible. The growth rate of the economy in the post-reforms period is higher than in the previous decade putting India among the top ten fastest growing developing economies. The rate of inflation has also been modest. In some sectors, such as software and information technology, the economy has performed exceptionally well, earning a name for Indian technical skills and entrepreneurial capability in the industrial arena. The latest estimates of poverty also show a significant decline in the percentage of the population in poverty in 1999-2000 as compared with 1993-94.

1.5 However, the task of reforms is far from over. Our growth remains below the levels achieved by other East Asian countries. We need to grow at much faster rates if we are to raise the standards of living of the mass of our people, create a sufficient growth of high quality jobs for the increasingly better educated new entrants to the labour force and bring about a sharp reduction in poverty. It is time to initiate the second generation reforms, building upon what has been achieved and what we have learnt in the first stage.

1.6 The scope of the reforms that are needed is wide, and in some ways extends beyond economics. But there is an underlying common rationale or philosophical basis for all of the interconnected set of policies that constitute Economic Reform. This rationale has been amply vindicated by actual experience, both within and outside India; it is based on the philosophical and practical insight that equitable and sustainable growth flourishes best in an environment of opportunity, freedom and individual incentive and enterprise. A free and competitive set of markets with opportunity for access to them by all citizens, encourages efficiency and growth, and harmonises best their interests as producers, consumers, workers, savers and investors.

1.7 Economic Reform is sometimes equated with liberalization, but it is better described as encouragement of free and fair competition in all economic spheres as a spur to efficiency and growth. The negative aspects of liberalization are decontrol, deregulation and reduction in governmental intervention and involvement. These "liberalization" initiatives are important, but they are only a part of the agenda for increasing free and fair competition. They have to be supplemented by positive efforts to create the institutions that make competitive markets function and to make sure that all sections of society have access to the market economy and the opportunities it creates. They also have to be accompanied by targeted poverty alleviation schemes aimed at those whom the markets cannot help.

1.8 Over the years there has been a substantial change in public and political perception favouring greater competition and recognizing the potential benefits from letting markets function. However, some important misgivings remain. These misgivings need to be squarely addressed if further progress in Economic Reform is not to be inhibited by avoidable misunderstanding.

Misgivings about Economic Reform: Issues and Responses

1.9 One common misgiving about the reform process is that it is elitist and that the poor, particularly in the rural areas, are not touched by it. There is some truth in this in the sense that the better off sections are most easily able to respond to market signals and seize new opportunities. In this process it is possible that some sections of our population, especially those in rural areas have benefited less. But the fault lies not in the reforms implemented but in the lack of implementation of reforms in other important areas such as agriculture and small-scale industry and most of all in the tardy record in delivering education and health care services. These deficiencies are not caused by the reforms. They predate the reform process making corrective action all the more urgent. Even so, to say that the poor have not benefited at all is not correct. The reduction in the rate of inflation for example, clearly helps the poor. Besides, the latest NSS data for 1999-2000 show a decline in poverty, a decline which bears out the findings of earlier surveys conducted by the NCAER.

1.10 In any case, from the policy point of view, it is important to emphasise that reforms should not focus only on the rich and ignore the rest. The essence of reform is to increase the productivity of all sections of society by making competition free and access to markets easier. Unless this process is broad-based and embraces all sections of society, there cannot be adequate acceleration in the rate of growth. Government has a major role to play in ensuring that the growth process is indeed broad-based so that the benefits are widely spread.

1.11 Another set of misgivings centres round fears of loss of national sovereignty or decline in what is sometimes called pride in Swadeshi. There is no doubt that pride in one's country, its history, culture and arts and crafts is a noble and essential ingredient in national prosperity. But let us be equally clear that what we need is pride in "Swadesh" and not in "Swadeshi" as such. We have to achieve national self-respect and self-esteem, and not national self-sufficiency in a narrow cause. National pride and self esteem are best promoted by ensuring that we have high economic growth and can produce good quality products that sell all over the world. It cannot be promoted on the basis of an economy producing poor quality, high-cost goods which need a protected market to survive at home and which no one would buy abroad. It is worth examining how China has succeeded in achieving a high rate of growth and virtual abolition of poverty on the basis of billions of dollars worth of exports of a wide variety of goods. It is that which has earned China respect in the world as an economic giant.

1.12 International trade is one of the major engines of economic growth. It not only enables us to obtain through imports things which are difficult or expensive to produce at home by exporting those where we have comparative advantage. It also allows new products and technologies to make their appearance in our markets and thus encourages domestic producers to upgrade quality and technology. Fast growing countries all over the world have opened up their economies and integrated with world trade. They have learnt to compete in world markets and to open up their markets to import competition. The WTO is an international organization that supervises the rules by which sovereign independent nations trade with each other. These are rules that are established by negotiation. Membership of WTO imposes certain obligations on all of us but it also provides us protection against unfair practices, particularly from the richer countries. In the absence of some international rules of the game, we would be even more at the mercy of the rich. The value of being a member of the WTO is best seen in the far reaching concessions that China has recently made to the US and to Europe – going much beyond what is required by the WTO – in order to gain their approval for its membership.

1.13 Direct foreign investment yields similar benefits as it adds to our investible resources, technical know-how and organisational capacity. What is more, foreign firms are often in a better position to assist us in exploiting foreign markets. Foreign investors are of course interested in the domestic market but we should not assume they are only interested in exploiting the domestic market. That happens only when the domestic market is so heavily protected that foreign investment is designed only to jump the tariff wall. In such cases, high levels of protection make the economy too high cost to be a suitable base to exploit world markets. However, given the right environment (i.e. low levels of protection), foreign firms could also use India as an export base for many products – as they are doing in China and even in Bangladesh and Mauritius. Indeed, given our skilled man-power, we can even expect to "Indianise" foreign direct investment in the sense that Indians will enjoy the highest positions of management in them both at home and abroad. This is already happening. The fear that foreign investors will swamp the Indian economy and dominate it is not only misplaced, it is dangerous. It creates an isolationist mentality which denies our young people the opportunity they need to make India count in world commerce and finance.

1.14 Some people talk of countries like India being marginalised in a globalised world. Globalisation is an unavoidable process which is taking place independent of us. It forces us to cope with it. There is no room in a globalised world for an economy delinked from world trade and foreign investment. The truth is that if we do not reform rapidly, and position ourselves to compete, we will be marginalized. There is no divine dispensation that gives India alone the power to survive and prosper as an isolationist island in a globalised world.

1.15 Another common misgiving about economic reform is that it amounts to a laissez faire philosophy in which there is no role or only a minor role for the government, and it implies the abandonment by the government of any responsibility for the outcome. This is incorrect. Economic Reform does not imply a minimized role for the government. What it means is a redefinition of the role of government – away from government ownership and intervention in economic matters and towards greater attention to social and economic infrastructure and to law and order, efficient justice, rule of law and, in general, to better governance. Even in the economic sphere, the government has a formidable and indeed daunting responsibility to maintain a sound fiscal and financial framework, and to establish an appropriate environment in which markets can function.

The Way Ahead

1.16 In our view, this is an appropriate time to shed misgivings and embark on the next stage of reforms with renewed vigour. This report outlines a set of initiatives in different areas which we believe will consolidate the gains already achieved and make advances in areas where progress thus far has been limited. We believe that the proposals outlined in this report represent a broad professional consensus on the directions in which we need to move to give the economy the additional thrust it needs to break through the 6.5 per cent growth achieved thus far towards higher levels of 8 per cent or more. For the sake of brevity we have concentrated on areas where much remains to be done and have devoted little space to those where significant progress has been made (e.g. financial reforms) or where our current approach is essentially on the right lines (e.g. monetary policy and exchange rate management).

1.17 To advocate Economic Reform does not mean that no mistakes might be made in implementing them or that there may not be side-effects to be taken care of. Nor does it mean that in a federal democracy there may not be legitimate constraints that may have to be accommodated. There is also life beyond economics that has to be tackled and taken care of. But all this does not detract from the essential rationale and justification for reform. The central question that we have to keep in mind is: with all the qualifications that might be made and care exercised, what is the alternative to Economic Reform that would be better? To criticise without charting a viable alternative course is not a responsible activity; and the verdict of actual experience is clearly in favour of persisting with reform with determination and due diligence, while keeping our eyes and ears open to address any problems that might arise in the course of actual implementation.

2. AGRICULTURE

2.1 One of the criticisms of the reforms thus far is that they have not focused sufficiently on what needs to be done for agriculture. There is considerable validity in this criticism and this imbalance needs to be corrected. More than sixty percent of our population is still directly dependent on agriculture, and although this proportion is expected to decline if growth in the non-agricultural sector accelerates sufficiently, this decline will at best be a slow process. A very large proportion of our population will therefore continue to depend upon agriculture and their living standards cannot improve unless agriculture registers higher rates of growth. Agricultural development is important not only for those directly dependent on agriculture. This sector also has the potential to unleash a virtuous circle of growth and poverty alleviation which is essential to put the economy on a trajectory of 8 per cent growth. For this, agriculture must register at least 4 per cent annual growth based on promoting efficient, equitable and sustainable use of resources. All this calls for a comprehensive reform agenda in agriculture, encompassing incentives, infrastructure, technology and institutions.

Domestic Market Reforms

2.2 There are a large number of domestic market distortions which have a negative effect on agricultural producers and which should be eliminated. In our view, if we move away from controls and towards freer markets in agricultural products it will provide agricultural producers with an environment in which they can benefit from efficiency and entrepreneurial dynamism.

2.3 We recommend the following proposals in this context.

(i) All controls on the movement and stocking of agricultural commodities (foodgrains, edible oils, cotton or sugar) across the country should be abolished making India one integrated market. The private sector (including foreign investors), co-operatives, panchayats, etc. should be encouraged to develop modern storage and bulk handling facilities for different commodities. This can be achieved by repeal of the Essential Commodities Act or its drastic revision which would limit its use to times of war, civil strife or natural calamity, and by encouraging large scale investments in marketing, handling and storage. This would not only lead to regional specialisation based on resource endowments, but also result in large scale savings of the produce that is being wasted today due to lack of proper storage facilities. In brief, it would promote higher efficiency, and thus lower costs, in production, handling and storage. It will also provide larger and more dispersed employment opportunities.

(ii) Levies on commodities like rice, sugar, etc., should be abolished since they ultimately serve as a tax on the processors and are passed on to the farmer. At present, the levy on rice mills is 75 per cent in Punjab and

Haryana and 50 per cent in Andhra Pradesh. Sugar mills were until recently subjected to a 30 per cent levy. This has been reduced to 15 per cent and we greatly welcome this step and urge further that complete decontrol should be the goal.

(iii) Credit margin requirements for stocks of agricultural commodities should be reduced. Farmers should be extended credit against hypothecation of their stocks. A warehouse receipt system should be introduced in foodgrain marketing, and we should aim at creating large grain companies for procuring, stocking and trading, in competition with FCI.

(iv) The present procurement policy should be drastically revised so as to limit Government purchases only for preventing a sharp fall in prices (i.e., to support prices) instead of Government buying all that is offered at pre-determined 'fair' prices. The role of FCI should be limited to minimum buffer stocking, i.e. not more than 10 million tonnes. To feed its PDS, the Government should invite tenders from private grain companies/traders to deliver a specified amount of grain at a place and timing determined by the Government.

(v) Taxes and fees on raw agricultural commodities should be rationalised. In principle, raw agricultural commodities should attract zero tax (including purchase tax, mandi tax, commission of agents, and so on, which in Punjab today accounts for about 11 per cent on wheat). This can be done by allowing big grain companies to buy directly from farmers without going through commission agents, and abolishing purchase/sales tax. Instead, one should work towards introduction of value added tax (VAT) in agriculture, which would help the growth of the agro-processing industry.

(vi) Futures markets should be introduced in all agricultural commodities being traded in bulk, especially wheat and rice in the grain segment. This would help in containing wide fluctuations in commodity prices as also cut down their costs of marketing by hedging their risk.

(vii) All controls on the distribution of sugar should be abolished and its marketing should be allowed freely as for any other agricultural commodity.

(viii) Groundnut and rapeseed-mustard processing should be de-reserved from the Small Scale Industry (SSI) list so that the processors can increase their scale of operation, enjoy economies of scale, cut down costs, and thus compete with imported oils on efficiency basis. Similarly, manufacture of farm implements should be de-reserved.

(ix) The Milk and Milk Products Order (MMPO) should be abolished. The MMPO is a back door entry to a licensing regime, restricting private sector investment in milk processing. India is the largest producer of milk but only 10 per cent of it is processed through the organised sector. There is no logic in restricting large scale private investment in milk processing.

(x) Abolish Retention Price Scheme for urea manufacturers, decontrol urea marketing and decanalise urea imports. Announce a flat rate subsidy to urea manufacturers, which should be gradually reduced as the market price of urea for farmers is raised to its import parity level. The existing plants can be compensated by a one time capital subsidy to enable them to operate efficiently in the new policy environment.

2.4 The policy agenda outlined above points out a clear direction: that producers/processors of agricultural commodities should operate in a free market at home as well as abroad. This should improve their incentives, encourage them to be more efficient and increase investment in agriculture and agro-based activities to tap its potential.

Foreign Trade Policies

2.5 Foreign trade policies relating to agriculture are an extremely important part of the incentive structure for agriculture. It is well known that a development strategy which provides the industrial sector with high protection through tariffs or QRs has an adverse effect on agriculture because high industrial protection leads to an over-valued exchange rate, compared to the rate that would prevail if protection were lower, and this has the effect of altering the terms of trade in favour of industry and against agriculture. Indian agriculture suffered from this distortion in the years preceding the reforms. One of the important advantages of the reforms has been the reduction in this bias as industrial protection came down and the exchange rate became more market determined.

2.6 More recently, however, considerable concern has been expressed on whether Indian agriculture would be adversely affected by a flood of subsidized imports under the WTO regime which will be able to enter our markets when QRs are removed with effect from April 1, 2001. This concern has been greatly exaggerated since it fails to recognize that although we have to remove QRs we have negotiated comfortable high levels of tariffs which give us considerable flexibility to use tariffs as the instrument for protection. Not only can we take resort to fairly high levels of tariffs in agriculture (100 per cent for primary products, 150 per cent for processed product and 300 per cent for edible oils), government can also resort to countervailing duty to counter actionable subsidies to deal with imports from countries which subsidise agricultural exports. It can also act under safeguard provisions to counter any surge in imports. In our view, government has enough flexibility under these provisions to ensure that agricultural producers are not threatened by any sudden flood of agricultural imports.

2.7 One of the problems that is likely to arise when QRs are removed is that sudden and large fluctuations in world prices may pose a threat to agricultural producers. We recognize that our producers are not able to deal on their own with such large fluctuations. However, it is possible to counter the effects of large fluctuations in world prices through the use of variable import duties operating within the tariff bindings we have agreed under WTO. We would recommend use of such devices rather than QRs to avoid disruptive effects on producers.

Rural Infrastructure and R&D

2.8 If agricultural growth is to be stepped up, there is a need to raise investments in agriculture, especially in power, surface irrigation and rural roads, all of which are generally in the public sector domain and in the States sector. However public sector investments in Indian agriculture have been declining in real terms since 1980-81. Private sector investment in agriculture (mainly groundwater irrigation and agricultural machinery) has been increasing, partly in response to improving terms of trade, but even this has slowed down in recent years. In any case private investment is not a substitute for public investment in all areas. In fact it can be argued that additional public investment in critical areas of agricultural and rural infrastructure is crucial and private investment would go up further once investment in such rural infrastructure picks up.

2.9 Investing in rural infrastructure is held up by lack of resources, and to mobilize these resources we must rationalise subsidies in agriculture by carrying out price and institutional reforms in power, canal irrigation and fertilizer sectors. To check the real costs of power and canal irrigation, which are basically natural monopolies, the role of independent Regulatory Commissions would be critical. The problems involved in reforming the power sector are discussed separately in a subsequent chapter.

2.10 Expenditure on R&D for agriculture is not covered under 'investments in agriculture' as defined by CSO but R&D expenditures are critical for the long-term growth of this sector. Public spending on R&D has been only 0.46 per cent of agricultural GDP during 1992-97. This is way below the average of about 1.5 per cent for developing countries as a group, and about 3 per cent in a developed country like the USA.

2.11 While there is need to increase public expenditure on R&D for agriculture, there is a much greater need to carry out major institutional changes in the functioning of our agricultural research organizations. There is reason to believe that our agricultural research organizations have become bureaucratized and are not functioning as research institutions should. They need to chalk out their own agenda of research, work with international and national organisations as well as private sector concerns and exchange personnel and students.

2.12 Inadequate seed replacement rates and uncertain quality of seed is a major constraint in raising agricultural productivity.

It is necessary to contemplate major reforms in the seeds sector on the following lines :

(i) State seed farms should be converted into joint venture companies with the private sector. The state should be a minority holder. Let the farms be managed by companies on a commercial basis.

(ii) Private seed companies should be exempt from land ceiling laws to develop, test and then multiply their seeds for sale on a large scale. We should be aiming, with the help of these companies, and in association with ICAR, to become a major supplier of seeds not only within India but also to the developing world. India has a comparative advantage in seed development and seed companies need to be given similar priority as is being given to software companies.

(iii) To facilitate the entry of seed companies on a large scale, contentious issues related to IPR will have to be resolved in a transparent manner, keeping the interests of farmers in mind.

2.13 Agro-processing is a major area for further development of the value addition starting with agricultural production. This sector represents a link between agriculture and industry and holds the prospect for creating good quality jobs in the non-agriculture sector in the rural areas. An urgent review of policies in this area is needed to identify the reasons why this sector is not developing as it has in other countries.

3. INDUSTRY AND TRADE

3.1 The first phase of reforms saw some very important steps in industrial and trade policies, especially delicensing of industry, abolition of MRTP restrictions on investment by large firms, opening up of areas earlier reserved exclusively for the public sector, liberalisation of foreign direct investment, progressive elimination of quantitative restrictions and substantial reduction in import duties. These steps were designed to increase domestic competition and progressively expose Indian industry to international competition. On the whole, industry has adjusted well to the transition thus far.

3.2 However, the transformation required in the industrial sector is far from complete. This is borne out by the following facts:

(i) The industrial sector has not yet shown the double-digit growth rates which are necessary if GDP growth is to accelerate to beyond 8 per cent.

(ii) Employment in industry has not expanded rapidly, reflecting the fact that labour intensive industries have not yet seen rapid growth.

(iii) Exports of manufactured goods have also not grown as rapidly as in many other countries.

(iv) The small-scale sector remains nervous about its ability to cope with the removal of quantitative restrictions on imports of consumer goods.

3.3 A second generation of reforms in industrial and trade policies is necessary to address these problems.

Tariff Levels

3.4 With the last quantitative restrictions on imports scheduled to be removed by April 1, 2001, an important aspect of trade policy reforms will be completed. However, the levels of import duties will still be very high. Although import duty levels have been reduced significantly from an average of 87 per cent in 1990-91 to around 34 per cent in 1998-99, our duty rates are still among the highest in the developing world.

3.5 In public debate, protection through high tariff levels is often regarded as an instrument for supporting the industrial sector. However, while this may appear to help an individual industry in the short term, high rates of duty protection do not contribute to the development of a strong industrial sector. They shield inefficiencies in domestic production, creating a high cost industrial structure which makes domestic industry uncompetitive across the board. It also leads to over-valuation of the exchange rate, compared to what would prevail with lower levels of protection, which in turn makes export oriented industries less profitable than they otherwise would be.

3.6 Recognising these adverse effects of protection, successive Finance Ministers in all post-reform Governments have stated their intention to bring our average tariff rates to the levels prevailing in East Asia, which would require a reduction from an average of around 34 per cent at present to around 10-12 per cent. We endorse this objective and recommend the following steps:

(i) Government should announce a five-year phased transition from an average import duty level of 34 per cent to an average of, say, 12 per cent by 2005. This implies a reduction of 22 percentage points over 5 years or a little more than 4 percentage points per year. This is a very modest pace of duty reduction; most other developing countries have reduced import duties much faster. Any tendency for imports to increase as a result of duty reductions will lead to exchange rate depreciation and this will offset duty reductions in allowing domestic industry to compete.

(ii) Priority should be given to lowering tariffs of basic intermediates (such as steel and chemicals) as this will have the maximum beneficial effect on downstream industry, especially small scale industry. It will also reduce, if not eliminate the many "tariff anomalies" which plague the system at present, with duty rates on inputs exceeding duty rates on outputs.

(iii) Duty protection for consumer goods produced by the small scale sector can be left at present levels for some time to give this sector more time to adjust. The reduction in input duties proposed above will help this sector to become more competitive.

3.7 In recent months there has been a great deal of public discussion on the threat of large volumes of imports of selected consumer goods from China. This has led to allegations of dumping and the need to take countervailing action. There can be no question that dumping is an unfair trading practice and appropriate action under the WTO rules should be taken in cases where dumping can be proved. However, we would like to note that not all cases of competitive imports are dumping. In many cases, the items being imported may be more competitive than domestically produced items simply because our domestic competitiveness is constrained by restrictions on scale of production which prevents the achievement of international quality levels and also prevents economies of scale. In such cases, it is not appropriate to look to ways of banning trade as the solution – we should examine in greater detail why Indian industry is unable to produce equally good products at comparably attractive prices. While imports spurred by hidden subsidies must be appropriately regulated, imports which reflect weaknesses in domestic production systems can only be addressed by strengthening our domestic production capacity.

Small Scale Sector

3.8 Small scale industry represents a vital sector of the economy, being a potential source of employment and also a nursery for future entrepreneurship. Unfortunately, this sector suffers from many disadvantages arising from market failures. It is, therefore, essential that Government should evolve pro-active ways of assisting small scale industries to overcome these disadvantages.

3.9 The Abid Hussain Committee on Small Scale Enterprises has gone into these issues in great detail and made a number of specific recommendations for providing positive support. A Group on Small Scale Industry has been recently set up in the Planning Commission on the same subject and it has submitted its interim report. We urge that the various positive support measures recommended by these two groups may be considered expeditiously.

3.10 However, there is one aspect of our policy towards SSI which does not exist in any other country, that needs to be reconsidered. This is the policy of reserving certain products exclusively for small scale production. The Abid Hussain Committee has pointed out that reservation is not an appropriate instrument for supporting SSI. Two of their arguments are particularly compelling:–

(i) Reservation in India covers some of the sectors where we have the maximum export potential, i.e. leather products, toys and until recently also garments. The result is that we do not have units which are large enough to give assurance to international buyers that we can produce the volumes and quality they want. Indian export performance in these areas is, therefore, very much poorer than South-East Asia. In garments for example, the negative impact of our policy was to some extent hidden by the fact that our garment exports are still "protected" by textile quotas under the MFA regime. Once this regime is dismantled in 2005, our exporters will have to compete freely with exporters in other countries. The recent decision to de-reserve garments is therefore timely and very welcome. However the logic applies to other sectors also. Unless the existing limit of Rs.1 crore on investment in these sectors, imposed by the current reservation policy, is removed, the ability of our units to compete in world markets will be seriously affected.

(ii) The scheduled removal of quantitative restrictions on imports in April 2001 has created a situation where foreign producers, irrespective of size, will be able to bring in products (subject to tariff protection) but Indian producers, including existing small scale producers, will not be able to expand investment and scale to economically efficient levels to compete with imports. This is completely illogical.

3.11 We recognise that the issue of SSI reservation is sensitive and there is reluctance to make any changes in this policy for fear that it will hurt SSI. However, we would point out that the policy of SSI reservation is unique to India and it cannot be said that it has produced an SSI sector which is strong and able to compete. The time has come to give up reliance on reservation as an instrument for supporting SSI. Instead, we should focus our efforts at supporting SSI units by other methods of promotional nature. The proposed change will be less disruptive than is often supposed because many businesses that have been deliberately fragmented to remain small, will re-aggregate to derive benefits of scale. In other cases, existing small scale units, that are at present prevented from expanding because of investment ceilings, will be able to grow in size, which is precisely what is needed for healthy industrial growth.

3.12 In case outright abolition of reservation as recommended by the Abid Hussain Committee is not feasible, then in the first instance, reservation should be abolished immediately for select products in which we have a strong export potential. Further, a mechanism should be evolved for phased elimination of reservation for other products over the next five years.

Industrial Restructuring

3.13 A more open trade and investment regime will force a substantial restructuring in Indian industry in which industrial groups will have to shed flab and concentrate on their areas of core competence. Inefficiently run units should either be closed or taken over by others who are able to run them efficiently. This has not happened because labour legislation makes it difficult to restructure loss-making units, discouraging others from offering to run them. Legal procedures have also made it easy for owners to prolong control over companies, despite defaulting on bank dues, often using sickness to extract more funds from the banks ostensibly for the purpose of reviving units.

3.14 If our recommendations regarding labour legislation are accepted this should take care of one aspect of rigidity. The other aspect is to do with laws relating to reorganisation and bankruptcy of sick companies. In most other countries, the procedure for reorganisation, bankruptcy and liquidation are dealt with under one law and procedure. In the United States, for example, when a company is unable to pay creditors it files for protection against creditors under "Chapter 11" of the relevant legislation. Reorganisation and restructuring for revival are explored within a court procedure. If this does not succeed, bankruptcy and liquidation follows.

3.15 In India, bankruptcy and liquidation is covered under the Companies Act and the judicial procedure takes place in the relevant High Court. The Sick Industrial Companies Act (SICA) created the Board for Industrial and Financial Restructuring (BIFR). We therefore have a two step procedure. A sick company has to report to the BIFR under SICA; BIFR then explores reorganisation and restructuring for revival. If this is not found to be feasible, it then recommends winding up and the issue is referred to the relevant High Court. The High Court then appoints an Official Liquidator (OL) to look into the affairs of the company to enable the subsequent bankruptcy and liquidation proceedings.

3.16 This system is dilatory and fundamentally flawed. By the time a company becomes sick and reports to BIFR, revival is extremely difficult, and the procedures take a considerable length of time. The promoters' incentive also is to keep creditors at bay as long as possible and to keep control of the company. Years go by before a company is referred to the High court for winding up. Winding up typically takes anything up to 20 years and beyond. The Official Liquidator is a relatively low level official without the wherewithal to conduct complex investigations into company affairs. The result is that rapid industrial restructuring, which is now very necessary, is almost impossible in the current regulatory scenario.

3.17 To correct this situation, the following are recommended:

(i) SICA should be scrapped and BIFR wound up to be replaced by a process in which defaulting companies are given time to work out an arrangement with creditors.

(ii) The Debt Recovery Tribunals should be strengthened so that creditors can go to these tribunals for debt recovery.

(iii) Companies Act should be amended to allow for reorganisation and revival where feasible and rapid bankruptcy or liquidation where necessary. Outside expert agencies such as accounting firms and consultancy companies should be empanelled and empowered under court jurisdiction to conduct the relevant investigation in order to hasten the process.

3.18 Paradoxically, provision for speedy change of management or liquidation will ensure that there is less sickness because promoters will have an incentive to take action early to protect their control over companies. It will also ensure that if a change of management is needed, it is effected at an early stage rather than later, thus making it easier for new managements to pull companies out of sickness.

Privatisation of PSUs

3.19 The policy of reducing government equity in public sector undertakings has been followed by all governments in the past ten years and has now evolved to the point where the government has announced its intention to reduce its equity to a minority in a large number of undertakings, including the possibility of a change in management control in many cases. Past experience in India as well as in other countries shows that government control makes it difficult if not impossible for PSUs to function as commercial organizations able to compete with other private sector units and also with imports, as they will have to do. There is little rationale for continuing to insist on government control over management in such cases. Recent experience in India also shows that except where PSUs are in a monopoly or semi-monopoly position, their commercial performance has been disappointing.

3.20 We therefore endorse the proposition that government should reduce its equity in all PSUs except those which have a security strategic aspect and allow them to function as private units. The modality of disinvestments can vary. It could take the form of a sale to the public or financial institutions creating a board managed private sector company or it could be sold to a strategic private investor. The resources realized from the sale of equity can be more profitably deployed in building essential infrastructure or in retiring public debt.

Labour Market Reforms

3.21 An area which has been untouched thus far but where reforms are now urgently needed is the labour market facing the organised sector in India, which is more rigid than in other developing countries. By advocating reforms in this area, we are not adopting an extreme laissez faire position opposing legislation to protect labour rights. On the contrary, we recognize that there are important social reasons why labour markets are unique and labour being the weaker party in employer-employee relationships, legislation to protect labour is necessary and exists in all civilised countries.

3.22 However, such legislation must be consistent with providing a structure of incentives that encourages labour productivity and provides employers with sufficient flexibility to reduce the volume of employment or restructure producing units (or in extreme situations even close them down) when changes in market conditions and technology make it unavoidable. Our labour legislation does not meet this test. This has the unintended effect of reducing new employment opportunities in the organised sector.

3.23 There are some changes in labour legislation that are critical and need to be implemented immediately. One of these relates to the provisions governing retrenchment and closure contained in Chapter VB of the Industrial Disputes Act. This chapter was added in 1976 and is applicable to all units with more than 100 workers. In these units, retrenchment or closure can be implemented only with the explicit permission of the Government, which in practice is hardly ever given. These provisions make it virtually impossible for units to reduce their labour strength or close down a plant even temporarily even if economic circumstances have changed, making it unviable to operate.

3.24 Although these provisions may appear to serve the laudable objective of protecting employment, their actual effect is quite the opposite. Because of the difficulty in retrenching labour if needed, employers avoid increasing employment by:

(i) Opting for more capital intensive technologies than are economically justifiable given relative factor prices;

(ii) Remaining within the exempted limit by resorting to multiplication of units rather than expansion, thus denying firms the cost advantages that could accrue from economies of scale;

(iii) Relying on temporary labour and rotating them periodically to avoid permanence, thus depriving firms of skill development in the temporary segment of the labour force.

3.25 The net effect is that our industry is less competitive, especially in labour intensive activities, than we would otherwise be. It also acts as a disincentive for inflows of foreign direct investment, especially in labour intensive industries. More generally, it makes it difficult for Indian industry to adjust quickly to changing circumstances, which puts us at a serious disadvantage in the era of globalisation and rapid technological change. To correct the situation, the following steps are recommended:

(i) The requirement of prior Government permission should be abolished. This provision does not exist in our competitor countries and continuing with the present situation will hurt our ability to grow rapidly

(ii) To protect labour rights, the compensation paid to retrenched workmen should be increased from the present 15 days average pay for every completed year of service to 30 days.

(iii) If this is not possible then the floor at which the present provisions apply should be raised to cover only larger establishments employing 1000 or more workmen. Alternatively, eligibility could be defined in terms of capital employed which would favour labour intensive activities. In any case, all units in EPZs as well as 100 per cent EOUs, should be completely exempted from these requirements and allowed to retrench or close down a unit subject to enhanced payment of compensation.

3.26 A second area where reforms are urgently needed relates to contract labour. The Contract Labour (Regulation and Abolition) Act, 1970 was originally enacted to regulate contract labour to avoid exploitation. But, in practice it has been interpreted as if its intention is to abolish contract labour and force enterprises to have all services performed by regular employees on their payroll.

3.27 Unbundling of the production process and its distribution is a characteristic feature of modern industrial organisations and leads naturally to much larger resort to outsourcing of both products and services, many of which were traditionally produced within factory premises. The present Contract Labour Act, and the accumulated case law associated with it, is totally at variance with this practice and frowns on contracting out of any services that are currently performed on the factory premises. It is recommended that the Contract Labour Act should be replaced by an Act which recognises that outsourcing of services is a normal activity.

4. SOCIAL INFRASTRUCTURE

Introduction

4.1 Freedom from ignorance, disease and fear, along with freedom from want, are the best guarantors for human development. But education, health care, water and sanitation services, which can ensure these freedoms, are not accessible to all. To ensure easy accessibility, we need public action in these areas if human development has to gather momentum. Together, these facilities comprise a nation's social infrastructure that is as critical as physical infrastructure for a widely shared and inclusive development.

Education

4.2 The importance of education cannot be overstressed. Literacy is the first step towards empowerment. Universal primary education is an effective anti-poverty measure that promotes equity. The economic returns, both private and social, on investing in education are high. A World Bank (1995) review for Asia shows these to be 39 per cent, 19 per cent and 20 per cent for primary, secondary and higher education, respectively. This was before the Internet. Now, the returns would be much higher.

4.3 The world is getting globalized and integrated through the information technology/internet revolution. To partake from the information revolution human skills and knowledge have become the entry fee. Thus, five years of primary schooling is no longer adequate, nor even eight years of schooling till middle school. We need schooling up to high school for all. The merely middle school educated will be as unempowered and underprivileged in the IT era as the illiterates are today.

4.4 The modern economy, certainly the knowledge economy, requires highly educated people. Primary education is critical and its importance cannot be overemphasized. For running a technology-intensive economy, we need to go beyond primary education and build institutions for higher education. Our experience of recent years has shown that a few high quality engineers and managers have made strong impact in various industries and on the economy as a whole. It is not an exaggeration to give credit for India's software revolution principally to seven institutions: the five IITs, NCST, and the IISc.

4.5 These institutions today face enormous constraints in terms of finance and operational autonomy. Their student intake is pitifully small when compared to the size of India's economy. A large increase in the number of institutions of this quality would have a powerful impact upon our economic growth. Such 'elitist' institutions are consistent with democracy as long as admissions are open to people of all classes. In fact, they provide a way for bright persons from poor and backward classes to advance themselves. The government should fund the capital expenditure of such institutions but give annual support only to needy students. This question of redefining the scope for financial assistance and assuring the greatest flexibility and autonomy to institutions of proven performance such as the IITs and the IIMs is so urgent that we would suggest the formation of an Expert Committee to make suitable recommendations which should be speedily implemented.

4.6 The average achievement of Indians in terms of years of schooling is very low due to a high dropout rate and because a large number of people never enrolled in school. Among people aged 25 and above, for example, the average years of schooling is 2.4 in India, compared to 5 in China, 7.2 in Sri Lanka and 9.3 in South Korea.

4.7 The main problem for elementary education is high dropout rates. In 1998-99, the dropout rate was 39.7 per cent for classes I-V, 56.7 per cent for classes I-VIII and 67.4 per cent for classes I-X. (Annual Report for 1999-2000, Ministry of Human Resource Development.)

4.8 Children often drop out when they find schools uninteresting and when they cannot keep up with others. Children from socially and economically disadvantaged classes often suffer from lack of nutrition, stunted mental development and very little stimulation to learn at home. Removal of these deficiencies is vital if these children are to be successful in learning at school. Pre-primary schooling is thus critical to the goal of effective elementary schooling for all.

4.9 It is also worth noting that the failure of poor enrolment and attendance has much to do with poor quality of supply. One of the most striking findings of the PROBE (1999) survey is that a great deal of motivation exists among parents to educate their children. Asked whether it is important to educate a boy, 100 per cent parents answered in the affirmative. The figure is slightly lower at 89 per cent for girls' education. Most parents also wanted a minimum of 8 years of education for their children.

4.10 *Education Policy Goals*

The foregoing suggest the main goals:

(i) Ensure 100 per cent effective enrolment in quality primary schools within five, if not three, years.

(ii) Reduce dropout rates through the primary and upper primary levels to less than 10 per cent so that at least 90 per cent students complete eight years of schooling.

(iii) Aim for 75 per cent enrolment in higher secondary (class IX-XII) schools of good quality and provide and support the private sector in the establishment of high quality, secondary education facilities in every taluka so that secondary schooling is available to all those who want it.

(iv) Enrolment in colleges and professional education should be raised to 20 per cent of the age group 20-24.

(v) Revitalize our university system.

(vi) Expand institutions of quality for higher education so that all those capable of becoming high quality professionals have the opportunity to do so. Encourage the creation of state-of-the-art professional research based education institutions in all disciplines. India should be a sought after place for higher education for people around the world.

(vii) Expand and improve the quality of vocational training.

4.11 Actions & Reforms to achieve Goals

(i) The number and quality of schools have to be improved. The existing programmes – Sarva Shiksha Abhiyan and District Primary Education Programme – being implemented with the participation of Panchayats and

Village School Committees, should be adequately supported.

(ii) Studies have shown that school meals significantly increase school attendance, especially among girls. Provision of school meals in primary schools should be made the norm. Giving foodgrains for school attendance is not a viable option to providing meals. Foodgrains are often distributed without ensuring attendance and also inflate enrolment numbers.

(iii) The physical infrastructure of school buildings, including the provision of drinking water and toilet facilities, should be improved. Toilets are particularly important to encourage attendance by girls. Adequate teaching aids and books should be provided to all schools.

(iv) The Integrated Child Development Services (ICDS) programme was initiated in 1975. Under it, through a network of Anganwadis, pre-school children, pregnant women and nursing mothers are provided education, nutrition and basic health services. The programme that is now estimated to cover only 12 per cent of the children in the country should be expanded to cover all needy children.

(v) This will call for additional resources that must be provided. Increased funding alone, however, will not fetch quality schools. Ensuring the accountability of teachers is a critical factor. But a faraway central authority cannot ensure accountability. To achieve teacher accountability, we have to look at the option of community participation. Thus schools should be placed under the control of local stakeholders through a local level body, a village education committee with representatives of parents and the panchayat, to monitor the performance of teachers, who should be employed by the local bodies.

(vi) The entire resources allocated for education do not have to be spent by the Government in directly running schools. Private schools can play a very important role in achieving our targets. To facilitate private initiatives, education should be liberalised and all entry-exit restrictions on and bureaucratic hurdles faced by schools and colleges should be abolished.

(vii) But private and even autonomous public schools have to be made accountable for their performance. This can be done through performance-linked Government grants. In measuring performance, we should not create a monopoly, but instead encourage a number of competing independent certification, accreditation and examination agencies.

(viii) One can give every child, in the relevant age group, a voucher of a specified sum and the freedom to select a school. Many countries, including those with high literacy rates, are moving towards the voucher system to improve the quality of their education. The education system of Chile is now almost completely based on vouchers. A transportation subsidy may also be included to make choice possible over a larger set of schools. We may try it out in a State or in selected districts.

Health

4.12 We have made much progress in life expectancy and mortality but we have a long way to go. While life expectancy at birth of 62.4 years in 1997 is nearly double that in 1951, it is much less than 72 years in Malaysia (in Kerala too). Again our national average infant mortality rate of 71 per 1000 live births should be compared with Kerala's 12. The high infant mortality rate reflects the poor state of public health, inadequate medical attention during pregnancy and at birth and poor post-natal care. To reduce infant and child mortality, we need nearly 100 per cent immunization, supply of clean drinking water and provision of sanitation facilities to prevent infections, and professional attention during childbirth. The coverage of these facilities is very inadequate today.

4.13 Public action is particularly important for the health of the poor as they are not able to take care of themselves to the same extent as the rich.

4.14 There is vast disparity between rural and urban areas in health care facilities. 84 per cent of hospitals and 75 per cent of allopathic doctors are in urban areas that account for only 35 per cent of the population. While 74 per cent of the hospital beds are in government hospitals, the richest 20 per cent of the population occupy these 6 times as much as the poorest 20 per cent.

4.15 We need to focus more on preventive health care for it will be cost effective. Yet, government has to provide curative health care for the poor too.

4.16 *Healthcare Policy Goals*

(i) Reduce all-India infant mortality rate from 72 per 1,000 live births to Kerala's IMR of 12 over five years.

(ii) Reduce all-India child mortality rate (age 1-5) to that of Kerala.

(iii) Expand health care infrastructure (health centres, clinics and hospitals) in rural areas to redress the large rural-urban disparity that exists, and improve the functioning of existing facilities.

(iv) Expand the coverage of ICDS programme and improve it, using the Tamil Nadu Integrated Nutrition Programme Phase II as the model.

(v) To do these, Government should mobilise NGOs and media in a national campaign. Best performing NGOs, Panchayats, district collectors and States may be given special recognition, awards and incentives.

(vi) These efforts can be more effective if access to clean drinking water is ensured as almost 80 per cent of the diseases in the country are water-borne.

(vii) Private sector should be encouraged to set up and operate hospitals in rural areas through tax incentives and through grants related to the number of poor patients treated. Professional societies may be asked to set up a system of accreditation and certification.

(viii) Urban-based doctors may be encouraged to spend few days a month in rural hospitals as honorary doctors. Their opportunity cost of time spent in such work should be admissible for tax rebate as charitable contribution.

(ix) The relatively well off should be required to pay for health care services. A variety of health insurance schemes should be made available for them.

Social Safety Nets

4.17 Most industrialised countries have created social safety nets to take care of their poor, their unemployed, their sick and their aged. Social safety nets provide relief in the form of minimum income support or cost reimbursement when a person faces unemployment or unexpected expenditure. They are important as they reduce the fear of destitution and sense of insecurity. Insecurity has a debilitating effect on society and, thus, on the economy. It discourages people from taking risks. If there are adequate safety nets, people can be more enterprising as the cost of failure is reduced. Above all, any humane and compassionate society ought to provide social safety nets to all its citizens.

4.18 Among the anti-poverty programmes, the following are preferable for their cost-effectiveness of income transfer and other benefits:

(i) A model employment programme should be designed based on the experience of various schemes such as Employment Guarantee Scheme (EGS), Employment Assurance Scheme (EAS) and Jawahar Rozgar Yojana (JRY) and should cover the whole country. It should constitute the major thrust of anti-poverty initiatives. Employment programmes are self-targeting, as bulk of the wages accrue to the poor, self-adjusting as per need for employment, and self-terminating. Also, when properly designed and executed, they create productive assets.

(ii) Integrated Child Development Services (ICDS) should be expanded and modified along the Tamil Nadu Integrated Nutritional Programme Phase II. This will serve the purpose of reducing mortality and poverty.

(iii) Significant progress has been made in recent years for group-based micro-credit schemes. These should be expanded to cover the entire country.

Resources and Delivery Systems

4.19 To provide education, health care and social security we will need large resources. The resources required would certainly have a high social rate of return and would be justified. Yet, we have to first mobilize the resources. If fiscal reforms are carried out, expenditure trimmed, appropriate user fees are levied on economic services provided by the government and non-merit subsidies greatly reduced, finding the resources would not be a problem. Without fiscal reforms, we cannot expect to make significant improvement in providing social services which means so much for the well-being of all, rich and poor.

4.20 Resources have to be effectively spent. How the services are provided determines the extent to which they are delivered to the intended beneficiaries. The suggestions made here argue for participation and control by local stakeholders, mobilization of private sector and NGOs, performance based support by government, monitoring by rating agencies, creation of competitive environment and giving people a choice to make competition work.

5. ECONOMIC INFRASTRUCTURE

5.1 There is a general agreement that the quality of economic infrastructure in the country is a serious impediment to accelerating growth and indeed may even make it difficult to maintain the growth rate already achieved in the 1990s. To succeed in today's globalised world we have to be competitive, but all the efforts of our producers to improve plant level efficiency will come to naught if the quality of infrastructure services such as power supply, telecommunications, roads, railways, ports, civil aviation etc. does not come up to necessary standards. Yet this is precisely the situation that prevails today. High power costs to industry and unreliability of power supply is making Indian industry uncompetitive. Transport costs are very high and transport time far too long with too little assurance of guaranteed time of delivery to enable our producers to be credible suppliers in export markets.

5.2 Improving India's infrastructure requires a massive increase in investment in all these sectors. It also requires much greater levels of efficiency to ensure low costs and good quality of service.

The resources needed for investment are simply not available with the public sector providing one reason for bringing in the private sector. Besides, continuation with exclusive public sector monopolies in this area will not provide the competitive pressure needed to improve services. This is a second reason for bringing the private sector into infrastructure.

5.3 Both the Union and State Governments have taken a number of initiatives since 1991 to attract private investment into infrastructure. These efforts have yielded some fruit – there has been an increase in private sector capacity in power, telecommunications and ports – but the response has been much less than was hoped for. The principal reason for this is that the pre-conditions for successful entry of the private sector are not easy to establish. The problems vary from sector to sector and we have commented below on each sector separately but there are few general problems which we wish to highlight.

(i) The first is the problem of "user charges". Investment in infrastructure can either be financed on the basis of reasonable user charges or on the basis of State subsidies. Most of our infrastructure sectors suffer from inadequate user charges (e.g. very low tariffs for agricultural consumers and domestic consumers of power, no user charges for roads, low user charges for railway passengers etc.). Since the ability of the State to compensate for low user charges by providing budgetary subsidies is extremely limited, it follows that user charges have to be raised if infrastructure is to be financed. It is important to note that this is true whether we retain infrastructure as an exclusive public sector monopoly, or bring in the private sector into this area. Rationalisation of user charges in infrastructure is absolutely vital.

(ii) Even if the user charge issue is resolved, it will still be difficult to bring in private investment if the regulatory regime is not sufficiently transparent to reassure private investors. The establishment of a regulatory regime that is seen to be fair to consumers and also sensitive to the legitimate needs of investors is absolutely essential if we want to attract private investors into infrastructure.

Although regulatory authorities have been set up in various infrastructure sectors, they have had teething problems in the early years, and this has been an impediment to attracting investors.

In our view, the establishment of rational user charges and credible regulatory authorities are the two critical features on which the success of infrastructure development will depend.

Power

5.4 The power sector was the first among the infrastructure sectors to be opened up to the private sector and yet it is in this sector that the greatest difficulty has been encountered. Private investment in the power sector has been substantially short of expectations.

5.5 The basic strategy followed in the power sector was to attract private investment in the generation segment with independent power producers (IPPs) expected to sell the power they produce to the State Electricity Boards. The flaw in the policy was the failure to recognize that the root of the problem lies in the financial unviability of the State Electricity Boards. The likelihood that SEBs will not be able to pay for power produced and sold to them makes it impossible for private power producers to achieve financial closure. This has made IPPs look for temporary solutions such as escrow arrangements and Central Government guarantees which simply do not address the core problem. What this means is that growth in power generation, transmission and distribution is unlikely to take place unless the problems of State Electricity Boards are tackled head on.

5.6 Reform of the power sector calls for action on several fronts, mostly on the part of State Governments.

- Power tariffs for consumers need to be rationalized with very low tariff levels for some consumers progressively raised to economically viable levels while very high tariffs to other consumers (e.g. Industry) are not raised. State Electricity Regulatory Commission have to bring about this tariff rationalization.

- The huge transmission and distribution losses need to be brought down. Privatisation of distribution in our view will help to bring down losses. In retrospect it can be said that it would have been better to have focused on distribution reform and privatization first in order to get the cash flow position on even keel rather than pushing with reforms in generation in the first stage. Even if the entire distribution system cannot be privatized there is merit in privatizing part of the system as superior efficiency shown by private operators in the privatised areas would help achieve better efficiency from the public sector in the rest of the distribution system. Privatisation of distribution must be implemented by State Governments.
- In order to privatize distribution some solution must be found to the outstanding dues of the existing system. These are reported to have mounted to Rs.30,000 crores. Unless this problem is satisfactorily resolved, privatization will be difficult. It can be attempted in parts of the system but this will only leave the rest of the system burdened with all the past dues, which is not equitable. Since a large part of these dues are to Central Government organisations (NTPC, Coal India, Railways, NHPC) the Central Government has a role to play.
- Regulators have to provide clearer indications of tariff policies over much longer horizons to reassure private investors if privatization of distribution is to succeed.

5.7 It needs to be understood that for progress to take place in this sector, reforms cannot be piecemeal. Drafting of the Electricity Bill 2000 is a step in the right direction: it constitutes enabling legislation for full scale reform in this sector. It would enable unbundling of the sector into generation, transmission, supply and distribution activities. However, implementation of these reforms requires determined action on several fronts.

Telecom

5.8 Although telecommunication services were opened to private sector investment several years ago, the effort ran into difficulties because of unrealistic bids submitted by private companies and also a perceived lack of a regulatory level playing field. Fortunately, these problems have been overcome because of a number of positive initiatives taken by the Government involving modifications in policy to take account of problems that had surfaced. The telecom sector has been characterised by high user charges for all except local telecommunication. Therefore, reforms in this sector have generally meant a reduction in tariffs. Accordingly, teledensity has grown from about 1 per cent in 1990 to almost 3 per cent now, with telephone connections growing at a rate of almost 25 to 30 per cent per year over the decade. Because of the availability of adequate economic returns in the sector the private sector is well able to enter the sector. Private sector mobile telephone services are now available in almost all parts of the country. The announcement of the National Telecom Policy 1999 and the consequent changes in policy have rekindled interest in the sector. Domestic long distance services have been opened to the private sector. TRAI has recommended the opening up of basic services to competition with no restraint on the number of operators. The Department of Telecom services has already been corporatised. We can therefore expect new telecom investment as soon as the Government announces the exact conditions for entry into these areas.

5.9 The new challenges in financing the telecom sector are concerned with the ongoing convergence that is taking place in the sector. The evolution of telecom services during the last decade has been such that there is excessive fragmentation in the provision of services between service providers- both in terms of different services and in terms of geographical coverage of each licensee. The key issue for the future will be evolution of a regulatory regime that recognises convergence and allows for single national service based licences. In view of the rapid convergence of telecom, IT and media, a new comprehensive statute, replacing the Indian Telegraph Act of 1885, should be passed by the Parliament.

5.10 It is observed internationally that telecom service costs are coming down relentlessly because of increasing competition and decreasing actual costs. For Indian industry to be competitive, it will be necessary for services to be priced in a similar fashion.

The following are suggested to achieve this:

(i) The existing level of licence fees, levied as revenue sharing fees, will not be sustainable and will have to be reduced. The Government must make clear that it only expects to meet administration and regulatory costs, along with universal service obligation charges, through revenue sharing, and that it is not interested in mopping up rents. This reduction in license fees would not be a bonanza for private investors since the increasing competition in the sector will ensure that the benefits are passed on to the consumer.

(ii) Service taxes can be levied as on any other economic activity for revenue purposes. The only area where rents would have to be collected would be from the allocation of scarce resources concerned with spectrum allocation.

(iii) Consideration should be given to allowing voice telephony over the internet since that will bring down the costs for users significantly.

As the coverage of telecom expands over time, a high proportion of the new users would be smaller users. As the sector is unbundled, it will be increasingly difficult to cross-subsidise local services from long distance services. Thus, the universal service obligation needs to be defined carefully and the universal service fund used to finance such services.

5.11 The present monopoly of VSNL on international long distance services is undesirable and a big hurdle in establishing a world-class telecom infrastructure in the country. Competition in the international voice services will improve services and reduce the present level of high tariffs. We welcome the government's announcement of advancing the date of private sector entry in this segment to 2002. We would recommend that procedures for allowing new entry be worked out expeditiously and advance action taken for issuing licenses so that new entrants can be operational at the earliest possible date.

5.12 The lack of bandwidth for both international and domestic connectivity is a major problem. For India to become an IT superpower, it is necessary to provide easy and quick access to sufficient bandwidth at a reasonable cost. The projects of the

Indian Railways and the Power Grid Corporation to set up optical fibre cable networks using their right of way along railway track/ transmission lines should be expedited.

Roads

5.13 The past two years have seen a welcome thrust in road development. The National Highway Development Project (NHDP), which entails expansion of the existing two-lane highways to four lane highways along nearly 6,000 Km. commonly known as the Golden Quadrilateral, and also along the cross-country corridors that connect North to South and East to West will go a long way towards closing a critical gap, though we would emphasise that it will still leave us only with four-laned highways. The National Highway Authority of India (NHAI), the implementing agency for the project, has already started upgradation on selected stretches. About 590 Km. of the Golden Quadrilateral has already been converted into four-lane highway and over 700 Km. is under construction. Project preparation activities are in progress for the remaining sectors and contracting under the scheme amounting to 2500 kms is expected to be completed in the current fiscal year. This would be commendable and should be closely monitored.

5.14 Highways are difficult to finance exclusively through tolls and some other form of indirect user charge is therefore needed. The Government has levied a cess of Re. 1 per litre on petrol and diesel and the resources collected from this cess will go a long way to finance the ambitious road development programme that the Government has undertaken. However, these funds will not be adequate to finance the full programme as envisaged. Hence all other means of funding or leveraging existing funds should be explored. Tolls should be imposed on all four lane stretches of National Highways to ensure maximum inflow of resources and especially to provide for maintenance expenditure. The prioritisation of highway segments to be developed should also be based on the existence of adequate traffic levels to pay tolls. BOT operators must bear some traffic risk through the collection of tolls. Capital subsidies or annuity arrangements for financing roads should be provided only as supplementary financing and should be accompanied by imposition of tolls. Since all road users would be paying the cess, it is important that the Central road fund is set up in such a fashion that allocations are made in a fair manner as between national highways, State roads and rural roads.

5.15 Private Sector participation in road construction should be encouraged to the extent possible through the BOT/Annuity system. The experience of the last 50 years has shown that the EPC system has many drawbacks, such as poor quality of construction and later, poor maintenance. Under the BOT/Annuity system EPC and O&M contracts will be merged and given to the same contractor who would be responsible for construction and maintenance of the road during the concession period. Such a system would provide incentives to the contractor to ensure quality of construction in order to minimise O&M expenses later. This will lead to use of technologies which reduce life cycle costs of the projects and consequently reduce the cost of project implementation. Essentially, the private sector efficiencies would offset higher financial mobilisation costs and at the same time ensure superior quality construction within the specified time frame.

5.16 High density corridors have several deficiencies at present, in the form of missing links, weak and narrow bridges, and the absence of bypasses. These should receive high priority. There is also an urgent need for the introduction of new technology in the design, engineering and construction methods as also carrying out surveys through remote sensing techniques particularly in the upgradation of the roads which are covered by the HDC. Use of machines to improve both the quality and speed of construction need to be pursued more vigorously. One of the reasons for the use of inappropriate technology in road construction and maintenance lies in the practice of awarding a large number of small contracts. A review therefore needs to be made of existing outdated contracting mechanisms. The possibility of creating engineering leasing companies needs to be encouraged.

Ports

5.17 To achieve higher economic growth rates and attain higher efficiency levels, the share of trade in GDP will have to increase substantially. Expansion of trade and export competitiveness depends on the efficiency of ports. The current structure of ports is amenable to neither achievement of greater efficiency nor significant expansion.

5.18 Low port productivity in India is to a considerable extent a consequence of obsolete equipment, inadequate mechanised handling facilities, poor port management techniques and outdated labour practices. Port handling equipment needs upgradation in technology to keep pace with changes such as design and size of ship. Future ship sizes would be much larger, especially in respect of liquid bulk cargo. It is imperative that infrastructure facilities (e.g. the pumping capacity in case of tankers) provided in the port are compatible with the ship capacity.

5.19 Private investment in port infrastructure will have to be encouraged actively. Existing Port Trusts should be corporatised and turned into landlord ports that then invite different operators, both public and private, to invest in cargo handling and port infrastructure services. The corporatised landlord ports should concentrate on the development of common user general cargo facilities. Private sector operators will only perform when faced with competition. Thus, both inter-port and intra-port competition must be promoted.

5.20 International trade is witnessing an increasing trend in containerization. JNPT and Chennai ports which are capable of berthing mother vessels, need to be developed as mainline gateway ports connected by a rail/road bridge and equipped with efficient, modern container handling facilities. The availability of such inter-modal facilities will result in considerable savings in cost and time for ships from the West carrying containers destined for Chennai or beyond and those from the East carrying containers destined for Mumbai or beyond.

5.21 The pricing policy of port services needs to be such that it helps in raising resources internally. Cross subsidisation needs to be phased out. Tariff policy should be used as a instrument of rationing of port capacity i.e., higher tariffs should be charged for the most congested facilities/periods. In the same way differential tariffs needs to be introduced for discouraging old vessels. Tariff Authority for Major Ports (TAMP) should be developed as a statutory autonomous body and its orders should be enforceable.

Railways

5.22 The finances of Indian Railways are today in a parlous state. For the first time in almost 20 years, the Indian Railways were not able to pay the dividend on capital at charge to the Central Government. This situation has been reached due to the excessive politicisation of the railway budget. The setting of tariffs is not based on economic criteria - overall passenger fares of lower classes are too low and many freight tariffs are too high. Second, many new investments are sanctioned on uneconomic lines that are never completed. The share of railways in total traffic at present is 40 per cent. Large-scale cross- subsidisation of passenger services by overcharging certain categories of freight has deflected freight traffic from railways to roads. The railway share in freight traffic should be increased through qualitative capacity augmentation aided by corrective pricing policies and organisational change. Consideration should also be given to running dedicated container trains between metros.

5.23 The fare freight ratio (earning per passenger Km. *vis-a-vis* earning per tonne Km.) at present is 0.32, which is one of the lowest in the world. If it is increased to 0.5 as it was in 1951-52, it would result in additional earnings of Rs. 4400 crore. Reluctance to impose passenger tariffs which cover costs only prevents the railways from mobilising the resources needed to modernise and upgrade the quality of their services which is increasingly important for passengers. It also prevents the railways from undertaking essential replacement of overage equipment (including especially rails) which has serious safety implications. There is need to phase out subsidies both in respect of passengers and freight over a period of the next three years.

5.24 In order to promote inter-modal traffic for safe, efficient, customer friendly and faster movement of goods, there is a need to increase Inland Container Depots (ICDs). The establishment of ICDs should take place at the crossings of the three modes of surface transport i.e. rail, road and inland waterways in order to minimise costs and time. The Railways have to increasingly focus on the creation of rail hubs with sufficient warehousing facilities and accelerate the programme of containerisation not only to promote inter-modal transport but also as a strategy for increasing its own market share and catering to high-value traffic.

5.25 At present, the railway system is a monolithic departmental enterprise which covers provision and maintenance of the track network, operation of freight and passenger services, and also substantial production units producing rolling stock. There is no obvious advantage in integrating manufacturing of rolling stock (locomotives, coaches and freight cars) into the monolithic departmental enterprise. The existing six manufacturing units of Indian Railways should be split into independent profit and cost centres and thereafter corporatised.

5.26 The scope of private sector participation in acquiring rolling stock, particularly high speed wagons and new generation locos, needs to be enlarged gradually through innovative leasing schemes. The railways need to identify projects with a high rate of return for offering to the private sector. Further, to tide over the conceptual and procedural difficulties, the legal and tax framework for the leasing scheme requires to be simplified and streamlined.

Civil Aviation

5.27 Delhi and Mumbai are our main airports and each is well connected with the rest of the country as a regional hub. The high volume of traffic at these airports and their interconnection offer the most immediately viable opportunity for their upgradation to world class international airports. Other airports can be taken up subsequently for such upgradation depending upon traffic intensity.

5.28 There is a continuing need for the upgradation and modernisation of air traffic services such as navigation and surveillance facilities. New approaches in airport design to accommodate technological innovations like the new large aircraft need to be considered. Technological upgradation should be extended to cover the ground facilities by introduction of automation and computerisation, mechanisation of baggage handling facilities and provision of aero bridges etc.

5.29 Across the world, the trend is towards a very high percentage, ranging from 60-70 per cent of the total revenue of airport operations, being generated from non-aeronautical sources at major airports, whereas the figure for AAI at international airports is just 22 per cent. There should be a major thrust towards increasing the share of commercial revenue emerging from non-aeronautical sources.

5.30 Currently the revenue from the taxes imposed in the aviation sector in the shape of Inland Air Travel Tax (IATT) and Foreign Travel Tax (FTT) is credited to the Consolidated Fund of India, with only 10 per cent of FTT being given to the AAI. Taking into account the vast sums required for infrastructural development, there is a strong case for conversion of these taxes into a common Civil Aviation Cess, the proceeds of which should be credited to a national Civil Aviation Fund to be operated by the Ministry of Civil Aviation.

5.31 The organisational structure of airports need to be corporatised to enable entry of the private sector, both in greenfield airports and existing airport operations. The restructuring of the major airports (Delhi, Mumbai, Chennai and Calcutta) on long term lease basis is being considered for inviting private sector management in the airports. AAI could develop other airports with the lease rentals received from the lease of these airports.

5.32 In the context of a multiplicity of operators, including private operators, there is a need for establishing an independent regulatory framework in the civil aviation sector for ensuring economic regulation in the sector. The regulatory authority should be empowered to fix and revise tariffs in the sector.

5.33 The Domestic Air Transport Policy debars foreign airlines from equity participation in the companies formed for domestic air transport operations. This is not desirable because it debars those from participation who actually have the experience in airlines operations, while allowing the participation of those who may not have expertise in the airlines business. Therefore, there is a need to review and change the policy.

5.34 The expansion of international services to India has been seriously constrained by the inability of the national carriers to expand their own services through adequate investments. This has led to an inadequate expansion of bilateral traffic rights which are negotiated on an inter-governmental basis. In effect the inability of the national carriers to expand has constrained the expansion of foreign carriers providing services to India. The net result has been severe shortage of seat capacity for air travel to

India, especially from Europe. This is inconsistent with the needs of a growing economy, especially one which wishes to expand tourism. The governance of bilateral rights needs to be reviewed urgently with a view to expanding services.

6. FINANCIAL SECTOR REFORMS

6.1 Financial sector reforms have been an important part of the economic reforms from the very inception in 1991. Since then, a number of steps have been taken in the banking sector as well as in the securities market to bring our regulatory framework and prudential norms in line with the international practice. While some gaps remain, there is no doubt that progress thus far has been commendable and we are confident that the remaining gaps can be bridged fairly quickly. We would particularly emphasise the importance of bringing the norms and standards in the banking sector up to international standards as quickly as possible as this sector has come under increased scrutiny in all emerging markets following the East Asian crisis.

6.2 The opening up of the insurance sector to new private players is an important new initiative which has got off to a good start. It will yield significant benefits in the years to come.

6.3 We endorse the recent initiative by the Government to seek changes in legislation to reduce government share in equity of the public sector banks to 33 per cent. We note that the present policy envisages a reduction in government equity while "retaining the public sector character of the public sector banks". In this context a note of caution is in order. The proposed reduction in Government equity below 51 per cent is clearly a move in the right direction, with significant potential benefits in terms of enabling the Government to give our public sector commercial banks the commercial freedom they need to function as competitive institutions in commercial banking. In principle, they should be able to function as board managed banks, with boards composed of individuals representing the government as well as eminent independent professionals. Some of the key decisions regarding personnel and promotions should also be determined by Board policy and not by the government. While this transformation is made possible by the reduction in equity holdings it will happen only if the reduction in equity leads to a conscious decision to give banks the necessary autonomy to function as board managed institutions. Unless this is done, the reduction in equity with a continuation of effective government control as at present will yield little benefit in terms of creating independent banks.

7. THE FISCAL SITUATION

7.1 The fiscal situation is undoubtedly one of the most serious weaknesses in the economy at present and corrective action in this area is urgently needed. The combined deficit of the Centre and States was around 10 per cent in 1999-2000 and is likely to be much the same in the current year. This is marginally higher than the level of 9.2 per cent reached in 1990-91, just before the crisis. The damage caused by high fiscal deficits is well appreciated, but it is worth repeating. The consequences of a high fiscal deficit depend upon the way the deficit is financed. There are three possibilities.

(i) The deficit can be financed largely by monetisation. While some monetisation is acceptable and even desirable, excessive monetisation leads to uncontrolled expansion in money supply and an increase in domestic inflationary pressure, which in turn will make Indian goods uncompetitive against imports and also in export markets. Inevitably, this will also put pressure on the exchange rate and lead to instability in the exchange markets. Inflation also is highly inequitable in the sense that its impact is the highest on the poor.

(ii) The deficit could be financed by borrowing in domestic financial markets. This is what has been happening in India of late and the result is that real interest rates become very high. In recent years the government has been borrowing at around 11 per cent when inflation averaged around 5 per cent. This implies real interest rates of 6 per cent for government borrowing, which means that private sector financing has to be at real interest rates of 8 per cent or so for the best corporates and correspondingly higher for others. With such high real interest rates, private investment is bound to be choked off, which is exactly what has happened. Large government borrowing not only pushes up interest rates and discourages investment, it also has the effect that banks have no incentive to look for good creditworthy borrowers as they can happily lend to the government at high interest rates.

(iii) The deficit could be financed by inflows of external funds. This is effectively what happens in countries where the capital account is open and there is a large fiscal deficit and it is presumed that the authorities are committed to a fixed exchange rate policy. The rise in domestic interest rates on sovereign debt attracts an inflow of foreign funds into the debt market. This moderates the rise in interest rates compared with (ii) above but it has the effect of unduly appreciating the exchange rate and also leads to a build up of foreign debt, often of the short-term variety. Such capital flows are volatile and can reverse very quickly, leading to an unsustainable situation. This mechanism was the cause of the debt crises in Latin America in the 1980s. Fortunately, the mechanism is not relevant for India because we do not have an open capital account.

7.2 With option (iii) ruled out, the choice we face is between allowing monetisation and risking high inflation, with all its attendant dangers, or accepting very high interest rates with the resultant squeeze on private investment. We have rightly avoided the monetisation option, but we are therefore faced with the consequences outlined in (ii) above i.e. high real interest rates and a crowding out of private investment.

7.3 It is important to note that high fiscal deficit would crowd out private investment whatever use the government makes of the funds it borrows. If the fiscal deficit is high because the government is making large investments in the economy, it could be argued that while private investment is being squeezed out, the economy at least benefits from the public investment especially if such investment took place in critical infrastructure where there are large gaps at present. Unfortunately, the large fiscal deficit which the Centre and States are running today is not caused by large public investment. In fact, a large part of the borrowing is only financing current expenditure. Both the Centre and the States are running large revenue deficits which have to be met by borrowing. Further borrowing is then needed to finance capital expenditure. While the fiscal deficit has increased in the past several years as a percentage of GDP, public investment as a percentage of GDP has fallen steadily.

7.4 Since the fiscal deficit equals the net increase in outstanding public debt, the outstanding debt of the Centre and the States combined has been rising steadily due to continuing fiscal deficit. The combined debt to GDP ratio is now around 65 per cent. This is too high. It leads to a high and rising interest burden and we have reached a situation where we have to borrow even to service the debt. This is clearly unsustainable. It will squeeze the capability of the system to finance productive expenditures from the Budget in future.

The Need For Correction

7.5 Clear targets should be established to bring the fiscal situation under control over the next 3 to 4 years. The Eleventh Finance Commission has recommended reducing the combined fiscal deficit of the Centre and States to 6.5 per cent by 2005. This involves an improvement of about one half of one percent per year in the fiscal deficit which is quite modest. It could be argued that a bolder effort is needed which could bring the combined deficit down to 5 per cent by the end of the Tenth Plan period i.e. 2006-07. One cannot be very precise in this area, but there can be no doubt that unless a substantial reduction in the deficit is achieved we cannot expect to raise the rate of growth of GDP to around 8 per cent, which is currently being discussed, and which is also needed if we want to make a significant impact on poverty and to provide growth in good quality employment. Instead, we face the prospect of continuing stagnation in private investment and inadequate public investment in the critical sectors of economic and social infrastructure, especially in rural areas.

7.6 Continued high fiscal deficits indicating the possibility of high inflation and financial crisis, could lead to a loss of investor confidence in the economy, with adverse effects on FDI and FII inflows. A sudden collapse of the type witnessed in East Asia in 1997 is not likely but a loss of investor confidence would certainly lead to a loss of growth momentum and possibly also create serious pressure on the balance of payments. In short, even maintenance of the present growth rate of around 6 per cent per year may be difficult, if real interest rates increase further and there is decline in public investment because of rising interest burden.

7.7 It is important to emphasise that a fiscal correction is needed in both the Centre and the States as performance in both levels of government suffer from fiscal stress. The fiscal situation of State governments is known to be extremely weak and many governments have even found it difficult to pay salaries. However, the Centre's performance is also highly unsatisfactory. Despite relatively healthy growth rates in the post-reforms period, the ratio of Central tax revenues to GDP actually declined from around 11 per cent in 1990-91 to 9 per cent in 1999-2000 whereas the expectation was that the tax-GDP ratio would increase over this period. It is interesting to note that States tax revenues as a percentage of GDP have at least remained stationary, whereas the Central tax-GDP ratio has actually fallen by over 2 percentage points. The poor performance of the Centre in mobilising tax revenue in turn has meant that the States have received much less by way of their share of Central taxes than was originally projected. The States have also suffered from the large increase in expenditure on government salaries forced on them by the Centre's decision in 1997 which went much beyond the Fifth Pay Commission's recommendations.

7.8 In the next two sections we outline the elements of a fiscal correction in the Centre and the States separately. Since it is important to avoid a fiscal correction based on a squeeze on public investment, the focus of the correction in both the Centre and the States must be on improving revenue mobilisation, as well as on containment of unproductive current expenditure.

Fiscal Correction at the Centre

7.9 The Centre has already taken two commendable steps in the current year. It has appointed an Expenditure Reforms Commission and it has introduced a Fiscal Responsibility Bill in Parliament. However, legislation by itself will not guarantee fiscal discipline – there could always be departures from targets and the Fiscal Responsibility legislation only requires that these departures would have to be explained. It is necessary to identity some critical areas for policy action which would bring about a significant reduction in the Centre's fiscal deficit over a three to four year period while also ensuring the quality of deficit reduction. Some of the critical areas where action is needed, are given in the following paragraphs:.

7.10 Revenue Mobilisation

(i) As pointed out above, the Centres' tax revenue in relation to GDP has actually fallen by about 2 percentage points over the past ten years. We should aim to recover this ground over the next four years. We have the following specific suggestions.

(ii) The basic strategy of lowering tax rates and broadening the tax base has worked extremely well in case of personal income tax where revenues have increased steadily despite reductions. We recommend continuation of this strategy with no increase in rates and a major effort at base broadening. The Corporate tax rate strategy has also worked well and needs no modification at present.

(iii) Revenue from customs duties has fallen as a percentage of GDP and this was to be expected. The strategy of moving towards a regime of low customs duties is a worldwide phenomenon and we need to continue on the same path. In the case of agriculture an increase in customs duty is appropriate in anticipation of the removal of QRs on 1st April 2001, especially since the present WTO regime permits industrialised countries to retain very large agricultural subsidies. For the industrial sector, we recommend a clear announcement of a phased transition from the present relatively high rates of customs duties, to the levels prevailing in East Asia over a three to four year period. Reduction in average duty rates may lead to some lack of buoyancy in this area though the liberalization of QRs as consumer goods is likely to increase revenue because these goods attract higher rates of duty.

(iv) Tax collection from excise duties as a percentage of GDP have fallen steadily through the 1990s. There is no reason why this should have happened and this is the principal area where corrective steps are needed. Experience in other countries shows that tax policy and administration reform, including the reduction in the number of rates, elimination of exemptions and deduction and simplification of procedures, can bring about greater buoyancy without an increase in tax rates. It is widely believed that this has not happened in India because there are innumerable exemptions and other loopholes in the excise systems which encourage evasion and corruption. The system of duty credit under Modvat is reportedly being widely misused, primarily because of certain provisions introduced for the benefit of the small-scale sector. These loopholes need to be plugged as a matter of urgency and the Budget for 2000-01 should give top priority to addressing this issue.

7.11 Expenditure Control

(i) Despite frequent talk by successive governments of the need to control non-Plan expenditure, remarkably little has been done in this area. The Expenditure Reforms Commission, which is going into the issue in depth, has begun submitting its reports. We would strongly recommend that the Government should announce that it will take decisions (whether positive or negative) on the recommendations of each report within six months of the receipt of the report. The forthcoming Budget could be used to announce decisions on some of the reports that have already been submitted by the Commission.

(ii) Downsizing of the Central bureaucracy has to be an essential part of the process of controlling non-Plan expenditure. We understand that detailed studies have been conducted recently, by a Committee headed by the Cabinet Secretary, to identity areas where the Central government Ministries/Departments could be reduced in size, including abolition of parts of certain organisations.

Even though the actual saving from implementing these recommendations may be small, their signal effect is substantial. We strongly recommend that some decisions on these pending recommendations be taken and announced in the Budget for 2001-02.

Interest payments account for a very substantial part of total government expenditure and while these payments are unavoidable it is important to eliminate practices which unnecessarily increase the burden of interest. In this connection, we recommend an urgent review of the present system of administered interest rates for national small savings, the public provident fund and for the public account. These administered rates effectively put a floor on the interest rate structure even when inflation falls. Persisting with relatively high rates of 11 per cent on National Savings Certificate and on the PPF effectively prevents banks from lowering term deposit rates and thus ensures a higher interest rate structure for government borrowing and for the private sector than is strictly necessary. We would recommend that the interest rates on these instruments should be lowered to a level no more than 2 percentage points above the inflation rate of the previous six months. The details of calibrating these interest rates with inflation can be worked out, but if implemented, this proposal would allow a drop in interest rates of as much as 2 percentage points, which would reduce the interest burden on the budget. It would also lower commercial interest rates generally, with favourable effects on investment.

(iii) There is a tendency to think of all Plan expenditure as necessarily productive while non-Plan expenditure is treated as unproductive. This is a mistake since maintenance is a non-Plan item and there is little point in adding new assets when maintenance of existing assets is neglected. Besides, detailed studies by the Planning Commission have shown that many Plan schemes in the Central Government do not achieve desired results and are continued simply because of the vested interest of the Central ministries which operate these schemes. We would recommend that for the 10th Plan period beginning 2002, all existing Plan schemes should be deemed to have ended and new Plan schemes should be approved in each sector only on the basis of a careful assessment of the efficacy of these schemes in achieving targets. These schemes should pay as much attention to modernisation and replacement of unproductive assets and their upgradation as to creation of new assets.

(iv) The present system of a "pay as you go" pension for government servants is unsustainable in future especially since pension payments are indexed to the cost of living and also to the minimum pay of the grade in which the individual has retired. Continuing with such a system amounts to living with an actively ticking fiscal time bomb. It may not be legally possible to alter the term of pension for existing employees, but we would recommend that all future government employment with effect from a date to be notified, say 1. 4. 2002, should be on new terms involving a fully funded pension with a defined contribution system. The present pension system involves no explicit contribution by the employee but it has an implicit unfunded obligation by the government to meet pension payment in future. The implicit premium in the present system as a per cent of salary should be computed, and treated as part of the gross salary for future employees to be automatically deducted and paid into an individual retirement account which is then invested in the capital market. The accumulated contribution for each employee, with income and capital gains accrued over the vesting period can then be used to buy a pension at the time of retirement. All over the world, pension reform involves a switch to such fully funded systems and we should make the switch now.

7.12 Subsidies and user charges

(i) Rationalisation of subsidies is a critical area for revenue mobilisation and the Central Government can give a valuable lead to the States by taking some hard decisions in areas which are in its purview. The following suggestions indicate some of the "hard decisions" which the Government should, in our view, be willing to take:-

(a) **Food Subsidy :** This is a politically sensitive area but it is important to point out that with the latest announcement of additional subsidy (beyond the BPL category) the total food subsidy will be Rs. 10,000 crores. Only a very small part of this amount actually goes to the poor. Nor can it be said that the farmers are the principal beneficiaries. The inefficiency of the FCI is built into the food subsidy numbers and this could be quite large. The Expenditure Commission should be asked to go into the whole issue of how best we can achieve our twin objectives of providing a reasonable level of support prices for farmers and some support for the consumption of the poor. This could be treated as a priority item of special reference to the Expenditure Commission.

(b) **Fertilizer Subsidy :** The Expenditure Commission has submitted its report and a decision should be taken and announced for the next fiscal year.

(c) **Kerosene :** Despite the recent increase in the price of kerosene supplied through the PDS this item remains heavily underpriced (it is less than half the market price) and the cross-subsidy is borne by petrol and aviation turbine fuel. The announced intention of Government is to eliminate the Administered Price Mechanism in petroleum products by 1.4.2002 after which date the subsidy on kerosene will have to be borne by the Budget. If prices are not raised, the subsidy bill on kerosene which is approximately Rs. 8000 crores, will have to be added to the Budget. The Budget simply cannot bear such a burden given the other fiscal pressures on the system. It is therefore essential that kerosene prices are adjusted substantially to come much closer to market prices before 1.4.2002. As a rule of thumb, we would recommend that the difference between the PDS price and the market price should not exceed 20 per cent if black marketing of kerosene, which is very extensive, is to be stopped. This means PDS kerosene prices need to be raised in stages by about 60 per cent over the next fifteen months.

(d) **Railway Passenger fares :** At present second class railway passenger fares are much below costs which provide an implicit subsidy of about Rs. 3000 crores. The railways are also desperately short of resources even to undertake basic safety related expenditure on track renewal. There is no reason to believe that railway passengers as a class deserve such a large subsidy. Passenger fares should be increased in a phased manner to cover costs over a three year period. This will bring in much needed resources and also enable the railways to reduce freight charges which at present are pitched excessively high making the railways uncompetitive *vis-a-vis* road transport for moving freight. The Central Government has advised State Governments to set up State Electricity Regulatory Commissions to depoliticise power tariffs. The same logic applies to railways. There should be a Rail Tariff Fixation Authority which would fix economic railway fares. Subsidies to reduce fares below this level should be explicitly provided in the Budget if resources are available.

(e) **Higher Education :** Fees charged in universities are abysmally low and at the same time our universities are desperately starved of funds. This has led to steady erosion of standards. University fees accounted for 20 per cent of the cost of running universities and colleges in the 1960s but this has dropped to 5 per cent today. There is a case for a sharp increase in central university fees. If lead is given by the Centre for Central Universities it can be picked up by the States. The fees for Delhi University are Rs.15 per month, unchanged from thirty years ago.

(f) **Postal Deficit :** Postal charges are another area where user charges have been kept at very low levels leading to a postal deficit of Rs. 600 crores. The enormous growth in the courier industry, which charges much higher rates, show that there is a substantial capacity and willingness to pay for quality service.

(ii) We recognise that each of the expenditure containment proposals listed above may appear to be politically sensitive. However, they are, in our view, unavoidable if we are really to make credible progress towards reducing the fiscal deficit in the Centre without squeezing public investment. In the absence of concrete steps by the Centre in this area it is difficult to carry any credibility in urging the States to take action to enforce fiscal responsibility.

Fiscal Correction at the State Level

7.13 The fiscal situation in most States is near collapse with shortfalls in Plan expenditure of 30 per cent compared with targets in the States taken as a group. In the poorer performing States the shortfall will be even greater. While the devolution provided by the Eleventh Finance Commission eases the pressure somewhat, it does not solve the problem and all States will continue to be under severe fiscal strain. Yet our targets of raising our rate of growth to 8 per cent and more call for substantial investment in social and economic infrastructure especially in rural areas which can only be met if the resource position of the States improves.

7.14 The areas where State Governments need to act are well known and are similar to the areas where Central action is needed. For example, improvements are desperately needed in Sales Tax administration and property taxation. The bureaucracy has grown much faster at the State level than at the Centre and serious efforts at downsizing are needed. In practice this may require reducing the size of State Cabinets, which are often very large and typically encourage proliferation of staff down the line.

7.15 Rationalisation of user charges is another obvious area where State performance is seriously deficient. The most obvious area for rationalisation is power tariffs. The combined losses of the State Electricity Boards amount to Rs. 20,000 crores and this is due to a combination of low tariffs for certain categories and massive leakages in distribution owing to inefficiency and corruption. Similar problems arise in water charges for irrigation which at present cover only one fifth of the estimated maintenance cost. Such low charges do not help farmers since they have only led to neglect of maintenance and consequent deterioration of the irrigation system. State Road Transport Corporations make losses aggregating to about Rs. 1500 crores, much of which is due to uneconomic tariffs.

7.16 These problems are well known and have been extensively documented in the Mid-Term appraisal of the Tenth Plan recently released by the Planning Commission. The Centre has in the past limited itself to urging the States to take corrective action. We believe that in addition to persuasion and urging the Centre should also set an example by addressing these problems in the Central sphere. An announced plan of action on some of the areas outlined in the sections above would create credible pressure on the States to do their part.

7.17 We also believe that the States should be given an incentive to undertake such adjustment. To this end, we recommend that the Planning Commission should be directed to work out an arrangement whereby, from the Tenth Plan onwards i.e. starting 1.4.2002, half of the normal Central assistance to be State Plans should be provided on the basis of a quantitatively worked out fiscal reform plan, decided jointly with the State Government, the Planning Commission and the Ministry of Finance. Release of Central assistance during the year should be linked to achievement of milestones of policy action agreed by the States as part of the Tenth Plan exercise. In the event of non-performance, the amount should be set aside in a non-lapsable fund to be released later to the State as and when promised performance levels are achieved.

7.18 We recognise that the above proposal may be questioned on the grounds that it introduces an element of conditionality in the release of Plan assistance which may appear to be a departure from existing practice. However, we note that even the Finance

Commission transfer, which until recently were completely unconditional, now include an element linked to performance. Plan assistance even in the past has been notionally linked to Plan performance, although the linkage has not been strictly enforced. The nature of the current fiscal crisis in the States is such that unless strong action is taken, the situation will only continue to deteriorate. There is therefore a good case for introducing performance linkage for at least a part of Central assistance.

8. CONCLUSION

8.1 The discussion in the foregoing sections has briefly catalogued the rationale for economic reform and the specific areas which need to be addressed in the second generation of reforms in major sectors of the economy. We have sought to demonstrate not only the desirability of reforms but also their sheer necessity to provide every Indian with the opportunity to release as well as realise his/her full potential. In our view, it is only with the release of the productive capacities of every citizen that the country will achieve its rightful place in the family of developed nations.

8.2 Much has been written and spoken of in the last many years since economic reforms were launched about the need to develop a political consensus around the core reform programme, so that specific reform measures enjoy support cutting across party lines. We would seek to revisit this theme here to stress that the need for a political consensus on economic reforms is no empty slogan. By sheer experience India has demonstrated that there exists broad political support to the reform programme, as has been proved by the transition of several Governments in the last five years through the political space. The world at large now does believe that the reform process in India is irreversible, but would certainly like to see an acceleration of its momentum, so that the goals that seem so easily within reach can be rapidly attained.

8.3 While emphasizing the need to build a political consensus, we are conscious of the percolation of reformist ideas from the Centre, where economic reforms were initiated, to the States in recent times. We are heartened to note that in the past few years several political parties, covering the entire spectrum of political thought, have held power in various States and have taken up and continue to sustain bold reform programmes embracing a wide range of activities. Thus, in our view, a nation-wide and broad-based consensus to reform our economy and to put the individual States and the country as a whole on a path of higher productivity and growth is already in place. What is required now is for this consensus to be built upon and carried over into the realm of policy and implementation.